RECON

1

CAPTAIN Lester A. Niles ran along the Avenue de l'Aeroport. The machine-thunder of helicopters beat from the runway landing zones. Two hundred meters ahead, cars and trucks lined the curb. A crowd stood at the fence—rescuers, journalists, Lebanese police, and civilians. Marine sentries crouched behind the fence and watched the onlookers and the highway. Lebanese in passing cars slowed to gawk at the blast-stripped trees and gray devastation where a bomb had destroyed the Battalion Landing Team building that morning, murdering hundreds of United States Marines as they slept.

Past the one-story concrete building housing the Support and Service Group, Niles cut along the traffic circle to a checkpoint. A barrier of sandbags, steel oil drums, and concertina wire channeled traffic to a narrow entry. Two sentries stood inside a sandbagged guard post, their M-16 rifles in their hands. An LAAW rocket—light antiarmor weapon, capable of penetrating 300 mm of steel plate and destroying any car or truck—lay on the sandbags, ready to snap out and fire.

A sentry stepped out to block Niles, the young man shouting a command. But rotor-throb overwhelmed his voice. A CH-46 helicopter rose from the runway a hundred meters to the west, carrying away wounded Marines to surgery on the *Iwo Jima* offshore.

Niles stopped. The Marine battalion commander had issued shoot-to-kill instructions to all sentries. The two sentries at the gate eyed him, their rifles in their hands. He slung his rifle over his shoulder.

1

Dust swirled as a stake-bed truck low-geared out of the compound. Niles glanced in the back. A Marine sat on the tailgate, staring down at the asphalt. In the truck, a tarp covered the bodies of Marines. Dust gray boots and gray hands stuck out from under the tarp. The driver eased around the traffic circle, going slow to the improvised morgue near the west runway—he had no reason to speed.

Waiting for the rotor noise to fade, impatient, his jaw clenched with rage, Niles removed his helmet, then wiped gray dust from his face to show the sentries his craggy Anglo features. He wore blood-splashed Marine camouflage pants, a bloody flak vest, and web gear. Gray dust had obscured the green camouflage patterns. His bare arms—deeply tanned and bloodstained—stuck out of the flak vest. Blood had clotted on Niles's sleeves, and he had cut the blood-stiff sleeves off at his shoulders.

Throughout the morning, he had helped take dead and wounded Marines out of the wreckage of the barracks. Then Lieutenant Shaffik Hijazi of the Lebanese Armed Forces had come with an emergency message.

A thin, wiry man of sinew and hard muscle, Captain Niles looked older than his thirty-eight years. Born into the poverty of Harlan County, Kentucky, he grew up hard. He had started working for his family at eight years old, shooting rabbits and squirrels to feed his brothers and sisters. Later, when his growth gave him strength in his arms and back, he worked in his uncle's mine, gouging coal from the earth. Then another uncle offered him the job of driving untaxed liquor from the mountain distillery to the towns. He drove for two years before his arrest. The judge offered to dismiss the charges if Niles enlisted in the armed services that day. Like his father before him, Niles joined the Marines. On his eighteenth birthday, he volunteered and qualified for the training program of the Force Recon Company at Camp Pendleton, California. He then went for airborne training at Fort Benning, Georgia. After two tours of combat in the I Corps of Vietnam—running reconnaissance patrols along the demilitarized zone and the Laotian border, he applied for Officer Candidate School. He returned to Vietnam as a very experienced second lieutenant and led Recon patrols—wearing North Vietnamese or Khmer Rouge uniforms and carrying Soviet weapons—into Laos and Cambodia. Since then, he had served in the United States, the Caribbean, Central America, advancing in rank as he continued his education. He had served as an instructor to the Lebanese Air Assault Battalion since November of 1982.

Standing there, waiting for the noise of the helicopter to fade, he thought back over the past twenty years—ambushes when he had to leave the bodies of his friends, the long waits for medevacs with his hands over the gaping wounds of lung-shot eighteen-year-old boys, the faces of hundreds of dead Marines after fire fights—and he could not remember a day worse than this day, 23 October 1983.

Pain and rage. The State Department dreamers. Ignorant politicians and bureaucrats mouthing vainglorious rhetoric, then sending brave young men into a maelstrom of war and atrocity fueled by religious hatred, class struggle, and ruthless dictatorial ambition—sending Marines to stand with unloaded rifles against the Syrian Army and the fanatics of Lebanon and Iran. Rules of Engagement denying the Marines the right to fire in their own defense, requiring the death of Marines before a Marine could fire back. Now the bombing of the barracks.

And the Syrians and Iranians had not yet killed enough Americans. A Lebanese officer had given him warning of another attack. Niles had to get to a trans-Atlantic telephone.

The rotor noise died away. "You see I'm a Marine?" His anger brought out his Appalachian accent. "I'm no Shia infiltrator. You need identification to pass me?"

"The headquarters compound is now restricted to essential personnel only."

"I'm Captain Niles. Liaison to the Lebanese Armed Forces."

"Pardon me, sir."

"Sir, we saw you come in from over there—" The second sentry pointed his rifle toward the slums of the Burj al-Branjneh Palestinian camp, where the tenements overlooked the northern perimeter of the airport. "From where those shits are shooting—"

3

A bullet banged into a steel drum a step away. Reflexively, Niles dropped down to a crouch behind the checkpoint sandbags. Bullets tore past the checkpoint.

"Don't know how you made it here, sir. They're shooting at us nonstop."

Squinting against the afternoon glare, Niles peered over the barrels. The Marine Support and Services Group building shielded the Marine compound from one section of the slum. But blocks of tenements with hundreds of windows had an unobstructed view of the airport. Niles scanned the roof lines three hundred fifty meters away. The snipers could be firing from any of the windows or rooftops. Another bullet slapped into the sandbags at the back of the checkpoint.

"See them?" a sentry asked.

"If I saw them, I'd shoot them." Putting on his helmet, he sprinted through the open area, then veered through a gate and into the shelter of the MSSG building.

Down an access road, Niles saw the dust gray ruin of the Marine barracks. When the suicide driver had crashed the truck into the lobby and detonated the cargo of explosives, the blast had sheared the four-story complex off its foundations. Nothing remained of the structure, only thousands of tons of broken concrete—intermixed with furnishings, equipment, and Marines. A gray dust of pulverized concrete covered everything.

Voices still screamed from the wreckage. American and Lebanese rescue teams worked with heavy equipment and bare hands to free trapped Marines. A slab of concrete edged with tangled strands of reinforcing steel hung from a crane as rescuers dug through the debris. Journalists followed a team carrying away a corpse, flash units blinking as the photographers recorded images for the newspapers of the world.

Niles rushed to the Marine Amphibious Unit Headquarters. A sergeant stepped out of a sandbagged guard post. "You with the command?"

"Captain Niles, Liaison to the Lebanese Air Assault—"

"Didn't recognize you, sir." Saluting, the sergeant motioned him through the doors. Niles ran up the stairs to the

4

second floor. Hurrying down the corridor, he glanced into
the cubicles of the intelligence staff. Officers and clerks
worked in pressed fatigues. Niles continued until he found
an office with an unused desk and telephone. He closed the
door and dialed zero.

"Operator, this is a priority call to Lieutenant Colonel
Devlin, in Washington, D.C., at the following number—"
Niles recited the number from memory, then waited. He
stared out the window to the adjoining airport maintenance
building. Over the roof, he saw the ridges of the Shouf
Mountains. The building blocked any sniper fire from the
Shiite ghettos of Hay al-Sollom. The phone finally rang in
Washington. A woman answered.

"Mrs. Devlin? This is Captain Lester Niles, calling from
Lebanon. I apologize if I woke you up."

"No, Captain, you didn't." Mrs. Devlin spoke with the
precise and measured diction of an eastern university graduate. "Are you calling from Beirut?"

"Yes, ma'am. I'm calling from Marine headquarters. I
need to speak to the colonel."

"Oh, you are *the* Captain Niles. Anthony has spoken of
you."

"Surprised that I'm worth the mention. Is it possible I
could speak with the colonel?"

"He was called to a meeting very early today."

"Special Operations?"

"I don't believe so. His aide called with a number in case
of an emergency."

"This is an emergency."

"I know. One moment, I have the number here . . ."

Niles wrote the series of numbers on the bloodstained tan
of his arm. "Well, thank you. Hope I have the pleasure of
meeting you some day."

"Captain, are you all right?"

"Yes, ma'am. I wasn't even here at the airport last night."

"Is it as bad as it looks on television? They say fifty
Marines are dead."

"It's worse. There might be three hundred men dead."

"Oh, good Lord . . ."

5

"Got to go, Mrs. Devlin, thank you very much." He broke the connection. "Operator? Operator, the colonel was not at that number. Try this number . . ." Again, Niles waited.

A neutral voice answered. "Code, please."

Niles read off the last four numbers.

The line switched. Another voice answered. "Council."

"I need to speak with Lieutenant Colonel Devlin."

"The advisor and his staff are in a meeting. Would you like to leave a message?"

"This is an emergency. Can you put the call through to Colonel Devlin?"

"An emergency?"

"I'm calling from the Marine Amphibious Unit Headquarters in Beirut. I need to speak with Colonel Devlin."

"There are several offices represented in the meeting. Who is Colonel Devlin with?"

"Special Operations, Joint Chiefs of Staff."

"Just a moment, sir."

A helicopter passed overhead. Niles cupped his hands over the mouthpiece and waited, listening to the electronic hiss of the satellite relay.

Noise and voices came. "This is Colonel Devlin."

"Colonel, this is Niles in Beirut."

"What is the situation there? We're getting conflicting statements."

"You have a television there?"

"It looks bad."

"It's worse. Colonel, they wiped it out. Every man in that building is dead or wounded. Three hundred or more."

"How did that truck get in the compound?"

"How'd that kamikaze get in? He drove in through the gate. But that's history, sir. I've got information that the militias are talking about hitting the airport in force."

"You gave this information to the commander?"

"No, sir. I'm not going to bother. Sir, a week ago I got that information about the Syrians and the Pasdaran—the Iranian Revolutionary Guards—planning a bombing. I passed that information to the intelligence staff. You know that's a fact because I forwarded a copy of it to you. And now we've got hundreds of dead Marines. The men working rescue are taking continuous sniper fire and I've got word that the Hizbullah—that's the Party of God, the militia organized by the Iranians, led by Iranians and Syrians—that they're talking about hitting us. Look, sir. You know I'm in a peculiar position here. I've been here a year and the unit commanders change every few months. I know what goes. I got the sources. I want to do something about this information. Can you get me Special Operations authorization to go out there?"

"Go where?"

"Hay al-Sollom."

"You're willing to go into the militia-controlled areas alone?"

"No, sir. Not alone. I'm not crazy. I'm not looking for martyrdom. I got men who'll go with me. American and Lebanese."

"As a recon unit?"

"We'll look for the Hizbullah force that's forming up. Call down artillery or gunships if they're actually out there."

"We're in a meeting now with National Security Advisor Reisinger. I'll discuss it with him."

"That man can most definitely make it happen. If you can get the okay, I'll go out at dark."

"I'll try. We're discussing who did this. If I can suggest your action as a recon for information, are you willing to do that?"

"Anything you say, sir. But let me save you the suspense. I know who did it. The Syrians and the Iranians."

"Not a militia gang?"

"Sir, the men here thought they got hit by a nuke. It was a professional hit. Perfectly planned, perfectly made, and perfectly executed. No militia did this. Not the Hizbullah. Not the Phalange."

"If I get the authorization, how will I contact you?"

"Send a cable—yes or no. I'll be in the area of the Third Platoon of Charlie Company, near checkpoint 76."

"There may be a problem with—"

A lieutenant stepped into the office. He saw Niles—dusty,

7

blood-splotched—sitting on his desk. "Who are you, soldier? Why are you in here? Don't call your family from my telephone."

Niles thought of the wife he had divorced fifteen years before—she wouldn't care if he lived or died. And his children? They did not face any danger today. The Marines came first. "Do what you can, sir. A lieutenant wants his phone back."

"Keep me informed."

Rushing out, Niles wove through the crowded corridor, then down the stairs and out of the building. A white flash startled him, reflexes throwing him to the side even as he caught himself—it had not been the flash of another bomb.

"You Marines are very jumpy!" A young Frenchwoman with a camera laughed.

Pushing the woman aside, Niles elbowed through news crews waiting at the door to the headquarters building. The young woman—a slender blonde in designer jeans and a white sweat shirt stenciled with the warning Don't Shoot, Journalist in three languages—laughed with a cameraman holding a video camera. The woman raised her camera to take another photo of Niles.

Niles ran north. At an intersecting road, he caught a ride with a truck delivering ammunition to the perimeter outposts. They stopped first at Charlie Battery—a unit with the responsibility of providing mortar and artillery support for the Marine compound.

"You ready to put out some fire from those one fifty-fives?" Niles called out to a cannoneer.

"Quit the jokes." The Marine took a case of 5.56mm ammunition and dodged away through incoming sniper fire.

The truck continued around the perimeter. In the back of the stake-side truck, Niles crouched down beside the wooden crates. He heard the hammering of a Marine's M-60 machine gun returning fire at the distant snipers.

Only a few rifles and machine guns against thousands of fanatics, Niles thought. He listened to the Marine counterfire, thinking of the hundreds of men already dead and how many more would die if a militia force hit the Marine perimeter. Sorrow took him for a moment, his thoughts trapped in a cycle of numbers—how many families woke up this Sunday morning to radio reports of their sons dying in Beirut? How many young widows stared at televisions, hoping they would not recognize a corpse? How many fatherless children? He forced the thoughts away, concentrating on the threat of an attack. He could not bring back the dead. But he could stop the fanatics from killing more young Americans.

Midpoint on the runway, he banged on the cab of the truck. The driver slowed and Niles leapt down to the perimeter road. He ran to the trail paralleling the dry streambed of the Nahr al-Ghadir, a seasonal river winding down from the Shouf Mountains.

Bullets cut through the trees and brush. Marines at sandbag bunkers motioned him down, but he continued. Rifles answered the sniper fire. He heard an M-60 firing short bursts. A few meters short of the bridge and the checkpoint there, Niles cut into the brush and went down the river embankment.

Hundreds of meters away, across open fields of dry grass and weeds, snipers fired from the tenements of Hay al-Sollom, a Shiite ghetto once controlled by the Amal, but now dominated by the Hizbullah and Iranian Revolutionary Guard. Months before, when the Amal held the district, before the State Department threw American support to the Christian rulers, the Marines had patrolled the streets to enforce the armed truce between the Amal, the Israelis, and the Phalange. The Shiite people greeted the Marines as saviors and protectors. Now the fanatics of the Hizbullah, advised by Iranian and Syrian officers, fired on the Marine positions around the airport from the windows and rooftops.

Exposed to the snipers, Niles zigzagged to a bunker. Living branches of bushes bent and tied to the sandbag walls camouflaged the position. Ten meters farther, the embankment fell away to the sand and trash of the dry Nahr al-Ghadir.

"Niles coming in," he announced. He ducked through a green plastic tarp covering the door. The muzzle blast of a machine gun slammed his ears. He pulled a pair of valved hearing protectors from a pocket and screwed the protectors into his ears.

Sergeant Leon Vatsek sprawled behind a tripod-mounted M-60 machine gun, triggering accurate bursts of heavy 7.62mm NATO slugs at snipers hiding in the tenements. A dedicated body-builder, Vatsek weighed two hundred and forty pounds—all hard muscle. His sharp, Slavic features—sharp nose, brilliant blue eyes, a slash for a mouth—gave him a malevolent look. A Recon Marine like Captain Niles, he served as an instructor to the Lebanese Air Assault Battalion. A black belt in karate and judo, he taught hand-to-hand combat to the recruits. And as an armorer, he taught the maintenance of weapons to the Lebanese technicians.

Another Marine crouched at the side of the bunker. Sergeant Jesús Marical Alvarez, of the Battalion Recon Platoon, had escaped the bombing only by chance. At six in the morning, his squad had completed a predawn security patrol of the airport. The other Recon men returned to the BLT barracks. Alvarez walked north to the Lebanese Army compound for a Sunday breakfast with Niles, Vatsek, and a group of Lebanese soldiers. At six twenty-two A.M., the truck bomb destroyed the barracks. Alvarez lived. All the others in his unit died. Tearing through the debris of the Recon quarters with his bare hands, Alvarez found only corpses and broken concrete running with blood. Shock had left his dark features drawn and gaunt.

"Vatsek! Stop killing them. Just for a minute."

The sergeant ceased firing. But he kept his eyes on the distant tenements.

"Gentlemen, I just came from the Lebanese compound. I talked to this officer there, an officer of the Islamic confession, a Shia in fact. He had information that—"

A three-shot burst interrupted the captain. Vatsek laughed. "Got him . . ."

Niles continued. "This officer told me the Hizbullah, a k a the Party of God, plans to hit the compound from Hay al-Sollom."

"They're coming to get us?" Vatsek smiled, his white teeth and prominent Slavic cheekbones twisting into a death's-head grin. "Is that a promise? I'll requisition a starlite scope and ten thousand rounds of linked seven six two."

Niles talked over his sergeant's interruption. "This is of serious concern to me, as a mass assault could wipe out whole sections of the line. Once they get through the line, it's hand-to-hand."

Vatsek raised an arm—the sleeve tight over muscles, his wrist thicker than most men's arms, the striking edges of his hand calloused from striking canvas sacks filled with gravel—and made a fist. "Ready. To. Go."

"Is is true?" Alvarez asked. "What he told you?"

"The man is reliable. And a friend. Whether the information is true, that's to be determined."

"What did intelligence say?" Alvarez looked out the gun slot at the crowded slums of the Shiite district, only a few hundred meters away. "They have the same story?"

"Didn't talk to them. I called Washington. Made a direct request to go out and confirm the information."

Alvarez snapped around. "Please repeat that, sir."

"I requested authorization for a recon out there. I asked them that can say yes."

"The colonel?" Vatsek asked, not joking now.

"The colonel will relay the request."

"I volunteer," Vatsek told the captain. "When does the word come?"

"Soon. But I don't think there'll be a role for you out there. Alvarez, you speak some Arabic and you can pass as Arabic from a distance. I'll take you if you volunteer."

"Me? Look like a local?"

"And some of the fellows from the Air Assault. They volunteered to do revenge hits. But this won't be that. The bombing is history. Payback can't change it."

"Then what exactly will I be volunteering for, sir?"

"To stop the fanatics from killing more of us. We'll go out, capture uniforms and weapons, then move around and watch. Maybe put down snipers. Dangerous, but not crazy. Exactly what you were trained to do."

"Sir, my courses didn't cover any urban recon."

"You'll learn."

11

"And out of uniform?"

"Standard procedure on extraordinary patrols is to wear the uniforms of the enemy. The colonel and I wore the uniforms of the People's Army of Vietnam. Walked around in Cambodia and Laos. Tonight, if you volunteer, we'll try for Syrian uniforms. Syrians shave. Take us a month to pass as Revolutionary Guards."

Alvarez laughed quietly. He stroked the stubble on his face. "A month? Okay, I volunteer. If you get the okay, sir, I'll go with you."

"Got no use for me?" Vatsek asked.

"You'll be our long-distance backup. We have to break for it, we'll come straight back to you."

"I won't argue with you, sir. But if you need me, I'm ready to go. And my M-60 with a starlite scope."

"I won't forget. Alvarez, you and me will go over to the Lebanese compound and recruit our assistants. For you, Sergeant, I'll requisition a few thousand rounds of linked."

Hours later, Captain Niles crouched near the trail along the Nahr al-Ghadir. The white disc of the moon lit the fields and tenements of Hay al-Sollom. Concealed in shadows, Niles watched the Marine perimeter exchange fire with Hizbullah positions. The fighting had escalated to long-distance fire fights, the militia gangs continuously firing Kalashnikov rifles and machine guns, shooting rockets from the distant rooftops at the improvised Marine defenses. The exposed and outnumbered Marine outposts had requested artillery to silence the militia bunkers. But the 155mm howitzers of Charlie Battery did not fire. The Marines requested mortars, nothing came.

Niles had assembled his men and equipment. The Marines and Lebanese waited in the bunker. Three English-speaking Lebanese troopers had volunteered. He knew them all from training and trusted them. As Sunni Moslem nationalists, they opposed the radical Shiite factions that wanted to throw Lebanon into the Islamic revolution. They had volunteered to join the patrol without demanding a complete briefing.

That afternoon, when Niles had explained that their role

would be to impersonate Hizbullah, the Air Assault troopers took Niles to a storeroom where they grabbed Soviet weapons from shelves and pulled militia uniforms—bloodstained but laundered—from plastic bags. Intelligence squads of the Lebanese Army also employed the uniforms of their enemies for reconnaissance patrols.

The Lebanese Army storerooms had provided small, citizen's band radios. But the troopers had cautioned that the radios had been purchased in a local shop. The radical and Islamic militias had identical radios.

The Marines and Lebanese then returned to bunker on the embankment of the Nahr al-Ghadir to wait.

But the authorization to proceed had not come. Niles thought of the political conflicts in Washington. Perhaps Colonel Devlin had not won the approval.

How many more Marines would die?

And at that moment, he decided to go without the authorization. He knew he risked his career—and it did not matter. If he did nothing, if the Marines suffered more losses—dead and maimed—because he feared the loss of his pension, his career with the Marines had meant nothing.

Yet he had to also consider the other men. All of the soldiers—American and Lebanese—risked their lives. Vatsek and Alvarez also risked the end of their careers, if not prison terms for breaking discipline.

He would lie to Alvarez and Vatsek and take the responsibility for the unauthorized action. They might get a few months filling sandbags. He would accept the risk of prison. He would accept that risk so that Marines did not lose their lives—for nothing—in Beirut.

Resolved, Niles silently walked the thirty meters to the bunker. He slipped through the green plastic tarp blocking the faint light. Inside, the others prepared for the action.

Three Lebanese Air Assault soldiers helped Alvarez with a Hizbullah uniform. One soldier—Lieutenant Shaffik Hijazi—wore the olive green fatigues of the Lebanese Army. Clean-shaven Hijazi, a young Lebanese officer studying to be an international attorney, had trained at Fort Benning, Georgia. He would remain behind with Vatsek. The other

Lebanese—Hussein and Gamal—wore the mismatched uniforms and beards of militiamen. They would go to Hay al-Sollom. White headbands marked with blood red Arabic script identified them as fighters for the Hizbullah. A photo of the Ayatollah Khomeini decorated the plywood stock of Hussein's Kalashnikov rifle.

Gamal carried two weapons—a folding-stock Kalashnikov and the most common heavy weapon of the militias, a RPG-7 rocket launcher. He wore the special Soviet pack required for his RPG-7. He had loaded one safety-capped rocket in the launcher and carried six more in his pack. Gamal spoke Arabic with Alvarez, repeating words for the Chicano Marine, trying to teach him to speak simple phrases without an accent. Strong, with muscles rivaling the body-builder Vatsek, Gamal came from a war-ravaged village. He had lost family to all the foreign invaders of his country—the Palestinians, the Syrians, and the Israelis. But he had become a good friend of the Chicano from the East Los Angeles barrios. Gamal feared that Alvarez might mispronounce a simple word and betray his nationality.

Niles unfolded a map and spread it out on the dirt. "Ready to go?"

"Un momento, por favor," Alvarez answered, switching from Arabic to Spanish. He adjusted the buckles of frayed Soviet web gear. "I look cool, Captain?"

"What about your hair?" Niles indicated the sergeant's regulation Marine haircut. "The Party of God ever wear helmets or hats?"

"They wear caps sometimes," Hussein answered, passing black watch caps to Alvarez and Niles. He had learned English in a private school, then lived for years with an uncle in New York. His hope to be a men's fashion importer/exporter to the Arab nations had faded as the civil war continued. "I have one for him and you. But Captain, your face is wrong. You must not be seen."

Pulling the cap over his hair, Niles grinned, then pulled the cap down over his face.

Vatsek laughed. "Hiz Boo Lah, the Unknown."

Niles put on ragged militia fatigues. He wore his own

boots. Old, mismatched web gear, a Kalashnikov rifle, and 7.62ComBloc magazines completed his Party of God costume. All his American gear and identification would remain with Vatsek.

"The checkpoint there—" Niles pointed to the far side of Hay al-Sollom district, where a bridge crossed the river. "We can walk the al-Ghadir creek all the way there. Chances are, any movement of crazies in from Baalbek will come that way."

"And the streets from West Beirut?" Hussein asked. "There are many militias—and the Palestinians—who would join a fight against the Marines."

"If we could cover the other routes, we would. But we can't."

As the others studied a map of Hay al-Sollom, he rubbed brown camouflage grease stick over his face and neck and hands to darken his Anglo skin. The sergeants had not asked if the authorization had come. They assumed Niles would not move without clearance for the action. If the action led to a court-martial, he would state that he had lied to the men . . .

"You understand what goes with the radio?" Alvarez asked Vatsek.

"Yeah, don't use it." The sergeant pressed the transmit button and heard the other radios click. "Toy . . ."

"They don't have the range, but if we do call you—"

"Don't give you away. I'll talk trash. Make like we're screwing around on the line here. Mister America to the Green Gang, come in."

"Mister America?" Alvarez asked. "Who's that?"

"Me."

"You mean, Mr. Godzilla."

"Godzilla? Give me some credit, Zoot-suit! That lizard did all his damage with his gluts and tail. No upper body development at all."

"Okay, Señor King Kong."

The two sergeants gave the radios a last check as they argued call-names. Niles inspected his Kalashnikov, stripping it and inspecting the components with the beam of a penlight. He returned the bolt to the receiver, snapped the receiver closed, and jammed in a magazine. He looked to the others.

Alvarez nodded. The Lebanese soldiers picked up their weapons. Niles gave Vatsek a left-handed salute, and without a word, led the others out of the bunker.

Moonlight gave the Marines vision but denied the concealment of darkness. Crouching in cover, Niles paused to allow the eyes of his squad to adjust. He scanned the Marine line and the distant buildings of Hay al-Sollom. Intermittent riflefire continued along the Marine line. The hammering of automatic weapons came from the Lebanese Army position on the bridge over the river. Niles saw no sentries.

Rising, Niles zigzagged through masses of brush, exploiting the shadows and branches for concealment. The weapons noise covered the faint cracking of the dry weeds as the four men crept down the embankment to the dry streambed.

The Nahr al-Ghadir flowed only in the winter and spring months, runoff from the Shouf foothills coursing through a winding riverbed southwest of Hay al-Sollom, dividing that district from Ashuefat to the south. The riverbed—actually a deep gulley—ended at the Beirut International Airport runways. There, storm drains carried the flow under the runways to the Mediterranean. The Marines had outposts on the south bank of the al-Ghadir. The Lebanese Armed Forces maintained a checkpoint at the north end of a bridge leading from Hay al-Sollom to the Marine outposts in the south. Hundreds of meters of open fields separated the Shiite district from the checkpoint and outposts.

In the summer, the natural flow failed and the gully carried only a stream of sewage from Hay al-Sollom. The Marines called the Nahr al-Ghadir 'The Shit River.' Tonight, a light wind came from the east, carrying away the stink of the open sewer.

Niles led the line of men toward the bridge. Rifles continued firing from the LAF checkpoint. Marines fired from their position beside the road, their high velocity bullets shrieking overhead to hit somewhere in the Shiite district. But the Marines guarding the road had no downward view into the streambed. Only the Lebanese on the bridge could see the streambed.

Years of trash made the streambed look like a landfill. Black filth—glistening in the moonlight—cut a deep channel through the litter. But winter flooding had banked sand at the sides of the gulley. Niles walked silently in the clean sand, staying at the extreme side of the streambed, where the squad's uniforms would not contrast against the moonlight-brilliant sand.

A rocket shrieked past the Lebanese bunker and exploded somewhere in the Marine line. A roar of rifle and machine gun fire answered from the Lebanese and Marine bunkers. Niles rushed under the bridge, blind for the seconds he blundered through the absolute darkness of the night shadow of the bridge. He found his way with sweeps of his boot tips, using his toes like the antennae of an insect. Past the bridge, he motioned for the others to rush. The chaos of firing weapons covered the noise of their boots on trash and leaves.

If Niles had had responsibility for this area, he would have sealed the approach to the Marine lines with walls of coiled concertina wire, then mined the streambed. But the State Department had vetoed all static defenses of lethal capability. Even minimal defenses conflicted with the Marine peacekeeping assignment.

But the lack of defenses now served his purpose. Leaving the fighting behind, the four men followed the riverbed to the northeast. Soon they passed under a footbridge that had linked Marine Combat Post 69 to a Lebanese Armed Forces position on the other side of the river. Combat Post 69 had been abandoned in September after months of escalating warfare between the Marines and the Shiite and Druze militias.

Niles knew the area. At one time, the Combat Post and the Lebanese Armed Forces position had guarded one side of Hay al-Sollom from the Israelis. Fields and buildings had surrounded the CP. After the withdrawal of the Israelis, the Shiite militias attacked the LAF position, attempting to force the army out of the district. The first attacks failed.

Then the militias directed their weapons at the Marines. The Marines drove back the gunmen with rifle and machine gun fire. To prepare for a sustained assault, the militias used earth-moving equipment to gouge trenches into the open fields. They built bunkers. The Rules of Engagement did not allow the Marine platoons stationed at CP 69 to fire on the militia work crews. Only after the militias launched their attacks from the completed trenches and bunkers—sniping, raking the CP with heavy machine gun fire, blasting the position with rockets—did the Rules of Engagement allow the Marines to return the fire. Buildings had also overlooked CP 69. Shiite snipers fired down on the Marines. Without the authority to use sufficient firepower to destroy the bunkers sheltering the militias or the buildings concealing the snipers, the Marine commander knew that CP 69 would eventually be overrun. He ordered their withdrawal. Without the support of the Marines, the Lebanese Army position fell. The militias took the soldiers prisoner and looted the compound. The Shiites then tortured the LAF officer to death as an example to the soldiers.

A distance of approximately five hundred meters separated the abandoned LAF and Marine positions from the airport perimeter. Niles estimated they had only three hundred fifty meters more to walk. Continuing fifty meters past the footbridge, Niles signaled the others to halt and wait. He crept up the steep embankment into a clean cool wind.

The area seemed as he remembered, the jagged roof lines of blasted buildings, the dead trees, the trench-scarred fields. The Shiite neighborhood around the ruins of CP 69 stood silhouetted against the glow of the airport, the buildings gray in the moonlight, the shadowed, narrow streets black voids—all the street lights and neon shot out or shattered by shrapnel during ten years of fighting. A few residents remained—cracks of yellow lantern light showed through sandbagged windows. Niles studied the roof lines of the highest apartments—the natural positions for militia lookouts. Despite the moonlight, the distance and shadows defeated his vision. He looked to the other side of the al-Ghadir.

There, he saw lighted windows. All the windows opened

to the Shouf Mountains, away from the fighting around the airport. Scanning the rooftops, he saw movement, but as he watched, his eyes defined the shapes as laundry flapping with the wind. The buildings blocked his view of the militias firing from Hay al-Sollom.

To the north, he saw only the brush and trees lining the river. He eased down the slope to the waiting men. They continued north along the side of the sewer, moving more slowly, placing their feet carefully in the littered sand. They passed places where children had played with tires and scrap plywood—which indicated an absence of mines or booby traps.

After counting a hundred steps, Niles stopped and listened. He heard Alvarez moving behind him. Niles signaled the sergeant with a hiss. Crouching down, his Kalashnikov pointing into the darkness, Niles listened. He heard the distant sound of weapons and the wind rustling branches. He turned his head slowly, trying to turn his ears toward any slight sound. Except for the weapons and wind, he heard only the creaking of the ligaments in his neck and his own breathing.

They moved again, advancing a few steps before he heard the voice. Niles stopped in midstride and dropped to a crouch. The voice came and went with the wind. Turning, he motioned Alvarez forward. He touched his ear and pointed in the direction of the sound.

Alvarez nodded. They crouched side by side for minutes, listening. The voice continued, pausing rhythmically, continuing, but too distant to be understood. Gamal left his position at the end of the line.

"Prayers," he whispered.

The Americans realized they had listened to the amplified voice of a mullah. Somewhere in the distance, loudspeakers blared out evening prayers. Niles continued on.

The streambed narrowed, forcing them finally to walk in the stream of sewage. Niles stayed at the edge of the wide stream, feeling the filth seep into his boots, every slow step bringing a wave of stink as his boots broke the scum. Branches overhanging the stream provided cover from observation. But the leaves scraped over their hands and webbing as they brushed the branches aside, dry sticks clicking across their weapons. Niles concentrated on making every step in the scum silent, making the motions of his hands through the leaves slow and soundless. He almost fell over the corpse.

His boot sank into the rotting flesh, and the vile stench hit him, his whole body shuddering with nausea. Knowing what lay below him in the black filth, he clamped down on his throat and stepped over the corpse. He forced himself to take several more silent steps before breathing.

Simultaneously, he heard the voices on the bridge. He advanced until he rounded a curve in the embankment and saw lantern light. Retreating, he heard Alvarez and the Lebanese gasping in the overwhelming stink of sewage and decomposition. He warned them with the hissed words, "Bridge. Checkpoint."

Niles went slowly up the side of the embankment, angling through the dry weeds. His hand found plastic and slick chrome. Tracing the outline with his hand, he felt a handle and shattered locks—a briefcase, shot open and looted. A kidnapping and murder? A robbery? A militia execution? It did not matter to the corpses dumped here. Niles edged forward until he saw the road.

Lanterns illuminated a checkpoint, posters of the Ayatollah Khomeini identifying the militia manning the position as the Hizbullah. Headlights approached. Three militiamen left the concrete block and sandbag bunker. A car snaked through curving rows of oil drums set in the road and stopped. A militiaman went to the driver's window with a flashlight. Voices came to him but he could not understand the Arabic. The militiaman checked the driver's identification, then shined the flashlight inside the car. Niles saw bearded faces and fatigues.

The militiamen motioned the car to continue. The three gunmen returned to the bunker. Niles watched shadows and light shift in the firing slots set in the bunker walls. Music came on, the sensual rhythms and insinuating words of Donna Summer blaring into the night.

Faint crackling announced Alvarez. The sergeant seemed to flow up the slope, his hands smoothing the weeds aside, his body rising to pass over trash, then going flat again, his boots silently pushing him ahead. He whispered, "Disco?"

"Three Party of God. Wait here."

Continuing to the top of the embankment, Niles stayed below the scraggly weeds and scanned the area. A wide, tire-rutted lot lay between him and the road. Dark buildings adjoined both sides of the Nahr al-Ghadir. Plywood covered the windows of the ground-level shops. Trash had drifted against the doors. No lights showed in the windows of the second- and third-floor apartments. The area seemed deserted except for the Hizbullah militiamen.

For the minutes that Niles watched and listened, no other cars came. He finally eased down the slope to Alvarez.

"Move Hussein and Gamal within listening distance of that checkpoint. We'll listen, we'll wait. Then we'll take it."

2

FROM the leather-upholstered comfort of the UNESCO limousine, Fahkr Rajai and Iziz Kalaq viewed their victory. Their chauffeur allowed the long Mercedes to idle past the ruins of the Marine barracks. Fifteen hours after the bombing, under glaring floodlights, American and Lebanese rescue workers continued to search for Marines in the gray wasteland of shattered concrete and debris. Jackhammers beat relentlessly. A crane pulled a slab up as a team of men in dust-grayed uniforms cut at steel reinforcing rods with power saws, sparks spraying from the discs. Men with flashlights risked their lives to look under the suspended mass of concrete for trapped men.

A rescuer pointed at a form in the wreckage and medics rushed under the hanging slab. A Lebanese ran with a stretcher. But then a medic stood and motioned the others back. They had found only another dead man. Photographers pointed their cameras at the twisted gray corpse and their strobe units flashed. The two young men in the limousine—Rajai the Iranian and Kalaq the Syrian-born Palestinian—laughed.

Horns sounded behind the limousine as other cruising onlookers demanded a view of the spectacle. The chauffeur touched the accelerator and the Mercedes eased forward, passing the rescue vehicles, ambulances, video trucks, and taxis lining the scene. A bulletproof and soundproof glass barrier separated the driver from the rear passenger compartment. Distracted, Kalaq shouted into the microphone.

"What now?"

22

"Shall I circle again?"

"Of course!"

"It is perhaps not wise," Rajai cautioned in his formal Arabic. "For us to be seen as too interested in the bombing. They cannot but notice this car, and therefore, the two foreigners within. Why not have him return us to my car and my guards? We will go immediately to where the militias will fight."

"Uh-huh." Kalaq found a Marlboro and lit it with a silver lighter. He pressed the intercom button again. "Do not go back there. Take us back to the café."

"And tomorrow," Rajai continued. "And for weeks, there will be thousands of photos published. We cannot risk touring our victory. But many photographers will have recorded images of our revenge for our pleasure and memory."

Kalaq laughed smoke. "You are right! Thousands of photos. I will cover the walls of my office with dead Marines. A theater of their defeat."

They laughed again, Rajai in his polite and reserved way, Kalaq almost barking. The project to bomb the Marines had brought together two very different young men.

Rajai wore his expensive French suit with ease and conservative elegance, every detail of his tailoring and grooming correct. A French expatriate barber styled his hair and beard. Exile from the Shah's Iran had made Rajai an international traveler. He spoke several languages and knew the cultures of the Middle East and Europe.

Kalaq dressed in a discounted polyester suit that he wore like military fatigues, unconsciously pushing the sleeves above his elbows, the slacks spotted by weapon lubricating oil. He had the habit of jerking at the knot of his tie to ease the constraint at his throat. His curly hair hung over his collar. His mustache blended with his heavy beard stubble. Born in Syria, he spoke only Arabic and basic Russian—learned during his training in Yemen.

"Those Marines!" Kalaq laughed. He took quick drags on his cigarette, his hand slashing the air, clouding the compartment with smoke. With his other hand, he swept back his curly hair. Then he jabbed at the release of a walnut-

23

veneered compartment. A table folded out. "A drink to our victory. Do you drink?"

"Alcohol? No."

"Iranians. Some are very strict. Others steal my vodka." Kalaq splashed the clear liquor into a glass. He gulped down the vodka and filled the glass again. "The Marines are amateurs. They come here. They think they know war. A delusion. They read too many comic books. They are amateurs in this business of politics and killing. All their money and weapons and ships. For months they kill no one—how did they think they could earn respect? Now they are defeated and they know they are nothing. Maybe they will run back to Europe. Or the U.S.A. It was a good sport to kill them—not like fighting the Zionists. That is fighting. But I think the game is over, they will go. The next action will be more difficult."

"Perhaps," Rajai commented. He touched the switch to drop the power window. Cold night air thinned the smoke and the smell of alcohol. The limousine left the airport highway, going east through the crowded Burj al-Branjneh district. This route would take them away from areas controlled by the Lebanese Armed Forces. Rajai watched the ravaged shops and apartments flash past. The wars had jammed this Moslem district with refugees from other areas of Lebanon—Shias from the south, Palestinians from the coast, Sunnis from East Beirut. The residents and refugees had crowded into the existing apartment buildings, then occupied the fields, building shacks and haphazard tenements. The doubled and redoubled population had overtaxed the utilities, leaving residents without water, electricity, or sewers. War had destroyed other conveniences —cutting off telephone service, blacking out the street lights. Many tenements occupied by refugees had only kerosene lanterns for light.

"And if they stay, we will kill them. What does it matter? They can do nothing. We are too strong."

"I am in agreement with you." Rajai gave his full attention to the raving Palestinian. Kalaq had killed without reason. Drunk with the mass murder of the Marines and the Russian alcohol, the Palestinian became very dangerous. Any wrong word might offend him. Rajai chose his words carefully. "But the response of the Americans will remain unknown until they attack—or do not attack. They are powerful. But without the will to act. There is no leader with the will to strike back in revenge—only that clown president. And his committees of fools and hacks."

Kalaq laughed. He lit another Marlboro from the butt of the one he smoked. "It was good to see. I am glad that I did not fly back to Damascus with all the others."

"They feared the revenge of the Americans. They feared without reason."

"It is the Americans who must fear. The wrath of the oppressed of the world shall not be satisfied by a few American dead. This was a defeat for the Americans. But it was not an annihilation of their imperial forces. It is a shame that they will go and deny our fighters easy targets. It will be very difficult to follow them to Europe or America."

"More difficult, but not impossible. Others have."

"Are you involved in another action?"

"Actions here in Beirut. You will see. We go there."

"In Europe? The U.S.A.?"

"No. I must be content with my assignment here."

"With the Party of God?"

"The faithful of the Party of God are not as experienced in war as your Palestinian warriors, but they fight. If they are encouraged and supported, they may be victorious. You will see."

"I do not trust them. They fought against the Palestinians. They welcomed the Zionists."

"They are not politically sophisticated. But they are devoted. They accept the teachings of the Ayatollah. Soon, they will take Lebanon from the Christians. When Lebanon joins the Islamic revolution, they will be our allies in the struggle against the Zionists and the Americans. And your allies."

The young Palestinian turned to him. He stabbed the air with his glowing cigarette to emphasize his statement. "Fahkr, you may be my friend. But Palestinians have no allies. Even the Syrians exploit us. We are alone in the world—without a nation, without allies."

"I can only hope to prove you wrong."

"Events prove my words true."

The limousine slowed. Rajai looked ahead and saw the taillights of stopped cars. Militiamen stood at the side of the boulevard, shining lights at the passengers. As the driver braked to a stop in the line of waiting cars and trucks, Kalaq took out his identification.

"You must conceal the alcohol." Rajai pointed to the bar compartment.

"Of course. This is not Syria. We will take this limousine on your tour, yes?" Kalaq asked him. "Why change cars? Your guards can follow."

"I would prefer that we did not," Rajai responded. He did not want to argue with this killer. He phrased his objections very carefully. "We can have no confidence in the discretion of the driver. He cannot hear us, but he can remember where—"

"The driver is one of us. I trust him."

"My friend Iziz, you may trust the driver, but I know my instructions. No one outside of the group is to be trusted."

Kalaq laughed. "Suspicious like a banker. A banker who thinks of everything, every detail. That is what the others said of you. You know every name. You know every detail. The bank clerk, they called you. I am surprised you were not with the command group. Why did you not return with them?"

"I have my assignment here. Who am I to question my role in the struggle?"

A flashlight illuminated the interior. Kalaq put his UNESCO identification against the glass of the window. Though he also carried papers issued by Syria and the Popular Front for the Liberation of Palestine, he presented his UNESCO identification at most checkpoints. Posing as a functionary of the United Nations Educational, Scientific, and Cultural Organization assured safe passage through the maze of Lebanese politics and religious conflicts. Even the Christian Phalangists passed Kalaq through their checkpoints. Rajai wondered if Kalaq would dare to present his UNESCO identification at an Israeli road block.

The militiamen signaled the limousine to continue. The driver steered through the rows of concrete obstacles, then continued east through the ghettos.

"Maybe I will have an operation for you," Kalaq began.

"An operation?" Rajai asked. "Against Israel?"

"Or Europe. When I have the command, I will need all my friends."

"Oh, when you have your command. You are very ambitious. I believe that will come soon." Rajai masked his disdain with flattery. The alcohol-drinking, chain-smoking Kalaq would never command more than a few squads of teenagers. Though the PLF commanders in Damascus valued his recklessness in combat, Kalaq lacked the education and discipline to plan an attack. The Syrian commander of the Marine bombing had used Kalaq to enforce security—by street murder or capture and execution. But Rajai could not dismiss Kalaq as only a vicious gunman. The handsome young Palestinian had the charisma to lead other young men—until the Americans or the Israelis killed him.

"I demanded a group. They told me I will have a command when opportunity comes. A man of action must not hesitate to seize his destiny."

"Of course, I know nothing of that. I am only . . . as you say, like a clerk, seeing to endless details."

The limousine slowed at a brightly lit café. Kalaq saw a group of foreigners. "She is here! There, you see her? Ah, my little French starlet, you are mine this night."

Two foreign men sat with the blond woman. The woman wore white jeans and a dust-soiled white sweat shirt. She toyed with a camera, peering through the viewfinder to look at the other patrons of the café. The men had aluminum equipment cases at their feet. Palestinian guards sat near the foreigners, Kalashnikov rifles in their hands.

"Journalists! Why are they here?" Rajai demanded.

"To interview me. And to accompany me on the visit to the militias attacking the Marines."

"No. They cannot see me. They cannot photograph me. They cannot know I—"

"They are friends, they—"

"No." Rajai threw open the door. Jerking his briefcase free of the Palestinian's legs, he rushed across the street. He kept his face turned from the café. Kalaq shouted out:

"I will see you in Hay al-Sollom, my sly friend Fahkr!"

Across the street, his old Mercedes waited. Rajai kept his face turned from the foreigners until he sat in his Mercedes, one of his guards blocking him from the cameras. Only as his Mercedes accelerated away did Rajai risk a glance back.

The group stood on the sidewalk. Surrounded by the other foreigners and the Palestinian gunmen, the blond Frenchwoman embraced Kalaq.

That whore, Rajai thought. Any shame for an interview. And Kalaq. How could he pretend to be a leader when he did not have the strength to resist the sins of the west?

Rajai knew his judgment of Kalaq to be correct—a fighter, a leader of other fighters, but unworthy of command. Yet fighters had value. Tomorrow or the next day, Rajai would receive a report on his night with the foreign woman. Details to add to his files. Kalaq had offered Rajai a role in his future action. More likely, Rajai would offer Kalaq a role.

If he sent Kalaq against the Americans, Americans would die. And perhaps Kalaq. But what did it matter? Money and weapons created armies of martyrs.

Alone with Angelique Chardon in his limousine, Kalaq watched her lips form the words of her questions, the movements of her hands as she gestured. She sat far from him, her back against the opposite door, her cassette recorder in her hand. Passing cars illuminated her features and hands like a woman seen in a dream. The scent of her perfume and the smoke of his cigarettes brought memories of the casinos of prewar Lebanon, when he had served as a teenage bodyguard for PLO chieftans. As the cars passed, she returned to a silhouette against the lights and scenes of moonlit streets.

The Palestinian guards preceded the limousine in their Land Rover, the French cameramen followed in their van. Chardon interviewed Kalaq in the bulletproof luxury of the limousine as the line of cars wound through the South Beirut slums.

"The Americans are denouncing the attacks on the Marines and French forces as terrorism. What is your response to that?"

"This is a war of liberation. We fight as we must."

"You say 'we.' Did your group participate in the attacks?"

"It is so unusual for a Frenchwoman to speak Arabic. And you do not speak as if you learned in a university. How did you come to speak my language?"

"My father worked in the oil fields. We did not want to live in the British enclaves, so we learned to speak Arabic."

"And where was this?"

"Kuwait. Saudi Arabia. My experience there has helped my career. But please—" She laughed. "I am interviewing you. My life is of no interest to the people of France."

"But to me, you are very interesting. You know the Islamic traditions, yet you dress—as if you were in Paris."

"I am a modern woman. Does that offend you? Are you a Shia?"

"No! I am a socialist."

"What of the Islamic revolution?"

"There are many roads to freedom."

"Do you fight in alliance with the Party of God?"

"Am I allied? No."

"You are taking me to their fighting lines. You must have some alliance—"

"No. We fight the same enemies—the Zionists and the Americans. But we do not coordinate our struggle. My people fight only to liberate Palestine—through revolution and armed struggle."

"Struggle against Israel—"

"The hated Zionist entity."

"And the United States."

"The imperialists who arm and pay the Zionists."

"And revolution?"

"The overthrow of the corrupt Arab regimes that permit the Zionists to exist. The few thousand freedom fighters in Syria and Lebanon cannot defeat the Zionist-American war machine. Only when all the Arab peoples unite in a single nation and launch a united attack can we reclaim our ancestral homes and the holy shrines now held by the Jews."

"There are rumors that Syria and Iran and the Popular Front participated in the attack on the Marines—"

"Who told you that?"

"Many people."

"And I thought you sought the truth. Instead you record the lies of the enemies of the revolutionary states."

"What is the truth?"

"Did not some Islamic group make a claim? The Holy War? I heard it on the radio."

"Yes, there was a call to a radio station—"

"There! They admit it."

Chardon laughed, leaning back. "You are a comedian. You have a reputation—"

"And you are beautiful." Moving across the seat, Kalaq grasped her hand and held her recorder up to her lips. "I want a tape of your laughter. I will play it as a song in my times of isolation and hardship."

She did not take her hand from his. "You have a reputation of brutality. What is your comment on that?"

By the lights of a car, he saw her watching him, her face leaping from the darkness, her blue eyes fixed on his eyes, her hair suddenly glowing, then dark as the lights streaked past.

"My comment?" He kissed her hand.

Laughing again, she pulled her hand from his grip and pushed him back. She spoke an English word. "Valentino."

"What does that mean?"

"Val-en-ti-no. An American movie star who played Arabs in the silent movies. Dark and handsome. Very romantic."

"I am no play actor—"

The limousine slowed. Flamelight lit the interior of the limousine as the driver stopped behind the Land Rover. Kalaq glanced out at the street. He saw blast-shattered buildings on one side, shanties of scrap lumber and sheet metal on the other. Ahead, flames leaped from oil barrels set in a line across the street. Forms moved against the fires.

A voice came from a walkie-talkie on the seat: "They will not allow us to pass."

"Who are they?"

"Shiites. Of the Amal."

"How many?"

"Only four boys."

"Offer them some money."

Kalaq turned to Chardon. "You see? We are not allies of the Shiites. We fight the same enemies. But they believe we are enemies, also."

The limousine intercom chimed. "Mr. Kalaq. I think there is a disturbance."

"What?" As Kalaq lifted the radio to speak, a silhouette came to the limousine. He spoke quickly into his walkie-talkie, "Be ready." A hand knocked at the window. Kalaq powered down the window.

A Kalashnikov barrel came through the open window. Chardon shrieked and pressed herself against the far side. The face of a teenage militiaman looked inside. Kalaq spoke smoothly, without fear. He kept the transmit lever of the walkie-talkie depressed.

"What is wrong? Why do you threaten workers of the United Nations?"

"What do you want in our district?"

"Nothing. We are only driving to the highway. Please do not point your rifle at us. This reporter is terrified."

"You are Palestinians. You come with soldiers and weapons. What do you want here?"

"Those men are my bodyguards. We are going to a troubled area. Please lower your rifle. Thank you, we are no threat to you. May I show you my United Nations identification? Will that end this problem? Here is my identification—"

In one motion, Kalaq brought a 9mm pistol from under his jacket and shot the teenager in the face. Simultaneously, rifles fired long bursts of full-auto. Kalaq threw open the limousine door and fired a second bullet through the head of the dying militiaman. He took the teenager's Kalashnikov.

Rushing from a doorway, a middle-aged man shouldered a rifle. Kalaq triggered a three-round burst through the man's chest, staggering him back. Shots from the Palestinians in the Land Rover hit the dying man again.

Kalaq scanned the street. An old man shuffled for the

safety of a doorway. Kalaq snapped a single shot through the man's back, spinning him to the sidewalk. Beyond the fires in the barrels, two shadowy forms ran for the tenements. Firing a long full-auto burst, Kalaq dropped the running forms—and a woman screamed in agony. No one else moved on that side of the street.

Glancing behind him, Kalaq saw the Frenchmen in the mini-van videotaping the scene. He flashed a V-for-victory handsign.

A silhouette moved in the open window of a wood and sheet metal shack. Kalaq fired a burst through the wall, an arm flailing, children screaming.

Ahead, his men leaned out the shattered windows of the Land Rover to fire long bursts of 7.62ComBloc slugs into the bodies of other teenage militiamen.

"They are all dead?" Kalaq shouted out.

"All."

"Continue on!"

Chardon crouched in the street, flashing photos of the dead teenager. Kalaq grabbed the collar of her sweat shirt and jerked her back. The acceleration of the limousine slammed the door closed. Kalaq put the muzzle of the Kalashnikov out the window and sprayed unaimed automatic fire at the shops and apartments around the checkpoint. Cartridge casings bounced off the glass partition and fell on the seat.

Pointing the camera up at Kalaq, Chardon flashed photos of him shooting. The Kalashnikov's bolt slammed closed on the empty chamber. Kalaq glanced back to confirm that the mini-van followed, then looked down at Chardon on the seat.

"I am not a play actor." He pushed his lips against hers and felt her mouth open, her mouth soft and fluid, her tongue fluttering against his lips. Her arms closed around him as they rode through the streets of Beirut.

Hidden in the trash and weeds of the stinking al-Ghadir, they watched the Hizbullah bridge checkpoint for hours. Hussein and Gamal hid within listening distance of the bunker, Gamal crouching on the steep embankment below the bunker, Hussein a few steps away, flat in the weeds where he overheard the voices of the drivers in the cars and trucks. Alvarez watched the bridge and road from a few meters away. Niles lay twenty-five meters away. From his position on the embankment, he viewed the area around the checkpoint—the bunker, both sides of the bridge, his concealed squad, and the nearby buildings.

Niles saw only three civilians on foot in the first two hours—a man and teenager escorting an old woman out of Hay al-Sollom. They had hurried from doorway to doorway, looking around with fear, the men carrying suitcases and bundles. The gunmen at the bridge jeered at them and fired bursts of automatic fire over their heads. After the pointless shooting, Niles watched the roof lines and windows overlooking the checkpoints. He saw no sentries. The residents did not dare look out their windows.

Other civilians passed in vehicles—outbound, their cars and trucks loaded with children and possessions. Niles saw the drivers passing money to the checkpoint gunmen—payoffs to escape the district. He wondered where in the Koran the Hizbullah militiamen found inspiration for extortion.

Cars and trucks carrying militiamen passed in both directions. The men held rifles and RPG launchers. Posters of the Ayatollah Khomeini had been taped to doors. A Land Rover with a pedestal-mounted Soviet 12.7mm Degtyarev heavy machine gun paused at the checkpoint, the militiamen talking for a few minutes before continuing. Niles saw the same cars enter and exit, carrying the same number of men each time. Perhaps the groups patrolled the roads leading to the district or carried a few boxes of ammunition to the snipers firing on the Marine perimeter. But no trucks with masses of militiamen went through the bridge checkpoint.

Niles waited. Though the Hizbullah—and their Syrian and Iranian sponsors—might be using other routes to other assembly points, Niles reasoned that any attack on the Marine perimeter would come from Hay al-Sollom, where the fanatics of the Party of God controlled the streets and the

Syrians controlled the highways from the Iranian-occupied town of Baalbek. An attack from the north of the airport involved negotiations with the several Palestinian and Shiite militias of Burj al-Branjneh. The Lebanese Armed Forces maintained salaried informers in all those militias. No information had come of an attack from the north—only the secondhand report of an attack from Hay al-Sollom.

The approach of the Mercedes took Niles's attention. He saw no weapons, no posters of the scowling Khomeini. The old four-door sedan slowed through the snaking curve of obstacles and stopped at the checkpoint. A militiaman waved his flashlight over the interior. The sight of the bearded men in the white shirts and suitcoats put Niles into motion.

Slipping backward through the trash, he eased down the embankment, and dropped into the stagnant sewage. He moved quickly through the stench until he passed Alvarez. Hand-signing for the sergeant to follow, Niles continued to the bridge, then went up the slope to Gamal. The radio in the bunker played Arabic-language songs, the voices and orchestra covering the noises of Niles's rush up the embankment.

"Who is in the car?"

"The music," Gamal answered in bad English. "I not hear."

Niles whispered in Arabic, telling Gamal to be ready to capture the checkpoint and the militiamen in the Mercedes. Then he continued up the embankment.

Loud voices came from the road. The men argued over identification. Niles understood that they disagreed over the validity of a pass issued by the Syrian Army. One man said the pass had no value in Beirut. The other said that their Party officers recognized the Syrians as allies and therefore they must accept the identification. Niles slowly raised his head above the concrete of the bridge.

Wind-blown papers and trash had drifted against the steel mesh of the guardrail. Niles shifted until one eye found a hole. He saw the polished black sedan continue into Hay al-Sollom. The boots and the voices of the militiamen passed as they returned to the bunker. Niles moved again, easing up beside Hussein. The music and pop lyrics of ABBA covered his whispered questioning of Hussein:

"Who was in that car?"

"Foreigners. They did not speak very good Arabic."

"But who were they?"

"There was nothing said. Only questions about their documents. They came from the Bekaa with Syrian papers."

"In thirty minues, we're taking the checkpoint. You and Gamal will walk up there and shoot them. Understand?"

"Just walk to them? And shoot?"

"They'll think you are one of them. Tell them you are looking for the Pasdaran. Try to get the name of that one in the Mercedes. Any information you can. The sergeant and I will cover you from here. Then you will man the checkpoint until that Mercedes comes out. I want whoever was in that Mercedes."

"They were not Syrians."

"That's why I want them."

Niles slowly worked his way down the embankment. He stopped and gave Gamal whispered instructions in both English and Arabic. He wanted no misunderstandings. Then he continued down to the stream of sewage where Alvarez waited.

"We're taking the checkpoint in thirty minutes. I want to try to capture whoever was in that Mercedes."

"Who were they?"

"Hussein said they weren't Syrian. They looked Persian to me. Iranian. They came in from the Bekaa. I want them."

"We'll take the checkpoint and wait? Check papers and all that?"

"Affirmative."

"Respectfully, sir, you are one *vato loco*."

"You don't want to do this?"

"Ready when you are, sir."

They went up the embankment. Niles hand-signed to Gamal to join Hussein. Gamal nodded and shifted positions. The two Marines continued up until they could peer through the litter and garbage against the bridge railings. From

35

Niles's point of view, he looked into the bunker where the three Hizbullah militiamen shared a kettle of tea and shouted over the loud music. He saw only one man. He saw the hands of another when the militiaman gestured and the boots of the third under the table.

Glancing at their watches, the Marines and Lebanese waited. Hussein and Gamal tied their white, Arabic-lettered headbands around their foreheads. Niles straightened the cotter pin on a U.S.-issue M-67 fragmentation grenade.

A car of civilians passed through the checkpoint. The shouted threats of the militiamen confirmed Niles's observation—when the escaping family pleaded that they had no money, the gunmen threatened to burn the car. Children wailed. A woman prayed out loud for the mercy of Allah and the gunmen told her to be quiet. The woman shrieked and the militiamen laughed and told the family to continue. From his point of view, Alvarez had watched what happened and whispered to Niles:

"The *puto* grabbed her gold teeth. Right out of her mouth."

The militiamen returned to their bunker. Niles saw them pour tea over gold bridgework, then hold the stolen gold up to the light. For the last minutes of their lives, the Party of God holy warriors laughed and joked about the gold.

Niles screwed his valved hearing protectors into his ears, then hand-signaled Hussein and Gamal. Silently, they left their concealment. They walked directly to the bunker, their hands casually gripping their Kalashnikov rifles.

A militiaman in the bunker heard their boots kicking through the sidewalk litter and looked out. Seeing their ragged fatigues and white headbands, he put down his rifle. Hussein leaned in the doorway, left hand on the sandbags, right hand loose on the pistol grip of his Kalashnikov. Niles, only two steps away, listened as Hussein asked if the militiamen had seen a group of Iranian Revolutionary Guards in a truck.

"A truck? No truck. But some Pasdaran came through in a Mercedes."

"Why do you ask that?" another militiaman demanded. "What unit are you from? We do not know—"

Hussein fired, sweeping the bucking assault rifle from side to side in the narrow bunker, emptying the thirty-round magazine point-blank into the three Hizbullah.

Silence returned. Niles bent down the safety pin on the grenade and returned it to his thigh pocket. Alvarez left the embankment and casually walked to the bunker. Niles watched the rooftops overlooking the road. He saw no response to the noise of the riflefire.

"Captain!" Alvarez hissed.

"On my way." Niles scrambled up to the road. He pulled his black watch cap down on his head to cover his forehead and short-cut hair. He continued to the bunker, his eyes scanning the buildings beyond the bridge.

In the bunker, Hussein searched through the pockets of the dead men, taking out papers, money, and identification. Gamal and Alvarez heaved the dead militiamen into the stream of sewage below. Mock-solemn, Alvarez crossed himself and muttered a quick prayer:

"Ashes to ashes, shit to shit."

Niles watched the moonlit rooftops. "Hussein. Gamal. Get out on the road. We'll deal with this."

The Marines threw the blood-splattered table and chairs, the shattered cassette player, and stacks of Khomeini posters and newspapers over the railing. Dirt from the torn sandbags ran onto the concrete, covering the blood. The confined interior of the bunker stank of cordite and blood.

"Now we wait." Niles looked out a gunport viewing the road from Hay al-Sollom. "The Party of God punks said that Mercedes was carrying Revolutionary Guards. When they come back, we take them."

"Alive or dead?"

"That's their decision."

"Car coming!"

Niles shifted to where he could watch the checkpoint. Headlights approached from the east. A battered Peugeot sedan stopped. Hussein went to the driver's window. Gamal stood a few steps from the passenger side. The driver wore the rust and green camouflage uniform and beret of an elite Syrian unit.

Hussein demanded identification. An officer spoke from

the back, questioning Hussein. Niles could not make out the Arabic of the dialogue between Hussein and the officer.

A soldier in the front seat jerked up his rifle. Gamal fired through the windshield, killing the soldier. Hussein fired into the faces of the Syrian officers as Gamal fired again, the full-auto bursts of high-velocity slugs raking the car, shattering the windows and hammering the metal of the car. The engine raced as the dead driver's foot held down the accelerator.

"Damn," Niles sighed. "Alvarez. Back that car off the road, put it over there—" He pointed to the vacant lot on the east bank of the al-Ghadir.

Gamal and Hussein leaned through the shattered windows of the Peugeot and took weapons. One Syrian groaned and struck at their hands. Alvarez ran to the car and shoved the dead driver aside. He shifted into reverse and backed the Peugeot through the obstacles, then parked in the vacant lot.

Niles left the bunker, keeping his face down. In less than ten minutes, they had fired almost a hundred shots—the quiet action had gone dangerously loud. Hussein ran to Niles and told him:

"They asked about an Iranian. They asked if he had come through here in a black Mercedes with Pasdaran body-guards."

"What else?"

"Then they saw blood on my hands."

"You did all right. You did what you had to. A few more minutes and we'll get out of here. If the Mercedes comes, try to separate the leader from the others. If they fight, shoot them. But I want the leader alive."

Continuing to the Peugeot, he glanced inside. Three Syrians—two soldiers in the front seat and an officer in the back—had died instantly of chest and head wounds. But the fourth Syrian still lived. Alvarez eased the officer out of the back seat and inspected his wounds. He pressed his hands over a froth of blood.

"He's got two sucking chest wounds," Alvarez told Niles. "A through-and-through with a compound fracture to the left arm. A gut wound. A near-miss along the side of his head."

Laboring to breathe, the officer choked and coughed blood, then said in British-accented English: "Americans . . ."

Niles had seen men wounded like this. The Syrian had only minutes to live. In Arabic, Niles told the Syrian not to move, a medic would come soon.

"Americans who speak Arabic. Don't lie to me about a doctor. You killed us, but you are defeated."

"You are not dead yet," Niles told him. "Answer my questions and we will try to keep you alive."

"I tell you nothing—"

Niles put his knee on the Syrian's bullet-shattered arm. Shrieking, his mouth spraying blood, the Syrian thrashed against the agony. Niles repeated, "Answer my questions and we will try to save your life. Who is the Iranian?"

"Rajai!"

Taking his knee from the Syrian's arm, Niles asked, "What is his full name?"

The Syrian struggled to breathe. Blood streamed from his mouth. "Rajai," he gasped out. "I only know Rajai."

"And what does he do?"

"He is with the Pasdaran . . ."

"Where will the Hizbullah assemble for the attack?"

No answers came. Choking, struggling to breathe, the Syrian convulsed as he drowned in his own blood. Alvarez rolled the man onto his side to try to clear his air passages, then gave him mouth-to-mouth resuscitation. The breath bubbled out of the bullet wounds in his lungs. The Syrian stopped moving. Alvarez searched for a pulse.

"Dead."

"Go work the checkpoint. No more shoot-outs. Don't stop anyone. Just wave cars through, unless the Mercedes comes. A few more minutes, then we're out of here."

"Even if we don't get the Iranian?"

"Can't risk it. This has gone wrong."

Working alone, Niles searched the dead Syrians for identification and documents. He found only identification cards and photos of their families. Going through the Peugeot, he found carbon copies of lists, typed in Russian and Arabic.

The numbers and Soviet names indicated weapons and munitions.

He stripped the corpses of their uniforms and equipment. In the trunk of the Peugeot, he found a ten-liter gas can, cans of oil, tools, ropes, and a plastic tarp. With the rope and tarp, Niles bundled up the uniforms and equipment.

Headlights interrupted him. Niles went flat on the rutted dirt and watched. A line of vehicles—a Land Rover, a gleaming midnight blue limousine, and a Japanese passenger van—slowed at the rows of oil drums in the road. Gunmen rode in the Land Rover, the muzzles of their Kalashnikov rifles out the windows. Niles watched the gunmen, noting their polyester sportscoats, their shaved faces, their barbered hair. No Arabic scrawls on the Land Rover identified their religious or political faction. They looked like hired soldiers, probably bodyguards for the official in the limousine.

Hussein motioned the Land Rover past. The driver of the limousine braked and held out documents, but Hussein told him to continue. Hussein shined a flashlight through the limousine's dark windows and stared at what he saw. The mini-van followed a moment later, a video camera recording the checkpoint scene.

Niles waited until the sounds of the vehicles faded before moving. He shoved the stripped bodies of the Syrians back into the old Peugeot. Finally, he spilled the gasoline from the ten-liter can over the bodies and the interior, soaking the foam upholstery with the gasoline, then poured a line of gasoline to the embankment. Done, he shouldered the bundle of captured uniforms and equipment and started down the embankment. He signaled the others with a low whistle.

Running from the bunker, Alvarez crossed the lot to Niles. But Hussein and Gamal did not leave the road. "We should've stopped that United Nations limo for a search, sir."

"It was a UN limo?"

"UNESCO. That Arab had a blonde and bar. The high life."

Niles pointed to the Lebanese troopers. "Get them over here. We're on our way out."

"Sir, they told me they're willing to risk it and stay. That Mercedes could come through any minute."

"I'm not willing to risk it. Taking this checkpoint was a gamble. And it's not going right. I want us out of here before we lose."

"Yes, sir. On my way."

Crouching, Niles waited. Alvarez ran back to the bridge. Hussein and Gamal rushed down the embankment and into the filth of the al-Ghadir. Alvarez followed, crawling backward down the slope, using a rag to erase their boot prints. He rearranged trash to cover any signs of their infiltration. Niles watched the road, his rifle ready.

This incursion had failed. Niles had not risked his life and the lives of his men to kill a few militiamen and Syrians.

Though his squad had monitored the traffic on this road, they had not seen any activity within the district. He knew only that no transports had passed through the checkpoint for three hours. If the Hizbullah had already massed their forces in the empty tenements of Hay al-Sollom, the Marine line would receive no warning until the assault. Or the assembly of militiamen and weapons might begin in an hour or a day.

The observation of the Iranians and Syrians operating with the militias confirmed information from Lebanese intelligence. For months, sources had reported the presence of the foreign liaison officers. The reports had not detailed their activities. Niles had hoped to take and interrogate the Iranian. He could not risk the wait. He had only the identification of the dead Syrians and their list of weapons and munitions.

But he now knew the name of an Iranian who worked with both the Hizbullah and the Syrians: Rajai.

Niles saw Alvarez and the Lebanese moving silently through the black stream below him. He motioned them to continue, then put the muzzle of his Kalashnikov to the trash in front of him. He fired once, gasoline flashing into flame and the line of fire racing to the Peugeot.

By the orange light of the burning car, Niles obscured his trail with a stick, scratching out his boot prints and scattering trash. He wanted nothing to remain to identify the killers of the militiamen and Syrians as Marines.

"Won't know what hit them, sir," Alvarez commented when Niles joined the others.

"Or what will hit them again."

3

ANGELIQUE Chardon packed her suitcase. In two hours, she would take the afternoon ferry to Cyprus, then fly on to Paris. She rushed through her updated reports on the bombing of the United States Marines. Reading that morning's Arabic language newspapers, she marked sections of the columns with her red pen. She marked a number beside each section. In a newpaper published the day before in Damascus, she found a quote of the Syrian Defense Minister Mustafa Talas. Then, translating as she typed, she went number by number through the sections, writing her French dispatch first draft from the Lebanese and Syrian newspapers.

She worked near the sliding glass balcony door of her rented room, the newpapers spread over the desk and the bed. Pausing in her translation of a paragraph of rhetorical Arabic to the straightforward French required by her Paris editor, Chardon stared out at the trees of the park below her hotel. The balcony overlooked one of the parks along the Corniche Pierre Geymayel. Over the tops of high-rise apartments, she had a view of the Shouf Mountains. The flowery Arabic phrases reminded her of the revolutionary nonsense Kalaq pronounced. Laughing at her one-night lover, she returned to her work. She completed translating and editing the articles of the other journalists very quickly—their writing would appear in Paris tomorrow under her name.

Glancing at her watch—only another hour—she cleared her desk, slipping her typed copy into her briefcase, throwing the newspapers in the corner. She set her Sony by the typewriter and plugged in the headphones. As the tape

43

played back the resonant voice of Kalaq raving, she translated and typed. The Palestinian's statements did not require a studied translation—she had heard it all many times, in Arabic, French, and English. Kalaq only repeated the propaganda of his faction.

She included the personal questions he had asked her—let the magazine readers in France read of her childhood in the Gulf States, let the readers imagine the scene of the Palestinian gunman eyeing a Frenchwoman as they rode through the war. But she cut his request for a tape of her laughter and the saccharine hand-kissing. Instead, the shooting ended the interview.

The photo of the dead boy, the sequence of Kalaq firing his rifle—the interview and photos would take no more than two magazine pages. On the plane to Paris, she would scribble out a romantic description of the dark-haired Iziz Kalaq, the poet and freedom fighter, charming and ruthless—she would not mention his tobacco-foul breath and premature ejaculation. She finished typing the interview only seconds before the telephone rang.

"Your car is here," the deskman told her.

Throwing the interview into the folder of copy sheets, she locked her briefcase and her portable typewriter. A horn sounded from the street. She searched through her rented room to confirm she had forgotten nothing. Rushing out, she struggled down the stairs.

Plywood had replaced the glass in the hotel's door and street windows. Running through the shadowy lobby, Chardon pushed the door open with her suitcase and hurried into the midday glare—and stopped. Two bearded men, their hair cropped prison-short, the forms of pistols at their waists visible through their polyester jackets, waited at a white Mercedes. Chardon saw no taxi. The two gunmen stepped toward her and she spun, trying to return to the hotel. Hands grabbed her.

A man spoke to her in Persian. She hit him with her typewriter case and simultaneously dropped her suitcase on the feet of the other man.

"Angelique!"

44

Recognizing the voice, she turned to see Fahkr Rajai. Elegant as always, Rajai took her arm and escorted her back to the Mercedes. His guards brought her suitcase and typewriter. "Why did you run?"

"Your men. I thought they would kidnap me. How could I know it would be you? I did not expect to see you here."

He pushed her into the back seat and sat beside her. "And I did not know you would leave without informing me."

"It doesn't matter. I will be back soon. I must go to Jounieh for the launch to Cyprus."

"We will take you there. Tell me of your evening with Kalaq. Or was it the night?"

Chardon snapped open her briefcase and gave Rajai the typed interview. "This is what I wrote of the evening. Do you want me to tell you of the night?"

"How can your sordid affairs interest me?"

As the driver guided the Mercedes through traffic, Rajai read the French article. Chardon watched him, waiting for a reaction. But his face showed nothing. She had met this strange man a year before, when he worked with the exiled Mujahedeen. Unlike the other Iranian men she knew in Paris, Rajai had not pursued her. This elegant schemer had never invited her to his chateau, hotel, rented room, or back seat. In fact, she had never seen him with a woman. Yet he watched her the times they talked, his eyes fixing on her breasts, the lines of her thighs under her skirt. Did she mistake those stares? Had he been one of the political prisoners emasculated by the Shah? Did he have no interest in women?

It did not matter. She did not want to risk their business relationship to discover the sexual identity of this Iranian who looked like an Italian mannequin. He paid too well and provided too many introductions to other strange creatures of Middle Eastern politics and war—like Kalaq.

"Is this all?" Rajai asked, returning the interview to her.

"What did you expect? A detailed strategic and political plan on the recapture of Palestine? An existentialist interpretation of the Palestinian experience? Another chapter for the Koran? Kalaq is no thinker. He only talks."

"And what of his time in Hay al-Sollom?" Rajai asked, turning, watching her. "He followed me. How did you pass the Hizbullah?"

"The Amals stopped us on the highway, but the others—"

"There was a checkpoint on the bridge."

"Nothing. They did not stop us."

"Did he or any of his men speak with them?"

"No."

"And in the district? Who did he contact? Names, streets, places, times."

Chardon shook her head no. "We only taped the shooting. We asked a militiaman to fire at the Marines but he refused. So the cameraman had Kalaq's Palestinians shoot. Then a patrol came and told us to leave. He met no one. No one talked with him. It was all—" she remembered the thrill when Kalaq shot the boy, then the noise of Kalaq's rifle slamming her senses. If he had only proved as much a lover as a killer—"a waste of time and videotape."

"Why do you return?"

"It is my editor's decision—"

"Tell him that events forced you to stay. The attacks against the Americans will continue."

"How do you know this?"

"I am only telling you of a rumor."

"And the French?"

Rajai shrugged. "I have heard nothing of that."

"But the Americans?"

"That, I have heard. Perhaps tonight."

"He has already told me to return."

"Were not the other rumors correct? And now you have excellent coverage of the victories."

"My editor would not allow me to call the attack on the French legionnaires a victory. The word will be terrorism."

"Words. We will take you back to your hotel."

"But I must call my editor."

"You are a modern woman. Make your own decision."

Chardon surrendered. "Take me back."

The Mercedes stopped in front of her hotel. "You are there."

Rajai pushed her from the car. The bodyguards dumped her cases on the sidewalk. Chardon struggled back to the hotel entry, spitting out curses in three languages. But she would never curse Rajai to his face. She could not break contact with him—she needed the money and names the arrogant little mannequin supplied. Without his Swiss checks financing her travel and expenses, without his calls alerting her to terrorist actions before the event, she had no hope of maintaining her flow of copy to newspapers and magazines. Her earnings from her articles and interviews did not meet her expenses. Somehow, she must end her dependency on the Iranian—find a staff position on a magazine, marry a banker—anything to escape from Rajai.

Lines of tracers arced across the moonlit fields. Colonel Anthony Devlin crouched in the darkness, his eyes searching the shadows and tangles of brush for the bunker. Fifty meters away, he saw the Marine CP-69 and the Lebanese Army bunkers on the bridge across the Nahr al-Ghadir.

Ahead, Devlin heard a distinct single shot from a 7.62-NATO weapon, followed by a three-shot burst—an M-60 machine gun. He rushed toward the hidden machine gunner and called out:

"Niles!"

A voice answered from the weeds. "Who's there?"

"I want to speak with Captain Niles."

"Don't know who you're talking about."

Devlin left the shadows. He wore a gray business suit and the gray cloth seemed to glow in the moonlight. Crouching, he held his black briefcase in front of him. He moved forward several steps, then crouched again, his eyes searching for the voice. Grass and low brush sloped down into the darkness of the streambed. He scanned the embankment but saw no one.

A rocket shot out from a tenement three hundred meters away. Devlin dropped down flat. Flame sprayed from the fields across the al-Ghadir, the sound of the explosion coming an instant later. A shadow moved beside him. A pale face with high Slavic cheekbones spoke to him:

"Are you Colonel Devlin?"

"Correct."

"I'm Sergeant Vatsek—"

The colonel remembered Sergeant Vatsek from fact-finding visits in August and early September. The son of Bolsheviks driven from Russia by Stalin's purges, the sergeant had an unusual understanding of the Soviet threat to the Free World. The Force Reconnaissance noncom somehow moved silently in the dry weeds.

"—just a second, Colonel. Shaffik, put it to them," Vatsek called out. "I got to talk with this man."

Steps away, a point of electronic green appeared, then went dark again. An M-60 fired a three-shot burst of 7.62-NATO.

"Over here, Colonel." Vatsek led him through the brush. The sergeant's shoulders looked almost a meter wide. "Get some shelter. That's my apprentice Shaffik back there. First Lebanese Air Assault Battalion. I mounted a starlite scope on a righteous M-sixty and we're trying to kill us some E-rannies. But the fact is, we need artillery."

They came to a camouflaged bunker. "Captain? Colonel's here . . ."

Devlin crouched behind a low wall of sandbags and waited. He heard low voices in the bunker speaking Arabic and English. A plastic blackout curtain parted as the sergeant went in. Weak light spilled out as silhouettes shifted in the doorway. The curtain fell back. A hand gripped his shoulder.

"Well, it's Colonel Marvel."

Friends for fifteen years, they shook hands. Devlin laughed at the old nickname of 'Marvel.' As an ambitious young intelligence lieutenant in Vietnam, his code name had been 'Captain Marvel' or 'Mr. Marvel.'

"As always," Niles continued in his harsh Appalachian accent. "You came through. Still in your D of C uniform. Look at that. Gray flannel camouflage for the war of the bureaucracies."

"I flew all night. I thought your offer required immediate action."

"Imagine you shake them up, talking tough and actually trying to do it, too."

48

Colonel Devlin cut short the jokes. "What's the situation?"

"The situation? We got two hundred men dead and fifty more missing and the sentries are now permitted to load their rifles. Yes, sir. It is official."

"What about the assault on the airport?"

"Nothing much from my sources. But you can see what's going on. Those gangs over there are trying to kill more Marines. The men on the perimeter request artillery and zero—it is inconsistent with our peacekeeping presence."

"All that is changing. There'll be a new man in command tomorrow."

"The Secretary of State resigned? Finally!"

"No. They replaced the commander here. The new headquarters unit is already on the ground."

"It wasn't the Marine commander who made the rules. But he'll take the blame for following State Department instructions. Nothing will change until the State Department understands that this isn't a peacekeeping operation anymore. That's why I called you to make the offer. There's no point in talking to our commander. You did get the authorization, right?"

"I did. And I took that authorization and flew out before they could reconsider. But there are conditions."

"Don't tell me, I'll guess. No loaded weapons."

"No U.S. weapons, equipment, or uniforms."

"Just like old times. We got all that."

"And a secondary mission. They want you to observe and report on the Iranians and Syrians in the area."

"They want prisoners?"

"No. Only your observations."

"What if I take prisoners?"

"Question them over there. And don't bring them back."

"The Iranians and Syrians came into Hay al-Sollom in September. You saw it, you brief the council."

"I don't qualify. Can you organize a unit and send them out there by tomorrow night?"

"Sir." Niles hesitated for a moment. "You and I go back a long time. I Corps, the incursions."

"Since I was a lieutenant."

"Right, we go back a long time. And look at us now. You a colonel in the Pentagon, and me—" A penlight flared—"and me, a captain in the Syrian Army . . ."

Niles waved the weak beam over his uniform. He wore the rust and green Soviet-style uniform of the Syrian Army. "Ready to go now. We went last night."

"Without authorization."

"The authorization didn't come. Had to do it. And we're ready to go out again."

"That was an unwise—that was an absolutely crazy thing to do. You would face court-martial."

"Yeah, I know. I'm just out-and-out loco. But someone had to do it."

"What did you see?"

"Syrians and Iranians. Didn't see any concentrations of Party of God militia. But I got some documents. And I got a name. An Iranian named Rajai of the Revolutionary Guard who works as liaison between the Hizbullah and the Syrians."

"How did you do this?"

Niles described the observation and capture of the checkpoint, then the interrogation of the wounded Syrian.

"What will you do tonight?"

"Take a walk through a different part of town. Look for a few hundred Party of God fanatics. Suppress some snipers. Why don't you come in and meet the other fellows?"

They pushed through the blackout tarp. In the bunker, Devlin saw four M-16 rifles propped against the wall. Two sets of USMC field gear—flak vests, folded camouflage fatigues, web gear, boots, and dog tags—lay in neat stacks. Two other stacks contained similar uniforms but with the different web gear of the Lebanese Armed Forces.

A group of five men gathered around a map. Only Sergeant Vatsek wore Marine fatigues. Captain Niles and a dark-featured Chicano wore the uniforms of the Syrian Army. Two Lebanese wore the mismatched uniforms and beards of militiamen. White headbands marked with blood red Arabic script identified the two men as fighters for the Hizbullah. All four men had Soviet Kalashnikov rifles. One of the Lebanese also carried rockets and a launcher.

Folding the map, Captain Niles introduced the others. "You know Sergeant Vatsek. This is Sergeant Alvarez—"

"The captain thinks I look like a Syrian."

"More than I do. And you most definitely look more like a Syrian than Sergeant Vatsek."

"I could wear a chador," the sergeant joked, meaning the black head-to-foot gown of traditional Shiite women. The Americans and Hussein laughed. Hussein explained the joke to Gamal and the group laughed again at the idea of the hulking, two-hundred-forty-pound weight lifter hidden under a black chador.

"You'll go with us when we recon Russia." Niles took grease-stick camouflage from his pocket. He smoothed the brown paste over his tanned Anglo face as he continued the introductions. "And my Lebanese friends are Hussein and Gamal of the Air Assault Battalion. Graduates of my courses."

"What do the headbands say?" Devlin asked.

"Oh, this?" Hussein pointed to the Arabic script. "It is a vow to become a martyr. Which I hope is not my fate."

"Came true for the shee-it that wore it," Vatsek told Devlin.

"Hussein and Gamal happen to be gentlemen of traditional Islam," Niles explained to Devlin. "Of what is called Sunni. They do not agree with the teachings of the Shias—"

"Do not agree!" Hussein protested against the captain's mild phrasing. "They will persecute my people. If we don't fight them, Lebanon will be like Iran. Or they will destroy the country and then we will be part of Syria."

"Enemies of all the world," Gamal added, pronouncing the words slowly. He talked in Arabic with Hussein. They argued. Alvarez joined in the argument in halting Arabic.

"How will you maintain contact with the perimeter?" Devlin asked Niles. "You have radios?"

"We have radios but we can't risk calling back here." Niles slipped his walkie-talkie from one of his magazine pouches. "They're only citizen's band. Alvarez played with the frequency, but he told me we can't trust it."

"The militias have got ones just like ours." Alvarez turned away from the Arabic argument to explain the radio problem. "Probably bought them at the same shop on Hamra. Rinky-dink things probably don't have the range to make it back here. Through all the buildings and all that. A very serious chance we'd just announce ourselves to the militias. We'll mostly be using ours for Morse code."

Niles looked to his men. "Ready to go?"

They nodded. One by one, they pushed through the plastic tarp.

"What do you estimate your return time to be?" Devlin asked Niles.

"From where?"

The colonel looked across the moonlit fields to Hay al-Sollom.

"Me, go there?" Niles asked, incredulous. He rubbed the dark greasepaint onto his face. "We're not going there. I deny any suggestion that we would violate the Rules of Engagement. But you can expect us back from where we're not going sometime before dawn."

4

EXPLOITING the shadows of the narrow, deserted streets, Niles led the others through Hay al-Sollom. Fighting had ravaged the district throughout the preceding decade—the attacks of the Phalangists early in the civil war, the Israeli artillery and air strikes of 1982, the small arms battles of the Shiites and Israelis during the occupation, then the street battles of the Shiites against Shiites. Streets had become piles of rubble. Many buildings had lost the upper floors or the balconies overlooking the street. Every shop, every tenement, every wall, every rusting street sign, bore the marks of war—the pocking of bullets and fragments from shells and rockets of all calibers and types.

The residents had rebuilt and repaired again and again. Walls had become abstract mosaics of bricks scavenged from rubble. Scrap metal became shacks. Wood and steel members from fallen buildings reinforced the walls and roofs of damaged buildings. Then, to stop bullets and shrapnel from explosions, the residents had added sandbags.

Thick walls of sandbags protected shops. Sandbags stacked on balconies and blocking windows provided safety for families on the upper floors. Sandbag bunkers on the street corners and rooftops protected the militiamen who guarded the area from other militias.

Niles led Alvarez and the Lebanese Air Assault volunteers through the deserted streets. Listening for Hizbullah patrols, his eyes scanning the windows and moonlit rooftops, Niles walked silently, his hand on the pistol grip of his Kalashnikov. He faked the arrogant swagger of the Syrians he had observed. Unless his voice or face identified him as an American, no militiaman would fire at a Syrian uniform. The militias feared the Syrians. If a gunman shot at a Syrian patrol, the patrol answered with rockets, then artillery, regardless of civilian casualties. The Syrians had no Rule of Engagement other than overwhelming firepower.

Twice, when he spotted lookouts watching the streets, he had ignored them, keeping his face turned. Hussein and Gamal had waved as they passed. The lookouts had not left the safety of their bunkers to question their comrades and the Syrian officers.

Niles knew Hay al-Sollom. He had first come to the district in the winter of 1982. After training Lebanese soldiers throughout the day, he changed into civilian clothes and walked through the districts of South Beirut. He carried a camera to pass as a journalist. Practicing his first words of Arabic, he went from street stalls to shops to cafés, watching the people of the war-shattered district. Years before, he had enrolled in through-the-mail anthropology courses with the University of North Carolina. He studied and wrote when his duties permitted. Learning of the Shiite position in the Lebanese society, he thought he might write a graduate study on the transition of the minority to majority.

He had felt closer to the Shiites of this ghetto than the Christian bourgeoisie of East Beirut. In East Beirut, wealth and traditional privilege kept the civil war far away. The Christians of East Beirut still enjoyed French restaurants and expensive shops and clean streets. Here, the Shiite people suffered with every shift in alliances, yet they continued to open their markets and peddle their products and answer the prayer calls to the mosques.

At first, the Marine force at the international airport brought the common people of the district some safety from the wars between the militias. The people greeted Marine patrols with flowers and cold soft drinks. But later, the American administration in Washington openly supported the Christian minority against all the other ethnic factions of Lebanon. This involved the United States in the ruling elite's denial of the right of a democractic government— representing the actual populations of the country's non-

Christian communities—to the people of the nation. Lebanese of all faiths saw the Marines as only more militia in Beirut.

As late as June, Niles still had friends in Hay al-Sollom. He visited cafés and made awkward conversation in Arabic or talked with acquaintances who spoke English. He took notes and photos. Some of the Shiites knew he served with the Marines at the airport—he had trained their sons. One young soldier had introduced him to a widowed cousin. He and the soldier and the young woman—a mother of two children—talked in a café and laughed at his very bad Arabic. Later, when the soldier invited Niles to his family for a dinner, he saw the woman only for moments as she carried food to the table and dishes away. The soldier assured him that in a few years, his father and the woman's father would see that the American might make a good husband for the young widow.

The shift of power from the nationalist Harakat Amal Shiites—originally known as the Movement of the Deprived—to the pro-Khomeini Islamic Amal militias had ended his visits to the ghetto. No foreigner from Europe or the United States could walk in safety after the radical Islamic Amal took control of the streets. The radical militias—reinforced by Palestinians returning from exile—began the sniping and mortaring of the Marines. Then, in September, the Syrians and Iranians appeared with their allies the Hizbullah. The Harakat Amal leaders organized an evacuation of the district's civilians and the war began. After months of continuous fighting, Niles returned to streets he had once enjoyed, streets now deserted: by night, the domain of fanatics.

The empty streets reassured Niles. With the civilians hiding in their shelters and the militia lookouts staying in the security of their bunkers, the disguised Americans and Lebanese feared only a face-to-face encounter with a Hizbullah patrol. And the only patrols they saw passed at a distance, blocks away and in vehicles, the militiamen cruising the district in cars and trucks. No foot patrols challenged them.

But after an hour of zigzagging through the center of the district, they had seen nothing of a massing of militiamen—

no trucks, no crowds of men with rifles. Niles signaled the others into the doorway of a gutted shop.

"Willing to walk down to the streets facing the airport? Where they're shooting at the line? The crazies will be down there. In numbers."

"You taking a vote on this, sir?" Alvarez asked.

"You're all volunteers. Those streets will be serious. It'll be more than a walk-through. Just listen—"

They all heard the distant hammering of automatic weapons.

Gamal answered first in his slow, awkward English. "Why talk? We volunteer to fight. We fight or lose our country."

Hussein nodded. "We volunteered."

"It's cool," Alvarez added. "Their security is way, way loose. We walk in, we walk out. No problem."

"Not quite. I want to take out some of the snipers."

Alvarez nodded. "Yeah, why not? We did okay last night. They won't know what happened to them. Walk in, walk out."

Niles mimicked the sergeant's nodding. "Walk in, walk out. Uh, huh. Come on . . ."

Stepping out of the doorway, Niles led them a block north. He found a one-lane alley, a shortcut he remembered. A stripped and burned-out truck and heaps of trash clogged the narrow lane. The stink of burned wood and rot came from a boarded-shut furniture workshop. The buildings on the south side of the alley blocked the moonlight, forcing the four men to step slowly through the darkness. Rats scurried across their boots.

The sound of firing came clearly as they came to the end of the alley. Niles went to a crouch and looked out. At that moment, white light seared away the night, the scream of a one-hundred-fifty-five-millimeter artillery shell coming an instant later. By reflex, he dropped flat.

A flare. Niles shifted to put himself in shadow, then looked out again. The magnesium white light illuminated a street of dust and broken concrete. To the east, the street continued into the empty district. To the west, the street ended one hundred meters away at an intersecting street of tenements.

There, the Hizbullah militia had built a bunker on the ruins of a shattered building. Salvaged bricks and beams reinforced the walls and roof. The bunker had a direct line of fire on the northeast end of the airfield and the Iranian-trained snipers continuously fired Kalashnikovs and heavy machine guns at the Marine outposts. Return fire from the Marines punched into the sandbags without effect. Some rounds went over the bunker and ricocheted along the deserted street. At the street corner across from the rubble, he saw another sandbagged checkpoint. But he saw no one manning the position.

The tenements on each side—inhabited or not—made the approval of an artillery or gunship strike unlikely. Despite the terror bombing of the Landing Team headquarters, Niles knew that the Marine commander would not authorize counterattacks which might kill civilians.

As the parachute flare drifted down, Niles had minutes of magnesium daylight to examine the doorways and windows of the devastated street. He saw no sentries. Behind him, the others waited for his signal as they watched their sectors— the other direction of the street, the alley behind them, the roof lines.

Shadows slid up the street's buildings as the flare descended. Niles waited, watching the building next to the bunker. White light backlit a form moving along the roof. The flare finally sputtered out and darkness returned. Niles did not move.

A flashlight waved in the darkness. The light revealed an entry through the wall of the building. Two militiamen carried a heavy case from the building as another militiaman lit the path for them. They went into the bunker.

"Vatos coming from the east," Alvarez hissed, using the Los Angeles barrio dialect of his youth. "Jeeps, cars. We are not alone out here . . ."

Not taking his eyes from the bunker, Niles waited for the militiamen to reappear. The militiamen did not exit. But a glow of light remained in the building's entryway.

"They're coming this way . . ."

The Marines and Lebanese eased deeper into the alley as headlights approached. A line of vehicles rattled past—a

Lebanese Army jeep crowded with Hizbullah, a Mercedes taxi, and a Japanese pickup truck. Militiamen fired wildly, their Kalashnikovs flashing straight up into the night. The pickup dragged something, a thing of rags and gore. Niles leaned out. In the red light of the taillights, he saw an arm flail as the corpse jerked at the end of the rope. The Hizbullah turned the corner.

Watching the street and bunker for a few more minutes, Niles finally turned to Alvarez. "They've got that position on the ground. I think there's more of them in the building. I saw one on the roof and I think they're firing from up there, too."

"What's the plan?"

"Walk in there and persuade them to stop shooting Marines. But I want a look-see on that roof first. Officers, advisors, whoever."

Alvarez nodded. He briefed the Lebanese in whispered Arabic and English.

During a fury of counterfire from the Marine perimeter, Niles left the doorway. He stayed close to the shopfronts for cover, watching the roof line above the bunker. The rooftop flashed with the backblast of a rocket—and a rocket shrieked toward the Marine perimeter.

At the corner, he glanced inside the sandbagged checkpoint. No one. He stepped inside the chest-high rectangle of sandbags and sat on an empty ComBloc ammunition crate. Hollow concrete blocks set sideways in the sandbags provided firing ports. He peered out through a port, watching for movement on the intersecting street.

A hundred meters away, a building had lights in the windows overlooking the street. He saw the tailgate of a pickup truck stacked with crates. He saw no one at the pickup.

Leaving the checkpoint, he walked back to the others and motioned them forward. Niles kept his craggy Anglo features turned away from the street.

Alvarez and the two Lebanese followed him to the corner. Inside the rectangle of sandbags, Niles crouched so he could not be seen from the street or adjoining buildings. He explained their next action as the others eyed the area:

"There are some of them on top and some in the bunker. I will go up to the roof position first. You three will wait behind the bunker. Do not follow me. You fellows look exactly like the opposition. I could get confused. And kill you. Understand?"

"Up to the roof?" Alvarez asked. "Alone? No backup?"

"Move faster on my own."

"Maintain radio contact . . ."

Keeping his face down, Niles crossed the street to the rubble-strewn lot. The deafening noise of automatic weapons reverberated between the buildings. In the pauses, he heard return fire cracking into the front of the bunker. Alvarez followed him, then Hussein and Gamal. The four-story tenement shadowed the lot, keeping the area in darkness. Niles went to the adjoining tenement. The others found concealment in the weed-overgrown rubble.

Bombs or artillery shells had blasted through the walls of the building. Flickering amber light revealed smashed concrete walls and floors hanging by strands of reinforcing steel. Niles stooped down and ran his fingertips over the bricks and broken mortar. He felt the flattened, hard surface of a pathway trampled through the debris. Continuing inside, he stood still and listened.

A radio. Using the tips of his boots, he felt his way through the debris, finding the path the militiamen had cleared to a hallway. Amber light and the voices of an Arabic-language broadcast came from a room. He understood that the announcer reported on the bombings of the American and French peacekeeping forces. Niles advanced slowly, extending a boot and testing the sandy concrete floor for debris or trash before transferring his weight and beginning the next step. At the open door, his back pressed to the wall, he listened. He heard snoring and the rustling of plastic.

Easing down to a crouch, he looked inside. A kerosene lantern hung from the ceiling, the wick turned down to a glow. Stacked cases of ammunition—stenciled with the Cyrillic letters of the Soviet Union, marked over with Arabic—lined the walls of the room. He saw a battery-powered transistor radio on one of the cases, rags and a can of crankcase oil on another. Splintered wood and cosmoline-slick packing paper from opened ammunition crates covered the floor. Leaning farther, he saw boots.

Infinitely slowly, silently, he stepped into the room. A wounded militiaman—his left arm wrapped in gauze and tape—slept on packing crates of RPG-7 rockets. Bearded, wearing dirty fatigues, the militiaman clutched a clear plastic tarp around himself as a blanket. A Kalashnikov with a folded stock lay on the concrete floor. A prescription bottle had spilled out pills. The militiaman shifted in his sleep and mumbled in a drugged stupor, then snored again, his head back. The announcer on the radio continued reading the news of the bombings. Then the program cut to a tape of a celebration. Over the screaming of a crowd, Niles recognized a speaker proclaiming victory, victory.

Niles took an oily rag from the floor. Then, slipping out his Marine combat knife, he bunched the rag around the knife where the blade met the hilt. He aimed the point slightly to the left of the militiaman's sternum and pushed the point through the ribs, using all his strength and weight to drive the blade through the man's heart. As the man jerked reflexively, already dying, his eyes opened and his hands grabbed at the stranger leaning on his chest. The hands released Niles and he heard the militiaman exhale in one long, shuddering sigh.

The rag had blocked and absorbed the gush of blood. Only a small spot marked the wound. Niles crossed the man's injured arm over the blood and rolled him on his side, putting his face to the wall. The dead man looked like he slept.

Niles went to the door and listened for movement in the hallway. The auto-fire continued outside. Stepping into the hallway, he followed a pathway to concrete stairs. Voices and the sounds of men moving came from the roof. He looked up and saw the night sky four floors above him. Pausing for a moment, Niles quickly rechecked his web gear and pouches—the magazines of ammunition for his Kalashnikov, the Syrian Army pouch containing U.S.-issue grenades, his sheathed knife, the concealed CB radio. He confirmed the OFF setting of the radio switch. Nothing rattled. He went up the stairs.

Sprawled in the rubble behind the bunker, Sergeant Alvarez listened to the militiamen curse the Marines. He thought of all the hours with language tapes and books, struggling with the strange phonetics and meanings—only so that he could understand some locals bad-mouthing him. Looking up, Alvarez saw the ventilation ports flickering with muzzle flashes. Only a few minutes had passed since Captain Niles entered the building, and in that short time the militiamen had fired hundreds of rounds from their rifles and machine guns. The cold night air stank of cordite.

A 40mm grenade popped on the other side. The auto-fire ceased for a moment. Alvarez heard a militiaman laugh. Yeah, laugh, loudmouth. Won't be laughing tomorrow.

The Marines tried LAAW rockets next, the first rocket tearing past the bunker and exploding against a ruined building on the opposite side of the street, collapsing a section of wall into the intersection. The second rocket scored a hit. Bits of brick and concrete rained down on Alvarez and the Lebanese. Dust filled the narrow area between the tenements. The hit had no effect. The militiamen waited until the wind carried the dust away, then fired again.

Alvarez crawled over the broken concrete to Hussein and Gamal. "We've got to get out of here," he whispered to the Lebanese soldiers. "They hit that bunker with forty mike mike and LAAW rockets. Next thing up is a Dragon—" He meant a Dragon Antitank/Assault Missile. The Dragon, much heavier than the small LAAW rockets, destroyed heavy tanks or penetrated a meter of reinforced concrete. The wire-guided Dragon missiles could be fired with great accuracy. "—and chances are, we'll be the jokers who get wasted."

Trucks approached. Alvarez heard the revving of engines and down-shifting gears before he saw the headlights appear around a corner. He pressed himself into the rubble as a stake-side truck passed. Hizbullah militiamen stood shoulder-to-shoulder in the back. Posters of Khomeini decorated the doors of the truck's cab. White cloth banners—spray-painted with red Arabic script—hung on the sides of the truck.

"What does that say?" Alvarez asked Hussein.

"Praise the martyrs of 23 October."

The truck continued down the block and parked. A second truck passed. The truck carried crates of munitions. Militiamen sat on the crates. Others crowded the open cargo area. Parking behind the first truck, the militiamen followed the others into the building.

A white Mercedes raced down the street, then braked to swerve around the concrete in the street. Alvarez saw a tinted window roll down. A bearded face peered out, then the Mercedes continued. Voices came.

"That is not Arabic," Hussein whispered.

A few seconds later, the bearded man—in a suit and slacks, carrying a folding stock Kalashnikov—approached the bunker.

"Foreigner," Hussein whispered.

A second man in a suit—but wearing a vest of magazine pouches over the suit coat—stood at the sidewalk, watching the foreigner and the street. The foreigner walked past the rubble concealing the Marine and Lebanese without a glance and continued into the bunker.

Shouting stopped the auto-fire. Then a teenage Shiite militiaman accompanied the foreigner out the doorway. The foreigner shouted and gestured at the Shiite teenager until they reached the street. The foreigner pointed at the sand-bagged checkpoint and shouted out his commands. The teenager went into the checkpoint. The foreigners walked out of sight. A motor revved and sped away.

"Iranian," Hussein told Alvarez. "Syrians speak Arabic. His Arabic was not good."

"What did he say about trucks? He told the punk to watch for trucks?"

"Yes, trucks will come soon."

"Who will be in the trucks?"

"He said only trucks."

"This is it . . . come with me." Watching the sentry across

the narrow street, Alvarez crawled through the broken concrete and reinforcing rod to the blown-open wall of the next building. He directed the Lebanese soldiers to take positions at a side of the passage through the shattered apartment.

Taking out his CB hand-radio, he keyed the transmit twice to signal the captain. No response came. He keyed the transmit again. No response.

"Oh, man. I got to go get him. We found what we came looking for."

Taking the time to make every step silent, Niles slowly, patiently approached the roof. The shooting continued, but he did not risk exploiting the noise to cover a rush to the top. Only one more floor, two more flights, and he would be there.

A flashlight beam waved over the walls. Boots ran down the flights, equipment and weapons clattering. Niles rushed up the stairs to meet the Hizbullah militiamen. The first gunman saw the Syrian uniform and beret Niles wore and pointed the flashlight into his face.

In the last second of his conscious life, the first militiaman saw a tall man with hard angular features, his face aged by years of sun and exposure. The foreigner in the Syrian uniform had darkened his skin with brown paint, but his blue eyes and Marine haircut betrayed him as an American.

A shout almost cleared the Shiite's lips. But Niles rushed up the steps and drove upward with the stock of his Kalashnikov, putting all his strength into a perfect rising buttstroke to the underside of the militiaman's chin. The blow smashed the man's jaw closed on his tongue, shattering the teeth and lower jaw, the impact throwing his head back as the stock snapped off the rifle.

Niles rammed the muzzle of the Kalashnikov into the solar plexus of the second Shiite, doubling him, driving him backward onto the steps, the only sound the gasp of his breath exploding from his throat. Niles hammered both militiamen with the twisted metal and splintered wood end of the rifle.

The Shiites rolled down the concrete steps. Niles cut their throats and took a Kalashnikov—the barrel and receiver still warm from firing—to replace his broken rifle.

Rushing to the roof-level stairwell housing, he listened to the militiamen. Some fired Kalashnikov rifles. Two others shouted to one another as they fired a machine gun. Niles paused for one precaution. He found his valved hearing protectors and jammed them into his ears. Then he took two U.S.-issue M-67 fragmentation grenades from his pouch. Slipping off the safety clips, he straightened the cotter pins. Letting his new Kalashnikov hang by its sling, he stepped out of the stairwell housing.

The Hizbullah positions viewed the northern half of the international airport. Their lines of fire included the airport terminal, the Marine outposts, the vehicle yards, and both runways. Riflemen fired through fist-sized holes hammered through the concrete walls. The two militiamen working the PKM belt-fed machine gun fired from a gap in the wall. All the positions had been reinforced with sandbags. Only a perfect shot with a bullet or rocket could hit a rifleman, only mortars or artillery could knock out this militia position.

Niles slipped the pins from the grenades and bounced the olive drab spheres across the roof. Retreating to the cover of the concrete stairwell housing, he took out two more grenades and slipped the safety clips. A man shouted. A rifle scraped concrete. The bangs of the grenades stopped the movement.

An instant later, Niles let the levers flip free, then tossed the next two grenades to the other end of the roof line. After the two bangs, Niles waited, listening.

A man groaned. Slipping out of the stairwell, Niles circled around the housing and a series of heating flues. He scanned the roof for movement. None of the sprawled forms moved. Moving toward the dead men, he crouched to stay under the continuing fire from the Marine perimeter.

One of the machine gunners clutched at his wounds to his chest and throat. The other militiamen lay motionless in spreading pools of blood. Unless the Shiite militia leaders commissioned a forensic examination of the scene and the dead snipers, the Marine riflemen and their grenade launchers would get the credit for the kills.

A rifle clattered against the concrete stairs. Niles unsheathed his knife and went to the stairwell housing. Waiting, the knife ready, he listened for the boots of militiamen. Metal clinked. Niles crouched down and tensed to drive the knife up into the heart of the man who stepped out of the stairwell housing.

"Hey, capitán. Hey Zoot está aqua."

"Hey, Zoot the Noisemaker. I told you to stay down there."

"And I advised you, sir, to keep your radio on. We got trucks of crazies coming in. With Iranians."

"Let's get this done. The ammunition room on the first floor—"

"Saw it—"

"The two dead ones on the stairs go in there. Don't worry about noise. We're alone up here."

Niles jerked the dying machine gunner away from the sandbags. He dragged the man to the stairwell and threw him down to the landing. The lung and throat wounds would explain the blood. He stomped down on the back of the man's neck until the vertebrae broke, then dragged the second throat-cut rifleman down the stairs to the ground floor. Alvarez crouched in a doorway, his Kalashnikov ready.

"Captain, we—"

"Move it. I'm torching the dump."

Dropping the second corpse half in, half out of the room, Niles stepped over the dead man and grabbed the kerosene lantern.

"Captain!"

Niles broke the glass shield, unscrewed the fill cap, then tipped the lantern over on the oily rags. Flames spread over the crates. Alvarez stood outside.

"Move it!" Niles repeated.

"Out there—"

"What?"

"There's a sentry at the checkpoint."

"Why"—Niles looked back at the flames and smoke coming from the burning crates of ammunition—"didn't you tell me that before I—"

"Move it, sir."

They continued into the concrete wreckage where Hussein and Gamal crouched. Niles glanced out at the Shiite rifleman. He went back to the others and spoke with Hussein.

"The sergeant and I will hit the bunker. Watch the guard over there. Give you odds, three to one, that he will come to us."

Staying low in the rubble, Niles and Alvarez crept to the back wall of the bunker. The Shiite riflemen continued spraying auto-fire as before. A machine gun fired short bursts. The Marine return fire had slacked off. Niles passed the sergeant two of the M-67 grenades. He went to a rifle port, Alvarez went to the bunker's door.

"Marines on the line down there," Alvarez prayed, "do not send the Dragon—"

"Now . . ."

Dust exploded from the door and ports as the four grenades ripped the interior. Silence. The teenager left the protection of the checkpoint and ran across the street.

Ammunition popped inside the building as the flames finally heated the crated cartridges. Stopping in the path, the teenager watched the dust billowing out of the bunker. He cautiously continued. When he realized the noise of the exploding ammunition did not come from the bunker, he rushed to the doorway. Alvarez smashed him in the head with a brick.

"In there." Niles pulled the pin on another grenade. Alvarez threw the unconscious militiaman inside the door. Five seconds later, no one remained alive in the bunker.

"Don't know how it happened," Niles commented to Alvarez. "But someone put a forty-millimeter grenade through one of those little holes. Whoever he is, that Marine most definitely deserves a marksman's medal."

"Scored on a six-inch target at almost four hundred yards. A miracle."

"That's it. A miracle."

"Now take a look at the crazies down the street."

Signaling to Hussein and Gamal, Niles rushed to the street. The white Mercedes had parked behind the trucks. From his angle, Niles saw the Mercedes, two trucks, and the pickup. The building had a shattered marquee and display windows: a theater. Niles remembered seeing crowds of teenagers lining up for kung-fu movies and Egyptian romances. Now guards paced the sidewalk in front of the ticket booth. He scanned the buildings overlooking the street. Hundreds of possible lookout positions viewed the street—windows, balconies, shell holes through the walls, roof lines. A sentry could be anywhere. Niles did not like the odds of approaching the theater by the street.

"The Iranians came in that Mercedes." Alvarez had to raise his voice to speak over the noise of the popping ammunition. "And the boss Iranian told that punk to watch for the trucks that were coming."

"What trucks?"

"Didn't say. Said trucks were coming."

"Guards down there. Can't walk up to that address."

"Ah, yes, sir. Do not like the looks of this street. Even in our Syrian camouflage."

"Instead, we will detour."

"To where?"

"Out into the fields. Cut behind these buildings and come back across from that theater."

"Sir! We got men with starlite scopes pointed this way. And they will shoot us."

"Didn't hit these Hizbullah."

"They had mucho concrete between them and the incoming."

"Then we'll stay low. No other way."

"We got Vatsek back there with an M-sixty. And he does not miss."

"The street or the fields."

Engines approached. Niles and Alvarez went flat in the rubble. Trucks clanked and rattled along the broken stones of the street. Ranks of bearded militiamen in white headbands and camouflage uniforms stood in the backs of two stake-side trucks. As the trucks passed, the militiamen looked toward the smoke and noise of the burning munitions. The trucks stopped at the theater. Militiamen leaped from the trucks, crowding the sidewalks and street, many running toward the Americans.

"You talked me into it, sir."

They doubled back to the bunker. In the noise of the burning munitions, they could not hear if the Marine perimeter positions continued firing on the bunker. A pathway curved around the bunker. Niles went first, running along the path, his feet scattering hundreds of empty rifle and machine gun cartridge casings.

The area behind the ruined tenements had become a dump. Past the bunker, pathways forked out, one path cutting across the fields, another path paralleling the rusted tangle of wire and posts that had once been a fence. But the path along the fence offered no cover.

Niles scrambled over the broken concrete and trash, glass and slivers of shrapnel cutting his hands, then turned to confirm that Hussein and Gamal followed. Alvarez came last. To the west, Niles saw the darkness of the runways and the Marine perimeter. Niles knew Marine snipers would have their starlite scopes focused on the bunker—and at any soldier in the area.

Bullets confirmed his assumption. An old bottle shattered. Sheet metal crackled. Dust and ashes sprayed. A bullet tore past him and ricocheted into the tenement.

"Down!" Niles warned the Lebanese as they passed him. He found the CB hand-radio and extended the antenna to full length. Curling into a mound of trash, he pressed the transmit and whispered: "Victor. Victor the Russian weight lifter. This is Actual. Old Man Actual."

A scratchy voice answered. "Yes, sir. This is Victor."

"How's the shooting?"

"Repeat, sir."

"How is the shooting?"

"Ah . . . great. Got some ragheads in the lines now."

"Do you have a positive identification on those individuals? Be advised they may be soldiers from another nation."

"All right! I'll request artillery."

"Victor, please don't. Be advised their identities may be in doubt."

"Question, sir. Am I familiar with this gang of payback warriors?"

"Affirmative. ¿Entiende?"

"Sí, señor."

"So pass the word, okay? I don't have a land line here."

Slipping the hand-radio back into his Soviet ammunition vest, he heard Alvarez hiss to him. Then he heard the voices from the bunker. Flashlights swept across the firing ports, the Hizbullah shouting and cursing as they found the corpses. A Kalashnikov jutted from a port and sprayed wild auto-fire in the direction of the airport. Niles crabbed across the slabs and stones and litter. The shooting covered his noise.

"Contact with Vatsek?" Alvarez asked.

"Said he had us in his sights."

No more bullets came at the four men. But they continued moving in dashes from cover to cover, running a few steps, crawling through garbage. Rats scattered. Twice they passed the ventilation pipes of shelters—music and the voices of the hiding families came up the pipes. The windows in the buildings remained dark. No one above ground risked lights. Niles counted the buildings they passed. After approximately a block, he stopped Alvarez and the Lebanese troopers.

Behind them, new militiamen had taken the place of the dead. Kalashnikov muzzles flashed as the Hizbullah sniped at the distant airport lights. Accurate Marine return fire cracked into the bunker. Sprawled in the cover of a trash heap, Niles risked a whisper:

"We kill them and there's more."

"Call for the Dragon. Waste that place."

"The leaders, we got to hit the leaders."

Searching two buildings for an entry, they found a faint path leading to a heavy wood plank door. Niles pointed to another building. Alvarez shook his head, no, and held up his hand for the captain and the others to wait. They crouched at the sides while Alvarez felt around the edges of the door. Then he gently pushed again and again. Finally, he reached in his pocket. Silver flashed as a blade snapped out of the push-button knife.

Alvarez slipped the knife between the planks. He motioned the others back, then flipped up with the blade and shoved the door as he jumped to the side.

The door swung open. They waited—expecting the blast of a booby trap—for a minute before glancing inside. Nothing moved in the dark interior of the tenement. Alvarez shone a penlight across the walls and floor of a narrow passageway. He went in first, his Kalashnikov leveled at the darkness. The Air Assault troopers followed. Niles pulled out his CB hand-radio again:

"Victor, this is the Old Man."

"Victor here." Static blurred Vatsek's voice.

"Be advised that hot spot needs the Dragon. Delta, Romeo, Alpha, Golf, Oscar, November. Zero bystanders. Many crazies. Hit them."

"Received. Will request Dragon zap. Be advised that requests don't mean shit."

Niles followed the others. He heard the chanting immediately. A slow, rhythmic beat accompanied the incomprehensible voice of a crowd.

The passageway entered a long, narrow courtyard open to the sky. Three levels of walkways lined by steel railings overlooked the concrete central courtyard. Laundry hung on lines stretched from rail to rail. A mortar hit had torn away a short section of the fourth-floor walkway. Boards bridged the gap.

Families struggled to survive here. Walls of sandbags surrounded several apartments on the ground level to provide makeshift bomb shelters. Light and radio voices came through the vents. Smoke drifted from one vent, the smell of spices and cooking oil filling the courtyard, almost covering the stink of the old tenement.

Narrow steel and concrete stairs creaked with the weight of the four men. The chanting covered the noises. Alvarez led the group up to the top floor, then motioned Niles forward. On the fourth level, the apartment windows and doors stood open, the interiors empty. Hussein and Gamal watched the apartments, their Kalashnikovs pointed at the shadows and doorways.

"Roof door open," Alvarez whispered.

Running his hand along the steps, Niles felt grit at the sides of a step, only worn concrete at the center. He continued up a step at a time, sweeping his fingers over a step, then the next and the next. Others had used the steps recently, but that meant nothing in a crowded building. Then he found the empty cartridge casing. By touch, he identified the short, tapered casing as 7.62ComBloc. He continued up the last stairs to the roof and slowly raised his head, listening for any movement. The chanting continued. He scanned the roof.

Laundry swayed on lines, the sheets and chadors moving with the shifting of the soft wind. Niles examined every silhouette and shape for movement, or the form of a militia-man, or the distinctive outlines of weapons. He checked the rooftops of the neighboring buildings.

Within reach, he found more cartridge casings and an empty cardboard tube. Other tubes lay on the concrete. The tubes had contained RPG-7 rockets. Militiamen had fired on the Marine perimeter from this building.

He finally left the stairs, Alvarez moving up to watch as Niles slow-stepped across the roof, his boots silent on the old tar and concrete. Mortars had punched holes through the roof and destroyed the rooms below. Standing behind the blowing laundry, Niles peered over the lines at the section of roof overlooking the street.

Explosions had shattered a section of the facade, littering the roof with chips and blocks of concrete. His angle of sight did not allow a view of the rooftops across the street. He signaled the others up, then motioned for Hussein to accompany him.

They crept forward toward the break in the facade, dropping to a crouch, then going prone and snaking through the debris. Niles checked his student's progress. Though the chant and beating noise would cover any sound, Hussein carefully removed the chunks of concrete, then brushed aside the dust and chips as he crawled forward. The young soldier had learned to move silently.

Hammering came from the bunker a block away as the gunmen aimed sporadic bursts of automatic fire at the airport. Niles and Hussein inched forward to the dropoff. Across the street and one floor lower, they saw the curved roof of the theater. Light fanned from the open door of a stairway. Militiamen in the white headbands of the Hizbullah watched the street. Two Syrian soldiers and a man in a casual suit stood apart. The man in the suit wore a Syrian Army ammunition vest over his coat. Niles could not see the features of the men.

"I think that one is an Iranian," Hussein whispered. "He spoke Farsi with the other one."

The chanting and the slow, rhythmic beat echoed in the street. Niles listened and realized what he heard.

In the theater, Shiites beat their chests with their fists as they proclaimed "Allahu Akbar"—"God is great."

Easing forward, he looked down on the street. Four stakeside cargo trucks lined the curb. He saw three Mercedes sedans and a Land Rover with a pedestal-mounted 12.7mm heavy machine gun. Groups of Hizbullah sentries guarded the front of the theater.

Niles had seen more than seventy militimen in two trucks. He doubled that to guess that somewhere between one hundred twenty-five and one hundred fifty Hizbullah militiamen had arrived in the trucks.

Other words emerged from the chanting. Someone in the theater raved. Niles could not follow the screaming. He turned to Hussein. "What is the preacher saying?"

"I can only understand . . . attack. He is telling them to attack the enemies of God."

Attack the enemies of God. A full company of chanting, suicidal fanatics less than five hundred meters from the few Marines manning the isolated sandbag outposts along the airport perimeter. Niles pointed to the Syrians and militiamen on the opposite roof.

"Watch them," he told Hussein. "I got to talk with Alvarez."

Moving back, he crossed the roof to the sergeant and crouched down with him. "Hear that?"

"The voices? Oh, yeah. God is great. Spooky shits."

"Four troop trucks. I calculate maybe one fifty of them in there. And there's a mullah or whoever telling them to attack."

"Attack who?"

"The enemies of God."

"Call for the Cobra."

"Go up there. Watch them. I'm going to try to call down payback with this toy radio." Continuing to the back of the roof, he looked down at the lights of the airport as he extended the CB radio's antenna.

"Victor. The Old Man calling Victor."

The line-of-sight transmission gave him clear reception of Vatsek's reply. "Victor here. Be advised no Dragon. No authorization. Cannot break policy. Read, chickenshit. Highest actual wants Dragons held in reserve. There's talk about tanks. Those shee-its out there can shoot at us forever."

"This is different. Put Mr. Marvel on the radio."

A moment later, Colonol Devlin spoke. "Marvel here."

"Aforementioned nationals confirmed. Repeat, your information is confirmed."

"Be advised mission complete. Withdraw field personnel."

"I want an air strike."

"Not possible. Repeat, not possible."

"There is a company of crazies staging for an attack. Repeat, one-five-zero crazies. Most definitely out for blood. I want a Cobra strike."

"What is the source of this information?"

Aware that his broadcast might be monitored, Niles switched to Spanish. "Agentes Señor Ojo y Señor Oreja." Eye and ear.

"I read. I will request. Be advised of report of tanks."

"Then time is most definitely of the essence. Repeat, one-five-zero crazies on their way. Hit them here or they hit the perimeter."

"Wait, actual. I will request. Over."

Crouching on the rooftop, Niles scanned the darkness between the tenement and the Marine lines. The Marine role as neutral peacekeepers denied the use of the mine fields,

barbed wire, and interlocking fields of fire required for a
secure perimeter. The Marines in the outposts had only their
rifles and a few squad automatic weapons. Niles had seen
the trucks of militiamen. Now Vatsek and Colonel Devlin
told him of the reports of tanks. The Hizbullah in the theater
might be only one of many groups gathering in the slums
around the international airport.

The Marine force had lost almost four hundred men, dead
and wounded, in the bombing. This left the Marines in the
airport complex without reserves. The bomb had also destroyed stockpiles of ammunition and rockets.

Though the battleship *New Jersey* waited on call offshore,
its 16-inch guns could not be used on Hay al-Sollom. The
battleship's secondary batteries of 5-inch guns could only be
used on the open fields outside the Marine perimeter. The
support ships *Iwo Jima* and *El Paso* also waited offshore
with Cobra attack helicopters and with more weapons. But
Niles doubted the value of the gunships in a defense of the
airport. Militia automatic-weapon fire had damaged the Cobras the few times the gunships appeared. And if the attackers entered the complex, the Cobras could not fire without
hitting the Marine defenders. The battle for the airport
would be rifle-to-rifle, hand-to-hand. Niles knew the Marines
would annihilate the attackers, but at what cost? How many
more young widows and orphans? How many more families
would lose sons?

A fifteen-second air strike on the theater by a Cobra could
eliminate four truckloads of the fanatics before they attacked
the Marines.

Waiting for the authorization, hoping for the sound of
helicopter rotors, Niles listened to the Hizbullah chanting
their prayer of hate.

5

HEARING his Revolutionary Guards muttering curses, Fahkr Rajai looked up from the 24 October edition of the *New York Times* to see yet another highway checkpoint. The headlights of his Mercedes illuminated a barricade of oil drums manned by bearded militiamen with Kalashnikov rifles. They wore photos of Imam Moussa Sadr on their fatigue jackets, the spiritual leader of Harakat Amal, the Movement of the Deprived. The driver slowed the sedan to a stop as the bodyguards lowered the muzzles of their rifles from the open windows. Through the tinted glass of his window, Rajai saw the forms of men surround the luxury sedan. One man leaned down and peered through an open window at the passengers inside.

Voices demanded identification. Rajai held up the newspaper to the dome light and resumed reading of the strike against the United States Marines. A courier had brought air express copies of American and French newspapers from Damascus to the Iranian Embassy for all the diplomats to enjoy. Other copies had been forwarded to Tehran for the commander and his staff of explosives technicians.

Though he did not read English as easily as Farsi or Arabic, he understood the words of the headline celebrated the victory—

**BEIRUT DEATH TOLL AT 146 AMERICANS;
FRENCH CASUALTIES RISE IN BOMBINGS;
REAGAN INSISTS MARINES WILL REMAIN**

Only one hundred forty-six? A lie meant for the American people. The Mercedes bumped over sandbag speed barriers, then accelerated away from the Amal militiamen. Rajai continued reading the *Times*. He knew that the bomb had killed or maimed every Marine in the building. All four hundred. The explosion of the TNT and hexogene instantly killed every American in the basements and first two floors. Perhaps a few on the third floor survived to be maimed by the falling slabs of concrete. Only the sentries on the roof had any chance of survival.

Nothing less than annihilation justified the months of surveillance and planning. Agents masquerading as street vendors had detailed the Marine routine. European journalists took thousands of photos of the interior of the buildings. Then the search through Baalbek militias for the religious psychopaths to drive the trucks. Rajai had been the only Iranian working with the militias and their Syrian advisors from the beginning. His other countrymen—officers and technicians of the Revolutionary Guard, others from the Ayatollah's secret police, SAVAMA—had come three weeks ago with the explosives. Under the supervision of Syrian and Palestinian technicians, they assembled the explosives. Yesterday the officers and technicians had returned to Damascus and Tehran to accept the glory:

U.S. SAYS TERRORISTS TIED
TO IRAN MAY HAVE SET
OFF THE LETHAL BLAST

Even the United States acknowledged Iran as the victor. Rajai laughed again at the last line of the headline—REAGAN INSISTS. The words brought the mental image of the retired movie star at a television press conference. In his imagination, he saw the aging matinee idol—his hair slicked, his face tanned with cosmetics—attempting to play the role of a world leader by mouthing rehearsed statements and posing for the video cameras. The elected movie actor could not speak without a script. Any unexpected question brought nonsense from his mouth that forced his press secretary to issue immediate clarifications and explanations.

How would the actor-president and his staff of hacks explain this annihilation?

One of the column headings brought more laughter—

'DON'T LEAVE US,'
TRAPPED MEN CRY

Leaning to Akbar, the bodyguard who shared the back seat with him, Rajai pointed out the heading and translated the English words. "They are weeping, pleading to be saved—" He acted out a scene of a Marine clawing for air and screaming.

Akbar did not laugh. A grim veteran of five years of war, he had fought for the Revolution from the first days, seizing a rifle in the street riots against the Shah, then becoming one of the Guards of the Revolution. He proved himself utterly loyal to the Ayatollah Khomeini, obeying without question the orders to arrest and execute Mujahedeen allies during the purges, then volunteering for the trench warfare of the Iraqi front. Rajai had checked through his file personally before accepting the man as his bodyguard. His scarred face an expressionless mask, Akbar watched Rajai mimicking the struggles of a dying Marine, then looked back to the street.

At that moment, Rajai decided to liquidate him. The soldier had protected Rajai throughout the past months, every hour of the day and night, riding in his Mercedes, standing guard outside the meetings, sleeping in the court-yard of his villa in Baalbek. Akbar knew by sight, if not by name, the Syrian officers, the Palestinian technicians, and the Lebanese militia leaders who had worked with Rajai. His capture or defection—or any talk in the future to someone who worked for the Western intelligence agencies—would compromise the mystery of the Islamic Jihad. What a reward for Akbar's courage and absolute loyalty—the execution wall. A joke.

The driver slowed again, weaving through the curves of a series of barriers. The stink of sewage hit Rajai. Hizbullah militiamen manned this checkpoint on a bridge over the Nahr al-Ghadir. Scowling portraits of Khomeini marked the end of Amal power. Past this checkpoint, fighters trained and armed by Iran had the authority to act in the name of the Islamic Revolution.

No one walked on the streets. Despite the early hour of the evening, no shops remained open. Only a few lights shone in the hundreds of windows overlooking the empty boulevard. Rajai heard firing, the far-off sounds of rifles and machine guns.

Again, the demand for a pass. The bearded faces of militiamen with headbands proclaiming themselves as warriors of Allah stared at Rajai in his suit and tie, his barbered hair and razor-sculpted beard. One grabbed for the *New York Times* in his hands.

"He is a foreigner! He is reading the pornography of Satan!"

The stupid creature called for assistance. A group of Hizbullah converged around the Mercedes. Kalashnikov rifles banged and scratched on the door. Hands reached inside to take the newspaper but Rajai folded it and placed it in his briefcase. His bodyguards talked quickly in their awkward Arabic, attempting to explain the privileges of an officer in the Iranian Revolutionary Guard. Finally their leader appeared. He recognized the Iranians from other visits to Hay al-Sollom and shoved the crowd of ragged militiamen away.

"Do not bother our comrades! They come as allies in our revolution and you greet them with this trouble? My brothers, how can I help you?"

"We are expected at the prayers for the martyrs," the driver told him.

"Oh, yes. At the cinema. My men will take you there."

"My driver does not need a guide. We were there last night."

"But there is fighting with the Americans at the airport. And last night the Phalangists attacked us. Three of my men died here. I would be failing in my responsibilities if I did not provide an escort."

Several militiamen crowded into an open Land Rover. Posters of Khomeini glared from the doors and tailgate. Rajai could not understand the blind devotion of the Lebanese proletariat to the mullahs. His knowledge of Iran's culture and history rationalized his country's surrender to the mullahs, but these Lebanese did not share that tortured history even if they shared the same Shiite faith. Amal idolized Imam Moussa Sadr. The Islamic Amal and the Hizbullah worshiped the Ayatollah Khomeini. Sadr had already disappeared into the execution cells of Libya and Khomeini had retreated into madness. Neither mullah, nor any of the thousands of mullahs controlling the villages and towns and cities of the Shiite domain, offered the Persian and Arab societies a future: only a descent into the medieval past. Yet the devoted came by the millions, offering their lives to the madness of the Shiite myths, giving hundreds of thousands of their sons to the vast yawning grave of the Iraqi front, condemning their daughters to lifelong isolation within the woven prison walls of the black chador.

Of course, if Rajai ever expressed his thoughts out loud he would be immediately imprisoned, if not executed on the spot. He knew the terrible penalties for free thought and speech in his country—both Imperial prerevolutionary Iran and the Iran of the Ayatollah.

His father, a devout Shiite, had served in the Shah's Imperial Army as a captain in command of an armored unit. The rapid modernization—and the corruption, the captain believed—of Iran offended his traditional values. He spoke too freely of his concerns. A cousin in the Shah's secret police, the SAVAK, warned him to leave. Captain Rajai fled with his family to Iraq, where they lived in exile with the Ayatollah Khomeini in Najaf, one of the Shiite shrine-cities.

Without a salary, without a command, Captain Rajai promoted himself to colonel and took work where he found it, training the forces of the warring Arab states, sometimes the irregular forces of the Palestinians. His young son Fahkr often traveled with him. Fahkr already spoke the French of the international elite and the Arabic of Iraq. His travels taught him the dialects and politics of other nations—Arab and European.

A decade later, the Shah pressured Saddam Hussein to expel Iranian troublemakers from Najaf. The family went to Paris. This second exile enhanced Colonel Rajai's international contacts. The colonel continued working in the Arab nations but also expanded his list of clients to include the French-speaking nations of Africa. With his knowledge of American, Soviet, and European armored vehicles Colonel Rajai trained elite units of tribal armies to use superpower military aid. International arms dealers occasionally contracted Colonel Rajai to demonstrate weapons in South America. Fahkr attended French colleges when he did not travel with his father. Sometimes he acted as a courier between his father and other devout exiles from Iran. Again, Fahkr learned—the politics, the organizations, the personalities of exiled leaders. But he ceased to only observe and learn. In the years of the Ayatollah's residence in France, Fahkr Rajai exploited his father's reputation to ingratiate himself with the future leader of Iran.

After the triumph of the mullahs, the Rajai family returned to Tehran. The middle-aged Colonel Rajai advised the new force of street fighters and assassins, the Revolutionary Guard, in the art of military organization. The young, multilingual Fahkr Rajai led platoons of Revolutionary Guards in search of royalists and liberals.

Then the mullahs turned on their fellow revolutionaries, the Mujahedeen. The Mujahedeen believed in a socialist Islamic society ruled by laws and elected secular leaders. Thousands of the Islamic socialists had died by torture or the firing squad in the prisons of the Shah's secret police, the SAVAK. The Mujahedeen had fought side by side with other Iranians to depose the Shah, then paraded in the streets to celebrate the return of Khomeini. In the years of the purge, Rajai went name by name, address by address, down the official membership lists of the National Liberation Movement. Thousands died by torture or the bullet or the noose in the prisons of the Ayatollah's secret police, the SAVAMA.

His performance in the pursuit of the heretics won the trust of SAVAMA. After shattering the Mujahedeen organization in Tehran, the SAVAMA sent Rajai to France to infiltrate the exile organizations there. The SAVAMA intended to dispatch Revolutionary Guard kill squads to eliminate the leaders of the expatriate factions in opposition to Khomeini. Rajai warned his commander in Tehran of the efficiency of the French security forces. But SAVAMA sent the killers.

Within days, the French police captured the assassins with their weapons—Rajai had anonymously informed on his comrades. His forewarning of the arrests gained the respect of his commander. Rajai continued his work with the Mujahedeen exile organization. His months of patience earned a position on the staff. He learned which leader ran the surviving networks in Iran, then requested a second Revolutionary Guard team—but this time with a French mercenary pilot and a plane to wait at a provincial airfield. The team kidnapped the network leader and flew him to Tehran for interrogation.

In the chaos of the disappearance, Rajai worked with the staff of the missing leader to salvage and reorganize the Mujahedeen networks in Iran. He never saw or heard a name, but he saw the safe where the staff put their lists. Booking a flight on the next Paris-to-Tehran flight, he burglarized the office and stole the lists.

Rajai returned to Tehran and supervised the liquidation of several Mujahedeen cells. His next assignment sent him to Baalbek, as an advisor to the Revolutionary Guard units working with the Syrians to combat the Israeli occupation forces. When the American president sent Marines to protect the Palestinians and Shiites from the Christians and Israelis, he coordinated the training of the Hizbullah militias and armed them for their assaults on the Marines. Then came the assignment to prepare for the bombing of the Marine headquarters.

Now with that victory on his record, he continued in his long-term liaison with the Syrians and plotted more attacks. As long as the Americans maintained a presence in Lebanon, Rajai would send fanatics to strike—at their soldiers, at the embassy diplomats, at the professors of the American University of Beirut, at their journalists, then at their citizens.

Tonight, the Hizbullah threw themselves on the Marine lines. Rajai expected a slaughter—of the Hizbullah militiamen and Marines. Shiite casualties did not concern him. He wanted more headlines, more photos of American dead and wounded on the front pages of international newspapers.

The Land Rover led his Mercedes through the narrow, war-ruined streets of Hay al-Sollom. Over the noise of automatic rifles firing, he heard the chanting of the militiamen, the ritual prayer and flagellation echoing in the streets as the militiamen vowed to embrace martyrdom.

Rajai thought of the *New York Times* column linking the bombing of the Marines to Iran. Let the Americans accuse Iran. Let them threaten Iran and plead with their European allies for a united response to terror. Let them isolate Iran and starve the people. Let the United States attack Iran.

The terror would not stop. The fanatics of Iran wanted to die, they sought death in their holy war. No American threat or counterattack would defeat the mass psychosis of his tortured people. And when the holy war against the American invaders left his nation ruined, then the Soviets would play their role and drive out the Americans.

Rajai wanted to lead his people into the twenty-first century. The creation of a new Iran required the destruction of the old Iran. As Josef Stalin had used the gulag and the Nazis to create a modern Soviet Union, Fahkr Rajai would use the madness of the revolution and a war with America to create a modern Iran—with Fahkr Rajai as the nation's leader.

Niles memorized the features and clothing of the young man who left the black Mercedes. Two bodyguards accompanied him. Like the Iranians who had arrived earlier, these men wore slacks and coats. But the one with the briefcase looked different from the others.

First, the briefcase. Who carried a briefcase in a war? The other men carried folding-stock Kalashnikovs. And his suit. As the young man walked through spots of light from the windows, Niles saw the lines of the trousers, the tailored fit of the coat across his shoulders, the conservative blue of the fabric—the young man dressed like a diplomat. He wore his hair styled and his beard neatly trimmed. Then he went into the theater.

"That one wasn't a militiaman," Niles whispered to Hussein.

"The soldiers with him, they look like the Iranians."

"Yeah, that they do."

Smoke drifted over the rooftop. A block away, the stockpiled munitions had burned out. Only a streak of acrid, greasy smoke rose from the tenement. The pops of single shots and short bursts of sniping continued. In the street, two militiamen carried a wooden crate of ammunition toward the bunker. Other militiamen stood on the corners of the block.

The chant stopped. In the seconds of silence that followed, Niles heard a militia leader shouting to his men to unload the rockets. Teams of Hizbullah worked in the backs of the trucks, passing crates of munitions to men in the street. Niles leaned out and looked straight down. Boxes and weapons lined the sidewalks, ready for distribution.

An amplified voice boomed in the theater. Hussein gave Niles a running translation. "They will attack, they will be the vanguard of the revolution, they will be the sword of God's revolution, they will drive the Marines into the sea—"

"This is serious." Niles left the facade and ran to the back of the building where Alvarez waited with a radio. "Did he get the authorization?"

"No call back yet."

"Sergeant, you willing to do something that is seriously dangerous?"

"I'm here. What could be more—"

"I want to hit them."

Alvarez laughed softly. "Oh, yeah . . . that would be seriously dangerous. But with what, sir? Rifles against a crazy convention? They've got it all—numbers, firepower, rockets."

"More widows if we don't. They'll overrun the line and run straight into the headquarters."

"If we do it, can we get out?"

A faint buzz came from their CB radios. They listened on their hand-radios as Vatsek reported: "This Victor. Strike denied authorization. Even Mr. Marvel can't get no satisfaction. I put out the word to the line."

"Yeah?" Niles spoke into his radio. "This is actual. Put

this word out to the line. Stand by for hot foot. Be advised, hot foot."

"What? Request repeat."

"Hotel Oscar Tango. Uniform Sierra Mike Charlie. Over." Niles turned to Alvarez. "This will be wild—" He went to the stairs and hissed to Gamal. He explained to Alvarez and Gamal what he needed. "This kid is going to walk out on that street and pick up a crate of rockets and a launcher."

"I have six." Gamal pointed to the sack on his back.

"We need more. Bring in the crate and one or two launchers. Then you and Alvarez bring them up to me and Hussein on the roof. Now. Move fast and we can do this."

Niles ran back to the front. The amplified voice continued. "We're going to hit them."

Hussein stared at the American. "How? There are hundreds!"

"Won't be hundreds when we're done."

Below, Niles saw Gamal leave the street entry of the building. Gamal walked directly to the stacks of equipment and crates. He took a rocket launcher and a crate of rockets. Staggering with the weight, he started back. A militiaman stopped him.

Gamal swayed with the weight of the crate as the militiaman approached him. Niles saw the two men talk for a moment, then the militiaman took one end of the crate. Together, they carried the rockets into the building. The steel stairs at the street end of the courtyard rang with boots.

The militiaman appeared first, then Gamal. Niles smashed the Hizbullah's skull with a fist-sized block of concrete. Alvarez ran up the steps.

"His rifle and ammunition and web gear go to Gamal. I get the grenades," Niles told Alvarez. Then he pulled his combat knife and levered off the lid of the crate. He told Hussein, "All these rockets, pull them out of the tubes, get them ready." Then he motioned Gamal over to him. Niles pointed out the targets on the street.

"Your first rocket goes into that last truck, next rocket into that first car. Then all the other rockets, you point at the entrance to the cinema or at the roof and shoot. I want rockets through the roof and inside. We'll reload for you."

"Yes—yes—" Gamal stuttered as he stripped off his pack of rockets.

"Don't panic and keep putting out rockets. And keep the tailpipe pointed up in the air."

Alvarez brought a Kalashnikov and a vest with several magazines of ammunition. He gave the vest to Gamal. The militiaman had also carried Soviet fragmentation grenades. Niles laid out the grenades, then his remaining U.S.-issue grenades. He kept two of the M-67 grenades for their retreat.

A line of rockets stood ready for Gamal. Niles pointed to the Syrians and Iranians on the roof, telling Alvarez, "Hit them with the first burst, then the sentries. They're the only ones who can hit us." He looked to Gamal. "Ready? When we shoot, you hit them."

Gamal shouldered his launcher and nodded. Alvarez set extra magazines near his rifle and sighted on the opposite roof.

Taking a long breath, then exhaling, Alvarez snapped three quick shots into the standing Syrians and Iranians. Niles wasted ammunition, firing his Kalashnikov on full-automatic to kill the Hizbullah sentries on the roof. Gamal's rocket shrieked away, tearing through the last troop truck. Niles took the second launcher and fired the rocket into a truck parked in front of the theater entrance. The warhead punched into the diesel tanks and sprayed flaming fuel. Niles passed the launcher back to Hussein to reload.

Flames lit the street. As Gamal fired the third rocket, Niles pulled the wire pins from the Soviet serrated iron grenades and threw them as quickly as he could pull and throw. He threw two far down the street, then two in front of the theater.

Thirty seconds passed before the first return fire. Bullets chipped at the concrete, the deformed slugs humming into the sky. The high angle of their position denied the militiamen on the street any target. Following Niles's instructions, Gamal did not risk aiming after the first three rockets. Hussein passed him the reloaded launchers, then Gamal pointed at the curving auditorium roof of the theater and fired the rockets, the warheads shrieking into the tar and asbestos and exploding inside the auditorium. Other times, he only held the launcher out at arm's length and fired the rocket down at panicked militiamen rushing from the entrance.

The Marines could not lean out to fire on the street. Niles shouted out to Alvarez. "Get down to the back stairs. Don't let them get through the street door."

A rocket shrieked past, a miss, the warhead continuing hundreds of meters into the night and self-destructing. Niles chanced a glance down into the street—seeing flames, wrecked trucks, corpses, running men—and bullets punched into the concrete wall, fragments slashing the side of his head, spinning away his Syrian beret. He fell back and touched blood in his hair. Hussein came to his aid and Niles pushed him away. "Reload those rockets!"

Niles pulled the pin from an M-67, counted off two seconds, and dropped it down to the building entrance. Without risking his life again to look, he threw the next fragmentation grenade approximately twenty meters away, between the entrance and the theater. He saw that Gamal had only four more rockets to fire. Niles dropped another grenade in front of the entrance, then took a rocket launcher.

Aiming at the stairwell on the roof of the theater, he waited. He saw a form moving in the doorway and fired, the rocket hitting a step short of the doorway. Forms dived from the stairs at that instant but the flash tore through the concrete, shattering the stairs and housing, sending broken concrete across the domed roof. As Gamal fired the last rockets, Niles emptied his Kalashnikov at the remains of the stair shaft. He snapped another magazine into the rifle and motioned Gamal and Hussein back.

Rifle and machine gun slugs tore at the facade, impacts coming continuously, bits of concrete flying. A rocket hit low on the building, blast and flame roaring upward. Niles and the Lebanese troopers ran for the back stairs. Rifles fired in the courtyard. Behind them, they heard another rocket explode at their abandoned position.

The Lebanese went down the stairs first. At the top, Niles watched the front entry. Flames from the street backlit a form. He fired, and below him Alvarez fired, the two slugs dropping a militiaman among the other bodies in the courtyard. When Gamal and Hussein cleared the stairs, Niles rushed down.

Only Alvarez waited. "They're already out of here."

Hizbullah militiamen rushed through the front entry. Niles leveled his Kalashnikov and swept the entry with full-auto 7.62ComBloc while Alvarez fired single shots into two forms sprinting through the darkness.

The courtyard went quiet. At the far end, they saw a rectangle of flame. "Get back, Alvarez. Move it—"

"Rockets are next—"

"Move it!"

Alvarez backed out of the building. Niles went prone, his Kalashnikov resting on the walkway. He took an M-67 from his bag. Pulling the pin, he turned to the heavy plank door.

At the street, a militiaman appeared, a rocket launcher on his shoulder.

"Move!" Alvarez shouted out.

Niles spun and Alvarez fired once, the slug knocking the militiaman back. But the rocket flashed away. Niles fell, his hands closed around the grenade.

The passageway exploded, concrete and tiles showering Niles. But the rocket had gone high, hitting the wall above the rear exit passageway. Dust filled the passageway. Crawling, Niles put the armed grenade under a slab of concrete, then scrambled out the exit. Alvarez grabbed his arm and dragged him to the side as several automatic rifles hammered in the courtyard, bullets splitting the door, ricocheting from the walls.

"Cut across." Niles pointed toward the gully of the Nahr River. "Back the way we came." Alvarez tried to lift Niles to his feet. Niles twisted away. "Move it, sergeant."

"With you, sir."

Niles did not answer. He found a can in the trash piles around him. Pulling the pin out of the last U.S.-issue grenade, he put the grenade in the can and set it on the path from the exit. He fired a burst back into the building. "Now we go—"

Flames roared in the street. Rockets pinwheeled from the burning trucks, the warheads slamming against walls and careening off in spirals. Rajai stood in the lobby of the theater, his briefcase clutched in his hands. A mass of torn bodies blocked the theater door. Men screamed, clawing at the dead sprawled across them, twisting to free themselves from the carnage. Across the street, the firing continued as the Hizbullah fighters assaulted the gunmen who had attacked the gathering.

Akbar crouched at the side of the entry, watching the assault. No more bullets or rockets came at the theater, no more antipersonnel grenades exploded in the street. Rajai joined Akbar.

Bodies lay in the street. Rajai saw that his Mercedes burned. Wounded men crawled away from the flames. Groups of Hizbullah stood at both sides of a tenement entrance. One fighter with a rocket launcher leaped into the center with a rocket ready, but as his rocket shrieked away he lurched back and fell. The blast sent dust and smoke clouding from the entry. The man with the rocket launcher lay in the street, not moving, as other fighters rushed into the building, their Soviet rifles firing on automatic.

A militiaman emerged from the entry and motioned the groups of waiting men to follow.

"Who were they?" Rajai asked his bodyguard.

"They have not been seen."

Rajai saw fighters crowding through the entry. He started across the street and Akbar called him back. "My leader Rajai. It is not safe. You should not—"

"Then come with me."

Akbar shouted back to the theater. Three surviving Revolutionary Guards hurried out with rifles. Staying one step ahead of Rajai, Akbar preceded his officer into the building. Men shouted, rifles fired from the far end of the interior courtyard.

The tiny explosion lit the rear passage for an instant, the yellow flash silhouetting militiamen holding rifles, their forms twisting in the narrow passage. Rajai stumbled over a wounded man, the man screaming out. Akbar caught Rajai and led him to the side.

More screams came. A man staggered from the billowing dust, his body lurching oddly with every step. Rajai saw that the Hizbullah fighter had only one foot. Other men screamed and pleaded from a tangle of bodies and broken concrete. Militiamen dragged the dead and wounded out of the passage. Other militiamen stepped over the men on the pavement and fired.

Rajai hurried to the passage but this time Akbar stood in front of him and would not move. "It is not safe."

A voice shouted out, "They are running toward the Marines. They are Marines."

Hizbullah crowded through the narrow passage. Another explosion stopped their pursuit. Akbar pushed Rajai back to the shelter of a corner as more wounded staggered back. An officer shouted into the passageway. "Come back. This is a trap."

Bullets slammed into the men, throwing the walking wounded down, making the dead jerk. Small 5.56mm bullets from the rifles of the Marines hundreds of meters away pinged from the concrete. The heavier 7.62NATO slugs from the machine guns hit like hammers. Retreating men fell over the others—

A flash swept the passage of life, one of the small American rockets exploding in the confined space, the blast throwing concrete and fragments of men everywhere in the courtyard. Legless, the Hizbullah officer screamed as blood gushed from his stumps.

Rajai signaled his bodyguards to follow him. Still holding his briefcase, he led them from the slaughterhouse of the courtyard to the street. "Find the officers. If they are to attack, it must be now."

One of the Iranians ran to the theater, another to a group of Hizbullah tending to their wounded. Another explosion tore through the tenement as a second American rocket hit. Militiamen dragged wounded from the entry. A crowd of Hizbullah gathered there and took the wounded, rushing their bleeding and maimed comrades away from the flaming line of trucks and cars. Lines of wounded lay in the street. Attendants struggled to cram wounded into a single white Pinto station wagon.

A wounded man with tourniquets on both legs screamed and thrashed in the hands of four militiamen. The wounded man pointed at Rajai and raved: "You Syrian dogs did this. I saw your soldiers. Why did you attack us? Why?"

Rajai went to the raving militiaman. "You saw who attacked us?"

"Syrians! I saw Syrians! Syrian soldiers did this . . ." Convulsing, the man coughed blood. The other militiamen carried him away.

"Who saw the soldiers?" Rajai asked the crowd of Hizbullah. "Is there someone who saw who attacked?"

"Ask the dead," one militiaman shouted back.

Akbar returned with a Hizbullah officer. Blood covered the officer's hands. The officer stared around at the flaming trucks and the lines of wounded men. He did not look at Rajai until the Revolutionary Guard took his arm and turned him to Rajai.

"When will you attack?" Rajai asked.

"What?" The officer only stared.

"When will you attack the Marines?"

The Hizbullah officer walked away. Blood glistened in his short-cut hair and streamed down the back of his uniform. Akbar started after the man but Rajai motioned his bodyguard to stop. "Did you see others?"

"No."

"And the mullah?"

"He is injured. He fell off the stage."

"Syrians?"

"They are dead."

Rajai looked at the flaming trucks, the bodies in the bloodsplashed street, the militiamen helping their wounded. Only a few minutes before, this mass of Hizbullah would have assaulted and overwhelmed the few Marines guarding the airport runways. Now they only cursed the unknown enemies who had struck and escaped. Curses meant nothing to the newspapers and televisions of the world. The terror war against the Americans required American dead. And this incident offered only more anonymous Lebanese corpses. In a civil war that had already killed a hundred thousand, fifty or a hundred more corpses meant nothing.

No victory tonight. Rajai accepted that. But then, he had not lost. No cameras had recorded the attack. The killers of these Hizbullah did not even gain a fifteen-second video clip on the evening news. There would be no images of a successful counterstrike by Marines or American allies to diminish the Iranian victory of 23 October.

"Find a car," he told Akbar. "We return to Baalbek."

To plan the next strike against the Marines.

At the al-Ghadir, Niles turned and watched the fields as the others slid down to the streambed. He saw no militiamen pursuing his squad. Rifles and machine guns continued firing from the tenements of Hay al-Sollom but the Marine outposts remained silent. A few bursts of return fire came from the black form of the Lebanese Army bunker on the bridge. Niles watched the LAF bunker for sentries—he wanted no lethal errors.

Sliding down the embankment, Niles went west. Brush and weeds concealed the four men from the Lebanese bunker. They passed under the bridge, slowing to maintain their silence as they walked through the darkness. Niles placed his boots by touch, feeling for trash or brush before stepping forward. Above him, he heard music and the voices of the Lebanese soldiers. The music stopped. Voices faded away. In the total darkness under the bridge, Niles did not risk stopping—Gamal or Hussein might blunder into him. He continued through to the moonlight and crouched down against the side of the gully.

Auto-fire exploded from the bunker above him. Gamal and Hussein rushed from under the bridge. They took cover in the brush. Past the bridge, Niles saw dust clouding from the embankment. The Lebanese soldiers put out hundreds of rounds in wild full-automatic. Tracers ricocheted, spinning away. Niles could not see Alvarez. A grenade popped. The riflefire quit as the soldiers emptied their weapons. A belt-fed machine gun continued cutting the night with long bursts.

Alvarez rushed out. Niles broke from his cover and followed him.

"What are they shooting at?"

"Not me," Alvarez shouted back.

Behind them, the rifles fired again. Gamal and Hussein splashed through the filth and raced up the embankment. They shouted out their names.

"Lookouts coming in," Vatsek bellowed out. "Hold your fire!"

Alvarez follwed them, then Niles went up the embankment. A muzzle flashed point-blank. Niles threw himself to the side, rolling away through the weeds, then scrambling into the cover of a low bush. He looked up to see Vatsek firing an M-60 from the hip, sweeping the heavy machine gun from side to side to saturate the streambed.

White light seared the scene. The tiny point of a pop-up flare floated overhead, revealing a bloody Hizbullah militiaman sprawled in the sand. Vatsek fired another long burst into the corpse, spraying blood and flesh.

Without leaving his concealment, Niles called out, "I think he's dead."

Vatsek waved across the Nahr to the Lebanese soldiers at the bunker. "Nah. He lives on. Sunbathing forever at the Motel Allah. Just lay cool, sir. Don't want to have to explain you. Wait till that light goes out . . ."

The flare burned out and Niles rushed to the top of the embankment. He heard Colonel Devlin congratulating him, but he did not stop moving until he pushed through the plastic blackout curtain screening the Marine bunker. Colonel Devlin followed him inside.

Alone in the bunker, they sat in the darkness as Captain Niles described the improvised strike on the Hizbullah. Colonel Devlin listened. He did not debrief Niles, did not interrupt him with questions—later he would question all four men as a group. The colonel let Niles speak until he ended his story.

"Remarkable. A platoon could not have done it but four men did."

"Luck, Colonel. I used up all the luck I had."

"I don't believe in luck. Luck is discipline. Luck is preparation for an eventual opportunity. You prepared, you moved, you encountered a target of opportunity—"

"And we escaped. That gang of fanatics back there is not professional. If we'd been up against Pa-Vin, we would have been dead."

"But you did encounter a professional."

"Yeah, the Iranian. The executive with the briefcase. Maybe he was Rajai. But I don't believe it was his show. He had Pasdaran—Revolutionary Guards—with him, but they were his bodyguards. The same with the Syrians. They were professionals, but they were there to watch the crazies. Those Hizbullah—one of them may have driven the truck, but they didn't make the bomb. They didn't plan the bombing. That was professional work."

"The Iranian. You think you could recognize him? If we show you photos?"

"I memorized him."

"And if I could win the authorization, would you go after him?"

"Most definitely. I'm going to be thinking about hundreds of dead Marines for the rest of my life. And I want to be able to think that I got them justice. Most definitely I would chase that Iranian and anyone else who was in on that bombing. I would buy my own boots."

"That will not be necessary. And how did those two Lebanese soldiers do?"

"They did good."

"Would you foresee any problems with loyalty in a future action against other Islamics?"

"Sir, religion is not their motivation. They are Lebanese nationalists. They like living in the twentieth century. They went out against the Hizbullah because those crazies would give the country to Iran. I don't know if I'd want to involve them in what we're talking about. Rather have somone who speaks Farsi."

"Farsi. That may be difficult."

"There's got to be a Farsi-speaking Marine somewhere in the world."

"Tomorrow, I return to Washington. National Security Advisor Reisinger took me out of the Special Operations Division. I'll be with an office in the Council."

"Congratulations, Colonel. You're there."

"Temporarily. Only for this project. I'll brief my superiors on your observations and attempt to describe your success tonight without ending your career—If anyone, in the Corps or out, asks you what happened tonight, do not answer them. Only in my presence and with my authorization. Do you understand me?"

Niles laughed. "What happened tonight? I don't know what you're talking about."

"Exactly. I'll give the same instructions to the other men. However, I will say nothing of the future action. That is between you and me. It may be weeks before we can begin organizing a counteraction, so please be patient. There are many who will refuse to contemplate this. But I will not stop until we bring the murderers of those Marines to justice. I promise you that."

"Ready to go. Send the word."

6

STEEL gates blocked the Cadillac. As the driver displayed identification cards, the prison guards looked from the photos to the back seat of the old car, comparing the photos to the face of Abdulkarim Maranaki. A guard signaled the gate operator. The motor-driven gates rolled into the thick concrete walls and the car continued into the courtyard of Qasr Prison.

The chauffeur drove through the tree-lined courtyard, passing the administration building and the gates of two cell blocks, then stopped at the third. Maranaki left the Cadillac and went to the iron bars of the gate.

Two Revolutionary Guards sat at a table beside the walkway, drinking tea and arguing. They went silent when they saw him, standing quickly and opening the gates. They passed him without a document check. Other Revolutionary Guards stood inside the entry to the two-story brick cell block. Their conversation died as he passed. Maranaki pushed through the double doors to the quiet corridor.

Before the Revolution, this cell block had housed wealthy and influential opponents of the Shah. The windows of the cells overlooked landscaped grounds and pine trees. Tiled hallways and plaster walls painted with brilliant white enamel gave the cell block the look of a villa. The prisoners had enjoyed a recreational center and meals cooked by their own servants. Doctors and nurses tended elderly prisoners or prisoners suffering from long-term illnesses. This changed with the Revolution.

The Ayatollah had granted this cell block to the Guards of the Revolution for the detention of special prisoners. Most enemies of the Revolution went to Evin Prison for interrogation and—if not execution—Islamic reeducation before their release. The Revolutionary Guards held prisoners here in total isolation. Unlike Evin Prison, no other prisoners could bring news or take out information. No visitors came here. No prisoner had ever escaped from the cells—the windows now bricked over, the doors double-locked, the halls guarded by survivors of the SAVAK prisons. And as in Evin Prison, interrogations continued until death or total cooperation.

Pausing at the guard's glass-doored booth, Maranaki checked his reflection. The short, wiry officer prided himself on his coarse appearance. He kept his beard cut as short as his hair to emphasize his freedom from vanity. His beaked nose and heavy eyebrows jutted from his profile. He wore a black suit but no tie with his shirt. A tie would be a concession to European convention. Instead, he buttoned his white shirt tightly around his throat. He had discovered that this stark, uncompromising appearance unnerved the decadent and immoral prisoners seized by the Revolutionary Guards. Before the Revolution, he had taught the children of the poor in a small village south of Tehran. Now he taught lessons to the enemies of Iran.

Maranaki called for the guard who carried the keys. Without a word, the bent-backed young man—his spine twisted by beatings in the torture cells of the SAVAK—followed Maranaki and unlocked a double-barred door.

The cell stank. Maranaki entered alone. Closing the door behind him, he stood and stared at the naked prisoner chained to the wall. Loops of chain secured his outstretched arms. Another loop cut into his waist. More chain immobilized his feet. Excrement and blood puddled under the ex-officer in the Shah's air force. Maranaki and his assistants had subjected the pilot to a series of tortures, starting with lashing with a steel cable, progressing to electric shock, then to shock combined with injected chemicals. Though he had screamed and pleaded to be questioned, to be told his crime, they did not demand a confession or the names of other conspirators. They had investigated this pilot before arresting him and knew he and his family to be innocent of any counterrevolutionary actions. The object of the torture had been to make the pilot understand how much pain they could inflict, to make him fear life more than death.

"Open your eyes!" Maranaki demanded, his voice rising to a high-pitched shriek.

The young man lifted his head. One eye squinted, the lid heavy with a clot of blood where the lash of a steel whip had cut his eyelid. Blood had clotted in a line across his face. Many other lines of blood crisscrossed his body.

"Do you doubt this place is Hell?" Maranaki asked him.

Desperate to avoid more torture, the pilot gasped out, "I will answer. I will answer any question. Only what do you want to know? What do you want? How have I offended Allah?"

"We have your mother and father. Your brother. Your sisters."

"No! They are innocent. They know nothing. My brother and sisters are only children. They are all innocent."

But Maranaki knew this also. The pilot could have defected to America or Europe, like many other of the Shah's pilots. But he had remained in Iran rather than leave his mother and crippled father to care for his younger brother and sisters. He had flown in the war against Iraq until the lack of spare parts grounded the Iranian Air Force. He then volunteered for the front and commanded an antiaircraft battery, sending his air force money home to his parents. But his loyalty to Iran and his love for his family had condemned him to this cell.

"They are beautiful children. Your brother will go to the degenerates. Your sisters will be ours—"

The pilot jumped against the chains, a scream rasping from his throat.

"And your mother and father will cry for the mercy of Allah—"

"No, no, what was my crime? What is it that you want from me? What do you want?"

"Your martyrdom."

Without explaining, Maranaki left the cell. The twisted jailer secured the double locks. Maranaki went to the door of another cell. Inside, a sixty-year-old man slept on a cot. A hand across his forehead shielded his eyes from the light of the single glaring bulb hanging from the gray ceiling.

This man—a commercial airline pilot—had plotted an escape. He and another pilot had schemed to steal a cargo jet from a German company, intending to escape with their families to Europe. A suspicious technician had betrayed the pilots. Waiting until the pilots and their families had gone to the airfield, Revolutionary Guards took them in the act. The other pilot had thrown himself on the rifle of a captor to commit suicide. All the others—the dead pilot's wife and child, the old pilot's wife and children and grandchildren— went to Evin Prison. The pilot had not been tortured. He had confessed to every detail, taking all the crimes upon himself to free the families. But he had observed the interrogations in the cells of the prison. He knew the horror of the tortures.

"Criminal."

The white-haired pilot looked at Maranaki, his eyes steady. "Are you speaking to me?"

"You who sinned against the Revolution and Allah."

"I committed no sins."

"The sentence will be death."

Closing his eyes, the pilot seemed to sleep.

"But I can grant mercy to the others, all the others who would have accompanied you on your flight to the nations of Satan."

"What do you want?"

"You are a pilot. If you volunteer for martyrdom, your family will be freed from the curse of your sins."

After almost a minute of silence and thought, the pilot countered. "If you will free my family and the wife and baby of my dead friend, I will fly against Iraq."

Maranaki left the cell without correcting the pilot. The pilot had accepted the sentence of death in an attack. Let him believe that he would attack Iraq. When the time came and he learned the actual target, Maranaki would still hold his family. The pilot would not condemn his children and grandchildren to the horror of death in Evin Prison to save the lives of a few hundred Americans.

* * *

98

RECON

In an office of the Foreign Ministry, Under Secretary of Exports Abas Zargar listened to the report of the small, rat-faced torturer. Abdulkarim Maranaki stood in the Persian splendor of the office in his tight, badly fitted black suit, the sleeves emphasizing his bony arms, his pants wrinkled, his off-white shirt buttoned tight around his hairy throat. He described the backgrounds and qualifications of the two pilots, then detailed the dedication of both men to their families. As if he described the operation of a machine, he spoke of the threats against the innocent families in an even monologue, his voice a high-pitched drone.

Secretary Zargar listened without comment, stroking the lapels of his French-tailored suit. The absurd appearance of the little man—he looked like a rat dressed in black—created the conflicting impulses of laughter and dread. Even the Revolutionary Guards feared this fanatic in the tight suit and prison haircut. Would he see the foreign clothing of the secretary as decadent, as a sin against the relentless horror of the Revolution? Would Maranaki suspect corruption—rather than duty—as the reason Zargar often flew to Europe? Zargar resolved never again to wear a fine suit to a meeting with this fanatic—only a black suit of low quality Iranian cloth. If the Revolution continued to turn and devour its spawn, Zargar did not want to be one of the first taken in the next purge. A day's warning would give him time to escape to his apartment in Paris. Only after thinking of a good tailor in Tehran could he put aside his fears to concentrate on the planning of the attack on America. When the torturer-fanatic finally concluded, Zargar asked the most important question:

"Will they accept this action regardless of the target?"

"They have no loyalty to America."

Though the preparations for the attack required that Maranaki know the attack would be against Americans, secrecy did not permit this torturer to know who would die and where. He would learn only if the attack succeeded. And this made the two skilled, experienced pilots uncertain elements.

"Are you absolutely—"

"We will hold their families in Evin Prison. The pilots

99

know their families will suffer hell on earth if they lose their courage. And if they do, there will be a third pilot whose devotion to Allah and the Revolution is absolute."

"Who is this?"

"He has not flown an aircraft since the Revolution, but he came to us with the dream of martyrdom in a crash into the palace of the monster Hassan. This man gave two sons in the Revolution and his last son at the front. He wants to join his sons in Paradise."

"What is this man's state of mind?"

"He has lost his sons. Now he has only his life to offer to the Revolution."

"Can he be trained?"

"Yes. And I know when I tell him the target will be Americans, he will praise Allah in prayers of thanks."

Zargar dismissed Maranaki. "Good. We will proceed. Inform me if there is any problem with the pilots."

Alone in his office, Zargar considered the separate elements of the attack. He had a few minutes to think before his appointment with Fahkr Rajai.

This attack required skilled, intelligent pilots to navigate for hours along a difficult course before hurtling into suicide. Maranaki had found those pilots. The third pilot—the grieving father who sought out death—would enforce the martyrdom of the others. Zargar would confirm the background of the volunteer, then order a brief training session. The man would only need to take control of the plane in the event of a last-moment failure by the other pilots.

In Argentina, a Swiss agent—who received his money from Panama and believed he worked for Colombian drug smugglers—had already purchased a DC-4 airliner. An overhaul of the engines and mechanical systems by qualified technicians would be complete in a few weeks.

Days before, he had received a cable indirectly relayed from Mexico confirming the purchase of tons of dynamite in the United States. A second shipment of U.S.-made C-4 plastic explosive—purchased in the United States and shipped to Libya by an American ex-soldier—had already left Tripoli.

Now came the role for Rajai. The young Revolutionary

Guard intelligence officer had served for a year in Lebanon, supervising the formation of the Hizbullah militias and coordinating their actions with Syrian and Iranian objectives. His months of careful, tedious organizing had allowed the team of architectural and explosives specialists to exploit the weakness of the Lebanese government and the naiveté of the Americans. Though the Syrian and Iranian specialists had received the praise for the bombing, much of the credit belonged to Rajai. Zargar intended to offer Rajai a central role in the next action. Though the world would never know the sponsors of the attack, another victory against America promised glory and distinction within the closed society of the leadership of the Revolution.

The intercom buzzed and the voice of his clerk announced, "Fahkr Rajai."

Zargar left his desk to receive the young man. Framed in the oiled carving of the ornate entry and doors, Rajai looked like a French diplomat. Others had told Zargar of the young man's international knowledge and savoir faire, but his debonair appearance—an expensive Italian suit, a pale blue shirt and brilliant blue silk tie, his grooming impeccable—came as a complete surprise. How could this fashionable young man of Iran's Persian elite command units of fanatics? Waiting until his clerk closed the doors, Zargar rushed forward and greeted Rajai in French.

"What a pleasure to finally meet you, Fahkr. I reviewed your contributions to the Beirut victory and demanded that the leaders of the Guard allow me to personally request your assistance in this project."

"I was only one of many," Rajai replied in perfect Parisian French. "And I sacrificed nothing, unlike the martyrs. I bow in awe to their spirits"—The young man gave a perfunctory nod—"and offer my prayers."

"Yes, the martyrs. They will live in our prayers forever."

"I also pray," Rajai added with an ironic smile, "that we will have many volunteers for martyrdom. The Revolution cannot yet afford guided missiles."

Zargar laughed. He threw an arm over the young man's shoulders and walked with him to the desk. He indicated a velvet upholstered chair and took his own seat behind the desk. "All my years in Paris and I did not meet you until today. I seemed to know all the families in exile, all the students at the university. But somehow I did not meet you. How did that happen?"

"I often traveled with my father."

"And what degree did you take at the university?"

"I did not complete my studies. The university thought my father's business an unworthy enterprise and would not accommodate the many interruptions in my education. I made the choice to travel and learn."

"Experience rather than textbooks and lectures. Very good. Very pragmatic. Perhaps your wealth of experience with other peoples explains your success in Lebanon."

"I was fortunate to have the Americans and the Israelis and the Christians as enemies. My work only accelerated the inevitable."

"Do you work with Palestinians there?"

"Yes."

"All factions?"

"Yes."

"Even the mercenary Palestinians?"

"Many of the units are mercenaries. Ideology attracted recruits, but money maintains the forces. Leaders who have no money have no soldiers."

"Could you, with money, recruit Palestinian soldiers?"

"With money and a telephone, this hour."

"They must be loyal allies of Iran, ready to fight our enemies."

"They fight one another in disputes over the meanings of words. For money, they will kill our enemies."

"The enemy will be the United States—"

"They are all enemies of America."

"They must be soldiers who are brave, worthy of our trust, who obey without question, yet of no importance to Iran. If martyred, they can be no loss."

"There are millions of Palestinians. If a few die, their women will give birth to more."

"And they must have no knowledge of you, their sponsor. And they must know nothing of the action they guard. They will be dispatched, they will fulfill their role, and then—

through the unfortunate circumstances of the endless war against the Satans of the West—they will be granted martyrdom on a very distant front. If one or more are captured, they must believe the story they tell their torturers. But the story will be only a story, a clever illusion of truth."

Rajai considered this for a moment. "It can be done. Without great difficulty. I know it has been done many times before."

"Your file mentions that you once visited Argentina, Chile, and Nicaragua."

"My father sold weapons to those countries."

"And how is your Spanish?"

"Spanish? This operation will be in South America? Central America?"

"How quickly you understand. But you will not travel there. Do you have experience with other countries of the Americas?"

"In passing. To be truthful, my father had very little business there. But if you want Latin allies for an operation against the United States, recruit the allies in Paris. Or perhaps now, Nicaragua. If this will be an operation which pleases Nicaragua, I will recruit in Nicaragua. It will be impossible to conceal the recruiting from their secret police, so it must have their approval. If not, then Paris."

"But what of the French counterintelligence?"

"I will identify myself as a Libyan agent. The Libyans and the French have an agreement. It is common knowledge. If I plot the death of Americans or other foreigners outside of France, I may operate without restriction. I will be expelled only if I plot murder in France or the murder of French citizens."

"It will be Paris. But remember, this will be a stunning event in world events. Even the French may be obliged to act."

"What have they done after Beirut?"

"This will not be the killing of a few soldiers."

"What will be the target?"

"I cannot tell you that until the last days of the operation. Will you accept this assignment?"

Zargar watched the young man for a reaction. He saw

Rajai's eyes focus on the intricate, interlinked designs of the colorful hand-knotted carpet at his feet. Then he looked up, smiling with a charm sudden and strange from an officer of the Revolutionary Guards.

"Do I accept the opportunity to fly to Paris? Yes."

Zargar laughed. "Yes! To Paris! Consider it a reward for the victory of the twenty-third of October! Now we will discuss the details of your new assignment . . ."

As their conversation continued into the late afternoon, Rajai sat across the desk from the paunchy Secretary Zargar and studied his gestures, the inflection of his affected French, his pompous insistence that he controlled the operation. Rajai had understood this bureaucrat the moment Zargar had left his desk to shake hands and mouth effusive French. The bourgeois fat man had not conceived the operation and he would not execute it. He controlled nothing but the assignment of the details.

Two tests confirmed Rajai's first impression. The joke of martyrs as cheap missiles had tested the bureaucrat's commitment to Shiite Islam. Instead of ordering his immediate arrest and interrogation, Zargar had laughed. The joke of leaving the Bekaa for Paris had confirmed his estimation of Zargar. The bureaucrat had no greater joy than the decadence symbolized by Paris. And now he believed Rajai to be like him.

Point by point, as Rajai clarified the scope of his new assignment and discussed the organization of the Palestinian and Latin American mercenaries, he learned the limits of Zargar's knowledge. The bureaucrat knew the means of the attack and the device to be employed. But he did not know the target. Also, he knew only the approximate date of the attack.

When they concluded their meeting, Rajai learned another detail. Zargar told him to enjoy the trip to Paris, as Zargar could not travel until after the victory. Rajai walked alone through the dark hallways of the deteriorating Foreign Ministry—the offices had closed an hour before—and considered the comment. The commander—or the committee—heading this operation had limited Zargar's knowledge, then restricted his travel. Whatever the target of the attack, Zargar knew enough to win sanctuary in the West by selling the little information he possessed.

This attack would destroy a very significant target. Zargar had stressed to Rajai that all the mercenaries—Arab and Latin—would be liquidated. For the bombings of the French and American barracks, the Syrian and Iranian specialists had maintained tight security, but the attack required the cooperation of several militias. No one demanded the liquidation of the militia support units. But Zargar had stressed that the coming attack required absolute sterilization—no one could remain alive to bear witness against Iran.

Then, in a flash of the obvious, Rajai realized he would be liquidated also. He stood on the steps of the ministry as the gray, smoky evening descended on Tehran. Along the boulevard, a few lights flickered on. Motorcycles and cars raced past. A legless cripple from the Iraqi front guided a motorized three-wheeled scooter. Glancing at Rajai in his foreign suit and holding an American briefcase, the cripple sneered and called out a curse Rajai did not hear through the noise of the boulevard.

If he surrendered to his first impulse and fled to asylum in France or the United States, Rajai lost his chance to join the leadership of the Revolution. He had weeks to think and plan. The assassin would come for him only after he had completed his assignments.

Did Zargar know Rajai would be liquidated? No, he did not have the discipline to mask the knowledge. He would revel in his superiority over the condemned assistant. In fact, Zargar believed participation in this strike against America promised recognition and advancement for Rajai. As Rajai reconsidered his role in the operation and the position Zargar held, his thoughts calmed. Zargar, the fat, stupid bureaucrat, had survived the SAVAK of the Shah and the SAVAMA of the Ayatollah to hold a continuing staff position in a series of conspiracies against the United States of America.

To survive, Rajai knew he must change his role in the operation. He must cease to be a valuable but expendable lieutenant and become a director of operations. He could not wait for promotion—waiting meant liquidation. Instead, he would advance himself to the next logical position in the structure of the conspiracy—the office of Zargar.

The pompous, pleasure-loving fat man had survived the SAVAK and the SAVAMA. But he would not survive Rajai.

Randall Mason followed the rush of arriving passengers through the terminal. He scanned the travelers clustered around the pay phones but did not see Salah Freij. Continuing out to the sidewalk, Mason ignored the line of taxis and drivers. He stood at the curb and waited, his eyes searching the sidewalks and crowds for the Palestinian wearing a blue jacket and bright orange cap. Around him, businessmen entered taxis, travelers met their families, vacationers rented cars at the agency booths. Mason watched for Freij.

Mason wore jeans and a denim jacket. Lizard-skin boots added inches to his height. His Caribbean tan completed the carefully contrived image of Jack Brown, independent transnational entrepreneur. The thin, middle-aged businessman had left his wool suit and conservative identity in London at one the previous afternoon. He arrived at New York's J.F.K. International Airport as Jack Brown, an Australian-born legal resident of the United States who operated a gold mining company out of an office in Las Vegas, Nevada. Another flight took him to Chicago, a third to Los Angeles International Airport.

Mason closed his eyes against the fatigue. He longed for a gin and Valium. The uncertainty and anxiety of the business in the United States kept him awake throughout the flights as he reviewed every detail in his mind, thinking of a thousand different scenarios for failure—and years in an American prison. The jet roar of a plane startled him awake.

Beyond the taxis and the lanes of traffic, Salah Freij leaned against a fence. He wore a Los Angeles Dodgers jacket and a Kerr-McGee cap. With a mustache and long sideburns, the Palestinian looked Mexican. Mason went to a crosswalk and waited with a group of laughing elderly couples talking of Arizona. He crossed to the parking structure and a horn sounded. Not turning, not changing his course,

Mason continued to the center of the covered parking lot. He glanced behind him to see that no one followed, then cut through the rows of cars to another lane. Freij stopped a ten-year-old Chevrolet van beside him. Mason slid open the cargo door and got inside. He leaned between the front seats and asked:

"Any problems with the cargo?"

"All of it came," Freij told him as he continued to the toll booth. "No police, no government. No problems."

"And the loading of the truck?"

"Almost. It will be done tonight."

"Thank the Lord." Mason took a pint of Beefeaters from his travel bag and broke the seal. He downed a ten-milligram tablet of Valium with a gulp of gin. Lying down on the carpeted floor, he emptied the bottle and slept.

Five hours later, Mason looked out at the desolation of the Mojave Desert. To the west, the last light of day faded behind the Argus Mountains. The sulfurous stink to the evening air indicated that they approached Trona, a small town of mineral processing plants and independent mines. The United States Bureau of Land Management controlled vast sections of the desert and granted rights for the exploration of mineral resources. Hundreds of prospectors—working alone or as the employees of major corporations—searched the deserts and barren mountains for gold, silver, and strategic metals. Only the China Lake Arsenal and the Death Valley National Monument remained closed to exploitation.

Headlights flashed past. Freij maintained a steady speed through the rock foothills. The lights of the Kerr-McGee West End facility appeared. A vast expanse of a salt flat extended to the eastern horizon. The minerals of the ancient lake provided the raw materials for the conveyors, sifting towers, chemical pools, and column separators of the plant. Freij sped past the noise and dust of the facility—the industrial plant on the east side of the highway, the rows of identical trailers for worker housing on the west. Mason choked on the chemical stink and lit a cigarette. He forced himself to concentrate on the image of stacks of American currency, the green and black inks, the intricate geometry and scrolling of the engraving—only a fortune to be paid in one-hundred-dollar bills could induce him to come to Trona.

At the Circle K gas station and market, Freij turned off the highway. The van bumped over the rocks and rutted sand of the wide street. Mason saw groups of Kerr-McGee employees in the market parking lot, standing around their pickup trucks drinking beer out of brown paper bags. The lower classes of the world wasted their few hours of liberty in remarkably similar idylls: Welsh miners drank in pubs, Iranian laborers tea in cafés, Americans beer from aluminum cans. Only their wealth distinguished these Trona louts—as evidenced by their Japanese four-wheel-drive pickups and motorcycles—and the decline of the American military/industrial empire would soon strip them of their luxuries.

Small stucco houses lined the street. Pickup trucks and motorcycles parked in the driveways. Dogs barked. The lurid colors of television came from the windows. Mason loathed it all. How had this nation of ignorant, inarticulate, uncultured louts come to dominate the world? But tonight would be the last time he endured this desert town.

Freij parked at a sheet steel warehouse. The wide rolling doors provided for access by trucks or skiploaders transferring freight from the railroad siding running behind the warehouse. Beyond the rails, high chain-link fences blocked access to the Kerr-McGee Trona facility. Why the sulfur-processing plant required a high-security fence, Mason would never understand. Wages chained the employees to their work—with or without a fence, they could not escape. And who would want to steal sulfur?

"An old man came," Freij told Mason as they went to the warehouse door. "A miner. He said he mined gold for many years. Said we give him job, he help us find gold."

"You sent him on his way, I trust?"

"Told him come back next month, when boss here."

Unlocking the alarm system first, Freij then unlocked and opened the door for Mason. The door opened to an office with walls decorated with full-color promotional brochures of Dinkum Enterprises, Limited. Freij reset the alarm circuit, locked and barred the door, then unlocked the inner door.

The prefab steel sheet warehouse had a length of twenty-five meters, a width of twenty meters, and a ceiling height of six meters. Under the glare of work lights, Freij's three-man crew of Palestinians continued the tedious labor of unpacking dynamite from wooden shipping crates. The first man assembled an exact count of the paper-rolled sticks of dynamite into bundles. The second put the bundles into heavy-duty plastic trash bags, knotted the bags, then slipped the bagged bundles into empty five-gallon cans. The third man poured drilling mud—a thick, gray semi-fluid used by oil crews to seal the air space around drill bits—over the bags until he filled the can. A row of filled cans waited for lids and sealing tape.

A Mexican cassette played while the men worked. All the men had cut their curly hair short. They wore denim overalls and work boots. In the two weeks since a closed van brought them from the Mexican border, they had not left this warehouse, eating, sleeping, and working without seeing daylight or the neighborhood outside. Mason had provided cassette stereos and videotape decks for their entertainment. All the music and movies had English or Spanish lyrics and the television channel selector had been removed. The Palestinian crew did not know where they had worked these two weeks. When deliveries arrived, only Freij spoke.

Freij had already assembled the television and personal effects of his crew in preparation for their departure tonight. Only the empty dynamite crates and the Dinkum Enterprises brochures would remain.

A diesel truck and flatbed trailer had been parked at the far wall. Nylon straps secured a shipping container to the trailer. A ramp led from the floor into the cargo container. Mason crossed to the ramp and walked into the container.

Stacks of five-gallon steel cans stood from the floor to the roof of the container. The stacks went from wall to wall, without a hand's width of space between the stacks and the walls. The volume of cans would not allow the cargo to shift in transit. The cargo lacked only three side-to-side rows to be complete. The last layer of floor-to-ceiling, wall-to-wall cans would be solid drilling mud. Mason counted the number of unsealed cans remaining and the last black plastic bundles of dynamite.

Less than an hour's work remained.

In a white stucco house on the street leading to the warehouse, an agent of the U.S. Alcohol, Tobacco, and Firearms Bureau listened to the monitors of three radio receivers. Each receiver had a reel-to-reel recorder taping the incoming signals. Voices and echoing noises came from monitor speakers. The overweight, balding agent adjusted the volume on one receiver and noted the time on a log sheet. He shouted out. "They're moving out!"

"What?" In the small living room, another agent watched a football game. A man in his mid-thirties, the agent had the broad shoulders and hard body of a newcomer to the bureau.

"Shut it off!"

After reluctantly switching off the television, the second agent heard the sound of a diesel engine. "Is that the truck?"

"Look out the window," the other agent called back.

The agent went to the front windows and looked through the shades. He saw the lighted interior of the warehouse as men pushed the high doors to the sides. The warehouse went dark. By the street lights, he saw men carrying bags and boxes to a van parked outside.

A diesel cab appeared. From the other room, the agent heard the sound of the truck's engine transmitted by the contact microphones and transmitters placed on the steel building. Slowly, carefully, the truck emerged from the warehouse pulling a container shell on a trailer. As the trailer cleared the warehouse, men pushed the doors closed, then ran to the waiting van. The van followed the truck and trailer away.

"They're gone. White Chevrolet panel van, red semi pulling a trailer. White male Caucasian driving the semi. Phony Mexican driving the van. I saw three others get in the back of the van."

In the bedroom, the older agent telephoned the information to an address only two blocks away, a rental cabin in a motel across the highway. "You see them coming down the street? Get on them. I'm calling the office."

He hung up and keyed a number. "This is Alfred over here in Trona. Mason and his Arabs are on the highway."

Driving all night on dexadrine, Mason approached the Mexican border at ten in the morning. Signs in English and Spanish advertised businesses in Calexico and Mexicali, two small towns divided by the international border but depending on their geographic and political position for commerce. The trade between California and the Mexican state of Sonora created a two-way flow of people and commerce second only to the San Diego crossing.

Mason would exploit this international flow to move the ten tons of dynamite out of the United States.

But he would not drive the truck to the border. Leaving Highway 111 three kilometers before Calexico, he maneuvered the truck and trailer through the streets of Heber, a small town of Mexican-American agricultural workers. Several turns took him to a dirt lane of modest frame homes surrounded by large fenced yards. Freij followed him in the van. Chicano children watched the Anglo truck driver park the truck and trailer in a field already rutted by heavy truck tires. A semi-truck—the cab shell tilted forward to expose the engine and transmission—stood on concrete blocks at one side of the field. Freij stopped on the side of the dirt street and waited as Mason went to the cottage next to the field. He carried a notebook.

Luis Mendez, a gray-haired Mexican with a beer belly overhanging his belt, opened the door as Mason wiped his boots on the wooden steps. Like Mason, he wore jeans and a denim jacket. "Mr. Brown, you are exactly on time. No problems on the desert?"

"American deserts are nothing. Could drive kiddie carts out there. Rig I drove across the Nullarbo—three trailers. Like a bloody train. Here are the documents. Brought it all."

"The papers, yes. Very, very important."

"The documents on the truck, on the trailer, the container, the mud, the destination—everything you asked for and everything the port authorities in Mazatlán requested. My agent there will of course have copies also. But just so there won't be any misunderstandings on the highway, you have copies of everything."

Easing into an iron patio-chair, Mendez put his bare feet up on the porch rail. "Very good. And Mr. Brown, I know it is your business and of course it is all arranged, but if you must change your arrangement, I can drive the truck to Guatemala and go direct to the oil well. If things change."

"It's the company's decision. I know they don't want the truck going across the Guatemalan border. They think the sea is better. It's their problem. They think they can save money with a Mexican port and a Guatemalan ship. We will see, won't we?"

Nodding, Mendez leafed through the photocopies in the notebook. "Not my problem. I will leave today. Your mud will be there in two days."

"And then the agent takes it. So best of luck to you, Mr. Mendez."

"You are leaving already? You will not come in for breakfast? Or for coffee?"

Mason pointed to the van on the street. "My associate is waiting. Rushing back to Las Vegas. But I thank you very much for your kind invitation."

"Then adiós, Mr. Brown."

"Goodbye and all the best to you."

The Englishman hurried to the van. Seconds later, the van disappeared around the corner. Mendez waited on the porch, looking from the parked semi-truck and trailer to the dust hanging in the morning sunlight. Then he looked down to the cigarette pack bulging one of his jacket flap pockets and said, "So, gentlemen, did you hear everything?"

"Yes, sir," a voice called from inside the house. "You did great. Come on in."

Two young men waited inside. Both wore the work boots, polyester pants, and long-sleeved shirts favored by the local workers. But their boots and clothes looked new. Nylon jackets with the logo of International Harvester covered their shoulder-holstered pistols. Mendez gave them the notebook of photocopies, then took the microphone and transmitter out of his jacket pocket.

"Now the government takes the truck?"

"No, sir. You take the truck, as agreed, to Mazatlán. Exactly as you agreed."

In an eighth-floor conference room of the Federal Building on Wilshire Boulevard in West Los Angeles, a group of officers met informally to discuss Randall Mason. Larry Gelb of the Customs Department stood with his hands in the pockets of his slacks, staring out the window at the campus of the University of California, Los Angeles.

Gelb listened as Julia Sula of the Bureau of Alcohol, Tobacco, and Firearms briefed the officers of two other bureaus on the English weapons smuggler. The officers represented the Federal Bureau of Investigation and the United States Attorney.

"Sources in the Panamanian banks documented the transfer of funds," Sula told the men. In her severe gray suit and reading glasses, the dark-haired young Latina woman looked like a banker. She read from the typed summary in a flat, emotionless tone. "From the Bank of Azadegan—an institution wholly owned by the Iranian government—to Mason's account in Panama, then to his account in London. Surveillance observed Mason meeting several times with Iranians in London. Surveillance observed Mason departing for the United States in the casual clothes he affects for his role as Jack Brown, an Australian national. In New York, Immigration allowed him to pass his forged passport and visa without challenge. Surveillance followed him from New York to Chicago and then to Los Angeles.

"In Los Angeles, Salah Freij, a Palestinian who once worked with the Syrian-based Popular Front for the Liberation of Palestine, took Mason from the airport to Trona, a small desert town near Death Valley, where Mason had rented a warehouse for the operations of the fraudulent mining company he had established.

"Surveillance had already noted the arrival of tons of commercial explosive. We sent a man to look into the warehouse. He spoke with Salah Freij, who pretended to be a Mexican. Our man, who has many years of travel and residence in Mexico, observed that Freij is not Mexican.

"A few hours after the arrival of Freij and Mason, our teams in place saw a van and a truck towing a cargo container from the warehouse. Surveillance teams followed the van and truck to a town on the Mexican border and then to the house of a Mexican national with a history of involvement with drug gangs. This man has worked with American authorities for the past ten years. Mason then turned the truck and cargo over to the Mexican for transport to the port of Mazatlán.

"Mason then returned to Los Angeles for a return flight to London. Freij and three other Palestinians crossed into Mexico at Tijuana. We have a Mexican surveillance team following the Palestinians but we doubt the team will be successful in following the Palestinians until they exit Mexico.

"As to the explosives, technicians placed tracer beacons on the container and sent a team to Mazatlán to learn the destination of the explosives. We will follow the explosives until they are delivered to the end user."

Concluding the reading, Sula set down the typed pages. "Questions?"

George Harcourt, an assistant director in the West Coast office of the FBI, ran his thick, scarred fingers through his thinning hair. A fifty-three-year-old executive who won promotion after promotion for his daring in field work—sometimes using his karate and judo to subdue felons—he looked from Sula to Gelb. "Why, for heaven's sake, didn't you grab this jerk? You'll never get him extradited from England. And these PLO terrorists? You just let them wander off into Mexico?"

"We want to know where that dynamite's going." Gelb turned away from the window and paced the conference room. A thin, long-legged man who had also worked as a Federal prosecutor before transferring to the Customs Department, he consciously avoided speaking legalistic jargon. "Mason buys weapons for the Iranians. Then they put him to buying this dynamite. It has no military use. So what do they want it for? And for who? We arrest Mason, we lose any chance of following it to who'll use it."

"When do you foresee prosecution in this case?" Allan Rempel, the representative of the U.S. Attorney, asked the question which concerned his office.

"The English would extradite for the dynamite buy, wouldn't they?"

"I believe so . . ." A pale, overweight young man with black-rimmed glasses and wispy blond hair slicked sideways, Rempel stared at the far wall as he composed his thoughts. "Yes, they would extradite. But I believe they would view the illegal purchase of commercial explosives as less than world-threatening. And therefore, they would assign a very low priority to the case. Perhaps they would claim we had filed on the case only to bring him within jurisdiction, so that we could take him for violations which they do not consider to be crimes. I would anticipate a very lengthy delay."

"Then let's don't bother," Gelb told him. "Can you agree to that?"

"A continuing investigation. No problem."

"Any problem with that, Harcourt?" Gelb asked the FBI man.

"I don't like it. World would be a better place with him in a penitentiary."

"We want to continue the investigation indefinitely. Even if he comes into the U.S. again."

"And not take him? Then why bother following him?" Harcourt demanded.

Sula answered. "I am certain—absolutely—that a man of Mason's sophistication with weapons and munitions would know of the identification elements present in every commercial explosive manufactured in the United States. He cannot expect for his sponsors to use the explosives without betraying the source. And I believe that may be the object."

"What?" Harcourt asked. "Repeat that."

"He intends for the United States to be identified as the source of the explosives."

"Question is, why?" Gelb stressed. "So if we trace that shipment to where it's going, maybe we can find out who the

Iranians—or the Palestinians or whoever—are going to hit. And that'll probably answer our questions."

Harcourt did not accept that. "Answer your questions, yeah. But what's that worth if this Mason is out loose? When you get the information, it'll be too late to put him away. He could disappear. Take his money and retire. I'll go along with your indefinite investigation if it leads to something. When you get your information, what will you do with it?"

Gelb considered his response. He glanced at Sula, signaling that she could respond. She did not. "It's terrorism. Terrorism's on the news all the time. People in the Pentagon always talk about fighting terrorism. I'll take this to them. See if they can think of something interesting to do."

7

ON a tenth-floor balcony overlooking the beaches of the Avenue Ramlet el-Baida, Iziz Kalaq leaned on the railing and stared out at the blue horizon of the Mediterranean as Rajai explained the role for Kalaq and his Palestinians in the action. He listened to the details for minutes before finally interrupting Rajai:

"But you are saying nothing of the most important information. Where we assemble, the target, the day, and the time."

"I was not told. Therefore, I cannot tell you. However, the target will be of no concern to your force. You will not make the strike. Though you will share fully in the international glory—"

"And the pay."

"—your force will not make the attack. Others have volunteered for the joy of martyrdom."

"Unless the Americans counterattack."

"There will be no time for a counterattack." He glanced from his handwritten notes to the other balconies. He saw no one. Kalaq and his squads of Palestinian gunmen occupied the entire top floor of the apartment tower. And in the interior of Kalaq's apartment, where his Revolutionary Guards waited with one of the Palestinians, no one could overhear him. "When the unit of martyrs leaves for the target, your fighters will fly back to Lebanon. Regardless of the outcome of the attack—victory or failure—your unit will be gone."

117

"And if the Americans learn of this operation and attack?"

Rajai smiled at the question. "When have the Americans attacked? Before or after an action?"

"This will be in the Americas."

"The Americans will not even know you were there until long after the martyrs strike."

"You want twenty men. If there is no threat, why—"

"Twenty men and the technicians. There is always a threat of American action—or Zionist. We must anticipate even the impossible. Also, the fighters must be there to help the technicians."

"How can a man with a rifle help prepare explosives?"

"Your men . . ." Rajai considered his words carefully. He did not want to reveal the immense power of the bomb. "Your men may be needed to transfer explosives from one vehicle to another. There will be Latins there, comrades in the struggle. But I would not want them involved with the explosives. We cannot take any chances with errors due to misunderstandings. Your men will work at the direction of your technicians. That way, there will be no accidents."

"Another truck bomb? An embassy? Where?"

"My superiors will reveal the target only when I must know."

"They do not trust you," Kalaq laughed. "Rajai the loyal clerk. Why do the spymasters of Tehran not trust you?"

"I do not trust myself."

"Half the money will be paid before the action?"

"Of course. We can pay tomorrow. We will pay the second half when your group returns."

"Gold or dollars?"

"Dollars."

"I want all my money in advance."

"Only your share? There is no problem with that."

"And when do you want my men ready?"

"The second week of January. They must be ready to leave at the moment I call."

"And if your call does not come?"

"If my superiors cancel the operation, if the operation is compromised, then your unit will be paid."

"Good. This business is agreed."

"Must you not consult with your superiors in the movement?"

"No. This will be our operation."

"Good, Iziz. I had anticipated also paying your officers."

"Who will receive that money?"

"If they do not learn of this operation, if the participation
of your group remains secret, the money goes to you."

"Agreed. Total secrecy. They will not learn of this operation until after the victory."

Rajai returned his notes to his briefcase. "I need your
assistance on another matter. One of my countrymen needs
an escort to the airport. May I request the help of several of
your men?"

"Why does this Iranian need the protection of my men?
Why not send him in a taxi?"

"It is a political matter. And there may be some danger."

"A kidnapping? Then he must be sent back through Syria.
In a car or truck."

"No, you misunderstand. The danger is to me. My other
concern is that my compatriot leave Beirut without incident.
Only with the assistance of—"

Impatient, Kalaq cut off the explanation. "Four men?
Take them."

On a narrow street in the Shatila refugee camp, Rajai
waited in a Land Rover, watching the footpath that cut
through the broken concrete that had been shops and homes
before the Israeli bombardment of June 1982. Three-story
apartments—haphazard cubes with windows and twisting
stairways, constructed without plans as the population of the
camps increased—walled the street, blocking the late-after-
noon sun. Laundry flapped on lines strung across the street
as wind channeled along the street carried dust and trash.
The voices and laughter of children, the Arabic melodies of
radios, came from the windows near the Land Rover.

Two Palestinians with Kalashnikovs sat in the front seat.
One man dozed. The other man sat half-turned to Rajai,
waiting for his signal. At the other end of the long block, two
other Palestinians waited in a Volkswagen.

Fifteen minutes after they parked, a Palestinian patrol appeared—summoned by suspicious residents. Trucks blocked both ends of the street and gunmen approached the Volkswagen and Land Rover. Kalaq's men showed their identification and talked with the patrol, explaining their surveillance with a complex lie involving UNESCO. The patrol leader did not believe the lie. A handful of American ten-dollar bills resolved the problem. The patrol left immediately.

Women stared from windows. From time to time in the next hour, residents dashed along the street—men carrying their toolboxes, women with market bags. Everyone watched the parked cars.

As the afternoon light failed, Mohammed Farzan stumbled along the footpath. He wore torn jeans and a ragged windbreaker. Two years before in Paris, Farzan had sported the image of a rock star, playing guitar, wearing expensive jeans and leather jackets imported from the United States, drifting into a chic addiction to injections of heroin and snorts of cocaine—all financed by inherited wealth. After Farzan wasted the last of the money producing rock videos, Rajai paid him to join the Mujahedeen. Rajai then returned to Iran to lead Revolutionary Guard units. Farzan failed to report and Rajai stopped sending money. Farzan flew to Beirut to live on the charity of an uncle, but the uncle demanded the end of his use of drugs. Addicted, Farzan moved to a rented room in the squalor of Shatila camp and sold drugs to Lebanese students and foreigners on the Rue Hambra.

"There." Rajai alerted the gunmen.

They watched Farzan shuffle across the dirt street. He did not look to either side as he went directly to his apartment house. Taking his briefcase and a bundle, Rajai left the Land Rover and casually walked up behind Farzan as he stepped into his room. Two gunmen followed. They stood outside the door.

Rajai greeted the addict like a friend. "My dear Mohammed. All these months you have lived in Beirut and you did not tell me. I feared for you, but there was no one to ask."

"Who . . ." Startled, Farzan stumbled. He fell backward onto the wood slat bed, a board cracking under him.

Drugs had not provided a good income for the young man. Looking for weapons, Rajai saw only the furnishings provided with the room, a cassette player, a bag of dirty clothes, and a David Bowie poster. Farzan wore a beard over his gray face and his wrists looked like sticks. Rajai smelled the stink of rotting teeth.

"Mohammed, I am Fahkr," he said softly in Farsi. He had requested the use of the Palestinian gunmen because they did not understand Farsi. He could not risk his own Iranian bodyguards overhearing this conversation. "Your old friend Fahkr Rajai. From our student days in Paris. I saw you by chance on the street and followed you here. What has been the misfortune that has befallen you? Why do you live like this when you have friends?"

His face twisting into a smile that displayed his yellowed teeth, Farzan staggered upright. He looked like a grinning rat as he embraced Rajai. "Fahkr, I did not know you remembered me. Everyone else forgot me. I lost my money and my French friends. But now I see you again. I thank God for the strength of our friendship."

Rajai took a seat on a wobbling chair. On the table, he noticed a spoon with a scorched-black underside. "I feared greatly for you. I thought perhaps the hypocrites in Paris had associated us somehow. I fled when their suspicions turned on me, but I thought you would be safe. But then I heard no more from you and I—"

"Those Mujahedeen dogs! Hypocrites. They live in luxury and—"

"In decadence and corruption," Rajai prompted.

"Decadence! Corruption! And they talk revolution and sacrifice. I worked for them but they demanded I forsake my music and friends. And then . . . then all my money was gone."

"Mohammed." Rajai leaned closer and spoke very quietly. "I stopped sending the money because I thought you had been compromised. But my sources have told me that did not happen."

Backhanding the air as if waving away a fly, Farzan

laughed. "They suspected me of nothing, but—" He switched to English. "Good times! Sex and drugs and boogie-woogie—"

"Very good!" Rajai tossed the bundle to Farzan. He opened his briefcase. "There is clothing. You can leave this unfortunate city immediately. You have lost your papers and passport? You are free to travel?"

"I guard my papers like my life." Farzan reached into a box of clothes and cassette tapes. He found a plastic envelope with an Iranian passport and other documents. "I can go anywhere—even America. My music and my dreams. I have hoped for so long to go to America . . ."

"Perhaps America will be possible." Taking the papers, Rajai flipped through the pages of the passport. He saw the multiple-entry French visa—no void stamp had revoked the privilege.

"But how can I go there? I do not even have the bus fare to Jounieh."

"The Foreign Ministry will pay." Rajai held up five American one-hundred-dollar bills. "Here is the money. You will go to Paris. You will work—"

"But why should I return there?"

"You will work in Paris until I can transfer you to Los Angeles. There is a place there called Beverly Hills—"

"Yes! Where the stars of the cinema live."

"And many Iranians who plot against the Revolution. First you will go to Paris. You will go directly to the offices of the Mujahedeen. Make a story of fighting with the Palestinian Marxists. But your health forced you to return to Paris. So you want to join the resistance again. They will take you."

"But how will I live? They pay nothing to their workers."

"I have other friends in the organization. They will provide for you. Do as they instruct you and you will receive the money you need. Soon you will continue on to California. Put on the clothes—don't be modest. If I have failed to purchase the correct sizes, we will return the clothing to the shop tonight."

"I have only my joy to offer in return for your gifts, for your unselfish friendship."

Rajai turned his eyes away from the image of the addict's thin limbs, gray skin, and pustules. If the French customs authorities body-searched this pathetic specimen, they would not allow him into their country. Farzan pulled on the slacks and shirt. A fashionable American-styled sportscoat and American jogging shoes completed the transformation.

"A coat, new shoes—I am ready to travel."

"And here—"

"A hundred dollars? Thank you, Fahkr."

"It is nothing. Only an advance on your salary from the Foreign Ministry. If you need more, ask in Paris."

"Ask who?"

"I will inform my agents of you. They will come to you."

"What will my salary be?"

"One thousand United States dollars a month."

"But, Fahkr, Paris is very expensive! That is why I came to Beirut."

"We will see about your expenses also. But I cannot promise now. That I must discuss with our superior. Are you ready?"

"Ready? Ready for—"

Rajai took an airline ticket from his briefcase. "Your flight leaves tonight."

"But—but I have friends to inform. I have business to conclude—"

"Friends? Friends who allowed you to exist like this? I think you should leave these friends and business behind—come, I have a car waiting." Rajai took the addict's stick-thin arm. Farzan tried to jerk away. Calling out in Arabic, Rajai told the Palestinians to open the room's door.

Farzan saw the two men with rifles and panicked. Thrashing, he struck out at Rajai. A Palestinian immobilized his other arm and they walked him out to the Land Rover. He did not struggle as they helped him into the back seat. A Palestinian sat on one side, Rajai on the other. As they rode through the darkness of the narrow streets, the driver winding through the maze of the Shatila camp by memory, Rajai spoke soothingly to the addict:

"Perhaps I am rushing you away from Beirut, but when I see how you are living here, I feel sorrow. It is only by the grace of God that I have this opportunity from the Ministry to offer. Otherwise, I could only offer my own insufficient funds. But with the Ministry, you can receive the funds you require for only sending a few letters a month."

"Will there be danger?" Farzan whined.

"Was there danger before?"

"You were there to advise me."

"You are experienced now. And the Ministry expects only informal reports until you go on to Beverly Hills. Then, among the rich ones, then you will begin your long-term assignment."

"In Beverly Hills!" The addict nodded with enthusiasm. "In California. Near Hollywood. I could not have dreamed of this today. And now I am leaving."

"Very soon."

At the entrance to the airport complex, an Army checkpoint stopped the Land Rover. The driver used UNESCO credentials to avoid the delay of a search.

In the terminal, Rajai and the Palestinians waited with Farzan. They did not allow the addict out of their sight. Rajai talked with Farzan throughout the wait, detailing the information he required and describing how to gain the information in the Paris offices of the Mujahedeen. Finally, the airline announced the flight to Paris.

Rajai accompanied Farzan to the departure gate. There, in the crowd of wealthy Lebanese and departing journalists, Rajai passed him a card.

"Send your reports to him by air mail. He is now the head of all the operations against the Mujahedeen. Under Secretary of Exports Abas Zargar, in the Foreign Ministry, Tehran."

Minutes later, Farzar boarded the direct flight to Paris. Rajai waited in the departure lounge and watched the jet taxi across the runways. When the jet soared away, he went to the long-distance telephones and called the apartment of a Mujahedeen leader living in Auvers-sur-Oise, a village outside of Paris.

"I am a friend of the resistance to the mad ayatollahs. I am calling to tell you of an assassin coming to your organization. He is Mohammed Farzan . . ."

Blood-slick fingers pinched a fold of white flesh. A knife blade slashed across the fold, leaving a triangular flap of skin hanging. With the point, the knife cut two parallel lines down from the flap. Plier jaws gripped the flap and pulled away the strip of skin, jerk by jerk.

Shrieking, his scream of pain muffled by rope between his jaws, Mohammed Farzan thrashed against the ropes securing his naked body to the high-backed chair. He could not retreat from the agony. Ropes bound his head, arms, waist, legs, and ankles to the heavy chair. His drug-wasted body convulsed, his chest heaving as he sucked down gasps of air to power his choked screams.

Torture earlier in the day had left Farzan's fingertips charred. Blackened skin and blisters formed lines on his arms and legs. Strips of skin hung down and blood clotted on the floor. But his answers had not satisfied the Mujahedeen officers. The Iranian with the pliers paused as another man leaned down to their shrieking, gasping prisoner. The interrogator asked:

"What are the names of the informers in the organization?"

Farzan panted. He tried to turn to the interrogator, his neck straining against the ropes across his mouth and forehead, his eyes going wide and white against the gray of his face. He gasped out, "I don't know. He did not tell me. How can I know if he did not tell—"

With a jerk, the man with the pliers tore away more skin, then stopped as Farzan convulsed, shrieking. The interrogator leaned down and waited for an answer. Sucking down breath after breath, Farzan finally sobbed out, "I told you of Rajai—"

"We know of Rajai."

"And Zargan, the Foreign Minister of Commerce—"

"He is a new one, thank you."

"But Rajai did not tell me the names of his agents here."

125

"How would you contact these agents without their names?"

"He said they would come to me."

"I find that difficult to believe. When you were here before, you knew many French women. Are you protecting one of your women? Is the agent a woman?"

"No!"

"Who is the agent?"

"I don't know."

"Who are you protecting?"

"I told you the names! Rajai. Zargan."

"Then, Mohammed, I cannot save you . . ."

A butane blowtorch flared.

At the bar of the transit lounge, Randall Mason gulped down a Valium and two gins with tonic water. He paid and left the air-conditioned darkness, stepping into the warmth of the Hawaiian night. He wove through the crowds of departing and arriving passengers to an atrium. A long narrow roof sheltered the passenger walkway, but on both sides palms and flowers glistened from a gentle tropical rain. Mason wiped the concrete of a planter with a newspaper and sat there, rain splattering on ferns only an arm's distance away. He closed his eyes and dreamed of beaches. His body seemed to float, as if he lay in clear, warm water of a quiet lagoon.

Mason had received a telex and a first-class air ticket the previous day. He had flown from London to New York, on to Los Angeles, now to Hawaii. In thirty minutes, the next stretch of the flight took him on to Singapore, then Sri Lanka—and the final transaction of his brief but lucrative career in shipping weapons for the Iranians.

"Randall?" a voice asked.

Turning, he saw a young woman with olive skin and black hair. She wore her hair pulled straight back to accentuate her sharp features. A gold crucifix glinted at her throat. She wore a polo shirt with the words University of Florida, running shorts, and white tennis shoes. Small-breasted, with thin boyish legs, he guessed her to be twenty-one years old.

"Who are you looking for, miss?"

"For you, Randall." She sat with him, casually laying one hand on his thigh. "My name will be Linda Gomez. I'm a very good friend of Salah. I'm going with you to Colombo."

"And why will you go with me?" Slow with alcohol and Valium, he tried to take her hand off him.

She gripped his hand and leaned close to him, her lips touching his neck as she whispered, "Because I have instructions. Because you do not speak Arabic. I will help you with the transfer."

"Miss, perhaps there is a misunderstanding. I have my own associates there. Associates who speak English."

"You do not know the men who will take the cargo. The new men speak only Arabic."

"Oh. How convenient." He studied her features. Though she gave the name of Gomez, he recognized the Middle Eastern lines to her features—Palestinian.

"And I will travel with you as your lover to the resorts of Ceylon. It will all look very ordinary, the handsome man of the world." She caressed his face. "With his young girlfriend. My instructions are to do whatever is required to make the transfer successful."

"Well, my dear Linda. Please have no illusions—there will be very little required of you."

The public address system announced the boarding of their flight. Other passengers—Chinese and Thais and British expatriates—left the gift shops and bookstores. Gomez pulled Mason away, already acting like a woman with her lover. She clung to him as they checked through security and took their places in the first-class seats.

Drugged, Mason slept through the long, trans-Pacific flight to Singapore. He woke to find himself sharing a blanket with Gomez. Stewardesses guided him from the jet. He stumbled through the transit lounges to the next plane, an Air India commuter flight. With only an hour's air time to Sri Lanka, he could not indulge in the luxury of sleep. Cup after cup of tea cleansed his blood of thirty hours of Valium and alcohol, turning his stupor to impatient anxiety.

Linda Gomez showed him photos and maps of tourist

attractions, chatting with him and laughing mindlessly, the personification of the college girl with the older man. Mason smiled and nodded at the brochures but kept his thoughts on the transfer of the explosives.

The container ship had docked in the Port of Colombo. As a major transshipment point in South Asia, Colombo serviced hundreds of freighters a month. The facility assembled or divided cargos, using modern container transport systems and gangs of Sinhalese workmen to route shipments.

Mason had often used Colombo for the transshipment of materiel and weapons to Iran—helicopter parts from Latin America, aviation electronics from the United States, high-tech NATO rockets stolen from warehouses in Europe. The cargos had arrived in the Port of Colombo in containers, left in crates with forged documentation. The shipment of explosives did not require breakdown to crates—only the rerouting of the container to another freighter.

However, for this shipment, the Iranians had placed Palestinian guards on the freighter leaving Colombo. Why, Mason could not guess. He foresaw no difficulties with the transfer of the container. In the last minutes of the flight, he mentally checked off every detail.

None of his men had cabled him with problems. The supervisor had prepared the false documents. The government clerks had received their payments. Though the Palestinians serving as security created an unknown in the exchange, the Iranians had anticipated any difficulties by assigning the girl to accompany him.

At Katunayake International Airport, lines of complaining Sinhalese waited as customs officers searched their luggage and boxes for weapons. The recent Buddhist riots in which hundreds of minority Tamils died had panicked the nation with fears of revenge by the Tamils. But the customs officers only glanced into the suitcases of foreigners. Mason and Gomez cleared customs in minutes. The driver of the Hotel Intercontinental van waited for them in the lobby. Mason pushed through a crowd of porters grabbing for the luggage and threw the cases into the van. No other tourists came to the van.

They rode through the chaos of the Negombo Highway, the driver somehow avoiding the bicycles, roller-board cripples, transport trucks, buses, and three-wheeled Honda jitneys. Horns, engines, and shops with loudspeakers created an unending cacophony of noise. Gomez watched the passing scenes of tropical Asia. Shops lined the highway, signs advertising their wares in three languages—Sinhalese, Tamil, and British. Pigs nosed through the trash and discarded coconuts littering the muddy roadsides. Smoke drifted from smoldering heaps.

"Not like the tourist books, is it now?"

Gomez shook her head no.

"Colombo is worse. There, look."

Though dust and diesel soot from the highway covered the lush foliage at the roadside, an intersecting road offered a view into the radiant green of the flat countryside. They saw saronged boys walking along a macadam road cutting across wind-swayed rice fields. Wild tropical flowers lined the road. Then their speed took the image away.

"If we are forced to wait, I'll ring up a car hire agency. We'll motor up into the hill country. Beautiful there. Not like this."

They endured thirty kilometers of the highway before entering the filth and crowds of Colombo. The city had no expressways. The highway became an avenue of bumper-to-bumper vehicles, buffalo carts, and jitneys. Gomez stared around at the sprawl of decaying buildings and narrow, rutted streets. As the van crept through a jammed traffic circle, she shouted over the blare of a hundred horns:

"Why do people come here?"

"Clever media management, dear. Propaganda. The authorities ban all photography outside of the tourist areas. On the penalty of forced permanent residence."

At the Intercontinental, Gomez rushed into their room and closed the drapes on the view of the Gulf of Mannar. In the darkness, she turned on the air-conditioning and threw herself on one of the beds. "Finally!"

"My pretty lover overwhelmed by the beauty of Sri Lanka?"

"Completely!"

Mason checked his watch. "Then to work. My associates will still be in their offices."

The hotel featured a modern switchboard and a multilingual operator. However, the telephone system of Colombo had declined since the departure of the British in 1948. Connections crossed, relays failed to close, sometimes voices spoke over the ringing of the phone. But Mason persevered. The only alternative would be to walk across the city to the port offices. Three calls took two hours.

"And that is that, now we go."

In the tenth-floor restaurant of the Hotel Taprobane, Mason studied a series of forms. The first page bore the letterhead of the Colombo Port Authority. He read the strange Asian English slowly, searching for errors. A Sinhalese he knew only as Mr. Nilaveli sat beside him, watching as Mason flipped to the forms stapled to the cover page. Mason checked the official seals and every entry typed into the spaces—the fictitious company names, the numbers, the transshipment codes, the names of the agents. He compared the entries on one form to the following sheets. Any omission or error might block the transfer of the container to the outward bound freighter—and force Mason to remain in Sri Lanka to expedite the shipment.

Linda Gomez, in jeans and a University of Florida windbreaker, looked out at the harbor. She sipped from a tall arrack-and-cola. Below the hotel, thousands of lights illuminated the Prince of Wales Jetty. Freighters and cranes and trucks remained motionless, all activity stopped for the night. Unlike other ports, the loading and unloading of the vessels ended in the afternoon. No threat or bribe induced the supervisors and work crews to break their union statutes.

"A totally false document," Mason commented.

"Yes, yes, my dear Mr. Mason, all is in order," Nilaveli nodded. "The authorities will have no questions as to the validity of the papers. The cargo was from Mexico with the destination of Saudi Arabia. The cargo is presently from Saudi Arabia with the destination of Colombia."

"Your bank received the telexed transfer of funds from your cousin?"

"Oh, yes." Nilaveli smiled. "The generosity of my dear London cousin overwhelms this humble and undeserving fellow."

"When the ship leaves Colombo, you will receive the second payment."

"How can I ever thank my cousin?"

"When is the ship scheduled to depart?"

"Soon. I can promise no more than the immediate loading of your goods. The departure is out of my hands."

"It appears," Mason told Gomez, "that I will do business tomorrow, then we will see the sights while we wait for the ship to sail."

"We won't be waiting in Colombo! Tell me we won't."

"I would not be so cruel."

After another hour of drinks and talk, they left Nilaveli. Gomez giggled and staggered, unsteady with arrack. Mason endured her embrace as they waited for the elevator, then stepped away when the elevator doors closed.

"Am I so ugly," Gomez asked, "that you can't even pretend?"

"It's nothing personal."

As the elevator lurched to a stop, she pressed herself against him, kissing him, one hand clutching his crotch. Two sunburned, overweight foreigners laughed, commenting on her antics in Russian. Gomez clung to him through the lobby.

"Only doing my job," she teased him.

"And with enthusiasm. I'm sure your performance is effective. I only question if it is needed."

In their room, Mason took a bottle of gin from his luggage. He watched as Gomez stripped off her clothes.

"Valium? A drink? You'll need your sleep. We must be at the dock at first light."

"You English are cold fish." Wearing only panties, she searched through her luggage. Her long, slim legs flared to wide hips. She had a very narrow waist. A livid scar cut diagonally across one shoulder blade, marring the flow of her back.

She is very young to be involved in this, Mason thought to himself. He took a pill and gulped from the bottle. "Miss, didn't your superiors explain the situation?"

"What situation?"

"You are the wrong sex."

"They didn't—"

"Then they didn't know. I must apologize for keeping my private affairs private. They thought of you—as what? A bonus? A tart for my pleasure? But it is unnecessary for us to be bitchy about their error. It will only interfere with our work."

A wind from the northeast brought a light monsoon rain. Over the gray skyline of the Pettah slums, a gaudy dawn broke through the smoke and clouds. Mason and Gomez waited in a taxi on Sea Beach Road, watching the port workers crowd through the gates to the harbor. Betel vendors lined the curb, displaying their trays of leaf-wrapped portions of betel nut and shredded coconut. Other vendors dodged through the buses, offering umbrellas, wristwatches, and radio batteries.

Gomez stared out at the urban scenes, questioning Mason on the narcotic effect of betel, the history of the Pettah district, the rate of exchange of the dollar for the rupee—performing her role as the girlfriend of the international businessman.

As they waited to enter the harbor complex, Mason silently thanked the Iranians for sending the young woman. Security conditions had changed since his last trip in June. He knew that two tourists did not attract the same notice as a foreign man alone.

Police at the gates checked the cards of all the workers. Soldiers with Sterling submachine guns stood inside the gates. Before the communal riots of August, unarmed watchmen had served to block vendors and petty thieves from the complex. The police and soldiers reflected new concerns with terrorism. Mason hoped the security—as at the international airport—did not apply to foreign tourists.

A horn sounded. Nilaveli waved from his Fiat. Mason

paid the taxi driver and splashed through the street water to the Fiat. He opened a back door for Gomez, then he sat in the front with Nilaveli. Nilaveli joined the line of cars and trucks waiting to enter the gates.

"You didn't mention the security men. Will they pass us?"

"Of course, my dear Mr. Mason. Why should they halt you? Are you not my guest?"

"I'm a foreigner."

"A guest in our lovely Sri Lanka."

"Then why the security?"

Nilaveli smiled to Mason, his white false teeth startling against the South Asian black of his face. "Of course you have heard of the incidents of Tamil terrorism. Very unfortunate, but true."

A policeman leaned down to the window of the Fiat. Nilaveli presented his identification, then gestured toward Mason and Gomez. The officer nodded. Accelerating through the gate, Nilaveli waved to the soldiers. Other soldiers paced through crowds of workers. Policemen and soldiers at the doors of warehouses.

"Not bloody good . . ." Mason cursed.

"Do not trouble yourself. You will see that the officers do not concern themselves with foreign guests. Or with the business of the port."

Driving to the end of an access lane between the warehouses, Nilaveli parked his Fiat and ushered the strangers past a guard. Inside the warehouse, thousands of tons of crates stood in stacks three meters high. Only one forklift operated. Arriving pushcart workers squatted in circles and chatted, smoking cigarettes and spitting red betel juice on the concrete while foremen argued over paperwork. Nilaveli interrupted an argument and pointed to a page in a collection of papers. A foreman went to a telephone and spoke rapidly for minutes, nodding and gesturing into space. The foreman returned and explained to Nilaveli. Mason waited for the conversation to end. Nilaveli finally translated:

"The telephone is out of order. Come."

A few steps behind the two Sinhalese, Mason whispered to Gomez, "One must retain one's appreciation of the absurd on this lovely isle. Security men who do not question strangers. Workers who do not work. Talking for an hour on a phone that doesn't work."

They walked through intermittent rain to a mechanized wharf. Sinhalese technicians supervised the beginning of the work day, the loading of a rusted freighter with the name *Manhattan*. A crane above the ship creaked and groaned, moving a container from the wharf to the deck of the ship. Nilaveli and the warehouse foreman spoke with a technician. They compared papers. The technician finally pointed to the containers stacked on the deck of the *Manhattan*. Nilaveli returned to Mason.

"All is well. Your cargo is aboard."

"What? But we didn't bring the papers until this morning."

"All was ready yesterday, as according to your specifications. Through our long association, I have come to know your business. As you this very moment saw, I perfectly prepared the instructions. Is it now a surprise that the transfer went through without delay?"

"No, of course not. But I want to confirm that it's actually on the ship."

"Very well. Let us go."

On the deck of the freighter, Mason searched for the container while Gomez spoke quickly with a crewman. The crewman—a short, powerful Arab with curly hair and a beard—ran to Mason and guided him through the stacked containers. Mason recognized the container from Trona, California, by the color and dents. He checked the code numbers. The numbers matched. He examined the doors. No one had tampered with the locks or seals.

"This is amazing. The shipment is here. It is loaded. It has not been looted."

The crewman shrugged—he did not understand English. Mason hurried back to Gomez and hugged her. "Linda, you are a godsend. There can be no explanation but the supernatural. The work was done exactly as specified."

"Now do we get to play tourists?"

"An excellent idea. We cannot leave until the ship sails—why not enjoy the wait? To the hill country, we go."

"I want to walk back to the hotel. The map says it's an easy walk. I want to see the Pettah Mosque and the Fort and . . ."

Like lovers, they walked arm in arm from the port. Mason led the young woman through the narrow streets of the Pettah—the centuries-old colonial commercial district—to the red-and-white-striped mosque on 3rd Cross Street. Loudspeakers called the faithful to prayer. Moslem men in traditional white pants and shirts crowded around the mosque entrance. Shopkeepers in modern summer-weight suits stood in the shops lining the muddy street. A few women passed in the saris of the Sinhalese or Tamils, others in the pants and long dresses of the Moslems. The men watched the foreigners pass. All eyes followed Gomez in her tight jeans.

"I don't like them staring at me," she told Mason. She stepped into a narrow alley. There, she watched the passing crowds of Asians.

"Isn't visiting a mosque out of character," Mason asked, "for Linda Gomez, the Latin-American college girl?"

"This is important," she laughed. "I'm your little tourist girl, right?"

"Right."

A razor slashed across his throat. As his life pulsed from his severed arteries, hands pulled him back into the darkness of the alley. He called out in panic. Breath and blood sprayed from his open throat. He saw the bearded face of the Arab from the freighter and the faces of other men as they dragged him around a corner.

As they wrapped him in black plastic, as he died, he heard Gomez answer her final question to him:

"Wrong."

8

COLONEL Anthony Devlin sorted through boxes of black-and-white eight-by-ten-inch photos. He worked with his shirt sleeves rolled up and his collar open, his suit coat and tie hanging over the back of his leather upholstered chair. His appearance did not matter— he worked alone with the photos in the Victorian luxury of the wood-paneled office.

Hundreds of black-and-white prints covered the oak desk and spilled over the royal blue carpeting. Taking a bundle of prints from a box, he glanced at the index code accompanying the photos, then flipped through the sequence. The prints showed scenes photographed from videotapes.

During the day, he and a group of technicians had scanned hours of videotapes, running through the scenes at high speeds. Some taped sequences had excellent panning shots of streets and skylines. The colonel then detailed the technicians to locate the scenes on street maps and to make photos from the tapes.

Panning shots offered long, continuous images. However, camera movement created blurs. Broadcast static reduced some images to abstract pointillism. Some pans—of back-lit skylines or glaring midday streets—featured only high-contrast images without details. The colonel had instructed the technicians to photograph all the sequences for his personal evaluation. Years of experience with the electronics and computers of photo reconnaissance allowed him to guess quickly what sequences could be enhanced.

Quickly laying out each panorama, the colonel searched

for details in the scenes, studying the buildings, the streets, the Arabic-language signs. Where he saw armed men, he checked for uniforms or equipment which might identify the forces, marking the images for enlargement. He also marked silhouettes that suggested Soviet ZSU-23-4 mechanized gun mounts—or any other antiaircraft weapon. These would be checked against satellite reconnaissance.

His aides had offered to stay through the night to do the work. But the colonel took the task himself. A delay in the translation of Arabic and Farsi radio interceptions had stalled the work. Until he had translations of the intercepted communications, he could not proceed. Rather than leaving for home or joining in the all-night Situation Room debates on possible actions, he worked on the photo montages.

Devlin had been temporarily transferred from his desk in the offices of the Joint Chiefs of Staff to a borrowed office in the old Executive Office Building. He would work with the staff of the National Security Council for the duration of the counterstrike operation.

Despite the evidence linking Syria and Iran to the bombing of the Marines, the colonel did not believe the National Security advisor would recommend a direct military counterattack. Both nations shared borders with the Soviet Union. The Soviets armed and advised the Syrian army and air force. An old treaty with Shah Reza of Iran pledged the Soviets to defend Iran in the event of an invasion. The administration did not want to risk a confrontation with the Soviets.

He anticipated an attack on the gangs in Baalbek—by Niles and his Marines. Friendship and respect for Niles kept the colonel at his desk this evening, working with the photos. The colonel's aides had the technical expertise to assemble and evaluate the photos. But the aides did not know Niles. To them, the death or capture of the Marines would be regrettable losses of anonymous soldiers in a covert operation. To the colonel, the casualties would be the loss of a friend and several brave young men. When Niles and his volunteers went into Baalbek, the colonel wanted those men to succeed. And survive.

A knock interrupted his work. He called out "Come

in" as he gathered and stacked a panorama of a street.

Looking up, Devlin saw Phil Carpio. Carpio worked in the bureaucracy of the Central Intelligence Agency. He had been called into the counterstrike planning group to coordinate the flow of information from foreign intelligence sources. A balding, retirement-aged administrator who had flown combat missions as a young pilot in the Korean War, Carpio had worked closely with the colonel throughout the contingency planning.

"I'm sorry to tell you, Colonel. But they're shutting us down."

"What?"

"Todd called me. He's not my direct superior in the agency but I've been reporting to him for the duration of this project. He told me to clean out my office here and return to Langley in the morning. I asked who would take over my work with you. And he said it was over. Reisinger will talk with you tomorrow."

"They've decided to do nothing . . ."

Carpio nodded. "Thought you'd want to know first."

"Thanks."

"Stay in touch, Colonel. Call me if you need help. You know how I think on all this."

"I will. And thank you again."

Devlin stepped away from the desk. He stared out the window at the sights of the capital—the Ellipse, the white blade of the Washington Monument rising against the night, the streaking lines of traffic on the avenues, the blocks of lights where clerks and researchers and aides processed the decisions of the government.

Had all the history and power of his country come to mean nothing?

Media commentators would interpret the failure to pursue justice for the murdered Marines as a demonstration of the heavy responsibilities of world power. The bureaucratic frenzy to conceal official cowardice behind a screen of prepared statements and leaked memos and press conferences would be seen as a process of reassessment—the balancing of foreign policy with *Realpolitik*, public outrage with military limitations. The commentators would praise the administration for wisdom and restraint.

The futility of his work saddened and angered him. His role in the contingency planning of a Baalbek action, his intelligence duties in the Joint Chiefs of Staff, the past twelve years of his career—all for nothing. There would always be overwhelming political reasons not to respond to the terror of gangs and dictators around the world. As a Marine and as a man who had devoted most of his life to the military, he wanted to strike back at the gangs who murdered the Marines in Beirut.

Payback—a strike against the gangs to demonstrate that the murder of Americans had a price. Yet this would not be justice for the two hundred forty-one murdered Marines. The *Realpolitik* of the superpower confrontation in the Middle East denied any hope of destroying the regimes responsible for the bombing.

But there would be no counterstrike. Only the words of diplomats.

He thought of resignation. Twenty-four years of service in the Marines guaranteed a pension. Corporate presidents had already questioned him on his future plans and offered positions in their companies. His new salary—combined with his pension—would send his children to the finest universities. He could reward his wife's devotion with a summer home and comforts never possible on his service pay.

Could he time his resignation as a protest against the inaction? A final statement against the paralysis of his nation's leaders?

Quitting meant he had no chance to act against the paralysis. Others in the military and government shared his frustration. They had worked together—exploiting their contacts and technical resources—in an informal network of alliances. Resigning meant severing his links to officers and bureaucrats willing to act on their principles.

National Security Advisor Reisinger had told the colonel that the president himself had demanded a counterstrike against the Shiite terrorists. However, congressional and diplomatic restrictions limited the administration's response to the gangs to the empty threats of the Secretary of State and the cautious contingency planning of the Secretary of Defense.

He thought of Niles and the volunteers acting on their own against the Hizbullah militia. Armed with Soviet weapons, wearing the uniforms of Syria and the gangs, they had walked into the Shiite ghetto and hit the militia.

What if the colonel developed Niles's squad into a covert unit? Not another special operations battalion like the Delta Force, or the Army Ranger companies, or the various commando forces of the Air Force or Navy. None of those covert warfare forces—because of their size, logistics, and command structure—could operate secretly. Every department of the government exercised veto power over the special operations commandos.

What if the colonel created a unit so small it could operate independently and secretly? That could be funded without congressional oversight. That could be dispatched with a phone call. That could exploit moments of opportunity.

If he suggested this to the National Security Advisor, the colonel risked the instantaneous end of his career. But so what? Why not risk his career? His career had come to an end. He thought of Niles risking not only his career but court-martial and prison to act against the fanatics threatening the Marines.

The mass murder of Marines in Beirut, the terrorism against American embassies and civilian travelers—the crimes demanded a response. Justice or payback—whatever the word—but action to stop the criminals from attacking Americans again.

Devlin reknotted his tie and slipped on his coat. At the end of the corridor, an elderly guard insisted that he sign out. He scrawled his initials and went down the polished granite stairs to the lobby, then into the cold air of the night.

Striding across the lawns and sidewalks, the colonel crossed the narrow street between the Executive Office Building to the northwest gate of the White House grounds. The guards there watched as the straight-backed, gray-haired man approached. The colonel heard a radio in the gatehouse reporting details of an assassination in Beirut.

"Good evening, sir." The guard checked his watch. "Can I help you? Do you have an appointment?"

"I'm Lieutenant Colonel Devlin, Joint Chiefs of Staff, temporarily with the Council staff—" He unclipped the plastic-laminated identification card from his shirt pocket. The card showed his name, rank, photo, and the seal of the National Security Council.

"Are they expecting you, sir?"

"No. Has Mr. Reisinger left yet?"

"No, sir."

"That's the man I want to see. Call him."

As the guard dialed, the colonel scanned the windows of the West Wing. Lights showed in several offices. Limousines and drivers waited at the basement entrance. Secret Service men paced the sidewalks and lawn. Even there—in the center of the capital, guarded by thousands of police, thousands more Federal guards, the high technology of the fence protecting the president, and the president's police—the Secret Service watched for a threat.

"Sir, Mr. Reisinger is with the Secretary of State. But his secretary said to come in if you're willing to wait."

"I'm willing."

"Just a moment, sir. A man will need to walk you to the door."

Obsessive security. He had top clearance and they would not allow him to walk the hundred meters to the entrance. The leaders of the nation demanded near-perfect security—but what about security for the people?

As he stood at the gate, he heard the radio announcer report on a new communiqué from the Shiite gangs of Beirut. The colonel listened. Nothing new. Threats and demands. Remarkably similar to the statements of the Secretary of State.

A young Secret Service man, a walkie-talkie in hand, came to the gate. Together, walking in silence, they followed the circular drive to the White House West Wing. The colonel heard the whisper of a voice from the earphone the agent wore. The agent spoke quickly into the walkie-talkie. "Colonel Devlin is here."

Perfect security for the leaders. Inside, the colonel faced

two more of the presidential police. He signed the log sheet and waited again. The door of an old elevator slid open. Another uniformed guard stood inside.

"Colonel Devlin? They're expecting you upstairs."

As the old elevator slowly carried him toward the third floor, he reconsidered his decision. Twenty-four years in the Marine Corps, all opportunities for work in this administration, any chance to somehow influence the national counter-terrorist policy: it all ended if Reisinger refused to authorize a counterstrike on the murderers of the Marines.

If the administration did not strike back, he wanted out.

Teletypes clattered. Stepping out of the elevator, he saw staffers watching the paper roll out of the wire service machines as the typeheads printed lines. The colonel hurried on. Telephones rang in the offices he passed. He heard a printer running. At the end of the hallway, he rushed into the outer office of the National Security Advisor. A stenographer at one of the metal desks transcribed from a cassette tape, headphones over her silver hair, her thin hands flying over the keyboard of a desk-top computer. A group of staff workers crowded around another desk, their briefcases open on the floor. One young man red-lined phrases on a typed sheet while the others leaned over him to read his editing—aides rewriting a meaningless statement.

"Who's inside with Reisinger?" the colonel demanded.

An overweight aide stared at him, recognizing his face from a House hearing or a television appearance but not remembering his name or position in the government. The aide squinted at the plastic identification card on the colonel's coat before answering. "Mr. Samuel and his assistant. And Mr. Todd. And some other military men."

The colonel went to the secretary and leaned down on her desk to stop her typing. Pointing to the interoffice phone, he told her, "Colonel Devlin, to speak with Mr. Reisinger."

"He's in discussion with the Secretary of State, sir."

"Interrupt him."

Her hand hesitated over the button as she studied him over the frames of her half-glasses. "May I ask why?"

"Interrupt him."

"There is a Colonel Devlin here to speak to Mr. Reisinger

on an urgent matter." She looked up to the Colonel. "Would you like to step inside and speak with—"

He took the phone from her hand. "We'll talk in the hallway."

"What is it—"

Hanging up the phone, the colonel heard the inner door jerk open. National Security Advisor Reisinger rushed out, the aides at the desk turning around to stare. A tall ex-major in the Army Airborne, Reisinger had gone gray in the service of the president. Long hours and stress had lined his face and taken the tone out of his body. Only fifty years old, he looked sixty. A cigarette hung from his yellowed fingers.

"What is it?"

Motioning the advisor outside, Devlin followed him into the hallway. Teletype clatter and voices continued. The gray-faced, gray-eyed advisor took a drag on his cigarette and waited for the colonel to speak.

"When do we hit Baalbek? The photo reconnaissance is ready. The agent information on the Bekaa is ready. We have Marines in Beirut ready. We're ready to go ahead on the action."

The advisor exhaled his smoke before speaking. "Someone told you that we're breaking up the contingency group. Is that it?"

"True."

"What exactly is it that you mean, 'action'?"

"The armed forces of the United States have the ability to strike back. The question is: does the administration have the will? Or do the lives of its servicemen mean nothing?"

"You're not talking to a committee, Colonel Devlin. Spare me the rhetorical questions. What's this 'action' you're talking about?"

"I briefed you on the actions of the Marine Recon unit in Beirut. We can send in those same men. They'll target those gangs for air strikes and then get out."

"That's impossible."

"Sir, what is impossible is for me to remain in service to a government that initiates endless studies, issues ultimatum after ultimatum, prepares for every possible contingency— but does nothing."

"You'd quit? The Council? The Joint Chiefs?"

"And the Marine Corps."

"You feel that strongly about this? I wanted to keep you on as a specialist after this. You could make general. Another colonel did."

"I did not come to discuss that. I want some attempt at justice for two hundred forty-one murdered Marines."

Advisor Reisinger smiled. He took a long drag on the stub of his cigarette. Exhaling, he instructed the colonel. "All right, you're out. Write your letter of resignation. List everything you just told me—"

Silent finally, Devlin nodded. He had gambled and lost.

The advisor waited for a response. After several seconds, he continued. "Sign it but leave the date open. Bring it to me tomorrow. Just a moment—"

Reisinger rushed across the waiting room. He leaned into his inner office. "Mr. Todd—"

A thin, middle-aged man with the round shoulders of a lifelong desk worker left the meeting. He had pale features and gray hair. Decades of fatigue had marked dark circles under his eyes. His lips cut a gray line across his face. He wore a gray suit highlighted by a black bow tie. Reisinger introduced the pale, stoop-shouldered bureaucrat.

"Colonel Devlin, this is Richard Todd, special assistant to the agency's director of operations. Todd, the colonel heads the group planning the response to the event of October the twenty-third. He learned that we're writing off any possible response and he's resigning in protest. Convenient?"

Todd extended his hand. "Good. It'll be a pleasure working with you, Colonel. I know of your expertise and service. Mr. Reisinger told me about the Recon squad's fighting in the Moslem sections of the city. You and your men are unique. We need all the help we can get."

"As of tonight, we're dissolving your planning group," Reisinger continued. "Officially, any response to the terrorist bombing of the Marine barracks—air strikes, airborne assaults, whatever—is politically impossible. Unofficially, covertly, we'll be using your men to chase those murdering sons-of-bitches and put them in a hole. From tomorrow on, you'll be working directly with me. Mr. Todd volunteered the assistance of his staff in the future. I want an oral presentation tomorrow of the options. No American weapons. No tracing it back to the United States. Nothing will be committed to writing. If this goes public, you are gone. You think you can do this? This quick-and-dirty squad?"

Clattering machines, the phones, the voices in the offices, the couriers and staff hurrying through the hall—all the distractions of the bureaucracy receded. Devlin stood eye to eye with the advisor to the President of the United States.

"I can do it."

Twenty-two years of extraordinary duty in the military had prepared Anthony Devlin for this opportunity.

As a young man graduating from Yale, he continued his family tradition of military service by volunteering for the Marine Corps. The Corps offered him a staff liaison position with the NATO command. He declined the prestige appointment and volunteered for a combat post with a Marine Amphibious Unit on continuous station in the Mediterranean. A battalion commander recognized the young lieutenant's education and language skills and assigned him to the division intelligence office, maintaining files and processing thousands of routine updates of topographical and military details that would be required in the event of a war. He received an excellent rating from his officers but requested retraining and transfer to Force Recon, an elite unit responsible for preassault reconnaissance of enemy territory.

Recon platoons operate as extensions of division intelligence, a role which requires stealth rather than firepower. The Amphibious Reconnaissance Course trained Devlin to enter an enemy-controlled area, observe the enemy forces, and exit—unseen and unheard. He learned the basic techniques of insertion and extraction by boat or helicopter. For months his technical instructors drilled him on surveillance, mapping, engineering, communications, and coding. He then went on to scuba training in San Diego. Later, he received parachute training at Fort Benning, Georgia.

But the peacetime Marine Corps of the early sixties could not offer Devlin the action he sought nor the rapid promotion he deserved. Instead, the Marine Corps exploited his dual capabilities—intelligence staff officer and qualified Recon officer—in the instruction of counterinsurgency forces of Latin America. He learned fluent Spanish as he taught the sons of colonels and presidents to fight the real and imagined enemies of their regimes.

After two years, he volunteered for reassignment to the Combat Operations Center of the Military Assistance Command, Vietnam. He received a promotion and took charge of an office evaluating and summarizing the after-action reports of Marine Recon units fighting in I Corps, the most northern of the military regions of South Vietnam.

Lieutenant Devlin took this responsibility at a time of escalation in the war. Both the American and North Vietnamese strategists had abandoned the tactics of a war fought by small units. American-led counterinsurgency teams no longer faced peasant guerrillas. The infiltration of the North Vietnamese Army had accelerated to thousands of soldiers a month and the Hanoi forces attacked South Vietnamese positions in battalion strength, overrunning villages and bases, driving the South Vietnamese government out of remote areas. The United States countered by deploying battalions of American Marines and Air Cavalry backed by the combined arms support of a modern army—jet bombers, helicopter gunships, artillery, armor.

But the North Vietnamese avoided conventional battles. Breaking their battalions into platoons, the Hanoi generals exploited the mountains and forests to hide their forces, regrouping their lightly equipped soldiers to stage an attack, then withdrawing and scattering before the American battalions massed their overwhelming firepower on the NVA forces.

This confronted the Marine forces in I Corps with a war of attrition. The Marine Corps, with the historic mission of launching amphibious assaults on hostile nations and establishing beachheads for the landing of American armies, did not have the training or equipment to fight a static, endless war against nonconventional forces. Assigned to defend the American bases at Da Nang and Chu Lai, the Marine battalions suffered hundreds of casualties in meaningless skirmishes as they patrolled the villages outside the base perimeters. Outside the areas of Marine control, the NVA established camps to train intelligence agents, sapper platoons, and shock forces for assaults on South Vietnamese Army and USMC units. Supply dumps hidden only a few kilometers from Da Nang or Chu Lai provided logistical support for battles staged at the convenience of the NVA generals.

During months of inconclusive battles in which the NVA struck, then dispersed, Marine commanders evolved a new concept in the employment of reconnaissance forces in combination with supporting arms. This concept altered the traditional mission of reconnaissance patrols. In World War II and Korea, Recon Marines preceded amphibious landings, observing enemy forces and defenses, then reporting their observations to division intelligence. Intelligence officers interpreted the observations and prepared reports for the division command, which then directed infantry or artillery or air strikes to destroy the positions. However, the evolving technique in I Corps short-cut the traditional intelligence and command structure to link Recon units operating independently and distantly from their bases directly with artillery and air support.

The Marines based the Recon find-and-destroy concept on airborne insertion. Abandoning their dependence on the slow, short-range cargo helicopters usually employed by the USMC, the Recon units acquired fast, maneuverable UH-1 helicopters. The U.S. Army Air Cavalry had already proved the combat value of these helicopters as troopships in the Central Highlands of II Corps. Marines employed the new helicopters to transport Recon units deep into NVA-controlled areas. The capacity of the aircraft—a Huey troopship carried six to eight armed troopers—usually limited their patrol strength to no more than twenty men. A twenty-man patrol, which required four Huey troopships for insertion, could not expect their arrival to be unnoticed by the NVA forces in the area. This led to the deployment of units as small as only four men.

Stealth and patience—and phenomenal courage—characterized these Recon missions. As resupply helicopters would betray the presence of the patrols, each Marine carried

147

rations and ammunition for the duration of the mission—
often as long as a week. With the additional weight of the
radios linking the patrol to the standby artillery and airsup-
port, the Marines could not carry enough ammunition to
fight. They depended on silence and invisibility to survive.

After helicopters inserted the Recon units, the Marines
searched for the enemy. Sometimes they only waited and
watched, observing NVA supply routes or bases from a
distance. Sometimes they trailed NVA troop movements—
following so close to the NVA that Vietnamese-speaking
Marines listened to the leader's instructions. Marines then
radioed target coordinates to waiting artillery or aircraft.
The Marines adjusted artillery fire for effect or called in new
coordinates as the NVA units fled.

The units scored remarkable kills on targets of opportunity. Often, fire directed by four-man Recon units killed
more NVA soldiers than days of the combined fire of a
battalion of Marines searching for NVA forces.

Lieutenant Devlin foresaw unusual future applications for
the Recon find-and-destroy concept. His classified work in
the MACV offices had introduced him to the development of
weapons technologies to be introduced later in the war—
radar/computer enhanced bomb delivery, video-guided
bombs and missiles, remote sensors, electronic scanning,
and satellite-bounced communications. All the new technologies would have direct application to conventional warfare
in Europe, where American armies and the questionable
European allies of the United States confronted the massed
armored divisions of the Soviet Army.

But he saw no opportunity for rapid advancement in the
MACV bureaucracy. He could only hope for routine promo-
tions and eventual transfer to a Marine Amphibious Unit on
standby station somewhere in the world.

Gambling on the emerging role of technology in war, he
created a new position in the MACV bureaucracy for himself: he became the Technology and Innovation Advisor to
the Marine Recon units operating in I Corps. Though another junior officer took over the duty of summarizing after-
action reports from the Marine units, Lieutenant Devlin
continued reviewing the reports. But now he had the author-

ity to fly north to I Corps and personally interview the Recon units. He also had the authority to present the Recon commanders with new weapons and communications electronics. Acting as an intermediary between the MACV command center and the Recon units, he bypassed the conservative leadership of the Marine Corps Headquarters to expedite the flow of advanced technology directly to the individual platoons.

As his first project, Lieutenant Devlin diverted several cases of the new and still experimental M-16 rifle to Recon platoons. Much lighter than the standard-issue M-14 rifle, the small-caliber plastic and aluminum M-16 rifles allowed soldiers to carry more ammunition. The lieutenant listened to the comments of the individual Marines and reported their opinions to his superiors. The manufacturer immediately initiated a program to improve the standard-issue rifle. A parallel program developed a special operations variant of the M-16.

Another project introduced a passive light-enhancement scope under development for the British armed forces. Devlin distributed the scopes to riflemen of night ambush and night surveillance details. In combat, the Marines discovered the values and limitations of the electronic nightsights. Years later, an American company developed an improved device called the starlite scope.

Supply flights carried the lieutenant between Da Nang and Saigon several times a week as he initiated and evaluated projects. He became familiar with department heads throughout the MACV bureaucracy and Recon leaders everywhere in I Corps as he searched for weapons development to enhance the effectiveness of individual patrols against the NVA.

The development of ground control radar in 1966 allowed the lieutenant to demonstrate the ultimate destructive power of a single Marine radioman. Up until the summer of 1966, B-52 bombers flying from Guam Island could not be redirected in flight. A bombing run on a target could be canceled, but the bombers could not be directed to an alternative target. After his briefing on the new ground control radar, the lieutenant rushed north to Chu Lai. A flight of B-52s had already left Guam and he had only a few hours to instruct a radio man in the frequencies and codes required to lock into the observer-to-ground-controller-to-bomber communications triangle.

In Chu Lai, he found a Recon unit already waiting for heli-transport to a drop-zone. He had no time to brief the radio man. Instead, he grabbed a weapon and pack. He went with the squad into the forests of the Annamite Mountains.

Through the electronic optics of a light-enhancement scope, the patrol spotted an NVA platoon scouting an abandoned plantation. Lieutenant Devlin knew he could not justify a B-52 air strike on only twenty NVA soldiers. He lied to the air controller, reporting that he saw a company of NVA resting in the groves of trees. The other Marines promised to collaborate the lie in their after-action report. However, as they waited, a truck convoy of NVA regulars appeared. The trucks parked in lines, using the rows of trees as camouflage.

Hundreds of North Vietnamese disappeared in the instantaneous devastation in fifty-eight thousand pounds of explosive and steel.

Lieutenant Devlin received promotion to captain. The Recon Marines of I Corps called him 'Mr. Marvel.'

But in 1968, the people of the United States elected Richard Nixon to end the Vietnam War. Corruption and political turmoil in the South Vietnamese government undercut the continuing struggle against the North Vietnamese. When Captain Devlin completed his third tour of duty in Vietnam, his superiors transferred him to Washington, D.C. There, as a deskbound hero in one of the thousands of Pentagon offices, he coordinated the disengagement of Marine forces from Vietnam. He tolerated years of paper-processing and Congressional hearings while he waited for transfer to Europe. He married and became a father. As expected, his next assignment sent him to an office in the NATO staff where he prepared for Marine landings in the coming war with the Soviet Union.

Detente ended, the Soviet subversion of Third World nationalist movements continued, the Soviet Union modernized and reinforced the Red Army in Eastern Europe, but a naive idealist in the White House allowed the American Armed Forces to deteriorate. Underpaid American soldiers armed with obsolete weapons faced the most awesome military machine in world history. Congress voted only minimal funding for the research and development of new weapons technology.

Though Devlin received a promotion to major, he remained deskbound—only a commander of clerks—his ambition for a central role in the future of the Marine Corps frustrated by political leaders in Washington who had surrendered America's role in world events to the Soviet Union. Major Devlin studied law in preparation for a new career as an executive with a defense contractor.

Then came the seizure of the American diplomats in revolutionary Iran and the Soviet invasion of Afghanistan. The inability of American forces to react to the terrorism of the Islamic fanatics or Soviet conventional forces moved Major Devlin to negotiate another transfer, this time to the Special Operations Division of the Joint Chiefs of Staff. He tried to organize a covert Force Recon unit. He received a promotion to lieutenant colonel but no command of a Marine unit.

When the Army's new Delta Force went into Iran, Lieutenant Colonel Devlin cursed as the ad hoc rescue attempt disintegrated in the wasteland of the Dasht-e Kavir Desert. But in the disaster, he saw a victory for the Armed Forces: the White House amateur who had allowed the military to deteriorate to impotency had now demonstrated his incompetence to the nation. The next election installed a president who promised increased support for the Armed Forces.

Hundreds of billions of dollars flowed into the military, raising pay, funding training, buying new equipment, and financing research. But the new strength of the Armed Forces did not protect the United States and its allies. The enemies of the modern world—the Soviets, the Islamics, the Soviet-backed fanatics in Africa and the Latin revolutionary nations, the fascist oligarchies of Central and South America—did not directly confront the strength of the American military.

Instead, the Soviets increased their funding of terror. Palestinian gangs waged campaigns of murder against international travelers. The Islamics of Iran formed alliances with the neo-Stalinist Arabs of Syria and Libya to strike European and American embassies. The fascist elites of Latin America dealt drugs with the communist dictators of Nicaragua and Cuba, the profits financing death squads that murdered Latins and North Americans without distinction.

These unlikely alliances of convenience—the Soviet Union and Saudi Arabia with Iraq and Lebanon, Nicaraguans with Palestinians, Colombian bankers with Cubans, Iranians with North Koreans and Libyans—had one common goal: the murder of Americans in carefully planned but unpredictable acts of terror. The enemies of the United States would not expose their regular armies to annihilation by the Armed Forces of the United States.

The gang leaders sent squads of semi-trained volunteers on one-way missions. Despairing young men, psychopaths, religious fanatics—their leaders sent them to certain death for the victory of a few American dead and media time.

Colonel Devlin believed that the Third World War had begun. This war would not be fought with armored divisions or airborne battalions or intercontinental ballistic missiles, but by thousands of teenagers with Kalashnikov rifles committing suicide on prime-time television. And it would be a war directed by the Soviet Union. Though the Soviets could never exercise complete control of the assault on the western democracies—to do so risked proof of that control and counterassault by the United States—its allies would shame and bleed the United States with every murder of Americans, demonstrating the weakness and vulnerability of mankind's most successful experiment in government to all the other nations of the world.

Without risk of a devastating war with the United States, the Soviets could force America to abandon the leadership of the world. Fear of terrorism would force Americans to withdraw from international commerce. And the failure of the American military to counter terrorism would show American democracy to the world as ridiculous and impotent, a showplace of decadent luxuries but incapable of protecting its citizens and allies. The red star of the Soviet Union would become a symbol of security and order, the Soviet totalitarian system a model for the 21st century.

Colonel Devlin wanted the Marine Corps to play a central role in the war against terrorism. In testimony for Senate and House committees, he stated that international terrorist groups—Palestinian, Islamic, Marxist, fascist—represented the shock forces of the Soviet Union and that no conventional American unit could counter the terrorists. Again and again, he told audiences of senators, representatives, academics, department executives, and military officers that the threat required an extraordinary response. This gained the recognition of others in the government with similar views, but in the office of Special Operations, the colonel became known as an extremist. His superiors isolated him from all but the most trivial staff responsibilities.

Despite his hopes for the future, frustrated by desk work and bureaucratic routine, Colonel Devlin considered retirement. Then came the temporary transfer to the staff National Security Council and the opportunity to take action.

9

VATSEK led the platoon of Lebanese recruits through physical training. After warm-ups, he progressed to strength exercises—flutter-kicks, sit-ups, slow isometric punches. Then he went to push-ups, dropping down prone in the sand on his fists. The recruits did the push-ups with their palms down. Vatsek called out to the English-speaking platoon leader, "On their fists!"

The platoon struggled to keep up with Vatsek's count, their wrists buckling, sand and stones digging into their knuckles. The two-hundred-forty-pound sergeant beat out push-ups like a machine, every line of his muscles defined through the o.d. green T-shirt he wore. The platoon tired and struggled, some of the teenagers flopping down into the sand.

On the last push-up, Vatsek punched hard against the earth and jumped to his feet in karate sparring stance. He punched and kicked in a fluid two-count technique, returning to sparring stance after the kick. At twenty-five, he switched to the left side and started again. The recruits groaned. Some stopped. Vatsek moved along the front line of recruits, targeting a punch and kick at anyone not following the count. A punch to the chest sent one teenager flying back. A kick dropped another recruit. Vatsek shouted out, "Kick or get kicked!" He drove a kick into the stomach of a recruit gasping for breath.

Niles and Lieutenant Shaffik Hijazi watched from the side of the sandbag-walled training field. The head-high walls protected the recruits and their Marine trainers from snipers or car bombs driven into the compound.

"What an animal," Hijazi commented. He grinned to Niles. "After this, they will want to fight the militias. Anything to escape the sergeant."

"King Kong cuts no slack," Niles laughed.

"Line up!" Vatsek told the platoon. "Karate test. One line. Every man attacks. Line up and attack!"

Vatsek stood in the center of the sandpit in Shotokan karate sparring stance, his right foot a natural distance behind his left, his arms held low to cover his ribs. The Lebanese recruits crowded into a line and watched as the first soldier rushed their American instructor. His arm going back to swing, the soldier screamed out a battle cry. Vatsek waited as the distance closed, then snapped an easy front kick into the recruit's stomach. Breath exploded from the young man's body and he fell backward, doubled up and gasping. He crawled away.

The second soldier hesitated. The man behind him shoved him out. This soldier tried to employ karate techniques, front-kicking twice in the empty air as he advanced. As the soldier drove a third kick at Vatsek's torso, Vatsek stepped aside and shoved his shoulder, throwing the soldier sideways into the sand.

A third soldier shuffled forward in a cautious sparring stance, keeping his arms in front of his body, his eyes locked on Vatsek. The line of soldiers cheered the young man. Niles recognized him. "Hey, Sergeant. Watch out! He's a black belt."

"Oh, yeah?"

Lunging, the soldier jabbed at Vatsek's face. Vatsek slapped the punch aside, then blocked a punch at his gut. The soldier took a half step back and threw a roundhouse kick at Vatsek's head. A quick slap stopped the kick. Vatsek took a step back. "Yeah, he's okay. He can punch and kick—"

As the soldier lunged forward again, Vatsek spun and shot a back kick into the young man's solar plexus, throwing him backward through the air. He crashed into the line of recruits.

"But he can't fight. This is too fucking much. Weeks I've been standing out here drilling them and they think—"

Behind the sergeant, the recruits whispered, urging on the next soldier in line. As the sergeant talked, the soldier attacked his back.

"—that this is a French lesson, all yes, sir and no, sir. Polite and all that shit." Turning and taking a step, Vatsek threw a classic reverse punch. He looked like an illustration in a textbook, the geometry of his stance perfect, his back straight, his massive shoulders locking as his fist smashed into the center of the soldier's stomach. The soldier fell backward and groaned. The platoon of soldiers laughed—except for the next in line. Vatsek held the formal stance for an instant, then turned back to Niles.

"Captain, what can I do with these jerks? Weeks of training and they don't have the first idea of what's going on."

"They're teenagers. They haven't had ten years of karate."

"They're not going to live ten more years if they don't learn something."

Niles turned to Hijazi. "Show them something, Lieutenant. You're not a black belt but you can knock him around."

"God willing . . ." Like Vatsek, Hijazi followed a weight-training discipline. He stood less than six feet tall but weighed two hundred pounds. He had received hand-to-hand combat training at Fort Benning. And Vatsek had personally tutored the lieutenant in combat karate. "Sergeant! I challenge you!"

The recruits cheered their officer. The stocky Hijazi went to the center of the area and faced Vatsek. Standing straight, heels together, his hands at his sides, Vatsek formally bowed to the lieutenant before taking a sparring stance. Hijazi circled Vatsek, forcing Vatsek to turn to follow him.

Rushing, Hijazi threw a powerful kick at Vatsek's groin. Instead of down-blocking the kick, Vatsek pivoted to the side and scooped upward with his forearm as he simultaneously deflected a punch. One hand gripping the lieutenant's shirtfront, the other his belt buckle, Vatsek heaved him into the air and held him. Hijazi thrashed.

A camera flashed. Niles whipped around to see a thin

blond woman photographing Vatsek and Hijazi. He shouted out, "No photos of the trainers!"

She ignored Niles and continued flashing photos as Vatsek spun the Lebanese lieutenant around. Hijazi screamed. Niles rushed at the woman and grabbed her camera out of her hands. The strap around her neck jerked taut and she slapped at his face with one hand, clawing at his hands with the other. She cursed him in French. He understood every word but he didn't bother to respond. He only repeated:

"No photos of the American trainers."

Seconds later, Lieutenant Hijazi and Vatsek joined him. Speaking calmly in French, the lieutenant slipped the strap from the woman, allowing Niles to take the camera. The woman screamed as Niles popped open the back and pulled out a long loop of film. Without closing the camera, Niles handed it back to her.

"Sorry, but you knew the rules. You can look, you can interview, but you can't take the names or photos of Americans. You knew that."

The woman switched to English. "I thought he was French. The legionnaires allow us to photograph."

"Uh-huh," Niles nodded, grinning, watching her take the ruined film from the camera. He remembered her from the day of the bombing, weeks before. A very pretty woman, she wore no makeup on her slight features and white skin— only a touch of lipstick, like an afterthought. She wore her white blond hair pulled back and bound with a rubber band, accenting her thin neck. A loose, dark blue sweater contrasted with her white skin. Small-breasted, lithe, she had the body of a teenager. But the tight denim over her hips and thighs revealed a woman's figure. She wore no jewelry—no earrings or bracelets, no wedding ring.

Closing her camera, she looked up to him smiling. "You said interviews. Will you talk with a reporter?"

"Who you with, miss?"

"I am independent. But I sell to *Le Monde* and *Match*. Sometimes the American newspapers and magazines."

"You must be a brave young woman to work Lebanon."

"And you, too, American. Many Marines died here."

"Marines are cheap. Ask the State Department."

"I want to ask you—"

"Don't quote what I just said."

"But you'll talk with me?"

"Sure." Niles smiled at her. "Cost you a few beers."

"In West Beirut? That may be difficult. There is a prohibition against alcohol."

"Not everywhere. But let's make it easy. We'll talk here in the compound. Cost you nothing."

Niles led her along a walkway walled with sandbags. Since the bombings, the Lebanese compound had become a sandbag fortress. Shovel and bag details worked every day to shield sentries and personnel. Soldiers walked from the sentry posts to the offices to the training field without exposure to the snipers firing from the nearby districts. Niles and the young woman passed a group of soldiers placing wooden beams over the walls—soon the walkway would be a tunnel through sandbags, secure from snipers, mortars, shrapnel. Only a direct hit from an artillery shell or heavy rocket would threaten the soldiers.

"You are an officer?" she asked him.

"That I am. Disappointing?"

"No, but I did not think an officer would speak with a journalist."

"Well, this officer wants to talk."

"You are critical of your country's Lebanese policy?"

"You can't quote what I say. But it's not like this Marine doesn't know what's going on."

They came to the vehicle yard. Above the parked trucks and cars, banks of black clouds loomed on the eastern horizon. A cold wind brought the stink of garbage and tenements from the ghettos. "Ask your questions here. Don't want the Lebanese officers wondering what I'm talking about."

"What will be the American response to the bombing?"

"You read the newspapers. It's history."

"There will be no response?"

"Against who?"

"Your president said the Syrians and Iranians were responsible."

"Maybe he knows something I don't. Miss, I can't really—"

"Angelique Chardon."

"Pleased to meet you, Miss Chardon. Call me Lester. I can't help you with those questions. I thought you wanted to talk to me about my work here with the Lebanese."

"Have you overcome the hatred of the Moslems for the Christians?"

"I don't know if the word is hatred. All the soldiers are volunteers. They volunteered to serve in the armed forces. If they hated Christians, they'd be in the militias. We stress loyalty to the government, not the faith."

"But the government is controlled by the Maronites."

"Now we're talking politics. I can't comment on politics. But I am aware of the problems."

"Without changing the regime, the civil war will continue—"

"There it is."

"Do you believe your government will—"

"I can't talk politics. Not here."

Across the vehicle lot, a jeep stopped at the sentry post. Niles saw Marines inside—and he recognized Colonel Devlin.

Chardon did not take his refusal as final. "You are the only officer I've met who will talk. And I want to hear your thoughts on Lebanon and the civil war. If we meet somewhere else, can we talk?"

"Where?"

"On the other side of the city."

"Okay. But not now. I've got to get back to my duties." He saw one sentry check the identification of the driver. Another sentry walked around the jeep with an underview mirror—a rectangular mirror on rollers. A long handle allowed the sentry to wheel the mirror around the jeep and examine the frame and undercarriage. Only after the check for hidden explosives did the sentries wave through the jeep.

She gave him a card. "There is the phone number of my hotel. And the number of a message service. If one does not work, try the other one."

Free-lance reporters moved from faction to faction. Did

she want to develop Niles as a source of information? "Thanks. See you later. Maybe I'll call if I want to talk at you. Sorry about spoiling your film, but you broke the rules."

"I hope we talk again," Chardon told him as she walked away through the trucks.

Niles watched the jeep stop. A Marine left the jeep with the colonel. Niles did not recognize the tall, wide-shouldered black man. Two gold bars identified the Marine as a lieutenant. He wore a pistol belt and carried a poster-sized folder but no rifle. Glancing toward the sentry post, Niles did not see Chardon among the parked cars and trucks.

"Captain," Devlin called out. "Allow me to introduce you to Second Lieutenant Richard Stark."

"Pleased to meet you, sir."

"Lieutenant Stark is the son of a friend. When his father told me that the lieutenant had completed his Recon training only a few weeks ago, I offered him the opportunity to volunteer for your new unit."

"New unit, Colonel?"

"You are no longer a trainer." Devlin looked behind Niles and saw no one within hearing. "You now head a special operations squad directed by National Security Advisor Reisinger."

"And what's the special operation?"

"The capture for interrogation of the commander of the Revolutionary Guards in Baalbek."

Across the vehicle yard, Chardon braced her camera on the door of a truck and focused the zoom lens on Colonel Anthony Devlin of the Pentagon's Special Operations Division.

Why had he come from the United States to speak with the officer called Lester? How much would Rajai pay for this information?

In the Lebanese barracks, the three Marines talked in Niles's room, a whitewashed concrete cubicle filled by a steel cot, a shipping crate for a closet, and RPG crates for bookshelves. Anthropology texts, stacks of paperback books, a reading lamp, and a clock radio filled the improvised shelves. The radio blared Arabic music to cover their voices. A folding card table served for the briefing.

"Here are the transcriptions of Farsi-language communications." Lieutenant Stark laid down a thick notebook. "Names, code names, times, locations—all indexed. Here is a series of satellite photos of the town." Stark spread out several sixteen-by-twenty-inch black-and-white prints on the small table. The large format prints showed the streets and rooftops of buildings of Baalbek. In the fields around the town, the resolution showed foot trails over the broken earth. Tire ruts and trash circled a checkpoint on a road outside of the town. Stark pointed to the grid codes along the edges of the prints. "If you give the laboratory the numbers, you can get sections enlarged and enhanced."

"How much time?"

"Same day, but that does not include transport time. You can expect no better than second day. Here are the montages prepared by Colonel Devlin's staff in Washington."

"My ex-staff," the colonel corrected. "For secrecy, Reisinger dissolved the contingency group. I will have access to the same people in their usual offices, but I will be responsible for coordinating and assembling the work. There will be no one group of specialists and translators and technicians to assemble your premission intelligence."

"What about the agency?" Niles asked.

"There is nothing they can do. They lost most of their sources when the Israelis expelled the PLO last year. They lost their entire Middle East staff in the April bombing. Their Washington officers promised whatever is possible, but—"

"I don't want it. I don't want those spooks involved."

"A certain amount of involvement will be unavoidable."

"Whatever, Colonel. But I'm prejudiced. You remember how it used to be in Vietnam. A spook white shirt comes in with a list of names or a black box or a series of map coordinates—didn't mean shit to them how many Marines died. I don't want to be involved in an agency operation."

"This will not be an agency operation."

"Your word's good enough for me. Lieutenant, what are those pictures?"

Stark laid down the assembled strips of prints photographed from videotapes. Niles studied the panoramas. He referred to the coordinates, then located the views on the satellite photo. "Can I mark on this big print?"

"Here, sir." Stark passed him a grease pencil. "That can be removed with a cloth."

"The lieutenant's organized." Niles printed the number of one panorama on the satellite photo, then indicated the arc of view. "This is great. Almost as good as reconning it. Did you prepare these, Lieutenant?"

"No, sir. Not this material. But I took classes in computer enhanced photography."

"He knows the work," Devlin told Niles. "In the future, he can assemble any required photo intelligence."

"What languages do you speak, Stark?"

"French, sir. Some Spanish."

"No Arabic? No Farsi?"

"No, sir."

"You start studying Arabic today." Niles turned to the colonel. "We need a Farsi-speaking Marine."

"The agency has Iranian nationals on contract. Expatriates. Do you want to interview—"

Niles shook his head no. "Who knows who an agency man will actually be working for? I want a Marine. Born in Iran. Farsi his first language. Speaks English. Hates the Ayatollah. Thousands of Iranians escaped to the United States, there have to be some who joined the Corps."

"That will be difficult," the colonel answered.

"That's why I'm giving the job to the lieutenant. All these photos and intercepted communications are great, but we need to get into the Bekaa. I don't know how it can be done without an Iranian. We can't just walk in like—did you brief Stark?"

Devlin nodded yes.

"And you still volunteered to work with me?" Niles asked the young lieutenant.

"Yes, sir. This will be an extraordinary unit. I am very fortunate Colonel Devlin—"

"Fortunate!" Niles laughed. "Maybe. We'll be a squad going into Baalbek. I think we can do it. I'm betting my life.

But rationally, the idea of a squad getting in, grabbing the chief of the Pasdaran, and getting out is not very likely. You might want to reconsider—"

"Sir! I reviewed the agency information on Baalbek. I know what we face. I also reviewed your file and the files of Sergeants Alvarez and Vatsek. I cannot match your experience but I can offer my skills. Despite my inexperience in the field, I believe I can be instrumental in developing a unit which can undertake very unusual assignments and survive."

Niles nodded to the colonel. "You brought me a good man. He knows what we're doing. Problem is, I don't. Lieutenant, go back to Washington and assemble all the background material we need. Find a Farsi-speaking Marine. These photos are great but we'll need names, photos, thousands of little details."

The lieutenant took notes. "The agency is already assembling agent reports—"

"Can't get away from the spooks, can we? Put the technical work on the agency. I want you to get me that Farsi-speaking Marine. And one other piece of research—a woman reporter talked to me today. Her name's Angelique Chardon. She's French. She's a free-lancer working Beirut. I want copies of the articles she's written. Can you do that?"

"Yes, sir. Does she write in English?"

"Probably French."

"Then you'll need translations."

"I can read some French. I can understand it. I want to know why she wants to talk to me."

"She interviewed you?" Devlin asked. "Why is that suspect?"

"Hundreds of reporters working here in Lebanon. And a pretty young one wants to talk to me? Invites me to get together with her off the compound and listen to my views on Lebanon? Me? Something ain't right."

Snow paled the fields of the Bekaa Valley. The storm darkened the midday sky, bringing snow and freezing rain, concealing the eastern foothills in banks of churning gray

163

and black clouds. Angelique Chardon drove slowly on the slick highway, the borrowed Fiat lurching and shuddering on the broken asphalt. Truck drivers ignored the weather and road, hurtling past her, water splashing over her small car like waves.

She passed battered billboards. Once the signs had advertised hotels and restaurants serving the tourists visiting the pagan and Roman ruins outside of Baalbek. Even during the worst years of the civil war, tourists had braved the militias to enjoy the resorts. Now, no tourists came to the Bekaa. Scrawls of Arabic graffiti across the advertisements declared loyalty to the Ayatollah Khomeini and the Islamic Revolution. Weathered posters of the scowling Khomeini looked down on the highway. On one sign, splashes of paint covered figures around a pool—the decadent illustration of tourists sunbathing on the deck of a hotel pool had offended the morals of a militiaman.

For this drive to Baalbek, Chardon had not worn European clothes. She did not want to risk humiliation by the fanatics manning checkpoints. Though she could not hide her foreign skin and features, she had dressed in clothing appropriate to a Shiite woman. She wore gray trousers, a gray formless dress, a black overcoat, and a black head scarf. Only her supple—and water resistant—knee-high boots came from France.

Clusters of whitewashed houses appeared alongside the road. Rutted dirt lanes led off to villages and farms. She recognized the scattered concrete and rusting sheet metal that had been an industrial development—the Syrians had tried to hide radar vans and antiaircraft guns among the trucks and equipment. A month before, an Israeli air strike had devastated the complex as part of an attack on the Iranian Revolutionary Guards and Party of God militiamen quartered in Baalbek. Her coverage of the destruction had included photos of dead workers entangled in a wrecked factory. The Paris and London newspapers had paid extra for a follow-up article on the grief of the workers' families. There had been no mention of the Syrian radar and guns. The Syrians thanked her for the propaganda with an unrestricted press pass.

At the division in the highway, the trucks veered west. She took the east road to Baalbek. Lines of cars and trucks waited at a Syrian checkpoint. Trucks went to the right lane, cars to the left. Every driver and passenger left the vehicles as Syrian soldiers searched. The squads worked methodically, soldiers patting down the men while other soldiers looked under the hoods and in the trunks of the cars. One soldier peered under the cars and trucks with a long-handled, wheeled mirror. Resigned to long waits, truck drivers sat on their bumpers as soldiers searched through their cargos.

After a fifteen-minute wait, a soldier motioned her out. He stared at her white face a moment before demanding her identification and Syrian Army pass. He called out to his officer. The soldiers searching the car joked to one another about becoming Shiites if they could meet women like this one. They found nothing but her camera and notebook.

The officer asked, "Why do you go to the Baalbek?"

"To interview victims of the Israeli war."

"Yes, many victims of the—"

Shouts interrupted his comment. Soldiers stepped into the road to block an old truck veering around the line of cars. They raised their rifles. The officer shoved her identification into her hands and rushed in front of the truck.

Though the truck had the markings of a construction company, a Syrian soldier drove. He shouted out to the soldiers. The other soldier in the cab remained quiet, looking down without interest at the Syrian officer demanding that the truck stop. Then the foreigner's eyes locked on Chardon, and the wide-faced, blue-eyed Russian in the uniform of the Soviet Army smiled at the lovely Frenchwoman. Brakes screeching, metal rattling, the truck slowed to a stop on the opposite side of the highway.

And in the back of the truck, peering over the plank sides, the Revolutionary Guards stared at her as she stared at them.

The Syrian driver, the Soviet officer, the ragged Iranians: am image worth hundreds of dollars to an international news service, if she could photograph the truck and its occupants at an angle showing the Syrian, the Soviet advisor, and the

Iranian Revolutionary Guards crowding the back of the troop truck.

Her pulse raced as she returned her identification to her purse and calmly got in her car. She rolled down her window. The checkpoint soldiers had their backs to her. By luck, she had a 1:18 50mm lens on her camera and not a zoom. She leaned over her camera, popped off the lens cap, and guessed at an f-stop of 11—which allowed a depth-of-field from three meters almost to infinity. She switched on the motor drive and clicked off one frame to test the batteries.

Starting the Fiat, she put it in gear and eased forward as she picked up the camera and braced it on the door with only the lens' element showing. The sleeve of her black coat covered the camera body and shielded the lens from the rain. She glanced down to check the lens, then steered wide around the truck.

Soldiers motioned her past. Pointing the camera without looking, she swerved in a semicircle—as if avoiding the soldiers standing in the highway—around the construction truck as she shot the roll of film. She did not risk pointing the camera back as she drove away.

The road curved through a shantytown of abandoned workshops, warehouses, and shacks. She stopped the car and unloaded the camera as boys in ragged clothing peered through the windows. Feeling under the dashboard, she found a space between a cardboard duct and the shell of the glove compartment. She jammed the film canister there. Hands tapped at the windows. The boys wanted money.

She accelerated away. The boys ran after the car, throwing rocks. A rock banged off the trunk and she left the shantytown behind as she drove past shops and walled family compounds enclosing trees and homes. Hundreds of posters of Khomeini declared the area to be the territory of the Islamic Amal.

The freezing rain had stopped work in the fields and the streets. Men squatted under sheets of plastic, waiting for the rain to pass. Outside of cafés, tools and wheelbarrows cluttered the sidewalks. Women in soaked black chadors stood in doorways, waiting hand-in-hand with small boys dressed in brilliantly colored polyester jackets. She saw only two militiamen with rifles. They took shelter from the rain under the sheet metal roof of a service station.

Then she passed a line of Syrian vehicles. A Soviet ZSU— a tank with the cannon replaced by four radar-directed 23mm machine guns—parked with three heavy transport trucks. Each truck towed twin-barreled antiaircraft machine guns. Syrians manned the tank and trucks.

Unlike the soldiers of the checkpoint, who had worn the helmets of the regular army, the Syrians in the trucks wore the red berets of the Special Forces, a division of elite soldiers usually stationed in Damascus to defend the regime of Hafez al-Assad from internal enemies and commando assaults.

In October, apparently in anticipation of counterstrikes by the United States, France, and Israel in response to the attacks of 23 October in Beirut and 4 November in Tyre, the Syrian Army positioned its antiaircraft weapons and crews around the town, in the fields where buildings would not interfere with the radar tracking and the line of fire of the machine guns.

But when Israeli jets attacked Baalbek on 4 November, after the truck bombing of their military headquarters in Tyre, the gun crews did not down a single jet.

Now the Syrians placed the weapons in the town itself. And assigned highly trained gunners of President Hassad's elite Special Forces to man the positions. What did the Syrians anticipate? Another counterstrike by the Israelis? Is this why Rajai had instructed her to ask the Marines about counterstrikes against Syria and Iran?

Chardon cruised slowly along the highway, looking into the narrow roads cutting through the blocks of walled houses. But she saw no other Syrian troops or vehicles until the old construction truck appeared behind her. Sounding the horn, the Syrian driver raced to her rear bumper and flashed his lights. She swerved to the side of the road, letting the truck pass.

A hundred meters ahead, Revolutionary Guards in rain

slickers stood at the steel barrels and sandbags of another checkpoint. Chardon followed the truck and stopped. The Iranians in the back of the truck turned to stare at her.

The Revolutionary Guard drew recruits from the villages and the slums of the cities, where the miracle of the Shah's oil-financed rush into the twentieth century—secular education, the education of girls, civil government instead of the dictates of the village mullahs—had not only failed but generated a reaction of holy rage that overwhelmed the secret police, the army, and all the other revolutionary factions.

Chardon feared the Revolutionary Guards. She had known educated Iranians in Paris. The young men in the truck had no education other than the madness of the Ayatollah. She saw them staring at her hands and face. In the remote villages, men considered the sight of a woman's face provocative. Switching off the Fiat's windshield wipers, she hid behind the rain spattering on the windshield. Finally the truck clanked away.

Easing the car forward to the militiamen, Chardon rolled down the window and showed her passes—one issued by the Syrian Army, the other by the director of the Ayatollah Khomeini Hospital in the center of Baalbek. Militiamen leered through the windows but their leader motioned her to continue.

She did not drive to the hospital—the hospital director had issued the pass only to allow her meetings with Rajai. Speeding a few blocks, she turned onto a street overarched by olive and carob trees. Sodden bougainvillea spread across walls topped by ironwork spikes. Before the civil war, this had been a street of wealthy landlords and merchants. Now, Syrian army staff officers enjoyed the homes. Fahkr Rajai used one villa for his offices and quarters.

Revolutionary Guards recognized Chardon and pushed open the wrought-iron gates. She drove through to the courtyard. The early storm had stripped the trees, carpeting the courtyard stones with yellow leaves. Guards called out as she hurried through the cold rain to the house.

Hasani stopped her at the door. He worked in the office as a clerk. A short, anemic man, he wore a holstered Russian pistol at all times. Like Rajai, he had learned French as an exile. "Why are you here?"

"I must see Rajai."

"Why did you not call?"

"The telephone is out. I have something important. I must show it to—"

"He is not here. He will call when—"

"What? When will he return? I'll wait if I must, but I must show him—"

"He will not return for days."

"But—" Chardon saw Akbar, the scar-faced war veteran who served as the personal bodyguard of Rajai. He stood a few steps away, watching as they argued in French. Akbar accompanied his commander everywhere in Lebanon. "Did he leave money for me?"

"Money? For you?" Hasani turned to Akbar and spoke in Farsi. Chardon understood that the clerk speculated on her relationship with their commander. Hating herself, pretending she had not understood the Farsi obscenities, she explained:

"He told me to wait in Beirut for another action against the Marines. There was no action. He told me to interview Marines. To take photos of them. To gather information. And now I have important information."

"What information? I will tell him when he returns."

"I must show you."

Hasani joked again with Akbar. Chardon ignored the obscenity. Following him into the office, she turned and slammed the door in Akbar's face. Hasani returned to his desk. A glaring fluorescent light made his pale, sickly face glisten. He leaned back in his chair and watched her, waiting for her to explain.

Crouching down, she reached under her long dress and unzipped her boot. She took out the photos. Flexing the prints to straighten the curl, she laid the prints on the papers covering the desk and pointed to the closeup of Devlin:

"This American—who looks like a movie star—he is a general or a colonel in the Pentagon. He has been in magazines and newspapers. On television. He is a hard-liner. An expert on covert war. His department is called Special

Operations. I will send one of these photos to *Le Monde*. They will search their files and confirm that."

"Special Operations is the CIA?"

"They work with the CIA. This Marine." She pointed to Niles. "The Special Operations officer came to talk to him. He is an officer. He trains the Lebanese. He has many friends in the Lebanese Armed Forces. This is what I want to show Rajai."

"He is CIA?" Hasani pointed to Niles.

"How can I know? I only know that he is a Marine."

"And this other one?"

"The Negro? An aide. He carries papers for the officer. Perhaps they are all CIA. I don't know. But I will know about that one—" She pointed to Niles. "He will talk with me. With time, I may learn why he talked with that officer. But I need money. I have money in my bank in Paris but there is a problem and it is difficult to draw on my account here. If I do not get money, I must return to Paris."

"He left no money here."

"When will he return?"

"It is uncertain."

"Then send the money to me in Beirut. I am at the same hotel. I can stay only a few more days. If you want this information, I must get money."

She gathered the photos of the Marines but Hasani grabbed them from her hands. "I will keep the pictures for him."

"No! Pay first—" Chardon fought for the photos.

Hasani shoved her back and called out to Akbar, telling him to take the woman out of his office. "Now go."

Rushing past the scarred bodyguard, Chardon ran out to her borrowed Fiat. She sped from the iron gates of the villa cursing the Iranians. Desperate, she mentally totaled her travelers checks and the few Lebanese pounds in her Beirut account—only enough for another week. If she did not have a return ticket to Paris, she would be trapped in Lebanon.

If she returned to Paris, she could write a few color articles about the war in Lebanon. Or interview Middle Eastern expatriates. Or interview the friends and families of the bombed legionnaires. But she had no assignments. And a thousand other journalists could write color articles and interviews. Without pay for articles or an advance, she had no money for a ticket back to Lebanon.

Her editors wanted her on-the-scene articles from Lebanon. But she did not have the money to stay.

Driving through the narrow streets, she tried to think of a solution. Perhaps she could sell the photos of the Revolutionary Guards with the Soviet—with a story identifying the Soviet as an advisor. With that money she could stay in Baalbek until the attack the Syrians expected. Her writing and photos would be the first from the scene—if the attack came.

Then, over the shopfronts of a narrow avenue, she saw the Syrians working in the fire-gutted shell of an abandoned hotel. A group of Revolutionary Guards had occupied the hotel the year before and used it as a barracks. Israeli jets had rocketed the hotel during the 4 November raid. The explosions had blown holes through the walls but had not collapsed the floors or roof.

Syrians used pulleys and ropes to lift equipment to the third floor. Buildings blocked her view. Chardon continued another two blocks on the street before she saw the Syrians again. Now she identified the equipment hanging by the ropes:

A twin-barreled antiaircraft gun.

Swerving to the curb, she parked and watched the Syrians raising the weapon. This confirmed her guess—the Syrians expected an attack. But why place the antiaircraft weapon in the hotel rather than on the roof? The hotel overlooked the old center of Baalbek. Hidden inside the hotel, the guns could not be photographed by air reconnaissance planes or satellites. But the gunners could not track an incoming jet.

Helicopters. The Syrians prepared for an attack by airborne commandos—the Israelis? the Americans? The heavy 14.5mm antiaircraft guns could rake any helicopter assault descending on Baalbek. Chardon reached for her camera.

A voice called out in Arabic. Startled, she looked to the sidewalk to see a Syrian soldier motioning her away. He told her not to park there. A Revolutionary Guardsman walked with the soldier. Chardon laid her notebook over the camera.

Accelerating away, she searched for another view of the hotel. She saw a side street and slowed. Syrian soldiers blocked the street. Seeing Chardon's foreign face, an officer stepped out to stop her but she continued past to the next street. Soldiers stood there also. At the next corner, she turned in the opposite direction, winding through a narrow lane of vendor stalls, empty in the cold rain. She maneuvered past the poles supporting the plastic sheets tenting the stalls, then eased around the next corner. She went back three streets, then turned again.

Two Syrian soldiers stood in the doorway of a shop. They watched the Fiat speed past. She saw the hotel ahead. The antiaircraft gun hung from ropes, the barrels silhouetted against the clouds. She slowed and scanned the shopfronts. Merchants stood in doorways talking. A young man with one leg stood on his crutches and rearranged goods on display.

Looking down at the camera for an instant, she confirmed the f-11 setting, then pushed the focus ring to infinity. She switched on the motor drive, then thumbed the motor drive setting from single to continuous.

As she made a slow right-hand turn, she waited for the correct moment, then pushed down the motor button with her thumb, the motor power-winding the roll past the shutter in two seconds. Fear made her breathing difficult as she continued past the Syrian officer for the second time.

Leaving the town, she followed a potholed road to the groves and small farms in the hills. No one worked in the rain. She stopped on a dirt lane and scanned the area around her. Despite the sound of the rain on the Fiat, she heard her heart hammering in her ears.

If they stopped and searched her, the first roll of film identified her as an unwanted journalist. She risked only interrogation and deportation. The second roll, the photos of the antiaircraft gun hidden in the abandoned hotel, marked her as a foreign agent—Israeli, American, French, whatever nation the Syrian interrogators demanded she confess.

RECON

The second roll of film meant prison—perhaps disappearance into the torture cells of Damascus.

She hid both rolls of film in her underwear. Though the photos of the weapon placement risked expulsion from Lebanon, the photos also offered the freedom of United States dollars.

Returning to Beirut, she went directly to the Lebanese Armed Forces Compound.

10

FOR an hour after leaving his hotel, Rajai zigzagged through the center of Paris, riding the Metro from station to station and dodging through the after-work crowds before reboarding the Metro for another station. He left the Metro for a final time at the Champs-Elysées and boarded a commuter train leaving the metropolitan center of the city. Finally, three minutes before the meeting time, he left a train depot and walked out to the street. The van appeared exactly on the minute. As he stepped inside, the door locked shut behind him, then the van sped away, swerving through turns to disorient him and to lose any surveillance.

A masked Colombian gunman watched Rajai. Only the gunman's eyes showed through holes cut in a pillowcase, his eyes and dark skin contrasting against the bleached-white, starched cloth. His hands held an Israeli Uzi submachine gun.

A twelve-volt bulb cast a weak yellow light on the stained and battered interior of the van. The van smelled of chemicals. The gunman sat on the floor, leaning back against the door to the cab. Rajai stood at the other side of the van, holding onto a strapping loop.

Several times, he felt the van slow and stop, then continue. He rode for thirty minutes before he heard the driver jerk the parking brake. The back door opened.

Flashlight glare blinded him. Hands helped him down, then guided him a few steps. Rajai glimpsed an alley. A form stood in front of him and passed a metal detector over his suit, a sensor squealing at his cufflinks and coins. Someone took his briefcase and searched through the papers and bundles of American hundred-dollar bills. Another electronic device appeared. No sensor sounded. The searchers returned his briefcase.

Hands pushed him into a smaller van. The second van smelled of flour and sweets. Immediately, the delivery van accelerated away. Rajai waited as the driver sped through another twenty minutes of evasion.

Finally the second van parked. Metal wheels screeched, chains clanked. After the machinery went silent, the van's side door slid open. Rajai saw that the van had parked in an apartment's underground garage.

Two men in slacks and leather jackets watched him step out of the van. They wore sacks over their heads—the sacks made of red and black cloth, the melodramatic colors of Revolution. Only their eyes peered out through round holes. A third revolutionary stood to one side holding an Uzi, her size and curves identifying her as a woman. Like the men, she wore slacks, a leather jacket, and the red and black headsack. The revolutionaries wasted no words. The shorter man demanded to know: "What is the action?"

"Your group will have a role in an action. Another force will make the attack."

"What is the action?" the short man repeated.

"I don't know."

"You're only a messenger?"

"My commander cannot risk traveling. I have my role. And my role does not permit me to know every detail of the action."

"We are not mercenaries. We are not for hire. We fight only for Colombian liberation."

"Any strike against the Yankees"—Rajai used the idiom of the Sandinistas—"is a blow for all the struggling peoples of the world."

The taller man asked, "But you will not trust us to know why we risk our lives?"

"The details will be revealed as the planning continues. I assure you that your role will be vital. You will take your place in the vanguard of the international. This action will rewrite the future and go down in history as a—"

"History books don't stop tanks," the woman spat out. "In Cacalombia, the army has American tanks, they have American helicopters, and we have only old rifles. What will we get for fighting for you Arabs?"

"Your group will not be fighting. However, you will share fully in the glory and the rewards. Please allow me to brief you on your responsibilities, if you accept, and the rewards of—"

"We want antitank rockets," the woman stated. "And antiaircraft missiles. Don't even talk about your holy shit action if you won't pay in rockets and missiles."

"Your comrades searched this valise." Rajai held up his American briefcase. "Perhaps they informed you that I brought, as promised, the first payment for your group's assistance."

"We have all the hundreds we can carry," the short one answered. "Rockets and Sam-seven missiles. That will be the price. Nothing else."

"Weapons instead of money? Is that the only disagreement? If so, it is solved. You will receive what you desire."

The revolutionaries looked to one another. The woman nodded to the short leader. He turned back to Rajai. "Tell us what you know about the hit."

In the color-coordinated decor of a room in the Holiday Inn in downtown Washington, District of Columbia, Lieutenant Stark dropped a photocopy of a Marine's career file. He rushed to the television and fine-tuned the picture as a commentator announced the names and numbers of a French soccer team playing in Buenos Aires. Tape replays showed the players in action.

The telephone rang. Stark watched a slow-motion scene of the French forward players closing on the goal, passing the ball around the defenders. A Frenchman drove the ball past the Brazilian goalie. Only then did Stark answer the ringing telephone. "Room Three Zero Nine."

Through electronic hissing, he heard an operator speaking very awkward English, asking his name. "Yes, I'm Richard Stark."

The line switched. "How's it going, Stark? This is Niles."

"Yes, sir. Good evening, sir."

"It's morning here. Let's keep this informal. I'm calling from a public phone."

Stark guessed that Captain Niles meant an insecure telephone line. "Informal. Yes, sir, I understand."

"I'm calling to thank you for those articles. Very interesting reading."

"No problem with the French?"

"Nah, I struggled through it. I'm sending Devlin some very interesting photos. Maybe it isn't my job, but I promised that photographer some money. You think you could get Devlin to wire some more money to me? I tried to call him tonight but he's at a conference somewhere. The pictures tell the story."

"Photos coming . . . request for funding . . ." Stark outlined the message on a pad by the telephone. "How much more, sir?"

"Ten thousand this week."

"Ten thousand dollars? Did I hear you correctly?"

"Affirmative. Ten thousand dollars. And how's the search for the new employee going? The new man."

"Yes, sir. It's ongoing." Stark looked around at the several enlistment and specialty forms laid out on the room's extra bed. "I'm reviewing . . . their résumés."

"Get him. We'll need him. Immediately."

Hands in the pockets of his heavy coat, the collar up to cover his face, Niles walked quickly on the wide Corniche Pierre Geymayel, passing department stores, shops, and the steel-grated entries of private apartments. Early morning traffic sped past on the divided boulevard. An old man walking a dog saw Niles and stared at him—looking at his scuffed leather boots, his black slacks, and the gray wool overcoat. The old man's eyes fixed on Niles's face. Niles had cut his hair to the style of a militiaman, an even, one-length stubble. He wore the beginning of a beard. With his sun-darkened face and prison haircut, he no longer looked like a Marine.

The old man watched Niles. Niles rushed past and went right, leaving the Corniche and hurrying along a side street of offices and apartments. He checked the addresses. The buildings overlooked a park of bare trees and frozen grass.

A hundred meters up the block, he saw the hotel. Plywood had replaced the street-level windows of the hotel. A section of the street had been repaved where a rocket or shell had hit. Shrapnel had pitted the fronts of the buildings and punched through the steel of roll-up shutters. Across the street, the shrapnel had scarred the trees.

Niles eased the front door open and stepped from the brilliant early morning glare of the street to the semi-darkness of the lobby. He smelled coffee. Though a radio played in the office, no one manned the desk. He silently crossed the torn carpets of the lobby to the stairway.

On the fourth floor, he found the room of Angelique Chardon. He listened for a moment, but heard only the distant traffic sounds of the Corniche. Reaching under his coat to his shoulder-holstered Colt Government Model, he unsnapped the hammer strap. He carried the pistol with a hollowpoint in the chamber, the hammer cocked and the safety set. The leather thumb strap held the pistol in the holster. He slipped the auto-pistol free of the holster, then pushed it back: ready.

Only then did he knock. He did not trust Chardon. The articles from the magazines and newspapers detailed her meetings with all the factions and powers in the crazed Lebanese civil war. But Niles needed information on Baalbek—the photos proved that Chardon moved through the Syrian and Iranian sectors of the Bekaa.

A minute passed. Knocking again, he heard bedsprings squeak. The door opened a hand's width. Chardon stared at him a moment, her eyes flicking from his face to his clothing.

"Why did you come here?"

"The photos."

"Why did you not call?"

"I did. You're always out. I've got the money you want."

"Wait." She peered out at the hallway. "Is there—"

"I came alone."

"Did anyone see you come here?"

"No one downstairs."

"Wait." She closed the door.

The bolt locked. Niles heard furniture clatter and a balcony door slide open. Water ran. Niles walked back to the stairway and waited. Minutes later, the door opened again. Now she wore jeans and a pullover sweater. A dark scarf covered her hair. Water beaded the fine blond hair around her face.

"I did not recognize you."

Early morning glare came through the open balcony door. The light made the white room glow. Niles glanced at the bed, the closets, and behind the door. He crossed the room and looked into the bathroom. Nylons and underwear hung on the shower curtain hoop. He stepped out onto the balcony. Concrete partitions extended an arm's reach past the railing, providing privacy and security. Smooth, angled concrete formed the overhang. No one could surprise him from the adjoining balconies.

"Perhaps you quit the Marines?"

Grinning, Niles rubbed the stubble covering his head and face. "Does it look bad?"

"Shia chic." She laughed, pointing to a chair. "Your officers want the photos?"

Niles moved the chair so that he sat with his back to the wall. He took an envelope from his coat pocket. Spilling out the black-and-white prints, he found the two best of the rolls.

"This one," he showed her the print of the truck driven by the Syrian, with the Soviet in the front seat, and the Iranian Revolutionary Guards in the back of the truck, "went to a friend who thinks the Russians are the devil. This picture'll get him all fired up. Evil Soviet Empire and all that—"

"But what will you pay?"

"For the picture of the Soviet? Nothing. Isn't anything I don't know about. Try the wire services. They'll pay you more."

"Where are the negatives?"

"Here. Now this one—" He held up the print showing the Syrians placing the antiaircraft gun in the shell of the hotel. "This one's of more interest."

"How much interest? What will you pay?"

He took out a handful of ten-dollar bills. "Five hundred."

"What?" Chardon looked at the stack of bills. "The Syrians, they would kill me for those photos. The Israelis, they would pay thousands of American dollars. What is the price of a helicopter? What is the price of all the commandos in a helicopter attack? Millions of dollars! You offer me only five hundred?"

He waited until she went silent. "I didn't ask you to take the pictures."

"I want all the photos returned. Where are the negatives?"

"There in the envelope. Take them back. No problem."

"Of course you made copies."

"Oh, yeah. But I don't have any helicopter. And I'm no Israeli."

"But you are a Marine of the United States."

"Miss Chardon, when you brought me those rolls of film, you said you needed money. I called the government offices and asked about you. You are an accredited journalist. You write articles and you work with television crews. Pardon me for saying this, I'm not being forward, but you're as pretty as a movie star. You could go back to France and do okay. Why are you taking these pictures of Syrians and Soviet soldiers and gun positions?"

"It is my work. Do you question all journalists? Or only pretty women?"

"Antiaircraft gun emplacements are not your business."

"Mr. Marine, I will explain. My business is news in the Middle East. I speak and write Arabic. I know the countries and the peoples. When I write here, I can sell my writing. That is why I work here."

"But pictures of antiaircraft guns are not your business."

"Interest in the Middle East, it comes and it goes. After the bombings, I sold many articles. Now, no."

"So you thought you could make some money selling photos to us Americans. Why do you think we want the photos?"

"The Americans will launch a strike on Baalbek."

"There won't be any bombing of Baalbek."

"Then why will you pay me five hundred dollars?"

Niles smiled. "Because I want information."

"Five hundred dollars is nothing. The CIA pays millions."

"I'm not with the agency. But I'm willing to pay for information about Baalbek."

"For who?"

"Why do you care? I'll pay."

"How much?"

"Five thousand dollars."

"For what? Photos? Names? What?"

"You'll take me out there. Help me look around. Then bring me back."

Chardon laughed. Niles watched her, marveling at her white skin, her perfect features, the rose color of her lips— why didn't this woman get a job reading the evening news into a television camera? She pulled off the scarf over her hair and wiped her eyes. Tangled from sleep, the white blond mass of her hair framed her face, accentuating her features, shadowing her eyes. She leaned forward, looking him straight in the face as she said, "American, they will kill you. I know. I go there. Every car is searched many times. By the Syrians. The Iranians. If you are lucky, the Syrians will take you. If you are very unlucky, the Iranians will take you. And when they take you, they will kill me also."

"Why did you risk those photos?"

"For money."

"Then risk this. I'll be a photographer. I—"

"You have equipment?"

"I can get it. I won't look like a Marine."

"That's why you look different. You want to be a spy."

"And I'll have false identification."

"What nationality?"

"French."

"Vous parlez francais?"

"Assez de duper un Syrien, je crois."

She stared for a moment. "You can."

"Marines ain't stupid."

"And that day you took my film, you understood everything I said."

"I didn't take it personally."

Chardon studied his short hair, the black and gray stubble on his face, his scarred features. She glanced down to the five stacks of bills on the table. Then she added, "A cameraman can't have a gun. No pistol, no Kalashnikov. Not even a knife."

"I know."

"And what of the story? The story of a U.S. Marine spying on the Iranians in Baalbek? When can I write it?"

"No story."

"But when there is the attack, there will be a story."

"There won't be an attack."

"Assassination? Kidnapping?"

"If and when it happens, we'll both know what's going on."

"When must you go?"

"Now."

"Perhaps in a few days. When do I get the five thousand?"

"When I get back."

"If you return. If we return."

"There it is, Miss." Niles gathered up the five hundred dollars on the table.

"That money is mine."

"I thought you refused."

She pushed the prints and negatives of the antiaircraft position to him. "Take the photos. I cannot sell that to a newspaper—and you have already made copies."

Standing, Niles pocketed the envelope. "Until tomorrow or the next day."

"Do not come here again. Do I call you at the Lebanese barracks?"

"Call me at this number." Niles took a tissue from her night table and printed a telephone number. "Call me when you're ready to go."

Idling along a quiet street in the Beirut suburb of Hazmiye, the taxi driver pointed a spotlight at the fences and walls of the homes. Trees swayed as cold wind swept down from the Shouf Mountains. Few lights showed from windows. The driver swept the spotlight across locked gates and concrete block walls. Iron spikes lined the tops of the walls.

Vines grew over rusted barbed wire. The light paused on name plaques and numbers.

"There." The driver turned to Stark and Vatsek in the back seat of the taxi.

"That is the house?"

"This is the street. That is the address."

Stark counted out Lebanese bills. The driver startled as a rifle action clacked. Vatsek set the safety on a folding-stock Kalashnikov. He grinned to the driver. The driver returned the grin, showing his gold molars. He took the money from Stark and shoved the wad of bills in his shirt pocket without counting it. "Very good, sir. Thank you, good evening."

"And thank you, driver," Stark answered as he stepped out with his attaché case. "I don't believe you need to—"

The taxi accelerated away, Stark staggering off balance as the door tore out of his hand.

Vatsek gripped the Kalashnikov in his right hand and carried a cardboard suitcase in his left. "Don't think he liked us."

"Very few taxi drivers appreciate someone cocking a rifle behind them."

"Hey, Lieutenant. This is Beirut, not Washington. I'm not coming out in the dark without a weapon in my hands."

A voice spoke from the darkness. "Next time, wear hats."

"Only hat I've got is a steel helmet," Vatsek answered.

"Then get out of the street," Niles told him. The hinges of a gate squealed. A silhouette in a long coat motioned for them to enter. "I don't want the neighbors to know I got Marines coming here. Could waste the property values. You requisition the camera equipment, Stark?"

"Right here, Captain." Vatsek held up the suitcase.

"And that little tourist camera?"

"Yes, sir," Stark answered. "But I caution you. I tested it and the photo quality is not excellent."

"I'll see, I'll be using it tomorrow." By the light from a second-floor window, they followed the driveway toward the house. Brush and trees thrashed in the cold wind, leaves swirling around their feet. They came to a battered white Ford.

"My car. Looks bad, but it's got a new engine."

"A Falcon, sir?" Vatsek asked. "A Marine Corps captain driving a Falcon, sir? Even that Turkish faggot who peddles disco tapes to the recruits works out of a Mercedes."

"A stolen Mercedes, Sergeant. He tried to sell it to me. Without papers. I decided to get a car—with papers—that no self-respecting militia Napoleon would want to steal."

Debris covered the driveway. Glass flashed in the light from the second-floor window. Niles led them along a zig-zagging path through broken concrete. Waving a flashlight across the interior of the house, he showed them the gutted first floor. Only trash remained of the interior walls and the furnishings.

"Landlord would not tell me what happened here."

"Looks like an accident with an incoming one fifty-five," Vatsek commented.

"Or Marine noncoms."

"Why is it necessary for you to live away from the barracks?" Stark asked. Niles pointed the flashlight at his own face. The sight of Niles's beard and hair answered Stark. "Sir, I wouldn't have recognized you."

"Neither do the Lebanese sentries," Niles laughed. "They won't let me through the gate."

They went up a flight of concrete steps to the second-floor entry. Boxes furnished the apartment. The stark light of bare bulbs showed walls cracked by the blast on the first floor. Plaster had fallen from the ceiling. The floors had been swept clean to reveal interlocking patterns of hardwood. The French windows overlooking the garden and the lights of Beirut had been patched with clear plastic sheets. The plastic flexed as the wind shifted.

"Don't take off your coats, there's no heat. Only been here a few days. Take a seat, anywhere." Niles went to an alcove and took out a six-pack of beer. "Don't have anything else to offer you. What's the news from Washington?"

Sitting on the floor, Stark set his attaché case on a box. "Sir, I have the money you requested. A few miscellaneous items—radios and electronic surveillance devices. And some more information on that journalist."

"Question number one," Niles started. He popped the caps off beers and handed them to Stark and Vatsek. "Why is she here in Beirut? You see any pictures of her? She's beautiful. She could be on a Paris television show."

"Yes, sir. She is attractive. I called several French newspapers. She is very new to journalism—"

"She says she's a free-lancer." Niles opened the cardboard suitcase. First, he examined a cheap plastic-bodied 35mm camera. He flipped open the lens cover to power the camera, then pressed the shutter button quickly, listening as the built-in motor whirred. As Stark continued his briefing, Niles sorted through the cameras and accessories, fitting lenses to camera bodies, checking the function of the delicate equipment.

"Another description would be, 'very infrequently employed.' Her work in journalism is all very recent. Up until two years ago, she was a student and a part-time actress. She began writing about Middle Eastern exiles in France. Then she came to Lebanon. Her editors praised her unusual contacts among the Arabs and Iranians here. Also, she exploits her contacts to learn of events before the fact—she called Paris with the first reports of the 23 October attacks, one of her editors told—"

"What?" Vatsek interrupted. "Did she know about the bombing? Was this woman in on it?"

"I considered that. I read all her dispatches on the attacks and the aftermath. I don't believe she knew anything about the means or targets of the attacks. But I do believe someone told her to be awake and ready to move at six that morning. That would explain her immediate report. Allow me to continue. She has no training in journalism and this creates difficulties for the editors. But they buy her articles because of her contacts and her on-the-scene reporting."

"Then why is she desperate for money?" Niles asked. He pushed the button of a power-winder. "Taking those pictures of the Syrian antiaircraft guns was desperate. She knows what the Syrians would do to her."

"Two newspapers buy from her only infrequently. In times of crisis in Lebanon, they buy her work. No crisis, no sale."

"Did you get any idea of how much she made? What is a standard price?"

"A few hundred dollars for an excellent story with photos."

"Does she have an apartment in Paris?"

"Exactly my thought, sir. She has expenses here and in France. But she has another problem. I spoke with a managing editor who will not buy from her again. They had contracted with her to write day-to-day reports from Lebanon. It seems she took her reports from Arabic newspapers. She translated articles from newspapers in Lebanon and Syria, then sold the articles to the French paper. The editor I spoke with stated that this has created legal problems."

"So she's in trouble." Niles put the cameras and spare lenses into a padded backpack. "What about those interviews you sent me? Those didn't come out of Arabic papers."

"No, sir. Those are examples of her exploiting her contacts with radicals. Her association with radicals and exiles took the attention of the agency—but the April bombing of the embassy disrupted agency operations in Lebanon. The agency personnel who may have evaluated the value of Miss Chardon as a source are dead. The bomb also destroyed their files."

"Then I'm on my own."

"On your own? I don't understand, sir."

Niles raised the black plastic tourist camera and snapped the shutter. "I'm her photographer tomorrow. We'll be taking a drive. Taking some pictures."

"Where, sir?"

"Baalbek."

Leaving the line of passengers walking from the airliner, Rajai hurried across the asphalt to a waiting Mercedes. Akbar stood at the door, his scarred face scowling, his light sportscoat flapping in the freezing wind off the mountains. Hasani—the overweight clerk—waited inside the car. Another bodyguard stepped out to take his suitcase. A shout came from the landing area:

"Sir, you must go through customs and immigration! It is the law."

Saying nothing, Akbar pointed his Kalashnikov. No other shouts came. Rajai sat in the Mercedes. Akbar and the other bodyguard took their places and the driver put the car in motion, easing the Mercedes through the technicians and vehicles of the service area.

"The Palestinian Kalaq waits for you on the road," Akbar told him.

"Good." Rajai turned to Hasani. "What is it that I must see?"

"These." Hasani opened a folder to show the prints of Colonel Devlin and Captain Niles. "The woman brought these. She said this one"—he pointed to Devlin—"is a colonel in the United States Pentagon. A commander of secret operations. I could not confirm it. This one is a Marine officer in Beirut. He was an advisor of the Lebanese Air Assault Battalion."

"You have their names?"

"Not the colonel. But the captain is Niles. I paid for information on him. There are rumors, only rumors, that he fought against the militias. No other information."

"Who did he fight? And when?"

"I could learn nothing else. Now he has left the training school. There is no information about his present assignment."

At the Avenue de l'Aeroport, Rajai saw the scattered lights of the Marine base. Walls of sandbags protected every American position, as if their enemies would make the mistake of attacking alert and prepared soldiers.

"Put the photos away," Rajai told Hasani. The Land Rovers of Kalaq and his squad waited ahead. "Tonight, I will talk with the Palestinian, then with Chardon."

Kalaq rushed up to the door as the Mercedes slowed. He called out. "So, my clerk! How went the business with the guerrillas?"

Rajai left the Mercedes. Turning away from the stench of alcohol, Rajai endured an embrace. He whispered, "Say nothing more. My men are to know nothing."

"Of course! Secrecy!" Kalaq closed the door behind Rajai. "Now they cannot hear. What of the Latins? Is it arranged?"

"Yes. They will make the arrangements in their country. Are your men ready?"

"They wait. The fedayeen and the bomb technicians. When will the word come?"

"Soon. You have two trucks. I must talk with the woman, Chardon. Is it possible we can talk as we go there?"

"To that French whore?" Kalaq lit a cigarette. He spat out a fleck of tobacco. "Do not ask me to accompany you. Did you read what she wrote of me?"

"No," Rajai lied.

"Friends have told me what she wrote. She heard nothing of my passion, nothing of my vision. She wrote only the propaganda of the Zionists, the lies they broadcast of our movement. And me? I am a rabid dog, murdering innocent boys."

"Only I will speak with her. Take me there. We will talk. Then I will speak with her."

"Done." Rushing to a Land Rover, he told the driver and a gunman to go to the other truck. Kalaq took the steering wheel.

As they sped through the slums, Rajai detailed the limited role accepted by the Latins. "They will only secure the staging point. They will watch the surrounding area for unusual activity. If there is any contact with the national authorities, the Latins will react. Your men will remain unseen. Your role will not be known unless it is a victory."

"And what if the impossible happens?"

"The Latins will delay the police while your men evacuate. Then they will disperse. There will be no attempt at defense or negotiations."

"What of the bomb? We will leave it to the gendarmes?"

"No. It will be destroyed."

"My friend, there is no courage in this action. If we do nothing, we win. If we fight, it is only to run. How can this inflame the imagination of the masses?"

"My duty is victory. I will leave the inflaming of the masses to you."

"What mockery is that?" Kalaq demanded. "Do you sneer at the struggle of my people? Do you think that the rage of Palestinian masses will not some day inflame the world?"

A checkpoint silenced him. Screeching to a stop, Kalaq presented his UNESCO identification. Rajai looked back and saw his Mercedes. The second Land Rover had disappeared. He spoke carefully, watching the Lebanese Army soldiers around the truck.

"You need not continue past here, Iziz." Rajai spoke to soothe the Palestinian's anger. "I have told you what you need to know of the business. I can go to the woman in the other car."

"You have told me!" Kalaq accelerated away from the soldiers. "You have told me. I tell you this, the next time I will command the action. And it will not be one of your Iranian schemes. There will be blood and fire and the screaming of the dying enemies of my people. Victory or defeat? What is the difference if the world watches? That they see suffering and learn of the suffering of my people, that is victory."

"And I hope I can serve you when you command," Rajai answered quietly. "This time, as with the other action, we can only do as we are told. In the future, when you command, it will be different."

Rajai talked of the future for several minutes. He flattered and lied to calm Kalaq's drunken rage. The promises of bloody victory and international glory satisfied the Palestinian's demands. Kalaq drove straight, his eyes fixed on the distance, as if he dreamed of fame. He allowed Rajai to direct him to the hotel of the Frenchwoman.

"So what is this appointment with her?" Kalaq asked. "Are you arranging for the publicity of your action?"

"No." Headlights filled the interior of the Land Rover. Rajai looked back to see the Mercedes parking at the curb.

"Then what? Is she your lover?"

"No!"

"Then what?"

Rajai considered the possible lies. But why not the truth? To learn more of the Americans—to follow them, to question

Lebanese informers—he needed men who operated in Beirut. His men could not watch the Americans. He needed Kalaq and his gang. "She has identified two Americans who may be working against us."

"What Americans?"

"I know almost nothing. I must question her."

"I will wait."

Signaling his bodyguards to stay in the Mercedes, Rajai entered the hotel and hurried up the stairs. The sounds of televisions and radios and arguments reverberated in the old hotel. Cooking odors came from the hallways. At Chardon's room, he heard a radio tuned to a Damascus station.

She answered the door with a knife in her hand. Food smeared the blade. "Finally. Did you bring the money?"

Pushing the door open, he saw bread and a can of imported sardines on the table with an open bottle of wine. Then he saw that Chardon wore no dress or pants, only a long shirt. The side-cut of the shirttail revealed her long, white legs, shaved smooth, naked to her waist, the front of her shirt covering only her crotch. He stared until her laugh startled him.

"Have you no shame? Clothe yourself."

"I did not invite you into this room." She sat at the table, the tabletop concealing her nakedness. "Did you bring my money?"

"The check was deposited in your Paris bank, in accordance with our agreement."

"I need more." She spread sardines on a slice of black bread. "Did Hasani tell you of the Americans?"

"How did you learn of the colonel in Beirut?"

"I did as you told me. I talked to the Marines. I watched them. Then I saw Colonel Devlin. I recognized him from the television and took the photos."

"What did you learn from the Marines?"

"They tell me nothing. It is not like before. Your bombing changed it all. Now they will not allow me inside their offices. They will not talk. They do not allow photos."

"I had no involvement in the bombing." Rajai took a banknote from his wallet. "Here is one hundred dollars for the photos of the Marines. The photos are nothing, but I will alert our intelligence services."

"One hundred dollars? I have worked only for you for weeks and you give me one hundred dollars? How can you expect me to live in this city? To rent a car costs hundreds of dollars. Restaurants. Hotels. Look, I am already living like a refugee."

"It was not our agreement that I employ you, only that—"

"Was not all of November and December employment? Interviewing the Marines, watching them. If I could leave Beirut, I would write of the war in Tripoli. But no, Rajai wants me in Beirut."

"Here is five hundred more. But it was not our agreement that I support you."

"I need more. What of the Americans? What are they worth?"

"I cannot pay you more for the photos."

"What if you take the Marines prisoner? What is it worth?"

"The Marines?"

"I want twenty-five thousand dollars for the captain. One hundred thousand dollars for the Pentagon colonel."

"Impossible."

"It is not impossible. Your country is paying millions for weapons. I am offering you the enemies of your country. How much will you pay?"

"I do not have the authority to—"

"Then call your commander. If I can arrange for you to capture the Marines who are plotting against you, how much will you pay? You must have paid millions for the bombing."

"The bombing? I know nothing of that incident."

"You knew enough to tell me to be ready. How much for the Americans?"

"I will consult with my superior. Continue watching them. Perhaps we can make an arrangement. I can say no more."

"This money will be enough for another week."

Chardon started from her chair. Rajai turned away, opening the door quickly and hurrying out of the room.

"Afraid of the sight of a woman," she laughed.

Returning to the street, he saw Kalaq waiting in the Land Rover, a cigarette in his hand. He went to the window.

"The woman is working for the Americans."

"How do you know?"

"She is questioning me on the October bombings. Always questioning. She is a threat to our next action. If I want her taken and interrogated, will you do it?"

"Will she then be released?"

"No. She has no more value to me."

"Then she does not survive the interrogation?"

"No."

"May I invite my men to participate in this interrogation?"

"Wait. I must inform my superior. If they agree with my decision, then you may do as you wish with that whore."

As snow swirled against the windows of his office, Abas Zargar sipped imported Colombian coffee and reread his notes. His clerk typed in the outer office, the keys and line-end chimes loud in the silence of the Foreign Ministry offices. All the other employees had left their desks and offices at the end of the workday. Only Zargar and his clerk stayed into the night.

Early the next morning, Zargar was to meet with the mullahs and the Pasdaran commanders. They would question every detail of the explosives shipments, the vehicle and aircraft transfers, and the various groups of fighters. His future with the Ministry, and perhaps his life, depended on answering the questions.

Zargar carefully arranged the order of the copies in the stacks on his desk.

Telex codes detailed the movement of the American-made dynamite from California, to Mexico, across the Pacific to Sri Lanka, then the transfer to the freighter bound for Colombia. A note from the Palestinians hired to accompany the container confirmed the liquidation of the Englishman.

Other telexes confirmed the shipment of American C-4 plastic explosive from Libya to Cyprus to Colombia.

A folder of bank documents and mechanical checklists sent from Panama to Switzerland, forwarded to Paris, then hand-carried to Iran recorded the purchase and renovation of a DC-4 airliner. The long-distance airliner waited on an airfield outside of Panama City, lacking only pilots.

Reports from the fanatic Maranaki—the school teacher who became a torturer for the Revolution—told of the training and indoctrination of the three pilots. The volunteer pilot remained determined to join his sons in Paradise. The two prisoners had accepted their fate and believed the promises of their torturer to spare their families if they flew to their martyrdom.

And finally, the reports from Fahkr Rajai in Lebanon. Marvelous, Zargar thought as he reviewed each summary. The young man had accepted an awkward task in the preparations—the recruitment and organization of the Palestinian fedayeen and the Latin revolutionaries—and he had succeeded. With his summaries of his contacts with the groups, he included organizational charts of the squads and brief histories of the leaders. He had determined the responsibilities of each squad and negotiated payments—American dollars for the fedayeen, Soviet rockets and antiaircraft missiles for the Colombians.

Zargar closed the folders, confident of his presentation. None of the mullahs or Pasdaran could find fault with his work. Though they did not trust him to know the actual target and the date of the attack, he had guided the preparations as if he had conceived the project. The glory of this strike against the Americans would assure his position in the regime—not as one of the fanatics but as a competent and reliable technocrat, a man of value to whoever replaced Khomeini. No purge would claim him.

The clerk brought sheets of typed numbers and dates—the record of payments in dollars and gold to code-numbered squads. Zargar dismissed the clerk for the night. He read through the retyped accounts, checking the codes against the actual names of the squads. Then he assembled all the reports, telexes, and documents and locked the presentation in his office safe.

Gulping the last of his coffee, he slipped on his heavy wool coat and left the office. He could do no more on the presentation. The individual reports documented every movement of vehicles, fighters, explosives, and money. And the marvelous reports from Rajai even sketched the personalities of the hired fighters. Zargar would, of course, present all the work as his own, but in time, he would make known his appreciation to Rajai. Perhaps he could post Rajai in Paris. He knew the debonair young man would value the transfer more than money.

The parking lot guards had retreated to the warmth of the corridor. With their old G-3 rifles leaning against the wall, the gray-haired militiamen stood in front of a kerosene heater, drying their ragged cloth coats and soaked boots. Zargar passed them without a word and stepped into the blowing snow.

Freezing wind came from the north. Snow reduced the few lights on the street to gray glows. Only his Mercedes—property of the Foreign Ministry—remained in the parking lot. He turned his fur-lined collar up and stepped carefully through the snow crusting the pavement.

His mind continued checking every detail of the next morning's presentation even as he put the key in the ignition of the Mercedes—then his thoughts came to an instantaneous end as the solenoid cable shot voltage into two electrically fuzed 81mm mortar shells placed by a Mujahedeen assassin. The simultaneous blasts lifted the Mercedes from the pavement, tearing through the floor of the car, sending the doors spinning away, and throwing pieces of the interior for fifty meters.

As the guards crowded around the flaming wreck of the Mercedes, snow fell on sprayed blood and flesh, concealing the remains of Abas Zargar under crystalline white.

An early morning commuter flight took Colonel Devlin from Washington National Airport to Los Angeles International. Thirty minutes later, he stepped out of a taxi on Wilshire Boulevard and went through the security checks to enter the Federal Building. Clerks and administrators crowded the lobby, rushing out to lunch at the restaurants and cafés two blocks away in Westwood.

Noon had cleared the Customs Department offices. One

young woman worked at the reception desk, eating a lunch of carrots and fruit while she typed. He introduced himself as Mr. Devlin.

"Just a second." The typist studied the names and numbers on an intercom, then keyed a button. "Mr. Gelb, Mr. Devlin is here."

Thin and balding, Larry Gelb stooped from years of desk work. He welcomed the square-shouldered visitor from the capital with a handshake and ushered him into his small office. "How exactly did you learn of this investigation of the dynamite shipment?"

"Through the Joint Chiefs. I reviewed the briefing papers you prepared. Your link between the dynamite and a terrorist group may be unfounded, but it is a legitimate concern. I'm also interested in why you believe Mason deliberately purchased dynamite which can be identified as of American manufacture."

"Finally!" Gelb raised his hands in thanks to the acoustical tile of the ceiling. "Finally someone sees the obvious."

"I believe the phrase in your report read, 'Mason has the knowledge and experience with explosives to know, first, that dynamite has very little military value, and second, can be traced to the company of manufacture.' I did quote that correctly?"

"My associate Mrs. Sula prepared the briefing. She is sharp. I thought that Mason creep had made a stupid mistake. But he knows chemistry and manufacturing. Informers reported that he can analyze the explosive compounds of munitions to confirm the specifications. International scam artists have burned the Iranians for hundreds of millions but they never got a load of trash past Mason. He had to know about U.S. regulations requiring the micro-coding of commercial explosives. And that's why I sent the report to the Pentagon. And when no one answered, that's why I sent Sula back there. And now, a month later, here you are. Like I said, finally."

"The dynamite left the country for Mexico, then shipment to the Port of Colombo in Asia. Is that correct?"

"The container is now in Cartagena, Colombia."

"Colombia?"

"Closer to home, isn't it? Mason did a fancy ship shuffle in Colombo and sent the container of dynamite to Colombia."

"Do you have agents watching the dynamite in Cartagena?"

"In the port. A friend in the DEA said they'd try to keep an eye on it if it leaves the port. But it sounds like I have to go to the Colombians for help on it."

Devlin put a business card on the desk. "This is my office number. A switchboard can put calls through to my home. Ask your friend in the DEA to assign whatever number of men he thinks necessary to follow that dynamite to its destination. If there is a departmental problem, call me. After you have exhausted your resources and the resources of the DEA in Colombia, then I can take action."

"So it's Colonel Devlin," Gelb commented, reading the card. "And—didn't I see you on the news a few times? You were in uniform. Talking for the Joint Chiefs of Staff in front of a committee? About the Russians paying for terrorism? So you're with the Joint Chiefs?"

"No." Devlin shook hands with Gelb again. At the door, he said, "Call me. I'll resolve the problem."

11

SYRIAN soldiers blocked the road. In the freezing morning air, exhaust and steam clouded from the lines of idling cars and trucks. Ahead, a driver raised his hands as the hooded and gloved soldiers searched him for weapons. Other soldiers searched the car. An officer supervised the document check and search from several steps away. Across the road, an armored personnel carrier parked in the snow, a blanket-wrapped soldier behind a 12.7mm machine gun watching the vehicles.

In his old Ford, Niles studied the routine of the soldiers. The Syrians worked quickly, passing the cars through the checkpoint at a rate of one every other minute. At the right-hand shoulder of the road, other soldiers slowly and carefully searched the cargos of trucks. Niles looked over to Chardon and saw her watching him. "Here goes."

"Do not be concerned when the soldier calls over the officer," Chardon told him again. "I think it is only the officer who can pass foreigners. If he speaks French he will not speak very well. Tell him I have the pass to the hospital. If he only speaks Arabic, I will talk for us."

"Got it. Got it memorized."

"Nervous?"

"Why?"

Chardon laughed. Niles heard the shrill, forced sound of her laugh—the sound of fear. Only two cars ahead, the soldiers searched a driver. Niles spoke quietly to reassure Chardon. "Nothing strange about this not making me nervous. They know you. You got the papers. And most journalists I see work in groups. Say, why is that? You work

197

alone. Why don't all journalists work alone? Wouldn't they see more like that?"

"It is simple to understand. They do not know the language, they do not know the people—and they have no interest. So to go to a place, they must hire a guide. If it is a dangerous place, the guide wants very much money, so the journalists hire the guide together. Less money and the same article and photos."

"But you go out alone, don't you? You're like an anthropologist. On my field work, I go out alone to do research. Got to. If I go out with a whole gang of people, it disturbs the folk."

"Is that what you study? Anthropology? How interesting. You are a strange one."

"No more talking. This is it. We're next."

A soldier returned keys and documents to the driver of a Fiat. Exhaust clouding, the driver gunned the engine and sped away. Then the soldier motioned Niles forward. Niles eased the old Ford up to the soldier and stepped out into the cold.

Speaking Arabic, the Syrian demanded identification. Niles said nothing. He passed the forged French passport to the soldier. The passport carried the name of an imaginary Jean Monory. Seeing the cover and design, the soldier called over the officer. Chardon spoke in Arabic, explaining their assignment at the Ayatollah Khomeini Hospital in Baalbek. Niles pretended to understand nothing. Other soldiers gathered around the car.

The officer spoke to Niles in Arabic, asking his business in Baalbek. Niles answered in French that he did not understand. Chardon repeated her explanation of the assignment at the hospital. The officer took Niles's passport and glanced at the photo and immigration stamps. With handsigns, the officer asked for the car keys and Niles took the keys out of the ignition. Soldiers searched through the interior and trunk of the Ford.

The officer went to the other side of the car and talked with Chardon, looking at her Syrian Army pass and the letter from the director of the hospital. A teenage soldier

casually watched Niles, his hands folded over a Kalashnikov, the rifle barrel pointed at Niles's gut. The soldier
grinned and arched his eyebrows, glancing in the direction of
Chardon. Niles smiled back and pulled his coat tight around
his throat, listening to the soldiers searching the car complain about foreigners making trouble in Lebanon.

A soldier returned the keys to Niles. Chardon translated
the officer's instructions to Niles as they got into the car—no
photographs of the buildings bombed by the Israelis, no
photos of militia positions. Niles nodded to the soldiers and
waved, then accelerated away from the checkpoint.

"Was not serious," he commented.

"There is no problem with the Syrians, but the Iranians—"

"Are next. What was that about no shots of what the
Israelis hit?"

"He advised us not to take out our cameras until the
hospital. The Hizbullah watch all the streets."

Niles let the Ford coast along the highway. He scanned
the sprawl of shops, work lots, and shacks outside of
Baalbek, comparing what he saw from the road to the high-
altitude photos he had memorized. Going slower, he looked
into the muddy streets and the narrow trash-strewn lanes
between the lines of shanties.

A three-story warehouse rose above the squalor. Niles
rolled down his window. He took the black plastic tourist
camera from his coat pocket and flicked open the lens cover.

"What are you doing?"

"Taking pictures."

"No! The Iranians will see and—"

"No, they won't. They're hundreds of meters up there."
Without looking through the viewfinder, Niles pointed the
plastic camera at the warehouse and pushed the button once.
A motor automatically advanced the film. Waiting until the
perspective changed, he took another photo. As the car
passed the front of the building, he clicked off a series of
photos—the cargo doors opening to the highway, the
barbed-wire parking area where men in coveralls worked on
the company trucks, then a flat, snow-covered field marked
by two improvised soccer goals. Niles steered with one hand

while he pointed the camera back and snapped two more photos of the field, trucks, and warehouse from the opposite side.

"Patrol!"

"Yeah, I see them." Niles returned the camera to his pocket. Ahead, a line of Syrian soldiers carried black sacks of charcoal from a walled lot to a truck. "But they're no patrol. Keep cool."

"Yes, very cool! Close your window."

"No can do, Miss. Think of the money."

Maintaining an even speed, Niles studied the approach to Baalbek. He noted the walled homes, the blocks of shops and apartments, the few street lights and electric signs. Posters of Khomeini and the Lebanese Shiite Ayatollah Sadr covered the walls. At an intersection, he saw an enclosure of sandbags roofed by sheet metal. No militiamen manned the post, but the ashes of fires indicated that militiamen watched the street and highway at night.

Merchants rolled up their shutters for their first customers of the day. Clerks swept shops and sidewalks as women in chadors passed. Running across the highway, a group of teenage girls in chadors and head-to-foot coats and shawls forced Niles to stop—he guessed their age by their slim legs and laughter as they ran across the highway.

Niles memorized the clothing of the men. Shopkeepers wore cheap dark suits. Laborers wore polyester work clothes and heavy coats. Some men carried their tools, others drove Japanese pickup trucks loaded with equipment. He saw a crowd of militiamen lounging in the doorway of a teashop, rifles in their hands. They wore civilian boots, Syrian winter uniforms, and Soviet web gear. The gunmen confirmed what he guessed—the Islamic fundamentalists dominated this district of Baalbek.

"All the town like this? Controlled by the Shia gangs?"

"Perhaps. I do not know. I have only visited the hospital. No farther. But I do not think all the people are radical. The Syrians support the Iranians and the militias, the militias control the people. Terrorize the people. Some people tell me they hate the militias. But they can do nothing."

"Who?"

200

"The people?"

"That hate the militias."

"Forget that thought, Marine. You will find no collaborators here. There, that is from the bombings last week."

Only blackened trash and ashes remained of a gas station. Water stood in craters. High explosive had flattened the sheet metal buildings, throwing the twisted panels everywhere. The hulks of burned-out trucks stood in a line along the side of the lot. An aluminum Land Rover had melted in the fire. The riveted-steel light poles on the highway showed hundreds of nicks and gouges from shrapnel. Though the adjoining buildings showed no bomb damage, the fire had spread the length of the block, gutting shops and the second-floor apartments.

Niles saw the white oil drums and sandbag bunkers of the next checkpoint. "Here it is . . ."

Militiamen checked the cargo of a flatbed farm truck, looking under tarps at an engine block and boxes heaped with grease-black parts. One boy unscrewed the filler cap of an oil drum and poked inside with a stick. The driver stood at the cab, showing the militia leader a clipboard of papers. In the back of the truck, a teenager with a Kalashnikov slung over his back noticed the passengers of the old Ford and called out to the others. The search of the truck ended, the leader motioning the driver to continue.

As the truck pulled away, Niles eased forward. A militiaman shouted out and rushed in front of the Ford, pointing his Kalashnikov at the windshield. Another militiaman banged the butt of his rifle down on the hood. Chardon saw a muzzle pointed at her face. Crying out, she startled back, pushing herself backward across the street, trying to retreat from the rifle.

Militiamen pointed rifles at Niles. Easing the gearshift into neutral, he turned off the motor and pulled out the keys. He put both hands out the window and asked in French if they wanted to search the car.

The leader jerked the door open. Another man pulled Niles out and threw him against the car. As Niles raised his hands, a Kalashnikov stock slammed him in the back, the flat side of plywood stock hitting him. His shirts and heavy coat absorbed the blow. He faked a gasp and bent sideways.

Chardon talked fast in Arabic, too fast for Niles to comprehend every word. But he understood most of what she said as she explained she had a pass from the Syrians and the Revolutionary Guard, that she had come to Baalbek to interview those who suffered the wounds of the Zionist crime, that she could take the story of the crime to all the people of the world. The militiamen interrupted her with shouts and curses, demanding she be silent.

Hands spun Niles. Rifle muzzles jammed into his gut. He relaxed his abdominal muscles and pretended to fold over the rifles. The militiamen crowded around him, demanding in Arabic to know why he had tried to run the checkpoint. Niles repeated in French that he did not understand.

Finally, the leader called out to a militiaman in Farsi. That militiaman asked in halting French for his passport. Niles straightened. He twisted his face into a nervous smile and made his raised hands shake slightly, as if he verged on panic. The militiamen glared at him, their eyes fierce in the masks of their full beards and shaggy, short-cut hair.

Adrenalin coursed through his body. He focused on the simple act of reaching into his pocket and taking out the passport, then handing it to the militiaman who spoke French. Asserting his authority, the leader grabbed the passport and tried to read the pages. The French-speaking militiaman pointed to lines, translating the statements into Farsi, then Arabic for the others.

Behind him, Niles heard Chardon speaking in slow, calm Arabic. She read the pass prepared by the director of the hospital, telling the militiamen of coming to the Bekaa after an Israeli attack and taking photos of the destruction and the victims. After the publication in the European newspapers, the Syrian Army had recognized her as friend of the people of Baalbek and granted her the privilege of documents—

"Quiet!" the leader shouted out. Throwing the passport back at Niles, the leader rushed around the car. He demanded to see the documents issued by the Syrians.

Niles looked down at the passport laying in the mud and ice of the road, then at the faces and the rifles of the men around him. He did not chance stooping down. Instead, he turned to the French-speaking militiaman and asked, "Why the interrogation? Miss Chardon comes often to Baalbek. She said there would be no problem."

"Spies," the militiaman answered. "Israelis came to bomb our positions. Only spies could have located our positions. We must stop all the spies."

"But we are not Israelis."

"You think the Jew spies wear uniforms?"

The leader shouted out for silence and the militiaman turned away. He directed the others to search the Ford. Two other cars stopped at the checkpoint. Militiamen demanded identification from the drivers. When only one man with a rifle remained, Niles picked up his passport.

"You can go," the leader told Chardon. "But not alone." He motioned for Niles to get inside the car. Chardon slid to the center of the front seat, allowing the French-speaking militiaman to take the passenger side. She edged away from the militiaman, pressing her side against Niles.

Driving past the barriers, Niles felt Chardon shaking. He glanced at her and grinned. In French, he asked her if the Revolutionary Guard always interrogated her.

"No, usually they were polite—"

"We are not Revolutionary Guard," the militiaman interrupted. "We are the Hizbullah, the Party of God, the faithful of Lebanon."

Chardon directed Niles through the narrow avenues. In the main square, they came to a bomb-shattered and flame-gutted building. Niles slowed to look at the damage and the militiaman grabbed his Kalashnikov, banging the magazine and stock against the dash as he tried to point the rifle at Niles.

"No look!"

"Offices of the Revolutionary Guard," Chardon told Niles.

"No lies!" Twisting in the seat, the gunman pointed the rifle at her. "School!"

Niles felt her hand grab his thigh. But Chardon said nothing more, ignoring the militiaman and pointing out turns until they came to a two-story concrete building.

The stark, utilitarian design of the hospital contrasted with the old European colonial style of the nearby shops and apartments. White banners marked with red crescents draped the walls, identifying the facility as a hospital. But the militias had fortified the grounds and the building. Sandbags blocked the windows. Walls of sandbags protected the entry. Militiamen in a sandbag bunker checked the identification of the few people entering the hospital. And on the roofs of the shops and apartments across the avenue, twin-barreled antiaircraft guns pointed up at the sky.

As they turned into the driveway, militiamen stopped the car. The gunman in the front seat called out in Farsi, then told Niles to continue. Niles eased past the men and parked. The French-speaking gunman left the Ford and talked with the other militiamen, pacing and gesturing toward the foreigners—while he spoke in Farsi. Chardon whispered in French:

"They are all Iranians."

Niles nodded. He looked down. Her hand still clutched his thigh. He gave her hand a squeeze, then opened the door and stepped out.

"No! Wait—" She tried to pull him back.

Stepping up to the group of startled militiamen, Niles asked in French, "What is the problem?"

They stared. Finally, the French-speaking militiaman told Niles and the woman to take their equipment and follow him.

Carrying the cameras and a tape recorder, Niles followed Chardon into the hospital. Adults with gifts sat in the waiting room, staring into space. Framed posters of Khomeini looked down from the walls. One woman sobbed as a nurse talked with her. A doctor greeted Chardon, then called over an administrator. They talked with the militiamen. Niles watched the activity of the hospital offices and corridors. Looking back to the parking lot, he saw the militiamen watching him through a window. He smiled and pantomimed taking a photo. They pantomimed shooting him.

A stairwell led up to the second floor. Niles saw four Iranians come down the stairs. Two men wore suits and carried folders of papers. The other two—in fatigues, boots, and stained parkas—carried folding-stock Kalashnikov rifies. Niles turned away. He crossed the waiting room and pretended to look through the window of the reception office at the clerks working inside.

In the reflection of the window, he watched the stairs to the second floor. Niles waited for minutes as Chardon talked with the administrator and the doctor. He saw none of the hospital staff enter or exit the stairwell. Doctors and nurses and clerks hurried through the corridor and waiting room, going from office to office, but no one of the staff went to the second floor. Only a militiaman with a rifle went up the stairs.

Calling to Niles, Chardon introduced him to Mr. Raed and Dr. Nourbash. Raed spoke Arabic, the doctor some French. Niles only nodded and shook hands, then followed them along the corridor to the door of a ward. There, the nurse directed Chardon and Niles to strip off their coats and cover their clothing with hospital gowns. They washed their hands and faces, wiped off their recorder and cameras with alcohol; then the nurse opened the door and Niles smelled burned flesh.

Children lay in rows of beds, segregated into boys and girls, the areas divided by folding screens. Niles followed Chardon from bed to bed, photographing burned and maimed children as she questioned the children and their parents about the two attacks in the first week of January—the first flight of Israeli jets striking at dawn, the second the next day in the afternoon.

The nurses pointed out the victims of the dawn attack. After the jets hit the gas station, exploding gasoline had trapped sleeping families in their apartments. Chardon collected stories of panic and family courage from the fathers and mothers sitting at the beds of their children. A father told of saving his severely burned children and the children of his brother, but watching his brother die in the fire. Niles photographed the father—his hands bandaged, his face blistered, his hair gone—comforting his crying son. At another bed, Chardon heard how the collapse of a roof orphaned three boys. Niles composed a group photo of the brothers in the row of beds.

Staying back as the others talked, Niles watched the

victims through the viewfinder, listening as the children talked, waiting for the exact moment, then snapping photos of suffering and remembered horror. The Marine Corps had taught him photography and news photographers had taught him the routine. War had taught him to switch off his emotions and thoughts—no matter how pathetic these innocent victims of strike and counterstrike, he had to act the role of the calloused news photographer. If he failed, if he betrayed himself, he would not survive.

He finished the first roll of film and went to the window to reload. Looking above the rows of sandbags, he saw the signs of shops and the windows and rooftops of the second-floor apartments. He set the shutter speed on automatic and the lens on infinity, then reloaded the camera. He took a bit of gauze from a nurse and cleaned imaginary dust from the lens as he took two photos of the rooftops opposite the hospital.

Chardon listened to a last story from a burned girl, then began an account of the second strike. In the next series of interviews, children told of jets, explosions, and bullets, of their parents falling, of blood. Niles photographed a nurse injecting a legless boy with painkiller. Speaking into the recorder, the nurse described the scene of the town's wounded and dying crowding the emergency rooms and wards, then cars and trucks with casualties arriving from the Palestinian camp outside Baalbek, of victims of the Israelis bleeding to death after the overwhelmed hospital staff exhausted their supply of plasma. Niles took a series of photos of the nurse crying as she told the story.

In the early afternoon, the doctor returned to the ward. He invited Chardon and Niles to lunch. They crossed the street to a café. Merchants and a few orderlies crowded the warm interior. Taking a table outside in the afternoon glare and intermittent wind, the doctor and Chardon talked in Arabic while Niles checked his camera and lenses. He took a series of photos of Chardon talking with the doctor. The backgrounds included the hospital, the streets, and the surrounding area—including the antiaircraft guns on the rooftops.

A waiter brought tea and plates of spiced meat with rice,

canned vegetables, and bread. Niles ate and watched the hospital. Two sentries paced on the roof. Revolutionary Guards and squads of the Hizbullah patrolled the streets. One of the patrols saw the woman sitting at the table. They circled the table, speaking in Farsi, gesturing at Chardon. The doctor dismissed the men and apologized to her. Chardon explained to Niles that her lunching in public—with two men—had offended the morals of the gunmen. Niles only nodded and continued eating—while he watched the hospital.

The Iranians in the suits passed in a Land Rover. Niles lost sight of the men and their bodyguards when their truck entered the parking lot. But watching the second-floor windows of the hospital, he saw venetian blinds open. One of the Iranians looked down at the foreigners on the sidewalk. The second Iranian stood at the window for a moment, then the blinds closed.

After lunch, Chardon went to an adult ward and interviewed men. Niles took only a few photos—the burned and wounded men did not present the pathetic images he knew the newspapers wanted. Instead, he listened to the stories from the men and watched the ward. He saw that the orderlies did not take Chardon to speak to some of the patients. With French and handsigns, Niles asked a silent one-legged teenager if he lost his leg during the air raid. The teenager answered in Arabic that the Iranians shot him. An orderly told the boy to be quiet. Niles pretended to understand nothing they said.

The nurses did not allow Niles to accompany Chardon into the women's ward. While he waited, he paced, memorizing the number of doors, the distance between the doors, and the length of the corridor. He found a service elevator—which did not operate.

Arguing in Farsi, a group of Revolutionary Guards entered. Stopping, going silent at the sight of the foreigner in the hospital gown, the Iranians stared at him. One man spoke to the others. The Iranians continued up the stairs. Niles paced to the opposite end of the hospital.

The corridor ended at double fire doors. Outside, he saw a wall of sandbags sheltering the doors. Steel and concrete stairs came down from the second floor. A steel gate blocked the stairs. Guarding the gate, a militiaman leaned back in a chair, sleeping in the late afternoon sun.

Only a fire alarm secured the double fire doors. But looking outside again, Niles saw hundreds of cigarette butts littering the walkway—militiamen stood guard there at night.

Sitting in a chair, Niles folded his hands behind his head and faked sleeping. He watched the length of the corridor under his lowered eyelids. The hospital activity continued—orderlies pushing meal trays, nurses going from ward to ward, a doctor leaning against a nurse and stroking a breast. But no one used the elevator. And only militiamen went up the stairs to the second floor.

An hour later, Chardon ended her interviews of the women. She passed the camera and recorder to Niles and chatted with a nurse. He checked the camera. Three exposures remained. He took a shot of Chardon walking with the nurse, framing the photo to include the entry, the stairs to the second floor, and an orderly who wore the regulation uniform. Setting the camera on automatic and opening up the lens to f-1.8, he pushed down the timer-delay lever. Then, when they stopped to strip off their hospital gowns and reclaim their coats, Niles set down the camera on a cart and pushed the button. In the noise and voices, no one heard the camera take a timed exposure of the corridor. He reset the exposure and lens, snapping a last photo, then back-wound the roll and pocketed it. Playing the professional, he quickly checked and cleaned the film guides, then reloaded the camera. He snapped off two frames to advance the film, then put the camera in his equipment pack.

"We must hurry," Chardon told him in French, "if we want to return to Beirut before night."

"I know, I know."

Waving goodbye to the doctor and the nurses, they hurried out. No guards stood at the door. But in the parking lot, Revolutionary Guards sat on the hood of the Ford, waiting.

"You come with us," an Iranian told them in English. He wore pressed fatigues, a new Soviet greatcoat, and new web gear. On the collars of his coat, emblems of a raised arm holding a rifle identified him as an officer in the Revolutionary Guard. The other Iranians gathered around them.

Niles looked to Chardon, as if he did not understand.

She translated the Iranian's order, then asked, "Why are you delaying us?"

"For questioning." The Iranian officer looked directly at Niles and asked: "Who are you? American? Israeli?"

Niles turned to Chardon and asked in French what the soldiers wanted. In his peripheral vision, he saw the Iranian lunge, throwing a punch at his face, and he flinched back, turning his head so that the Iranian's fist hit his skull just above the hairline. The blow jarred Niles but he heard the Iranian curse, the Farsi obscenities becoming a shuddering gasp as the pain of the broken bones screamed through the Iranian's brain.

Other fists hammered Niles, hands grabbed him. He did not attempt to fight—he felt the muzzles of Kalashnikovs jammed into his back and gut, another behind his ear. Raising his hands and crouching, he protected his face and ears as the group of men all tried to beat him at once.

He heard Chardon shouting in French and Arabic, telling him and the militiamen that they had made a mistake, that she and her photographer had official clearance, that they assaulted friends. Then a shout from a man stopped the melee.

The Revolutionary Guards stepped back. Niles looked up to see one of the well-dressed Iranians from the second-floor offices. Chardon tried to explain the situation. The man stepped past her and spoke quietly to the militiamen in Farsi. He ignored Niles. Turning to Chardon, he said in slow Arabic:

"You will go with these men. I apologize for the inconvenience, but there are some questions."

"Where are they taking us?" Chardon asked.

"To a hotel. You must remain in Baalbek tonight. If you attempt to leave, you will be arrested. Again, I apologize for the inconvenience. I am Moinfar. Please call me if there are difficulties."

Militiamen pushed Niles and Chardon toward the Ford. But another shout from Moinfar stopped the rough treatment. The Revolutionary Guards stepped back, allowing Niles to open the door for Chardon. They sat in the back of the Falcon. Demanding the keys from Niles, one of the men drove. The officer rode in the front seat, holding a pistol in his left hand. Other militiamen crowded into a pickup truck and followed the Ford through the narrow streets of Baalbek.

"We interrogate you, American," the officer with the broken hand told Niles. "Then we shoot."

"We are French," Niles answered. Chardon said nothing, but Niles saw her trembling.

"Talk English."

"I speak only French. Miss Chardon speaks English—"

"Lie! Interrogate. In French. Man comes. He prove you lie."

That explained the polite detention. The Iranians wanted to confirm their French nationality but the interrogation required an Iranian who spoke fluent French. Niles's French had satisfied the Syrians and most of the Iranians. Maybe Niles had made a mistake. Or maybe the Iranians wanted to question Niles as a routine security check. That would explain the apologies to Chardon from the Iranian who worked in the offices above the hospital—Moinfar. But a French-educated Iranian would immediately hear his accent and limited vocabulary. And why the courtesy of the hotel? Because they needed to send for the French-speaking interrogator.

"So we return tomorrow," Niles told Chardon in French. "It is nothing."

Chardon stared straight ahead. He leaned back in the seat and watched the town scenes pass—looking for hidden antiaircraft emplacements and military posts—as he waited for what came next. He had until tomorrow to escape.

The Revolutionary Guards stopped at an old three-story hotel. Inside the arched entry, an old Lebanese woman rag-mopped the polished tiles of the lobby. The officer—his broken hand balled into a fist and wrapped with a cloth—

shouted for a clerk in Arabic. The old woman set aside her mop and shuffled to the desk, looking with hatred at the militiamen and Niles. But seeing Chardon, she smiled, showing white porcelain teeth and greeting the young woman in awkward, provincial French.

"Good evening, mademoiselle. May I offer you a room for the evening?"

"Good evening, madame," Chardon told her. "These soldiers say that my friend Jean and myself must stay here."

"Jean?" The woman looked out to the street. "Where is Jean?"

"I am," Niles told her.

"Jean is my photographer," Chardon explained. "We need a room."

"You are with him?" She glanced at Niles's gray-flecked beard, his short hair, his deeply tanned face. "Blue eyes! And I thought he was one of them."

"Pardon me, madame. I am ugly. But I am not an Iranian."

The woman laughed and pushed the hotel register to him.

Niles signed the register in the name of Jean Monory and wrote down his passport number. He saw that only six guests had stayed there in the past month.

"Please take the equipment," Chardon requested. "Perhaps I can arrange for dinner. Is there not a restaurant in the hotel?"

The old woman nodded. Niles started upstairs with their equipment. But he did not go farther than the first landing on the stairs. Waiting, he listened as Chardon dialed on the telephone.

She spoke in Farsi, then Arabic, very slowly asking to speak to—

Rajai—the name of the Iranian working with the militias in Beirut.

Niles listened as she spoke.

Struggling with Farsi, Chardon asked to speak with Rajai. The Iranian who had answered the telephone told her Rajai had gone. He asked her name and why she called. She did not speak enough of the language to explain her detention by the Revolutionary Guards. She explained in Arabic, but the Iranian interrupted:

"I do not understand Arabic. Why must you speak with Rajai?"

"Is Hasani there?" she asked in Farsi. "I want to speak with Hasani."

"Rajai and Hasani have gone."

"When will Rajai return? When will Hasani return?"

"I do not know. Perhaps tomorrow."

"Where has he gone?"

"That I cannot discuss."

"Is Akbar there? Akbar who guards Rajai."

"Yes. Why do you want to speak with Akbar?"

"Does he speak Arabic or French?"

"No."

"I must speak with Rajai."

Giving him the name of the hotel, she hung up. She saw her hand shaking. She had tried to exploit an opportunity twice—and failed. First, to bring the American to Baalbek and collect his money. Second, with the American's confidence, to trick him and the colonel into a trap and sell them both to Rajai. She had reasoned that if the Revolutionary Guards discovered the American's identity, she could immediately betray him to Rajai. But Rajai had left the country. If he had gone to a meeting somewhere in Lebanon, Akbar—his bodyguard—would be with him. Chardon now faced interrogation by the Revolutionary Guards—without Rajai to explain the role she played in his group, without Rajai to explain that she had brought the American as a ploy to lure him out of Beirut. She had gambled and lost.

Voices came from the street. Chardon saw three militiamen push through the door. Bearded, wearing wool caps pulled down over their foreheads, they grinned at her like a pack of dogs and Chardon shuddered with fear.

Tomorrow, a minute after the interrogation of the American began and the Iranians learned his nationality, she became the property of those ragged militiamen—those creatures of medieval Islamic rage. She could only hope for accidental death during the torture. Without the luck of a quick death, the horror would continue for years, unending. Or could she hope for escape with the American?

In the small second-floor room, Niles found no windows to the outside—only frosted glass louvers to the hallway. The room had no bathroom or toilet. He looked down the hall and saw a common bathroom. There, he found a concrete arabesque serving as a vent—but no window. Outside, he saw the night sky and the lighted windows of another building. He looked for another stairway and found nothing—no stairwell, no windows, no emergency exit—only the front stairwell leading down to the lobby—and to the third floor.

Niles paused and listened for movement below him, then went up to the third floor. A door blocked access to the roof. An old padlock secured the door. Feet came up the stairs and he rushed down.

"What will we do?" Chardon whispered.

"Speak French. First we have dinner."

"How can we escape? They are down there."

Niles studied the woman. Her lips trembled as she breathed. She looked terrified. What game did she play? Acting terrified because Iranians suspected her of being a spy while calling other Iranians? Rajai—could the name be only a coincidence? Looking at her, he did not believe she faked the fear.

"First we eat."

Returning to the lobby, Niles saw two Revolutionary Guards sprawled on the couches, drinking tea. The old woman smiled and nodded and led Niles and Chardon into a dining room. Warmth and the smells of bread and spices came from the kitchen. The woman explained that she had only soup ready but if they waited, she could somehow make a dinner.

"We have time," Chardon answered.

Niles kept quiet. He turned on the dining room lights and took chairs off a table. The door to the street remained locked and cross-barred. Rolling steel shutters covered the windows. Niles turned and saw one of the Iranians watching from the lobby door. He ignored the Iranian. Turning the dining room's radio to the Phalangist pop station, he turned up the volume, then sat at the table with Chardon.

"Now we can talk," he whispered through the noise. "They cannot hear us."

"I cannot hear you," Chardon laughed. She moved her chair around the table until she sat shoulder-to-shoulder with him. "You are a strange one. Why are you not afraid?"

"I have no time to be afraid. I am thinking."

"How can we escape?"

"Tonight."

Shuffling to their table with a tray of soup and bread, the old woman saw them sitting close together and smiled, showing her perfect false teeth. She nodded and smiled as she set the bowls in front of them.

"Will chicken be good?" she asked them in her awkward provincial French.

"Oh, very good," Chardon answered. "More than we expected." Niles only nodded.

"And wine?"

"Impossible," Niles said. He looked at the Revolutionary Guard watching from the doorway.

"The shit," the old woman cursed. "They come and tell us of Allah. You lovers can have wine. Even if you must take it to your room."

He started to correct the woman. "No, we only work—"

Putting her hand over Niles's, Chardon smiled to the woman. "Thank you. Perhaps it will make us happy. Tonight will be very difficult."

"Difficult!" The woman looked at the Iranians. "They made our city a prison. And brought the war. The shit. And now I must cook for them. But you lovers first."

She shuffled back to the kitchen. Niles felt Chardon's hands shaking, a slight, almost imperceptible quivering of fear. No one could consciously force their nerves and muscles to simulate that state. He wondered how she succeeded in controlling her fear and not screaming in panic—if she acted with him, she faked calm. Niles disentangled his hands and tore the bread, pushing the ragged hunk of bread into the steaming soup. He watched the Iranians.

"If we are in one room," Chardon told him, "it will be easier."

"True. But it will go bad for you if we cannot escape. They know you. It is me they want. You can tell them I lied to you. I lied and you hired me."

Chardon shook her head no. "Do you think the Iranians care? It would not matter what I told them."

Throughout the dinner, as the radio blasted French and English lyrics, Chardon questioned Niles, trying to determine what had triggered the suspicion of the Iranians. She had watched him throughout the day and she had not seen any errors in his impersonation of a photographer—in fact, she wished her cameraman showed his professionalism. He had remained quiet and attentive to the interviews, photographing her subjects as they spoke rather than demanding lighting and poses to display his camera art.

"But I forgot to put film in the camera."

Her laughter brought the Iranians. Chardon shuddered when she noticed them staring.

Only once did Chardon attempt to talk to the children in the hospital. Niles cut her off, telling her, "I've seen it all before. And no talk ever made a child whole again."

"But you fight," she whispered. "In Vietnam, in other countries, against the militias, you fight and kill. And you know that sometimes the bullets and bombs hit the innocent."

Niles noted what she said of the militias—he had never mentioned fighting the militias. But he only replied, "I always fought soldiers. Maybe if you ask the Syrians and the Iranians and the Palestinians, they will tell you why they place their weapons and soldiers near the homes of civilians."

From the kitchen doorway, the old woman signaled Niles and held up a wine bottle. She pointed up, meaning the room. He nodded. Smiling, showing all her gleaming porcelain teeth, the old woman returned to the kitchen.

"Now it gets serious." Niles left Lebanese bills on the table—for the meal and the rooms—and went to the kitchen.

Her back to the doorway, the woman worked at the sink, scrubbing at a scorched pan. She hummed along with the

radio's pop music. Niles scanned the kitchen. On a magnetic
rack over the cutting board, he saw a row of knives—long
carving knives, boning knives, short paring knives. One old
knife had a full grip and a short, wide blade. He reached out
and jerked the knife from the magnet and slipped it into his
coat pocket. The woman sensed the movement behind her
and turned.

In deliberately slow Arabic, Niles said, "Thank you."

The old woman scowled. "You think I am an Arab? Speak
our language. Here." Handing him the wine bottle wrapped
in a dishcloth, she waved him away. "Go with her, go!"

Niles concealed the bottle under his coat and walked
across the lobby with Chardon. She put her arm through his,
like lovers.

"Don't," Niles hissed.

"Why not? They think I'm a whore for working with a
man. They will be less cautious if we confirm their ignorance."

"It could go very bad for you."

"I know."

In the room, they saw the equipment bags open on the
bed. The recorder and cameras lay open, the cassette and
film rolls gone. Chardon searched through the bag. She
found no film or cassettes, not even the unopened boxes.

"They've taken the film!"

Niles shook his head no. And pointed to his coat pocket.

"And I have the cassettes." Laughing, she shook the
pocket of her dark coat and he heard the rattle of plastic.
"So they found nothing of—"

He reached out and covered her mouth with his hand, then
pointed to the hallway. Chardon nodded. Niles unwrapped
the dishrag concealing the wine bottle. The old woman had
twisted a corkscrew into the cork. Niles jerked open the
bottle and poured wine on the rag. He draped the rag over
the louvers to the hall. The smell of the wine filled the room.

Hands touched his back. He turned and she pressed
herself against him, holding him, her body shaking. He put
his arms around her, trying to reassure her, and she raised
her face and kissed him, her lips warm and fluid, her hands
clutching him. For a moment, he returned the kiss, his hands

grasping the slight form of her torso. She arched against him, her lips going to his face, his neck, and then boots scuffled in the hall. They heard laughter and the clatter of a rifle.

Chardon looked at Niles. Wanting her, simultaneously incredulous and cynical, Niles eased away from her. She grabbed him, trying to pull him back.

"Later," he whispered, his lips touching her hair.

"Why not now?"

"In Beirut." He turned his back and listened to the boots of the Iranians on the stairs. They joked and laughed, their voices echoing. He waited, listening, the stolen knife in his hand.

12

LOCKING the heavy carved doors behind him, Rajai
went to the desk of Abas Zargar and opened the folder.
The papers still smelled of the dead man's cologne. He
spread the typescripts and photocopies across the desk and
scanned the several languages—telexes in English and Farsi
and French, harbor forms in English and a strange Asian
scrawl, bank documents in English and Spanish, and pages
of typed numbers and dates. He immediately recognized his
own reports from Lebanon and Paris. With amusement, he
read the note of praise attached to a cover page, recom-
mending Rajai for more responsibility in the next operation
against the United States. That note had won Zargar's
position for Rajai—after Rajai had engineered the assassination of Zargar.

A joke, Rajai laughed, enjoying his victory.

Early that morning, the call from Iran woke Rajai in his
Baalbek villa. Rajai and his aide Hasani drove to Damascus
for a flight to Tehran. There, Rajai met with the five-man
committee of mullahs and Pasdaran officers who had conceived the attack against the United States. They told him of
the assassination of Zargar, an event that threatened to
disrupt the operation at its most critical moment—the assembly of all the diverse elements and groups in South
America. Circumstances forced the committee to throw the
burden of the operation on a new coordinator immediately.
They had already reviewed the candidates—they wanted the
coordinator to be Rajai. Like Zargar, Rajai spoke and wrote
the principal languages of the squads: Farsi, Arabic, and

218

French. No other officer in the operation had his unusual qualifications—and no other officer could take over the operation that day.

Rajai accepted the responsibility. The committee told him the strike would be launched from Colombia and that all his forces absolutely must be in place by 20 January—only ten days away. They gave him the briefing folder prepared by the dead Zargar, telling him the collection of papers provided every detail he required.

Alone in the Foreign Ministry office, Rajai studied the information for hours, reading documents spanning the months of preparation by agents everywhere in the world— Palestinians, Englishmen, Iranians. He read of the reconditioned DC-4 waiting in Panama and the pilots who would fly the airliner and its cargo of American dynamite and C-4 plastic explosive. He now saw the limited role of the Colombian and Palestinian squads he had recruited—they would be only a security force around a remote jungle airstrip. But he still did not learn the target or the exact date of the attack. The committee had not trusted Zargar and they did not trust Rajai.

He did not need to know. Satisfied with his overview, he sketched a timetable for the assembly, scheduling the Colombian guerrillas to secure and patrol the airfield and the transport of the Palestinians to Colombia to reinforce the guerrilla unit. Trucks were required to move the American dynamite and military explosives from the port to the interior of the country. Finally, at the last possible moment, the airliner and the pilots must be delivered to the airfield.

The intercom interrupted his work. His aide Hasani announced a call from Lebanon, then switched lines. Rajai heard the static and interference of the thousands of kilometers of cables and relays.

"This is Moinfar, from Baalbek. The journalist Angelique Chardon was here to interview and photograph patients in the hospital. The name of her photographer did not appear in any of the files—"

"What photographer?"

"Jean Monory."

"French? Did he have the correct identification?"

"Yes. But my men were suspicious of him and we detained him and the woman for questioning. We are holding them in a hotel. My men are maintaining a watch."

"Why did you not call me sooner?"

"I called your office in Baalbek many times. Even the Frenchwoman called. I have called Tehran five times. And each time with great difficulty."

"What are the suspicions?"

"He does not look like the other journalists."

"You questioned him?"

"He speaks only French. When you return, I would like for you to interrogate the man."

"Describe him."

Except for the hair and beard, Moinfar described the Marine captain photographed by Chardon.

"Take them both! Imprison them. The man is an American soldier."

Nothing moved in the hallway. Standing at the louvers, Niles listened to the sounds of the hotel. The radio played in the dining room, now tuned to the melodies of an Arabic station. A truck passed on the street in front of the hotel. Metal clanked very faintly somewhere. He smelled cigarette smoke. But he heard no voices or footsteps.

In a pause between songs on the radio, he heard ragged breathing. He listened for a few more minutes. The breathing outside became a snore.

Niles glanced at Chardon. She sat on the bed, her back to the wall, waiting. He eased the door open a crack. The snoring outside continued. Niles looked into the hallway. The angle allowed a partial view of the stairway landing.

Boots and fatigue pants extended from one side of the hallway. Niles pulled the door open and slowly stepped out, lowering his boot silently to the tiles before transferring his weight.

One of the Revolutionary Guard militiamen lay on the hallway tiles, sleeping, his folding-stock Kalashnikov by his outstretched hand, the fire-selector lever down to full-auto.

RECON

The other man leaned back on the steps, staring into space and smoking. His rifle leaned on the steps beside him.

Niles stepped back into the room and silently eased the door closed.

"The Iranians are there. There's no way out unless I put them down."

"Kill them?"

"Yeah. Can't get past them to the street or the roof."

"Then you must."

"I kill two of their men, you are out of business. You can't stay in Lebanon."

"I know that. Did you get the information?"

"Enough. Can't come back for more."

"Then you'll pay?"

"Five thousand."

"I have more information. If I must leave this country, I will sell that also."

"What information?"

"Of the Revolutionary Guard and the bombing of the Marines."

"Woman, we will talk about that. If we get out."

Outside, the radio's music continued. But through the reverberating music and singing, he heard the snoring of two men. He took a long breath of the hallway air—and smelled no tobacco smoke. He silently swung the door open and stepped out.

Both Revolutionary Guards slept, one on the hallway tiles, the other on the steps. Niles considered his action, then took the razor-sharp kitchen knife from his back pocket. Step by slow, silent step he approached the men. He stepped over the man sleeping on the hallway tiles.

The other Iranian slept on the stairway. He lay to one side, his face resting on his outstretched arm. Slowly, Niles crouched, the knife ready in his right hand; his left hand open and ready.

Driving the blade between the vertebrae of the man's neck, Niles felt steel scrape on bone. The Iranian exhaled and slumped, suddenly dead. Niles jerked the blade free and spun, one step taking him to the other man.

The Iranian's eyes opened and his hand clutched for the Kalashnikov. Niles dove onto him, his left hand going for the man's mouth, his right jamming the knife into the man's chest. The blade skipped over ribs. He jerked the knife clear and thrust again, the blade plunging deep into the Iranian's gut. Niles wrenched the blade sideways and blood fountained out over his hands.

A slow, shuddering gasp came from above him. He looked up to see Chardon watching from the doorway of the room, her eyes fixed on the scene of blood and death. Then her eyes met his and he saw her face alive with fascination and dread—and in that instant, Niles understood why she worked in Lebanon, a country of war and atrocity, risking her own life to interview and write of the victims, to observe and photograph the horrors.

Niles dragged the Iranian off the stairs and dropped him beside the other man. Jerking a fatigue jacket off one of the corpses, Niles wiped the blood from his hands and face and shirt.

"Get my coat," he told Chardon. "Get my pack. We are going."

He searched the pockets of the dead men but did not find the keys to his Ford. Unbuckling the web gear of the larger man, Niles slipped the suspender straps over his own shoulders and fastened the belt buckle. Four pouches carried a total of eight 30-round magazines. He took the folding-stock Kalashnikov and hinged the stamped-metal struts of the stock closed. Pulling back the cocking handle, he saw a cartridge fly away and felt the bolt close on the next cartridge. He palmed the fire-selector level to semi-auto.

Chardon held out his coat. She wore the day pack containing the recorder and cameras over her shoulder like a purse. He took his coat and put it on over the web gear.

"I'm going down there. There must be more than two of them guarding us."

The music continued in the dining room. Listening for voices or movement, Niles went down the tiled steps. Metal clattered. Pausing, he listened for the shuffling of the old woman. He heard only the radio.

He went to the bottom of the steps and crouched. The angle of the wall screened him from the lobby. To his left, he saw the registration desk. He leaned out and scanned the lobby. The door to the dining room remained open. No one sat at the couches. But on the table he saw the militiaman's fatigue jacket.

Advancing one step from the stairwell, Niles looked toward the street. No one guarded the entry. He cut to the right, walking quickly to the dining room door. Crouching down, he eased one eye past the doorframe.

An Iranian sat at one of the tables. He drank tea and read a magazine. As the man turned a page, Niles saw pink breasts jutting out from the chest of a blonde. The Iranian poured another cup of tea, the teapot clattering on an aluminum tray, then he turned the magazine on its side and studied the long centerfold photo of a nude blonde stretching out on the blue satin of a bed.

Niles eased the fire-selector lever of the Kalashnikov up to safe. He tried to silence the lever with his palm but it clicked against the stamped-steel receiver of the rifle, the metal-on-metal noise loud despite the radio's music.

The Iranian turned. Niles rushed the seated militiaman. Losing an instant as he startled back, the Iranian reached across the table for the Kalashnikov there. One hand knocked over the teapot, the other closed on the foregrip of the rifle. Niles raised his rifle and slammed the blunt end of the stamped-steel receiver down on the Iranian's skull. The man cried out and Niles smashed him again and again.

Stunned, the Iranian fell sideways, sprawling onto the floor. Niles kicked the chair away and brought the heel of his boot down on the man's throat. Choking, the Iranian clawed at his destroyed throat as his consciousness failed.

Doors slammed. Voices called out in Farsi. Niles snatched the rifle from the dying man and went to the doorway. He heard weapons clatter in the lobby and boots run up the steps.

A rifle fired on full-automatic, the hammering noise overwhelming in the tiled interior of the hotel. Other rifles fired quick bursts but the first rifle continued, spraying out an entire magazine. All the shooting stopped for a second. Niles heard men shouting to one another. Another man screamed, his voice shrill, his words long and drawn out with agony.

Niles chanced a glance, looking and snapping back his head. In that instant, he saw dead militiamen tangled at the foot of the steps. Other men—Iranians and Hizbullah—crowded on both sides of the stairwell.

Another burst came from the top of the steps. The Iranians and Lebanese did not return the fire. Niles swung out the steel strut stock of his Kalashnikov and put it on the floor, ready. He took the second rifle and confirmed a round in the chamber. Holding the weapon left-handed, he looked out again and saw what he expected:

The militiamen pulled ComBloc grenades from their webbing pouches. Sheltered by the wall, exposing only his hands and the left side of his face, Niles raised his rifle and sighted on a militiaman with a grenade in his hand. The Iranian spoke to a second man, then they both pulled the grenade pins and allowed the levers to flip away. Niles waited until they swung their arms back, then snapped single shots into their backs.

As the shots echoed, Niles pushed down the fire-selector to full-auto and swept the groups of militiamen, emptying the magazine in a wild, sweeping spray of bullets before leaning back behind the solid brick of the wall and throwing the rifle aside.

A burst gouged the wood door and the grenades exploded. Taking the folding-stock Kalashnikov, he rushed out the door. He sprayed one-handed fire in the direction of the gunman and slid flat on the slick tiles of the floor, bracing his rifle on his elbows and sighting on a bloody man with a rifle. Niles fired a three-shot burst into the man's chest, throwing him back, dead before he fell. No other fire came at Niles.

Wounded men cried out in the mass of bodies at the entry and stairwell. A crawling militiaman tried to raise a rifle. Staying prone for a moment, Niles fired single shots into the moving and wounded militiamen, then rushed to the wall beside the steps.

"Hey, Chardon!"

She ran down the steps, a rifle in her hands. Magazines of ammunition rattled in her coat pockets and the day pack.

"Back up there!" Niles searched through the corpses, taking more ammunition, finding three grenades. "We're not going out on that street—"

"What?"

"We go out that door, we get shot. Go! Back up—"

"But to where?"

Niles shoved her. "Go! The roof." Half turning, he watched the lobby as they ran up the steps. Niles paused at the dead men in the second-floor hallway. He dragged a corpse to the stairwell and put a grenade under the dead man, his weight holding down the safety lever.

Slamming the padlock with the wooden stock of her rifle, Chardon pushed open the door. Niles sprinted up the steps and followed her. Steps led to the roof. By the third-floor hallway light, he scanned the tools, buckets, and boxes cluttering the interior of the stairwell housing. He kicked a box against the door.

"Where did you learn to use a rifle?"

"I reported on the PLO," she told him as she passed a book of matches to him. "They taught me."

He found a can of roofing tar. "Up the stairs, get on the roof."

Papers and dust swirled as she shoved the door open. Niles pulled the pin on another ComBloc grenade. He put the grenade on the box and used the can to hold down the safety lever—opening the door would shift the can and cause the level to flip away. Running up the stairs, he closed the roof door.

Gusts of wind roared out of the east. The door banged closed behind them. The wind had swept the clouds away, leaving the night clear. Brilliant stars and a fragment of moon illuminated the rooftop, casting faint shadows. Niles surveyed the neighboring buildings, the night sky allowing him to see not only forms but details.

Niles went to the front of the hotel roof and looked down to the street. He saw his white Ford Falcon. In the center of the street, a cargo truck idled with the lights on. Several Revolutionary Guards crouched behind parked cars, rifles pointed at the entry of the hotel.

Shouts came from the end of the street. A group of militiamen ran toward the hotel. Engine whirring, a pickup truck skidded around the corner. More militiamen rode in the back.

Niles hurried back to Chardon. "Only got two or three minutes, then they'll close off the block."

They angled to the back of the hotel roof. A drop-off stopped them. An alley ran the length of the block. No ladder or fire escape went down to the alley. They went to the roof of the next building. The walls had been built brick to brick with the hotel. Scrambling over the wall, an easy step down put them on the roof. Niles looked for a way down but saw nothing. They wove through the wires and poles of clotheslines to a third rooftop, then a fourth.

At the last building on the block, Niles hurried around the edge of the roof, looking for a way down to the street. On one side, he saw apartment balconies overlooking an avenue of shops. In the front, he looked down the block to see the street crowded with trucks and militiamen. He rushed to a back wall—and Chardon had gone.

"Here!" She signaled him from a flight of stairs. Not waiting for him, she went down. The old wooden slats creaked with her slight weight.

A dull thud came from the hotel. An instant later, automatic rifles fired in wild bursts—the militiamen had found the grenade at the door to the roof. Niles followed Chardon. Pottery smashed. Chardon kicked aside the shards of the pot and continued down another flight of stairs. A voice called out from a window. Moving fast, Niles ignored the noise and voices and lights coming in on the windows.

Chardon continued to the ground floor. The stairs ended at a door. Niles motioned her back. Going flat against the wall and pointing his Kalashnikov with one hand, he turned the latch. He pushed the door open with his boot. The stairwell light revealed a narrow passage. Above them, footsteps crossed the third-floor walkway and two men talked in Arabic, asking who had broken the flower pot. Niles eased the door open and stepped out, holding the door for Chardon, then silently closing it behind him.

In total darkness, Niles moved by touch toward the alley. He heard every step of Chardon's fashionable boots on the concrete. Rats skittered. His hands found a lock handle.

Opening the door, wind brought him the smells of oil and garbage. Light came from windows. He scanned the alley, his eyes searching for movement or the shapes of militiamen, but he saw only windblown trash.

Niles dropped to a squat and crept out the door. Bins of trash higher than his head concealed him. Rising, he looked in the opposite direction. He saw the avenue a few meters away. Past the avenue, the alley continued through the next block. Keeping his back to the wall, he stood.

"All right," he whispered to Chardon.

She slipped out the door. In the darkness, her white face flashed as she turned her head from side to side. "Where now?"

"Next block." Keeping close to the wall, Niles dashed to the mouth of the alley. He pressed himself to the wall and looked around the corner. Chardon's boots clicked on the concrete behind him.

A Land Rover raced in the direction of the hotel. Niles heard the squealing of tires. He turned to Chardon. "Come on, time to make distance."

Niles sprinted across the avenue. Crouching in the shadows of the alley, he glanced at the rooftop of the building overlooking the avenue—but saw no one. Their pursuit had not reached that building.

They ran. Halfway down the block, he heard an engine with a bad muffler. He jerked Chardon to the side, pushing her against the wall. Crouching down in a doorway, he looked back and watched as a small pickup truck turned in the other direction, its unmuffled engine deafening in the narrow alley. High beams illuminated the alley from the avenue back to the hotel. Militiamen searched the trash heaps and doorways on both sides of the alley.

"Go," Niles hissed to Chardon. "We got a minute or two."

Staying close to the buildings, they dashed from doorway

to doorway, kicking through litter and stones. The echoing staccato from the truck's exhaust pipe covered their noises. They stopped at the next street.

The alley ended there, at a muddy and tire-rutted dirt street. Across the street, they saw only the wide doors of a wholesaler. No windows or doorways broke a stark brick wall continuing the width of the block. To their right, metal flapped and banged in the gusting wind. Niles edged out. Corrugated sheet metal covered the front of a shop. Sand covered the sidewalk. He saw a pale spill of cement in the street. Looking to the left, he saw only a long wall.

"That way." Niles pointed left, to a street thirty meters away. "We're almost out of here."

Then Niles heard shouts. Turning, he went flat and looked back. A second truck had stopped behind the pickup. The silhouettes of men filled the back of a Land Rover. Others gathered around the driver's window. Spotlighted in the headlights of the Land Rover, a militiaman pointed toward Niles.

But no shots came. The Land Rover accelerated away. Against the taillights of the pickup, Niles saw two militiamen run into the alley where he and Chardon hid. Niles pushed Chardon toward the banging corrugated sheets.

"We didn't make it."

Her breath caught. "What?"

He grabbed at the corrugated sheets, trying one, then another and another. Only wire secured the sheets. He found one loose and pulled it back. He held it for Chardon, then followed her into the interior of a gutted, roofless shop. By the moonlight, they saw stacks of lumber and bricks. Scaffolding went up two stories.

Tires splashed through mud. Headlights flashed across the screen of sheet metal and tires skidded to a stop. Men shouted. Niles went to the loose sheet and peered out. Above him, the wind continued rattling and smashing the corrugated sheets of steel.

Militiamen left the Land Rover. The driver jerked the hand brake back. Leaving the motor running, he stepped down from the seat. He stood beside the Land Rover and watched the search of the alley. Niles signaled for Chardon. She crouched down beside him.

"I'm going to take that truck," Niles whispered. He took the short-bladed kitchen knife out of his pocket. Slowly pushing the corrugated sheet aside, he slipped out. His Kalashnikov clattered across the steel and he stopped. The driver did not turn, the panels banging in the wind covering the noise of steel on steel. Niles angled across the sidewalk to the soft sand and mud of the street. Silently, he came up behind the driver. He paused, looking past the driver. Illuminated by the headlights, the Revolutionary Guards and Hizbullah searched the alley.

Throwing his left arm around the throat of the driver, choking off his voice and breathing, Niles drove the blade into the man's kidney as he dragged him backward. The driver arched, going rigid with agony. His hands grabbed at the arm around his throat. Niles twisted the blade, then kicked the man's feet from under him, turning him sideways in the air and falling on top of him. He pressed the driver's face into the mud. The man bubbled, then breathed mud. Niles pulled back the dying man's head by the hair and cut his throat.

Niles ran to the Land Rover and released the brake. He waited until Chardon threw open the passenger-side door and jumped inside, then jammed the transmission in reverse. Spinning the wheels in the mud, he whipped the steering wheel to the left, then shifted and accelerated, careening off the curb and fishtailing across the street, managing to force the truck through a skidding right-hand turn. Flooring the accelerator, he raced away from the militiamen.

"Do you know where we are? How do we get out of this town without hitting a checkpoint?"

"Go slowly, Marine. Or a patrol will shoot us without questions."

"If I drive slow, they'll know we're foreigners." Speeding through the old, narrow streets, he came to an intersection with a red traffic signal. Niles did not brake. Downshifting, the engine whining with rpm's, he swerved past the taillights of an old Fiat. Headlights filled the windows, tires shrieked—the corner had blocked Niles's sight of a truck coming from the opposite direction—but his speed took him past the truck's bumper. Niles shifted and accelerated, leaving the blaring air horn of the truck behind.

A block farther, he switched off the headlights and turned off the paved street. He slowed to an idle along a twisting road of one-story workshops and equipment yards. Junked cars rusted in weed-overgrown lots. The pavement ended. Pausing for a moment, he stepped out of the Land Rover and looked at the stars and moon, plotting his approximate compass bearing. He turned left at the next road, a muddy lane lined by slat fences and walls of piled rocks. No light came from the shanties. He continued for a few hundred meters before stopping. Niles cranked down the windows and listened. He heard only the wind through the fences.

"We're southeast of the center of town," he whispered. "You recognize any of those streets behind us?"

"We must continue." Chardon pointed straight ahead. "This road—I don't know, but there are roads to the farms. If we go on those roads, it is possible to avoid the checkpoints. I did. But they will search for us."

"They find us, it's their problem." Niles put the Land Rover in gear and lurched over the ruts and stones. "They ain't taking me. Maybe the Syrians would help you out, but I got no hope if they—"

"Marine, the Syrians could not help me. I also would have no hope."

"Great. Then we're in this together."

Leaving the shanties behind them, they passed orchards of winter-bare trees. The dirt roads on the outskirts of the town had no street lights. The shacks had no electricity—only lanterns. Niles left the headlights off and drove by the moonlight, maintaining an even speed through the darkness. With the windows open, he listened for other vehicles. He heard only the rattling of gravel against the fenders and wind tearing through the branches of the trees.

A wide intersection appeared. The straight black band of a paved road cut through the center. Other dirt strips converged at odd angles, the haphazard farm roads twisting along the lines of the terrain and the fields. Niles scanned the south—the ridges of low hills, the orchards and fields, the black band of the paved road continuing over a ridge. Looking to the north, he saw lights a kilometer away. He remembered these roads from satellite photos. The lights marked the houses on a rise outside of the village of Ain Bourday. By weaving through the back roads, they had already left Baalbek and Ain Bourday behind them. By memory, Niles plotted their way through the other roads and villages.

Distant noise warned him. He saw headlights to the north. Jamming the Land Rover in reverse, he sped backward, struggling with the steering wheel as the truck bounced over the road. He aimed the truck's rear bumper at a tangle of branches overhanging a low wall of stone. Not slowing until the absolute last instant, branches scratched the paint and he stomped on the brakes and the bumper smashed stone.

The pickup truck roared past on the road, its muffler loud even a hundred meters away. Militiamen crouched in the back. The pickup's high beams illuminated the broken asphalt of the road and both sides of the road. Niles watched the suddenly bright fields until the pickup went over the next rise. Silence returned. Branches scraped the Land Rover as the wind gusted.

Despite the early morning darkness and their isolation, Chardon whispered, "They are searching for us."

"No. That truck's taking the word to other militias."

"Then they will search."

"If they do a search, they'll wait for day. Our problem is checkpoints."

Niles put the truck in gear and idled to the road. Again, he listened, then accelerated across to another dirt road cutting through the fields. Almost frozen mud filled deep parallel ruts, forcing Niles to downshift for traction. But the mud silenced the wheels of the Land Rover. When they came to a group of houses, they saw cracks of lantern light behind heavy curtains. The curtains did not move as the truck passed.

After a kilometer, another rutted and rock-strewn dirt track intersected the road. Not much more than a wide footpath scarred by tire marks, the track angled to the southwest. Niles followed the track to the crest of a hill.

An asphalt road ran along the foot of the hill. To the south, they saw the lights of another village—Taibi. One point of light took Niles's attention. Outside of the village, a flame flashed and sank. He watched the fire.

"Can't go that way. Checkpoint."

"Then they are searching."

"Give you odds that fire is there every night."

"But then how can we pass?"

"Do you want to stop at that checkpoint? Maybe interview the boys with the guns?"

Her white face flashed as she turned to stare at him. "Why do you joke?"

"Then we'll just stick to the scenic route."

Scanning the land on the other side of the asphalt road, he saw the winding lines of tracks through the fields. He let gravity take the Land Rover down the hillside, then followed two ruts leading off the road. A slight rise blocked the sight of the militiamen at the checkpoint and Niles went faster over the ruts and stones. The wheels smashed into rocks from time to time, but he risked the noise to make speed.

They reached the north-south Bekaa Valley highway in minutes. Niles turned south and accelerated through the darkness.

"The headlights, American!"

"They've got men on this road."

"But you'll kill us."

A front wheel hit a deep pothole and the frame smashed the axle. The Land Rover went airborne for an instant, coming down at an angle. Niles fought the steering wheel, muscling the truck on line.

"Maybe. But if the Syrians or Pasdaran spot us, it's a sure thing."

Driving by moonlight, he watched the road ahead and in the rear-view mirrors for other vehicles. The clear, cold night allowed unlimited visibility. Kilometers away, he saw a line of red lights—truck brake lights and the small running lights of trailers. No distance separated the lights. Perhaps a line of truckers tailgated each other—but more likely they waited at a checkpoint where the north-south Bekaa Valley highway met the east-west highway to Jounieh. Then, he spotted his turn.

Another road led to the west. The high-altitude photos had shown a railroad a kilometer west of the highway. By memory, he followed the single rutted lane of mud and stones to railroad tracks, then turned south onto the maintenance road paralleling the rails. Years of neglect had left the maintenance road eroded and overgrown with weeds. But Niles saw tire marks. He wrestled the Land Rover over the road, stepping on the accelerator at every straightaway.

Covering four kilometers in only a few minutes, they came to the railroad crossing at the Jounieh road. He waited for a truck and trailer to pass, then turned west. Finally he turned on the headlights.

"We are away from them?" Chardon asked.

"No one but the Sixth Brigade between us and the coast. They might not be with the government anymore, but they don't take orders from the Iranians or the Syrians."

"A miracle! I thought I would die this night."

"Hey, woman. No miracle. I learned to drive on nights like this, running illegal liquor out of the mountains. What is this other information you've got? What is it that you know about the bombing of the Marines?"

"For what price?"

"You'll be paid."

"You have not yet paid for Baalbek."

"I've got the money and you'll be paid."

"And now I must leave Lebanon. I must negotiate a good price for the other information."

"It's not up to me to negotiate. But I can get the money. And I think I can get you help working in other countries. You won't go hungry."

"You are with the CIA?"

"Don't talk that shit to me. I'm no Harvard rich boy."

"I will talk of the information when I can talk of the money."

Niles stopped the Land Rover. He took the Kalashnikov

from her, palmed the safety up, and dropped the rifle behind the seats. Outside, the icy fields continued to the distant mountains, desolate and gray.

"I told you I'd get you out of Baalbek and I got you out. Here you are. Out. See how far those fancy boots get you."

Her hands clutched at the dash. She spoke in a tight, controlled voice. "No. They will find me and take me to the Pasdaran."

"Then talk."

Taking his hand in hers, she lowered her voice almost to a whisper. "But you are a good man. You would not—"

Niles pulled his hand away. "Hey, cookie. Don't confuse the issue. I told you I would get you out. It was my word. But if you don't talk now, you walk."

Chardon laughed. "You are a strange one. I cannot trick you."

"Maybe, maybe not. We've got hours before we get back to Beirut. Quit this shit about selling what you know to the CI of A. For all I know, the rich boys bombed the Marines. So you tell me what you know, I'll get you paid, I'll get you help when you leave Lebanon. Then you can try to sell the information to the agency."

"Okay, Marine." She pulled the door closed. "I will tell you what I know."

As they followed the winding highway from the Bekaa Valley up into the mountains, Chardon told Niles of meeting Fahkr Rajai during a series of interviews of the Mujahedeen exiles in Paris. The multilingual young man had introduced her to many members of the organization and often helped with the translation, verification, and editing of the interviews. He demonstrated an encyclopedic knowledge of the revolutionary movements in Iran. He knew the biographies of the leaders and the backgrounds of hundreds of minor figures. With his help, she gained a reputation as a specialist despite her limited understanding and experience. And in return, he asked only for duplicates of her interview cassettes and photocopies of her articles.

She described Rajai as an odd creature, simultaneously a meticulous clerk and charming diplomat, a slight young man who devoted his working hours to the organization and enjoyed the evening hour perquisites of an exile organization based in Paris—the international society, the fine restaurants, the arts. He saw no conflict—or never commented on the conflict—in the Marxist ideology of his revolutionary organization and the decadence of the French capital. However, unlike his comrades, he seemed to observe the severe moral prohibitions of Islam. Chardon never saw him drink alcohol or pursue Frenchwomen. And despite working together for more than a year, he never propositioned her. Nor did he frequent the prostitutes of Paris. Even other devout Moslems considered Rajai curious.

The kidnapping of a Mujahedeen leader and the theft of lists of members operating in Iran exposed Rajai as an agent of the Revolutionary Guard. Closely associated with Rajai, Chardon became suspect. She suddenly had no contact with the inner committees of the exile organization. The leaders forbid the exile membership to speak to her. Stripped of her contacts and sources, she had no interviews or articles to offer her editors. She left Paris for Lebanon, where her French and fluent Arabic allowed her to restart her career.

By chance, she met Rajai again in the Shia slums of South Beirut. He refused to confirm his Paris role as an agent of the Revolutionary Guard. Nor would he tell her of his new duties in Beirut. But he did channel information to her and introduce her to various militia and religious leaders. Her editors contracted for a series of her interviews.

Rajai demanded information in return. As before, he wanted duplicates of the interview recordings and copies of the newspaper articles. Chardon guessed that he used her work to confirm information from his own sources. But he also told her to gather other information—interviews of Multi-National Peacekeeping Force personnel and photographs of both the American and French headquarters.

Through her own sources in Beirut, she learned that Rajai served as a liaison officer between the Syrians, the Revolutionary Guard, various Syrian-based Palestinian gangs, and the most extreme militia of the armed religious factions in Lebanon, the Hizbullah—the Party of God. She feared the fanatics and did not risk questions. Instead, she noted what she learned of Rajai even as she followed his instructions.

In early October, she learned of Syrian and Iranian technicians working in one of the warehouses outside of Baalbek. Trucks came from Syria with a cargo that required a twenty-four-hour-a-day security detail of Revolutionary Guards. A Palestinian contact in West Beirut reported the arrival of an ex-comrade in Beirut. This Palestinian had deserted the Arafat faction of the PLO for explosives training in Syria. Her contact saw the Palestinian peddling souvenirs to the French legionnaires at the entrance to their headquarters.

Then, on the twenty-second of October, Rajai told her to be at the arrivals terminal of the Beirut International Airport at no later than six in the morning. She thought he wanted her to meet someone flying into the country.

Only after the massive blast did she realize that Rajai had played a role in the bombing of the Marines.

"And what work has he sent you since then?"

"After the bombing, he broke off contact. He may be in Lebanon, perhaps in Iran. I do not know."

Niles questioned her on dates and details and names, comparing what she told him to what he knew. He believed she told the truth about her work with the Iranian before the bombing. However, he knew she lied about the end of her contact with Rajai—she had called him in Baalbek. To confirm this, Niles asked, "Can you get in contact with this Rajai?"

"I think perhaps it is impossible. He will believe it is a trick for you Americans. How can I explain taking an American to spy on the Revolutionary Guard? I am sorry I did not reveal the information on Rajai before Baalbek. But I feared you Americans. And I feared Rajai. Now it is impossible."

"Yeah, maybe. But it's not too late to debrief you. This is something my commander and his staff have to get in on. They'll get all the background available on this Iranian and his gang, then question you."

Chardon remained silent for a moment. Then she asked, "When will this be?"

"A few days. We've got to move fast."

"And where?"

"Not here. Maybe Washington. Doesn't matter. We've got to get you out. Or you won't live to be debriefed."

"No. I cannot leave immediately. I must risk remaining a few days. I have business to conclude here before I return to Paris. Also, perhaps I can arrange for others to provide information for you. I cannot do that if I am not in Beirut. If you must question me very soon, is it possible your commander can come here to Beirut?"

"Yeah, but why are you willing to risk it?"

She smiled at him. "For money."

13

IN the late night silence of the Foreign Ministry office, Rajai stared at the schedule of movements he had prepared. He had worked for hours without pause. His eyes ached with fatigue, but he had accounted for every significant detail of the assembly of the groups, vehicles, explosives, and aircraft at the remote airfield in Colombia.

Uncertainties remained—weather, personal conflicts between the Colombian and Palestinian squads, the questions of local people, or a raid by the national police—but nothing beyond the ability or responsibility of the group leaders to counter. And Rajai knew he must trust the leaders on the scene to respond to what could not be anticipated. Chance threatened every operation with disaster. Rajai had planned for every foreseen need, then prepared for the impossible, but what could not be imagined required the intelligence and daring of the squads in Colombia.

The telephone jarred him from his thoughts. After the telephone rang for a full minute in the outer office, his aide Hasani woke and answered. The intercom buzzed a moment later. He heard the distant voice of Moinfar, calling from Baalbek:

"The woman and the American escaped."

"How?"

"After I talked with you, I sent a squad to the hotel. The American killed them all. We lost two more men searching the hotel and the streets. They took a car and escaped. We alerted the militias and the militias watched all the roads from Baalbek. But they escaped."

"Could they be in Baalbek?"

"No. The American and the woman passed through a Lebanese Army roadblock at Nabi. We have an informer there who told us. They are returning to Beirut."

"Is there no way to stop them on the highway?"

"We have no units in the mountains. It is the territory of the Army and the Phalangists."

"What did they learn?"

"They were in the hospital all day. The American watched my men. He knows of the offices on the second floor of the hospital."

"Then he learned nothing that the Israelis could not tell him."

"But now we must fear a bombing."

"Why did not the Israelis bomb the offices before? Nothing has changed. The jets will not bomb your offices because they will not attack the hospital. They may risk commandos and helicopters but not more stories of dead children."

"We are ready for helicopters."

"Then nothing is changed. Did they go to my headquarters?"

"No. My men escorted the car from the highway to the hospital. He will know only what the woman tells him."

Rajai paused. He visualized the highway through the mountains, the winding roads and sheer drops. Storms in December and the first weeks of January had covered the mountains with snow. The night and icy roads would slow the American and Frenchwoman. They would not reach Beirut until morning.

"What she tells that American means nothing. I do not fear the dead."

Rajai ended the conversation. Keying the intercom, he woke Hasani again. "Call Beirut. I will speak to Iziz Kalaq."

As the American drove the mountain roads, Chardon slept, her heavy coat pulled around her like a blanket. Hours later, the voices of teenagers woke her. Three Lebanese Army soldiers blocked the Land Rover, their weapons and heavy winter clothing monstrous silhouettes against the light of a fire. Niles showed an officer his false French passport. Chardon pretended to continue sleeping and considered her next action. Taking the American to Baalbek had ended her work in Lebanon—and she had earned only five thousand dollars. She needed much more.

Niles shook her as he accelerated away from the soldiers. "Wake up. We're on the coast road. At Nahr el-Kelb. Ten minutes to Beirut."

She looked to the west and saw the gray horizon of the Mediterranean. "It will soon be dawn. Let us go to my hotel first."

"Do you want to chance that?" Niles asked her. "Chances are, the Iranians are looking for you. They could be at the hotel, waiting."

"No. I did not have that address on my press documents. But others know of my hotel, so I must leave it for another. If I go immediately, there will be no threat."

"A beautiful young Frenchwoman is not invisible."

"Now I am beautiful. But only hours ago, you pushed me away."

"Won't now. Stay with me in my apartment. You'll be safe there."

"And we will be lovers?"

"If the situation requires."

Chardon laughed. In the Bekaa, he had threatened to put her out on the highway. Now he wanted to lock her in his apartment. The promise of information on Rajai had succeeded where the offer of sex had failed. "I know of a safe hotel. And I can dress to hide my face and nationality. No one will know who I am."

"A blue-eyed Shiia?"

"The Iranians do not have the organization to search all of East Beirut. I will be safe if I go to a new hotel immediately. Do we go there first?"

"Why not?"

"And the five thousand dollars?"

"You've got it today."

"Then we will talk of meeting with your officer."

She wanted no protection from the Americans. Protection, any restriction on her movement, complicated her plans. The escape from Baalbek had confirmed the suspicions of the Revolutionary Guards. Those fanatics wanted

240

revenge but they did not know of her hotel. Only Rajai knew her address and he had always operated independently of the main unit of Iranians.

The fanatics of the Revolutionary Guard could not search for her and find her quickly in East Beirut. She could risk going to her hotel. But Rajai had contacts with all the militias of Beirut—Islamic, Socialist, Palestinian, even the criminal gangs of kidnappers and assassins. She must contact Rajai immediately or leave Lebanon with only the five thousand dollars for the disastrous trip to Baalbek. And to deal with Rajai, she needed freedom of communication and movement. If Niles insisted on posting men at her new hotel, she became a prisoner—and lost the opportunity to profit on the naiveté of the Americans.

"First we go to another hotel. Then we call your officer, yes? Is my information so important to justify waking him?"

"You got it. I think he'll be flying out of Washington today."

Staring through the darkness of the park, Iziz Kalaq watched the hotel. A car sped past, headlights flashing on the windows of shops and other cars. The black forms of trees broke his view of the street, but he had a clear line of sight of the hotel entry less than one hundred meters away.

Few people in East Beirut left their shelters this morning. The truck bombing of a mosque the evening before had enraged the Islamic militias. Druze and Shiite artillery crews fired randomly into the Christian suburbs, the shells screaming down at odd intervals. Kalaq heard the false thunder of explosions as he watched for Chardon and the American.

A man left the hotel, the lights of the entry illuminating his face and clothing: Lebanese. The two-cycle whine of a motorcycle cut the quiet and the headlight wobbled away in the predawn. The simultaneous shriek-explosion of a shell covered the noise of the motorcycle, then the engine whine returned as the motorcycle raced east on the Corniche.

Kalaq sat in the back seat of a van parked on the Corniche Pierre Geymayel. Two of his fedayeen slept in the front seat while he watched the hotel entry. Smoking his ninth cigarette of the day, he took a long drag and felt it burn his fingers. He flicked the butt out the window. He looked back to the second van. The gray light of the eastern horizon backlit the forms of four more of his fedayeen watching and waiting.

Headlights stopped at the hotel. Kalaq strained to see the type of car. Then, in the trees of the park, he saw the swinging of the flashlight—the signal. He woke the fedayeen in the front seat of the van. His walkie-talkie buzzed.

"A man and a woman," the lookout told him. "Perhaps they are the American and the journalist."

"You are positive?"

"They are going into the hotel."

But the boxy form of the car blocked Kalaq's view of the entry. "Did you see their faces?"

"I think the man was a foreigner. The woman dressed very modestly. Not like the woman you described. I did not see her hair or face."

"Describe the car."

"It is a Land Rover. Very muddy."

"Did the man have a rifle?"

"I did not see."

Kalaq cursed under his breath. Until the lookout confirmed the identities of the man and the woman, Kalaq could not order his squads into motion. He leaned forward to the front seat. "Start the motor and signal—"

The driver immediately turned on the ignition. Revving the engine, he flashed the taillights to the van behind them. Then Kalaq spoke into the walkie-talkie again to alert the fedayeen waiting in cars on a side street.

"Squads number three and four, be ready. We think they have come. The moment we are positive, we will capture them."

Taking the Beretta pistol from his shoulder holster, he touched the extractor to confirm a round in the chamber. He gripped the pistol and stroked the oil-smooth steel of the slide. Flicking the safety off and on with his thumb, he thought of that night months before with Chardon—her words, her demands, her mocking laughter. That night he silenced her with a slap. Today he would take his revenge. First he and his men would enjoy her, then they would question her. After the screaming, when she had no more to say, he would stop all her words forever—with the pistol.

Then he would question the American.

Showing no concern, Chardon casually pushed through the plywood-covered doors of the old hotel. The chemical stink of disinfectant almost covered the smells of mildew, old food, and tobacco. They saw no one in the lobby. Niles rushed past the office and searched for the rear doors of the hotel. Chardon heard him rattle the chains securing the fire doors.

"Is it not as I told you?" she asked him. "Are you satisfied? They do not have the means to pursue me everywhere, you know."

"You could be wrong, Miss Chardon. Dead wrong. Let's go to your room."

As they passed the registration desk, she looked through the doorway of the office and saw the clerk sleeping on a cot. Niles took his short rifle from under his coat and preceded her up the stairs.

Niles moved quickly from landing to landing, his boots somehow silent, the rifle pointing at every shadow and doorway. No gunmen assaulted them. At her room, he took the key and motioned for her to stand to the side. First, he listened. But a radio in another room echoed in the hallway. He carefully turned the key. Going flat against the solid brick wall, he kicked the door open. Niles waited a few seconds before looking inside the room. He did not go inside.

"Do you expect an explosion?" Impatient, she pushed past him. "No one has entered."

"Don't turn on the light. There could be a bomb wired to it."

"But I can't see." She flicked the light switch and surveyed the room. "Everything is as it was."

"Positive? Check everything."

"I know my own room. And my possessions."

Niles left. She glanced into the hall and saw him standing near the stairs, watching the hallway. Closing the door and locking it, she went to the room's telephone. The clerk finally answered after a minute of ringing.

"I want you to place a telephone call for me. The operator will need time. Perhaps it will take a few minutes, perhaps longer. I must pack. I will pay you if you listen and call for me when the operator finally makes the connection."

"How much will you pay?"

"Five United States dollars."

"Done, mademoiselle."

She gave the number of the villa in Baalbek.

"That call will be difficult."

"Have the operator try. I know I must wait. Perhaps it will go through without delay because of the early hour."

Looking in the hallway again, she saw Niles at the stairs. She packed quickly. Her suitcase contained her clothing. She needed only five minutes to gather her few personal effects from the bathroom and closet and bed table.

Carrying only her typewriter and attaché case, she rushed to Niles. "Can you bring my suitcase? I will go to the desk to settle my account."

He nodded and she continued down the stairs to the registration desk. Slapping the bell brought the clerk stumbling from the office, a red-eyed young man wearing a New York Yankees sweat shirt. He reeked of tobacco and stale wine. Chardon asked: "Is my call complete?"

He picked up the desk phone and asked for the operator. At that moment, Niles came from the stairs. Chardon motioned for him to continue to the car.

"Have I received calls? Has anyone asked for me?"

"No calls. But a letter."

A statement from her Paris bank detailed the decline of her finances—a fact she knew.

"The operator said there are difficulties," the clerk told Chardon.

"Always." She took the receiver from the clerk. "Total my account while I wait."

Listening for the voice of the operator, Chardon watched the hotel entry. The plywood sheets over the blown-out windows blocked the sight of Niles. She counted the seconds, hoping his patience continued. The clerk finally returned with a long list of charges. Using a battered hand-calculator, he slowly keyed the numbers.

The door opened. Hiding the receiver against her side, she looked behind her to see the hotel's elderly janitor struggling to guide a two-wheeled shopping cart through the door. Past the old man, she saw the Land Rover at the curb. Niles crouched beside the Land Rover, watching the street, the bulk of the Land Rover shielding him. Then, glancing to the hotel, he saw Chardon at the reception desk. She pointed to the clerk working with the hand-calculator.

Niles called out, "Hurry!"

A voice spoke from the telephone. The old man still struggled with his cart in the open doorway. Turning her back on Niles, she blocked his sight of the telephone and said, "Just one moment."

The old man jerked his cart clear of the entry. As the door swung closed, Chardon raised the receiver to her ear. Someone spoke Farsi. She asked for a French or Arabic speaker as she pulled the telephone away from the clerk. The long cord stretched to the corner of the desk. The noise from the television continued. Turning her back to the clerk, she covered her other ear with her hand and leaned over the receiver, using her body to contain her words—no one could overhear her conversation. An Iranian answered in Arabic.

"This is Angelique Chardon," she whispered into the telephone. "I must give you a message for Rajai—"

"You! The Frenchwoman. You agent of the Americans. You are dead."

Her body went cold as she recognized the voice of Moinfar, the Revolutionary Guard leader from the offices at the hospital. If Moinfar had taken command of Rajai's staff, he had access to all the information on her and contacts with the militias of Beirut. She could not speak for a moment.

"You are dead, hear me? You will not live another day."

Taking a long breath, she forced herself to speak calmly. "Then you do not know of my work for Rajai? Call him. He will explain."

"What is this you say?"

"Call Rajai. He will explain."

"How can he explain the deaths of my men?"

"If I could have spoken with Rajai, or if I could have

explained to you, there would have been no killing. Unfortunately, the circumstances did not allow me to explain. The American forced me to escape with him. And it is better. He trusts me now. If you had discovered his identity, if you had imprisoned him, I could not help you now to capture a colonel who is an aide to the President of the United States."

"What? I knew nothing of this."

"I cannot tell you more. I told you of the meeting only to convince you of the urgency of my call. I must speak with Rajai immediately or this opportunity will be lost. Contact him. I will call again soon."

Chardon hung up. The call had changed everything—the Revolutionary Guards pursued her with the advantage of all of Rajai's information and contacts. She hoped her talk of kidnapping an advisor to the American president had won her time. But until she spoke with Rajai, she remained in danger.

She paid the clerk and ran through the lobby with her attaché case and typewriter, shouldering open the plywood door. Dashing to the Land Rover, she put her case of papers inside with her suitcase—

A roar and high-pitched shrieking tore the dawn quiet. For a moment, she thought an artillery shell had passed overhead, then she realized she heard the sound of engines and spinning tires. She saw Niles looking in all directions, trying to identify the source of the noise. Then he raised his Kalashnikov and fired toward the park on the opposite side of the street.

Chardon crouched behind the Land Rover. She still gripped her typewriter. In the street, a form with an outstretched arm fell backward. Niles fired again into the fallen man, then pivoted and aimed at an onrushing Mercedes, firing a long, hammering burst at the windshield. The windshield went white with shatters and the Mercedes drifted to the side, crashing into a parked truck. Momentum spun the Mercedes sideways to block the street.

A second car skidded to a stop behind the wreck. Men with rifles came out of both cars and took cover in the doorways and behind the parked truck. A grenade popped in the street and tear gas clouded into the gray morning light. Wind carried the gas into the park.

Rifles fired from the street. In the park, Palestinians sprinted from cover to cover to encircle Niles and Chardon. The gunmen coughed and cursed in the drifting tear gas. One man shouted commands to the others. And at that moment, Chardon recognized the leader: Iziz Kalaq.

The rifle of the American only delayed the attack. She had no hope. The call to Moinfar had been too late. She would die there on the sidewalk—

Unless she demonstrated that she did not work for the American. If she lived to be the prisoner of Kalaq, she gained the time to talk to Rajai, to explain . . .

Bullets zipped past her as she rushed at Niles's back. Swinging the typewriter case with all the strength of her panic, she brought it down on the back of his head, sending him sprawling facedown onto the sidewalk. And then she ran to Kalaq: "Iziz! Iziz! Take me to Rajai! I have much to tell him!"

In his peripheral vision, Niles saw a blur of motion. He threw himself sideways—but too late. The plastic and chrome case glanced off the back of his head and hit his shoulder. Bells rang and keys clattered, then the typewriter smashed on the concrete as he fell. Stunned but conscious, he lay on the sidewalk, blinking away the pain.

The gunfire stopped. He heard Chardon shouting out the name "Iziz" and then a confusion of voices speaking Arabic covered her words.

Iziz Kalaq, Niles realized. The leader of a Palestinian gang. Niles had read her interview of the radical-faction militiaman.

Under the Land Rover, he saw boots crowd around her long skirt. Men dragged her away. Others came for him. Niles pulled another 30-round magazine out of the ammo pouches under his coat. He looked up and saw two Palestinian gunmen run from the cover of the truck. Firing by reflex, not aiming, he skipped a burst of 7.62ComBloc off the sidewalk. Ricochets tore through the legs of the running gunmen, dropping them hard to the concrete. Cursing and screaming, they pointed their rifles at him. Niles brought the Kalashnikov to his shoulder and fired killing bursts through their faces.

Boots ran toward the Land Rover. He aimed at a boot and pulled the trigger. The rifle did not fire. He dropped out the empty magazine and threw it over the Land Rover. Men shouted out and ran in opposite directions. Niles jammed the new magazine into the rifle. Then he saw the boots running around the front bumper.

Jerking his legs up under him, Niles dove forward, his shoulder catching the man sideways in the knees. Cartilage popped and the gunman fell onto a parked Fiat, the tinny bumper clanging with the impact of his head. The Palestinian kicked Niles and tried to bring up his automatic rifle, but the magazine tangled with his coat. Jerking back the rifle's cocking handle to chamber the first round, Niles put the muzzle of his rifle against the man's chest and fired. At the same instant, the Palestinian fired.

The impact of a bullet spun Niles. He did not feel the wound or lose consciousness. Sprawling on his back, the rifle locked in his hands, Niles saw a gunman running toward him and he fired wild into the man's torso, slugs punching through the man's chest, spraying blood and bone out the back of his neck, two bullets to the face exploding his skull. The corpse fell next to Niles, the dead eyes staring at him.

The street went silent. Niles saw no one moving. Scrambling to the shelter of the Land Rover, he scanned the sidewalk. He saw only corpses. Then he searched for his wound.

Blood stained his shirt. And he saw a bent magazine. The bullet had hit one of his ammunition pouches, smashed through the steel of the magazine, then slashed through the flesh at his side. He touched the wound and felt only a shallow gouge.

Crouching, Niles rushed to the back of the Land Rover. He looked across at the park. In the gray dawn light, he saw militiamen with rifles escorting Chardon away, jerking and dragging her toward two vans parked on the Corniche.

If they took Chardon, Niles lost his contact with the gang responsible for 23 October.

Niles dodged around the back of the Land Rover and looked into the street. One dead man lay on his back, a tear gas canister still smoking in his hand. He saw no one else. Running back to the driver's door, he threw the door open and twisted the key. He pumped the accelerator and screeched through a turn.

A bullet punched through the back window and exited through the windshield, tempered glass spraying the interior. Wrenching the steering wheel from side to side, he zigzagged across both lanes of the street.

The vans raced away. Niles saw Chardon in the back seat of the first van, a white Toyota. The second van, a red Volkswagen, contained more gunmen. They did not see Niles as he accelerated along the curving side street. Downshifting as the street merged with the Corniche, he flashed behind the red Volkswagen as he forced the Land Rover through a right-hand power-drift.

He picked up the Kalashnikov off the front seat and aimed a one-handed burst back at the gunmen in the Volkswagen. He scored on the windshield of the van, the driver swerving into the curb.

The driver of the white van spotted him. Niles saw the man's shoulders move and he anticipated the right-hand turn onto a side street. He forced the Land Rover through a smoking-tire turn. Only fifty meters behind the white Toyota, he accelerated, racing through a quiet neighborhood of shops and apartments. The random shelling of the city had cleared the neighborhood streets of traffic.

A hand dropped a grenade from the van. Niles saw the steel oval bounce off the asphalt and go high over him. An instant behind him, the grenade banged. Bits of spent shrapnel tapped the Land Rover. He saw the brake lights of the van flash red. The tires smoked as the van swayed through an extreme left turn onto another street.

The street intersected at an angle. Niles guessed the Palestinian driver would follow the street back to the Corniche and then race for a crossing into West Beirut. He downshifted and drifted through the turn, sideswiping a parked car. The white van pulled ahead.

One-handed, Niles shoved the muzzle of the Kalashnikov

through the shattered windshield. The foregrip rested on the dashboard. The plastic and glass laminate of the safety glass held the rifle in place. On the straightaway of the street, he pointed the muzzle at the back tires of the van and hoped for a lucky hit as he squeezed off a round.

A long streak appeared in the hood of the Land Rover. But ahead, he saw thousands of bits of glass falling from the back window of the Toyota van. The van wobbled, then skidded through another left-hand turn. Niles did not risk Chardon's life by firing again. He powered through the turn, staying close behind the van.

They paralleled another park. Beyond the trees and walkways, Niles saw the Corniche. If they made the Corniche, they had only a one kilometer race to a crossing. Niles floored the accelerator.

More grenades came from the van. One went under a parked car and exploded, the other bounced high. The small charge popped above and behind the Land Rover. Dozens of bits of steel shrapnel punched holes in the aluminum of the roof.

A muzzle flashed from the back window of the Toyota and bits of the windshield cut Niles. He whipped the Land Rover from side to side to deny the gunman an easy target.

Then he saw the red Volkswagen van coming head-on. Standing on the brakes, controlling the skid with one hand while he grabbed the Kalashnikov with the other, he sprayed full-automatic fire at the Volkswagen. But he did not stop the driver from turning and blocking the street.

Two men left the far side of the Volkswagen. Niles jerked the steering wheel to the side, aiming the Land Rover for a space between two parked cars. He knocked a headlight off a Fiat and got the front wheels of the Land Rover over the curb, then bullets hammered the side, smashing the windows and filling the interior with flying glass.

Niles threw open the other door. Pulling out the Kalashnikov, he dodged around the parked cars as he reloaded the rifle. Bursts of fire raked the cars. Glass sprayed around him. He sprinted past the Volkswagen, the gunmen leaving their positions to follow him. Niles spun and threw himself flat. A gunman ran from between two cars and Niles dropped him with two shots through the chest. Blood frothed from the wounds and the dying gunman called out as he reached for his Kalashnikov. Niles triggered a coup de grâce.

Bullets smashed into the car shielding Niles. On his knees and one hand, Niles scrambled to the dead man. He dropped down flat behind the dead man's body as bullets punched into sheet metal and chipped concrete. A Palestinian teenager ran across the street, spraying full automatic fire from his Kalashnikov to cover his dash. Niles fired a long burst, the ComBloc slugs shattering the running boy's legs. Legs bending at impossible angles, his hand convulsively emptying his rifle, he fell in the street and screamed.

Niles pulled a new magazine from the pocket of the dead man and jammed it into his rifle. In the street, the wounded boy pleaded for help. Niles searched for other Palestinians.

The driver of the Volkswagen lay against the steering wheel, blood draining from bullet holes in his face and chest. Niles saw no one else in the street. Looking behind him, through the trees of the park, he saw the Corniche. But the white Toyota van—carrying Chardon—had gone.

Rifle ready at his hip, Niles ran back to the Land Rover. Bullets had ripped both back tires. He ran to the Volkswagen. The dead man's foot kept the engine going steady. Niles went around to the driver's side. Then behind him, he heard the wounded Palestinian teenager.

The boy lay where he fell, his voice rising and falling with cries for help. Niles went to him and looked at his wounds. Though the bullets had shattered bones in both legs, the blood flow had slowed. He would not bleed to death.

Niles had lost Chardon. But this teenage militiaman knew where the kidnappers had taken her.

Checking the Palestinian quickly for concealed weapons, Niles grabbed an arm and dragged him to the Volkswagen. The boy screamed and pleaded every time the motion twisted his legs. Using the dead driver's belt, Niles tied the boy's hands behind his back and heaved him into the Volkswagen.

Neighborhood people watched from windows and doorways, no one daring to call out, as Niles transferred his equipment and Chardon's possessions into the Volkswagen and raced away from the scene.

As he drove, he turned to the wounded teenager: "You are alone. The others abandoned you. I have questions. Answer my questions and I will take you directly to a doctor. Lie and I will return and kill you. Stay silent and I will make you answer. And believe me, you will answer. Answer now and I promise you a doctor and a hospital."

Before Niles reached the Lebanese compound near the Beirut International Airport, the Palestinian had told him of Iziz Kalaq and his offices overlooking the Ramlet el-Baida.

Following the code names and commercial phrases established by the dead Zargar, Rajai typed cablegram instructions. An organizational chart handwritten by Zargar provided the actual names of the leaders and groups. Rajai had cross-checked the chart against the code sheet and the schedule of mobilization prepared by Zargar, But Rajai had rewritten the schedule the night before. He had not wasted time plotting an exact hour-by-hour timetable—it meant nothing in the execution of the attack. In rewriting the schedule, he subordinated all movements of secondary personnel to the loading and departure of the aircraft. Now the cablegrams went to each group.

Security did not allow him to delegate this task to Hasani. The series of cablegrams directly linked the Foreign Ministry office to the several groups assembling at the remote airfield in Colombia. For that reason, Rajai typed the forms himself—in the business jargon of Arabic, French, and English. The forms then went into diplomatic pouches bound for Iranian embassies in Cairo, Paris, and London. Non-Iranian operatives would take the forms to local offices and pay cash. If American antiterrorist investigators discovered the identities of the groups in Colombia, they could trace the forces back to their headquarters in Paris or Beirut or Geneva, and then the directives ordering the assembly to the cable offices—but no farther. The plan conceived by the mullahs and the Pasdaran commanders eliminated any chance of retaliation by the United States.

In the future, this would change. Rajai wanted a war with

the Americans. Only after the devastation of his country could he sever Iran from its history and religion. That war would be Year Zero and the first year of the future . . .

Fatigue brought these dreams to Rajai as he typed. Outside, he heard the traffic of Tehran, the trucks, the whining motor scooters, the blaring of horns. He heard telephones ringing in the other offices. He almost did not notice the ringing of his own telephone in the outer office. He waited for Hasani to answer. The ringing continued. Rajai picked up the nearest telephone on his desk, but heard nothing. He tried the second telephone, a modern European telephone with buttons and indicator lights for various lines. He punched buttons but the ringing did not stop.

Rajai rushed to the outer office. The door to the corridor stood open. Early morning clerks and bureaucrats glanced inside the office as they passed, noting the slim, well-dressed young man who had taken over the duties of the assassinated Zargar. Rajai grabbed the ringing telephone. He heard the voice of an international operator, then Moinfar spoke from Baalbek:

"It has been difficult to call you. The lines from Baalbek are very bad. The woman Chardon called and asked to talk with you."

"From where did she call?"

"The operator told me Beirut. Chardon told me she worked for you. She says she must speak with you."

"I have nothing to say to her. In the past, I used her. But now she has betrayed us to the Americans."

"I am not arguing for this woman, Rajai. But perhaps it is different than we believe. She said she brought the American here to gain his trust. Those are her words. She said she has a chance to arrange the capture of an aide to the American president."

"Forget the woman, she is no longer your concern. A team of technicians will bring radio equipment today. They will need a room for the equipment in my villa."

"It will be done."

"I return to Baalbek in two days. The equipment must be functioning then." Another telephone line rang. "Attend to that work. I will return in two days."

Rajai broke the connection. An international operator announced another call from Lebanon. This time the call came from Kalaq in Beirut:

"The woman is with us."

"Very good. You have your instructions."

"She tells us that she is working for you."

"That is a lie."

"I do not want there to be an error. I saw her fight with the American. She freed herself and ran to my squad. She says she took the American to Baalbek as a trick. You say this is a lie?"

Rajai closed his eyes against his fatigue. "Did I not tell you that you would leave Lebanon today?"

"My main unit is already in Damascus. They wait for instructions. If not for this job with the woman, I would be with them."

"Then why do you listen to the lies of that whore? There is no time to waste. Do as you were instructed."

"Then she lies?"

"And what of the American?"

"I will know soon."

"What?"

"I don't think he lived."

"You do not know?"

"It was only minutes ago. He attempted desperately to escape and I dispatched squads to take him. My men have not yet reported."

"Do as I instructed and join your men in Damascus. One other instruction. A joke on Miss Chardon. Did she have her camera and tape recorder with her?"

"No camera. No film. No tape."

"Do you have a camera there?"

"Yes."

"Photograph the interrogation. And record it."

Through the thousands of kilometers of telephone line, Rajai heard Kalaq laugh. "I will, my friend, I will. It will be my pleasure."

14

FOLLOWING the natural features of the jagged West Beirut coastline, the Avenue de General de Gaulle curves past a series of parks and beaches, runs straight along the Ramlet el-Baida beach, then rises to a hill jutting into the Mediterranean. The ten-story apartment tower used for offices by the UNESCO staff—and the Popular Front militia commanded by Iziz Kalaq—overlooked the Avenue de Gaulle and the north end of the Ramlet el-Baida beach.

Shaffik Hijazi stopped the delivery van at the side of the avenue. Sergeant Vatsek rode with him. Both the sergeant and the Lebanese Army lieutenant wore street clothes and Syrian web gear—the uniform of the Moslem militias. Niles had described the clothing of the Palestinians and the two men had dressed to match the description. Vatsek could not hide his size or foreign face, but he no longer looked like an American Marine.

They studied the front of the building. The foundations and parking lot of the office building had been cut into the hillside. From the avenue, Hijazi and Vatsek looked down on the entrance. Vatsek motioned for Hijazi to continue. Hijazi eased the van forward as Vatsek watched for the perfect angle on the Palestinians guarding the entrance of the office building.

"Stop, this is it."

The guards manned a sandbagged position outside the entry doors. One man paced on the concrete walkway. The other leaned back in a chair, reading a magazine. Unlike the gunmen described by Niles, the Palestinians wore keffiyahs—the black-on-white patterned headcloths of the PLO.

255

Vatsek watched for other guards in the sandbagged enclosure or militiamen inside the first-floor lobby. Seeing no other men on the ground level, he scanned the ten floors of balconies. He saw no one looking down.

In the distance, the artillery fire and explosions continued. The Christian radio had denounced the random shelling as terrorism. A Phalangist colonel threatened unrestrained retaliation on West Beirut. The Islamic leaders vowed to unleash the massed firepower of all the militias if the Christians did not end their terrorism. The threats and counterthreats had cleared the streets of traffic.

"Only four cars in the parking lot. Think the militia assholes closed down the city again?"

"There is talk of a truce."

"Truce, shit." Vatsek keyed a hand-radio. "In position. Wait one."

With a kit manufactured by the Swedish company of Interdynamics, Vatsek converted a scope-fitted M-16 rifle into a silent weapon. The black aluminum cylinder of the suppressor slipped down over the rifle's flash suppressor and locked. Then he loaded the rifle with a magazine of twenty Interdynamic reduced-charge 5.56mm cartridges. The reduced powder charges propelled the 5.3gram bullets at the subsonic velocity of two hundred seventy-five meters per second. The low gas pressure produced by the cartridges did not cycle the bolt, which eliminated the mechanical noise of the rifle. Vatsek pulled back the charging handle, then eased the bolt forward. He listened to the bolt chamber the first round. He thumbed up the safety and buzzed the others:

"Ready to go. Got two pukes in sight. No others outside. Don't see any on the first floor. Don't see anyone watching from upstairs. No civilians. This will be a walk-in."

"Think so?" Niles answered. "We shall see. Moving."

"Watch for me," Vatsek said to Hijazi. He took a last glance at the avenue. Wind swept the exhaust from the cars and trucks to the west. Papers blew west. Then he levered open a vent window and pulled a dark blanket over his head and arms and the rifle. "The second they drive into the lot, you got to let me know . . ."

Seen from the office buildings a few blocks away, Vatsek's

blanket-covered form inside the van would be only a shadow. A hundred meters away, the seated guard turned a page. The other man looked up at the van.

"Oh, shit."

"What?"

"One of the pukes is eyeballing us."

"The captain and the sergeant, their car—"

Vatsek saw the guard turn toward the parking lot entrance. Putting the plastic butt of the M-16 to his shoulder, Vatsek squinted through the telescopic sight and set the cross hairs on the Palestinian guard's temple. Vatsek had confidence in the zero of the sight. Lieutenant Stark had brought the Interdynamics kit from Washington three days before with the hand-radios and cameras. Shooting two 20-round magazines of the reduced-charge cartridges, the sergeant had proved to himself that—allowing for wind—he could put one of the low-velocity silent bullets within the 7-ring of a target first shot and every shot at one hundred meters.

But the man walked forward, taking several steps toward the parking lot. Vatsek put the sight on the reading man's forehead. He watched the smoke from the guard's cigarette swirl to the west. To allow for both drop and wind drift, Vatsek moved the cross hairs over to the hair above the man's ear.

"The car is stopped."

Vatsek saw the second guard watching the parking lot. Holding the cross hairs steady above the ear of the seated guard, Vatsek focused his will on the temple, imagining the thin bones and membranes protecting the brain, and he exhaled, slowly easing the trigger back.

He felt the cartridge fire and watched the head of the guard jerk to the side. The man did not move. Leaning back against the sandbags, his feet propped up on other sandbags, he seemed to sleep. The magazine slid from his hands. Vatsek pulled back the charging handle to chamber the next round and sighted on the back of the other guard's head.

Beyond the guard, he saw Captain Niles parking the battered old Mercedes. Vatsek put the cross hairs slightly to the left side of the guard's head and squeezed off the shot.

257

Staggering, the Palestinian fell—but not dead. Vatsek jerked back the charging handle and aimed again, putting the cross hairs on the man's forehead as he struggled to his feet, his face twisted with pain and shock. The second bullet punched through his right eye and he fell. Vatsek chambered another subsonic round and watched the guard through the cross hairs until he saw hands lift the dead man to his feet.

"They are there." Hijazi started the engine and let the van coast backward downhill.

At the parking lot entrance, he lurched forward into the lot, then parked the van next to the doors of the stairwell at the side of the building.

Throwing open the door before the van stopped, Vatsek rushed to the door and tried the knob. Locked. Hijazi left the van with his Kalashnikov ready.

Palestinians opened the door and Vatsek grabbed the muzzle of a rifle, pushing the rifle to the side as he snapped his leg up to kick—and he realized he faced Captain Niles in a bloody keffiyah.

"Be cool, King Kong!" Alvarez told him. He took the keffiyah off his head and passed the black-and-white cloth to Vatsek.

As the others went up the concrete and steel stairs, Vatsek wound the blood-damp cloth around his head and neck. He had served in Beirut throughout the summer and fall of 1983 but the Middle Eastern sun had not tanned his White Russian skin. And the sun only bleached his white blond hair whiter. Leaving only his eyes showing, he wrapped the cloth across the face. He smelled the hair oil and mints of the man he had killed and wondered if the man's family lived in the Palestinian ghettos north of the airport.

They took the stairs quickly, going directly to the tenth floor where Kalaq the leader had his apartment and offices. There, when he heard the sound coming from beyond the stairwell door, Vatsek stopped thinking about the families of the men he had killed minutes before.

The woman's scream continued without end, piercing the concrete walls of the building, echoing in the ten-floor-high stairwell column.

Alvarez tried the steel fire door. It did not open. Going to one knee, he peered into the three-millimeter gap between the door frame and the door. He studied the latching mechanism, then took out his knife. He slipped the blade into the gap and levered the mechanism. But the door did not open.

The scream stopped. In the silence, they heard laughter. Then, the scream came again. Alvarez struggled with the latch. The blade snapped. He jammed the blade into the latch and tried again.

As the scream echoed, Vatsek looked at Captain Niles. Niles stared at the locked door, his face showing nothing, but his eyes seeming to stare through the door at what happened beyond. And as Vatsek watched Niles, the scream shuddered and caught, then echoed again.

The captain closed his eyes, as if unwilling to imagine what happened. But Vatsek knew Captain Niles still saw the torture, eyes open or closed.

Peeling away the plastic paper, Kalaq stood with Hussain and Mohammed and watched the image emerge from the chemical film. First came the brilliant orange of the highway flare. Then the white of the woman's body. In the conference room, Chardon shrieked and pleaded, her words incoherent and rattling—her screams had torn her throat. Kalaq and two of his men watched the chemical process define the details: the strange, twisted lines of her limbs as she tried to escape from the searing pain, the blood around the reinforcing rod hammered through her hands and feet and into the table, the faces of the fedayeen gathered around the woman.

"This will be very amusing to the Iranian." Kalaq passed the camera to his aide Hussain. "Here. Take more. For me. For all of us. Use all the film. I must have photos for the comrades in Damascus."

Mohammed stared at the image of the Frenchwoman suffering. "And one for me. I want to remember that woman."

Kalaq laughed and clasped the man's shoulder. "Was she not as I said? Did she not tremble like a young girl? You must come with me to Europe. The women love the fedayeen—"

Shots cut off his jokes. At the end of the corridor, Kalaq

saw dust drifting around the emergency door. Plaster fell away from the door frame. The interior surface of the door had buckled and warped. Behind him, Mohammed moved reflexively, punching the elevator buttons, then grabbing Kalaq and jerking him toward the opening doors of the elevator.

They heard the second burst of automatic fire as the elevator doors slid closed.

Alvarez reached into the bullet-smashed hole and pulled the door open, then Niles ran into the corridor. The shooting had warned the Palestinians. In the confined space, he and the other Marines had no chance if he did not hit fast and hard.

A group of Palestinians stood in the center of the building. Niles sprinted at them, spraying fire from his Kalashnikov, the high-velocity slugs gouging the walls, shattering ceiling lights, throwing the men backward. When the bolt closed on the empty chamber, Niles threw himself flat on the carpeting.

Boots ran past him, Vatsek firing his rifle on automatic, raking the corridor. Hijazi followed. Niles jammed a new magazine into his Kalashnikov and shouldered the rifle, watching the doorways over the sights. A Palestinian appeared, rifle rising, and Niles squeezed off a single shot to the head as Vatsek turned and sprayed the doorway with a burst. Dead twice, the Palestinian fell back.

"Some of them got in the elevator!" Vatsek shouted out.

"We can't chase them." Niles ran to an open door and went flat against the wall.

A gunman inside the office fired out, slugs denting the polished stainless steel of the elevaotr. Plaster exploded in front of Niles's face as a line of bullets punched through the wall. Niles stumbled back and dropped down. Aiming from the floor, he angled his fire through the wall and up. A man screamed.

Vatsek rushed past the doorway and turned, firing two- and three-shot bursts into the office.

"Stop firing!" Niles shouted out in Arabic. "Surrender and you live!"

Moving too quick to see, Vatsek kicked something and then fired through the doorway again. Niles realized the sergeant had kicked a grenade back into the office. The bang shattered the windows and sent dust clouding into the corridor.

Niles dove through the doorway and hit a dead man. Crawling through the dust and smoke, he saw silhouettes against the window overlooking the Mediterranean. He fired low, dropping the men with bullets to the legs. They fell through the shattered sliding glass doors. Another burst came from the doorway and a Palestinian collapsed across the table.

The firing stopped and Niles heard only the gasping of wounded men. And despite the acrid cordite smoke in the air, he smelled another stink—burnt flesh.

"Oh, Mother of God," Alvarez choked.

Standing, Niles saw Chardon crucified to the table naked, with her arms and legs outstretched. He saw the bullet hole in her head that had ended her life. He saw Vatsek look at the dead woman's crotch and then turned away. Smoke stinking of burnt flesh and phosphorus rose from her abdomen, and Niles gagged on the stench and the understanding of what the Palestinians had done to the woman.

"Check for weapons," Niles shouted out. "Find the ones that are alive and keep them alive. Search through those other offices. Fast! We got to get out of here."

He turned to the gunmen he had shot at the sliding glass doors. One of the Palestinians had fallen on an upjutting blade of glass. Already gray with blood loss, he would die in minutes. The other man, semiconscious, called out to his god for an end to the pain of his shattered legs.

Niles looked to the balcony. An unconscious and bleeding man had a rifle in his hands. Niles reached out and took the weapon and a shot tore past his face. Looking out again, he saw a Palestinian on the next balcony beating at a glass door with the butt of his Kalashnikov. A rifle fired inside the office and the Palestinian staggered back and flipped over the railing. Niles scanned the other balconies before stepping out.

Looking down, he saw a white van racing across the

parking lot. Niles aimed and fired a burst. The van did not stop. Setting the fire-selector lever to semi-auto, he held the sights of the Kalashnikov on the roof over the driver and fired single shots until he emptied the rifle. The van turned onto the avenue. Niles grabbed a fixed-stock rifle and fired again as the van labored up the hill. But he did not stop the escaping Palestinians.

"We got one with a camera," Vatsek called out to the captain. "He has pictures of her with that flare in her—"

Going to the sergeant, he saw Vatsek holding a bleeding man against the wall, his huge hand clamped in the Palestinian's hair. Niles reloaded his folding-stock Kalashnikov. He chambered the first round and put the muzzle of the rifle under the Palestinian's chin.

"I was told to photograph," the Palestinian pleaded in English, his words becoming a wail. "It was my commander who did that terrible thing. Not me. I beg you, don't punish me for the crime of my leader. I am not—"

Niles jammed the rifle muzzle into the man's throat. The coughing, choking Palestinian held up his hands, as if praying. He tried to fall to his knees but Vatsek held him upright. "Who is your leader?"

"Abu . . . Abu Jihad."

Shaking his head, Niles turned to Vatsek. "He's lying. Do something nonfatal to him. Fast."

"Oh, yeah?" Vatsek studied the Palestinian for a moment, looking at his stubby legs and middle-aged paunch, his round face and double chin. Then, in one motion, Vatsek brought up his boot high and stomped down with all his strength on the knee of the photographer. The man screamed as the knee snapped backward. Vatsek continued through to the floor, breaking the knee back to a ninety-degree angle.

Looking into the gasping and crying man's face, Niles asked again, "Who is your leader?"

Panting for breath, his body twisting with pain, he finally answered: "Iziz . . . Kalaq."

"Where is he?"

"The elevator. I saw . . . I saw him in the elevator."

"Where did he go?"

"I . . . I do not know."

"Lying again. Do the stomp, Kong."

Screaming, the broken leg flopping, pivoting on the other leg and trying to push the Americans away, the photographer struggled. Vatsek stomped the other knee and dropped the Palestinian to the carpet, both knees bent backward.

"Where did he go?"

"Damascus!" He screamed out answers through the pain. "There are fedayeen . . . a unit waiting there . . . for orders from Rajai."

"Orders for what?"

"It is . . . unknown. The Iranian keeps it all secret. The photos . . . of the woman were for him. For him. He ordered the woman killed. I only did what . . . my leader told—"

"How many fighters in the unit?"

"Many. Twenty, thirty. Rajai wanted many men. Kalaq said . . . it would be a glorious victory against America, a strike . . . to be remembered in the history of the world—"

"Where?"

"It is unknown. A secret. Only the Iranian Rajai knows."

"And Kalaq."

"No . . . no . . . he does not know. He said he will not know until he arrives at the—at the place of assembly, where all the forces join together."

"What forces?"

"Comrades of the international struggle."

"Congratulations, comrade," Niles told the Palestinian. "You have won back your life. If you continue to cooperate, you will live. Sergeant, this comrade leaves with us."

"Not my comrade," Vatsek countered.

"Figure of speech . . ." Niles called out to the others. "Hey-zoot, Lieutenant. Gather papers, information, anything. We're getting out of here."

"These are offices," Alvarez shouted back. "I'm looking at filing cabinets of papers."

Hijazi called out, "Captain, please come here."

Niles hurried to an adjoining office. An inner office had been papered with color photos of the Marine barracks devastated on 23 October. The montage of photos showed the gray ruin and the splashes of blood, the crews of workers trying to rescue the wounded and recover the dead, the rows of torn and dismembered young men. He recognized photos of himself. In one, he comforted a teenager dying under a concrete slab. In another, he walked from the door of the Command and Intelligence offices—Chardon had taken that photo. Niles went back to the crippled Palestinian. He kicked him in a broken knee:

"The office with all the photos of the bombing. Whose office is that?"

"The"—he gasped back pain—"the office of Kalaq."

"Hey-zoot, get what you can out of there. Empty out the drawers, find telephone numbers, whatever, anything personal. Sergeant—can you get our comrade down the stairs? I think a booby trap on the elevator is a fact."

"Ten flights with that shit on my back?"

"Ten flights down."

"Will do. What about these others? The ones that aren't dead?"

Niles looked again at the outspread corpse of the young woman. He remembered Chardon holding him and shaking with fear as the Revolutionary Guards laughed. She had tried to make money off her radical contacts. Maybe she had tried to sell him out to the radicals or the Iranians, maybe not. But no one deserved the death she had suffered.

Crossing the office to a wounded man, Niles shot him.

One of the bullets had hit Mohammed in the back. Passing at an extreme angle through his body, the bullet tore through his lung and stomach before exiting through the left-hand pocket of his jacket. He had managed to continue driving for a block despite the wound. Kalaq pulled him away from the steering wheel and pushed him into the back of the van. He paused to wipe the blood off the seat before driving on.

Mohammed vomited blood and gasped out, "The University hospital . . ."

"No! The Americans will go there. It was Americans who attacked the office."

"I must . . . go to a hospital, Iziz."

"I will take you to our hospital. You will be safe there."

"It was . . . Americans?"

"I am sure," Kalaq lied. "I recognized the one with the

beard. The squads sent to capture him failed. They will be severely punished."

Kalaq drove over the concrete and earth planter dividing the north- and southbound lanes of the avenue. He did not want to waste time in the crowded streets of the metropolitan area. Flooring the accelerator, he raced south again, speeding downhill past the offices. He looked up at the tenth-floor balcony but saw nothing extraordinary. No riflefire came down at the van. Accelerating to the maximum speed of the van, he wove around the few cars on the avenue and continued south.

Retching and gasping, Mohammed struggled to breathe. His face went gray. Kalaq glanced back at his comrade. He saw no life—only the staring eyes and motionless chest of a corpse. He checked his watch—he had no time to deliver a dead man to a hospital.

Ahead, where a line of low cliffs interrupted the shoreline, the avenue curved east. Trash and the hulks of gutted cars covered the undeveloped area. Feral dogs searched through garbage. Kalaq stopped the van at the curve in the avenue. He jerked open the sliding side door and pulled out Mohammed.

The arm moved—Mohammed still lived. But Kalaq had no time for his dying fedayeen. He must speed to join his unit in Damascus. He could not stop at a hospital. Nor could he delay in Beirut to avenge the criminal attack on his office. The national cause of his people and the glorious mission he undertook in the name of liberation required his personal leadership. His fedayeen waited for him to lead them into battle against the Americans.

Dragging the bleeding man across the hard-packed earth, Kalaq dropped him behind a heap of concrete and rusting metal. A pack of dogs watched.

Running back to the van, Kalaq sped away, rushing to Damascus.

In a cubicle in the Marine Battalion Headquarters, Niles called Colonel Devlin in Washington—waking him at 2 A.M.—and brief him via a trans-Atlantic secure line. The electronics made the voice of the colonel monotonic, unnatural. After he had detailed his observations from the Bekaa, the story from Chardon, he then told of the interrogation of the man captured in the Popular Front office.

"Thirty militiamen?"

"That's what he told me, Colonel. Thirty Popular Front gunmen waiting for a signal to fly out. They won't know where they're going until they get there. But they will be working with gangs from other countries."

"What countries?"

"No way to know yet."

"About Baalbek, it is your opinion not to attempt the capture?"

"It is very likely a one-way trip. The woman got me in. Luck got me out. Luck and the disorganization of the Iranians. We can't count on that again. That's why the death of the woman is a catastrophe. She was the connection to the Iranian. The Iranian travels in and out of Baalbek. If we could track him in Beirut or in Europe, we could get him, no problem. But even if we went into Baalbek, there'd be the chance he wouldn't be there. Hate to talk negative, but there it is."

"Can we assume the leader of the Popular Front unit also has contacts with him?"

"Yes, sir. The woman told me that the Iranian introduced her to the Palestinian."

"Then the Palestinian is another link."

"But he's in Damascus, waiting for instructions to fly out."

"If you could capture the Palestinian, he could direct you to the Iranian."

"Sir, I have the Frenchwoman's papers. Notes, addresses, phone numbers. I can backtrack through her work. I can find others who had contact with the Iranian. I'll find him eventually."

"You don't have the time. The president's pulling the Marines out of Beirut. You—and all the Marines and all the soldiers of the multinational force—have reached the end of your service in Beirut."

"Sir, I'm out of all that. I'm operating on my own. I'm willing to stay on."

For a moment, he heard only line static as Colonel Devlin considered his offer. "Captain, you have been compromised by the Frenchwoman. We must assume the Popular Front and the Iranians will target you for capture or assassination."

"Target me? I'm an American. All Americans are targets. What's the difference if they know my name or not?"

"Captain, you are a very brave and dedicated soldier. We will study the situation as it emerges. But the American presence in Lebanon is ending. Prepare for reassignment of your team."

"As a team? With the others?"

"Of course. If you remain in Lebanon, you will not work alone. If we employ you in other actions, your team will continue working together. You speak Spanish?"

"¡Claro que sí!"

"And the other men?"

"Both sergeants. Check the file of the lieutenant for his Spanish. You need us in Central America?"

"There's a Customs Department case involving the illegal export of explosives. By an Englishman who works for the Iranians. Since this involves Iranians, the case was finally routed to my attention. Would you be willing to do this? A textbook Recon assignment?"

"An Englishman buying American explosives for Iranians? Any chance it's related?"

"We will be watching for the movement of the Palestinians into the area. How much advance time would you need to act on this?"

"Send a plane. We'll go. Put the lieutenant to assembling the equipment we'll need. But when we're done, I want to come back to work here. I remember that we lost hundreds of men here and that we haven't got the murderers yet."

Syrian Army soldiers guarded the transit lounge. Inside, Kalaq and the thirty fedayeen of the Popular Front waited. All through the day, they paced or talked of the action or slept on the bare wooden benches. Crumpled packs of cigarettes and hundreds of butts littered the floor.

In the evening, soldiers brought a meal of lukewarm tea

and bread with greasy rice. The officer supervising the guards refused to hear questions about their departure. After nine at night, Kalaq demanded to call the Popular Front offices in the downtown Cassion Hotel. The Syrians ignored him. Hour after hour, the fedayeen watched the lights of jets taxiing on the airfield, the noise of the engines waking the men who slept. Other Palestinians paced and talked, arguing their future in shouts.

The activity of the airport continued while they waited, flight announcements echoing in the corridor, passengers rushing to other lounges. The people represented all the nations of the Islamic world, men in the traditional white, women wearing the gray chadors of Pakistan, the colorful silk of South Asia, or the severe black of Iran. Others wore the styles of Europe. Kalaq watched them. They passed without a thought to the fighters held prisoner by the Syrians—he, who would fight for the cleansing of their world of the Zionists and Americans, he did not merit their interest. Only a European with a backpack stopped to look into the lounge at the fedayeen. The soldiers shoved him on his way without a word.

After midnight, the sounds of the airport went quiet. Only Kalaq remained awake. He smoked his last cigarette and tried to sleep on one of the benches. But the chill of the lounge kept him shivering. He returned to pacing, alone, stumbling with fatigue. He had not slept for days—organization details had kept him working throughout the past nights, the call to capture Chardon had come after only an hour's sleep, then the fighting and the long drive to Damascus. With the cold and his rage at the long, unexplained wait, he would not sleep this night.

Kalaq heard the soldiers demand identification, then a small man in a wrinkled black suit entered the lounge. He wore an old, fur-collared coat over his shoulder like a cape and carried a battered leather valise.

"Are you the contract workers from Lebanon?"

"Who are you?"

"Your travel agent. Who did you think I was?"

"I am Iziz Kalaq. Do you have a message for me?"

The agent glanced at a list. "No message. Only a ticket. To Italy."

"When will the plane come?"

"Tonight, tomorrow. There is a schedule with the ticket."

"Why have you come so late? We have waited many hours."

"Because this work took many hours. You think I have a computer? Wake the others."

As the men said their names, the agent checked a list and distributed the tickets. Some men went to Athens, then to Madrid. Others flew first to Cairo, then to Rome. Others went to Athens, then Rome, then Paris. No more than three men traveled on the same flight. The Palestinians turned to Kalaq. He signaled for the men to stay silent. The agent finished the distribution of the tickets. But when the agent left, Kalaq faced the questions of his fedayeen.

"The action will be in Europe?"

"Why is my ticket to France?"

"Why do we go to Italy?"

"They are scattering us everywhere!"

"My fighters! We are soldiers in a larger and grander plan. We must take the directions of the commanders. Understand that security does not allow for every man to know every detail. You knew this when you accepted your roles in the action. Now we know we are moving onward toward our destiny and our—"

"You!" a Syrian officer shouted out. He pointed at Kalaq. "A telephone call for you."

"This will be the explanation."

Soldiers escorted him to a telephone in the corridor. "This is Iziz Kalaq speaking."

"Did you receive the tickets?"

He did not recognize the voice. By the quality of the line tone, he guessed that the caller spoke from Damascus. "Yes, but only to Europe."

"Friends will meet your men as they leave their planes. They are to take the tickets and documents and continue. Is that clear?"

"What is the final destination?"

The line went dead. Kalaq clicked the receiver but the caller did not speak again. The soldiers took him back to the lounge. Smiling to his men, he declared, "Our patience is rewarded. From here, we travel quickly."

Fifty kilometers south of Riohacha, Peter Deak spotted the truck and trailer on the highway. The electronic pulse of the tracer confirmed his sighting. Taking the Piper Malibu up to a thousand meters over the swamps and rain forest, he cut his airspeed almost to stall. To the west, the Sierra Nevada de Santa Marta towered high above his plane. His altitude gave him a view of the convoluted valleys and ridges of the eastern ranges of the Sierra Nevadas and the peaks of the Sierra de Perija in the far distance.

Deak, a career officer with the Drug Enforcement Administration and a three-year veteran of the dope wars in Colombia, kept the truck in sight as the Malibu bucked updrafts. But the small plane had much more speed than this surveillance required. The truck never made more than one hundred kilometers per hour on the gravel highway. Minute by minute, even at stall speed, the plane gained on the truck, then left it behind. As the truck started the long, zigzagging upgrade to the thousand-meter-high crest of a ridge, its speed fell to only a few kilometers per hour. Deak climbed to three thousand meters and radioed to San Juan del César, thirty kilometers to the south.

"This is Malibu One, calling from the River plus fifty." The River meant Riohacha, fifty the kilometers from the town. "Is the man waiting at the crossroads?"

"That he is. Repeat, he is at the crossroads."

"Then I'm coming in. He can do the roadwork."

Ten minutes later, he brought the Malibu down at the asphalt airfield outside of San Juan del César, a small town at an intersection of highways. One road cut straight south from the coast, then meandered through the mountains. The other road ran northeast through the long César Valley to the Venezuelan border. Contrabandistas driving from the smuggling center of Maicao on the Venezuelan-Colombian border stopped at San Juan del César for beer and diesel fuel before continuing to the interior of Colombia with their untaxed trade goods.

The location of San Juan also served the DEA. Colombian nationalism required an isolated facility for the North Americans enforcing the drug laws of the United States. Using funds allocated by Congress for military aid, the DEA scraped the site out of the jungle, paved the airstrip, erected prefab hangars and offices, fenced the airstrip with chain link and razor wire, then applied tons of defoliant to the perimeter. A few platoons of Colombian soldiers guarded the *norteamericanos* from the local gangsters.

Heat radiated from the blacktop in silver, shimmering flashes. At eleven degrees north of the equator, the sun heated the field to incandescence every day before nine. Deak left the Malibu in the care of the technicians and walked through gusts of heat to the prefab quarters. He felt the heat of the asphalt through the soles of his jungle boots.

A tall, thin man made thinner by the food and climate, Deak no longer filled the slacks and shirts he ordered through a New York catalogue. But he had not adjusted his waist or neck size because he liked the comfort of loose clothing in the extreme humidity of the Guajira Peninsula. The loose cloth fluttered around his legs and torso. Despite the comfort, the temperature and humidity left him wet with sweat in seconds.

The air-conditioned cool of the office came like a wave. Here, inside the foam-insulated sheet-metal walls, the heat of the Colombian sun and the noise of the aircraft seemed distant. Deak saw Hector Alcaya—the day officer—studying teletype sheets while monitoring the radios. The humorless Cuban-American lived his work. A Marine Corps veteran, he had worked for a year as a Miami policeman before resigning in frustration at the impotence of law enforcement and the corruption of the community. He saw the drugs and the syndicates as a sin against God and country. Unlike Deak, Alcaya did not take the long view of the dope war:

"Look at this shit! These sons of bitches—" Alcaya pointed at a block of type on the long teletype sheet. "The

Colombians billed the administration for the use of a helicopter. A Huey! A Huey we gave them and we got to pay to use it."

"Makes sense to me." Deak took a liter of boiled water from the refrigerator. He dropped in a slice of lemon for flavor. "Think of all the money they lost."

"What money? Fuel and pilot time? We trained the pilots, we buy the fuel."

"A helicopter is a very valuable flying machine. They could be out moving coca paste if we didn't insist on enforcing laws. The operation may have inconvenienced them. Of course, they want us to pay."

"Sons of bitches. I say we nuke this shithole of a country."

"We don't have the warheads to do it. Besides, there are still some decent people here."

"Who? I want to know who."

Deak laughed. "Must be someone."

"Sodom and Colombia," Alcaya cursed.

"Relax. This is Guajira. You think like the States and you'll go crazy. Just to be here, we're winning. Any word from Jones?"

"He's north of the crossroads, waiting for that truck."

Deak considered the road downhill from the mountains. The road wound through valleys and hills. He did not remember any straight sections. "Truck won't pass him for another hour, minimum. And that's highballing. I'm going to go see a movie."

Weeks before, a raid on a jungle cocaine processing center had resulted in the seizure of tons of coca base, a processing factory, chemicals, and an entertainment center. Between shifts, the workers and guards had enjoyed an international selection of videotapes. Deak had personally overseen the destruction of the factory, using the kerosene and petroleum ether to incinerate the coca base and all the refining equipment. The colonel commanding the Colombian soldiers received the gang's weapons for resale to the death squads, the communist guerrillas, or other dope gangs—and the DEA officers took the video players, projection screens, and library of tapes.

RECON

Walt Disney's *Fantasia* needed no subtitles or dubbing. Deak lay back in an easy chair—taken from the personal quarters of a gang boss in another raid—and relaxed to the music and brilliant colors. The irony of enjoying a luxury captured from dopers amused him.

An hour later, the com-line woke him. Deak went back to the office. Alcaya told him, "No truck."

Deak took the radio microphone. "Crossroads, how's your radio reception?"

"Great, Malibu. Hearing you fine."

"Not me. The other radio station. You got the beat?"

"That's why I called in, sir. Heard it coming, getting stronger all the time, then it leveled out."

"But you still got it?"

"I got it. No malfunction."

"Well . . . damn. No more movies. See you in a while." Deak clicked off. "Got to go up there again. Maybe they parked for a siesta, maybe they broke down."

"And if they didn't?"

"I know where to look."

"Where?"

"Colombia."

Minutes later, at two thousand meters altitude, Deak followed the highway snaking through the low mountains. The impulses from the tracking unit in the container continued strong. The smugglers driving the truck had not found the pulse transmitter. Below him, he saw the intersection where a mud road to a village met the highway. He checked the agent watching the road:

"Crossroads, no traffic?"

"Yeah, traffic. Truckload of dopers hauling fertilizer to a farm."

"Don't jump to conclusions."

"Who else can afford fertilizer out here?"

"Your reasoning won't be admissible in court."

"Won't ever go to court."

"You young guys have an attitude problem."

Deak watched the black line of the road cutting through the rain forest. On both sides of the road, yellowed or blackened areas marked the efforts of the Colombian Department of Roads to defeat the forest with defoliants and fire. He passed over a steel bridge. The bridge went over a small river snaking down out of the mountains. He did not know the name of the river. The local people called it the Santo, but they also used that name for another river five kilometers to the south. The true Santo ran five hundred kilometers to the southwest, in the Magdalena Valley. Leaving the bridge far behind, he gained altitude quickly, scanning the zigzagging of the road up the eastern slopes of the Sierra Nevadas.

The pulse signal faded. Deak checked the signal. He had flown past the truck and trailer. Beneath him, he saw the vast panorama of forested mountains. Stark rocky crags with spots of snow crowned the Sierra Nevada de Santa Marta. The blue horizon of the Caribbean appeared to the north; he rose to five thousand meters, then banked through a long, slow turn, curving over the low mountains.

Reducing speed and altitude, he flew east-to-west, following the wide valley of a river. The pulse signal came strong. He saw the faint line of dirt road through the forest. Then he spotted the airstrip.

The gang had not cut a new airstrip. In the seventies, a marijuana syndicate had cut down the trees, burned the underbrush, and bulldozed a long landing strip. Regular flights had paid for the construction of a small village for the growers, processors, and laborers. Hidden between the mountains, cooled by winds down the valley, and with water from the river, the village did very well, making millions of dollars in the trade. But gang wars and government raids made the location—very close to the highway—undesirable. The syndicate abandoned the airfield. The first rains brought a regrowth of the saplings and palms. From time to time, other gangs cleared the brush and used the field for a few flights. But the development of hybrid sinsemilla marijuana in Hawaii, California, and Oregon depressed the international marijuana trade. The syndicates now concentrated on cocaine and operated from processing centers with less history and more concealment.

Deak scanned the edges of the clearings, looking for cars and trucks. A flash of reflected sunlight betrayed the truck and trailer. But a shadow covered part of the trailer. He focused binoculars on the trailer.

Men in green fatigues worked to cover the truck and trailer with camouflage netting. Deak did not change his speed or glide line. He continued west into the mountains, then circled back to the highway. Without breaking his radio silence, he returned to the San Juan del César airfield.

In the office, Deak unlocked the safe and took out a code book. He worked alone to write the message. The message went first to the Barranquilla office, then to Panama, then directly to Washington.

A courier hand-carried a decoded copy to Colonel Devlin.

15

AS the jet turned to the west, Niles looked back at the lights of Beirut. An escalation of the war of revenge between the militias had left many parts of the city without electricity. Without power, West Beirut remained black except for individual buildings with generators. Only kilometers away, thousands of lights defined the port and coast running north to Jounieh. Suburbs in the east remained lit. In the darkness south of the city, the crossed lines of the lights of the airport marked the Marine position. To Niles, the random pattern of the power failure created the image of a city shattered into sectors of light and darkness, the lights islands, the darkness like an ocean invading the land.

Exploding shells flashed in the blacked-out western sector. That morning, the Shias or Druze or Palestinians had car-bombed a Phalangist political office. The bombing had also killed or maimed several children walking to a school. The Phalangists took vengeance by firing hundreds of high-explosive shells into the slums of West Beirut—innocent, random victims avenged by killing and maiming innocent, random victims. Niles counted the flashes of explosions and multiplied by the kilograms of explosive per shell. He thought of high-velocity steel fragments shearing through flesh. More bodies for the morgues, more bandaged masses of suffering for the hospitals.

Then he thought of his year there and realized he and the Marines had only fought a delaying action against chaos. Hundreds of millions of dollars in military aid, thousands of Lebanese killed in militia wars, the sacrifice of hundreds of young Americans—all wasted.

276

"The City of Shit," Vatsek commented, staring out at the lights of ravaged Beirut. "Ragheads, Syrian Stalinists, Phalange Nazis, Iranian crazies, mystical motherfucking Druze—hope I never see your hellhole again."

Niles laughed. He stepped across the aisle to a swivel seat. The Air Force had modified the jet's passenger cabin for in-flight conferences. At the front bulkhead, the jet had six swiveling, reclining seats around a table for senior officers and diplomats. In the back, two lines of fixed, non-reclining seats faced the wide aisle. Fold-out tables provided work areas for every seat.

Across the wide center aisle, Niles saw Alvarez watching the city recede in the distance. He remembered the morning Alvarez had lost his platoon. The young sergeant had the same expression on his face now.

"At a moment of reflection and profound regret," Niles commented to Vatsek, "your obscene statement somehow—"

"Sorry, sir. I was just glad to be getting out."

Niles laughed again. "—somehow says it all."

"And what's there to regret?" Vatsek asked. "We're alive. I know a lot of guys who aren't."

"True, Sergeant. But there is the also the fact that we went in there to give a country a chance. And we failed."

"Not us. We didn't fail. We gave the people a chance. But the Lebanese let the gangs and gang bosses take their country away. You think people in the U.S. would let them take over a city?"

"Vatsek, I don't believe you understand the complexity of the problems. The colonial history, the religions, the dynamics of the religions and politics and class structure with the international forces."

"I don't care how complex it is. Beirut couldn't happen in the U.S.A. No gang would take over my town. I'd get together with the other guys and—"

"And make a militia," Alvarez interrupted.

"There it is, Sergeant Vatsek. Contradiction Number One. They all think their militia is the solution to the problem. Contradiction One of a list of a thousand contradictions." Niles looked past the sergeants to Lieutenant Stark, who sat at a back work table flipping through a notebook. "Lieutenant, the cablegram said you would provide a briefing in-flight."

Leaving his seat, the lieutenant walked to the front. As always, he looked like a Marine on a recruiting poster—perfect shave, pressed fatigues, mirror-polished boots. But days and nights of work in Washington had left his eyes bloodshot. He went to the tables at the front of the compartment and stepped over cardboard boxes and black fiberboard transit cases stacked under the table.

"Tired, Lieutenant?"

"No problem, sir. I'll get some sleep as we fly." Stark looked at a page in his notebook. He paused for seconds, staring at the typed sheet, then turned and pulled down a rolling map of the Western Hemisphere.

"Four days ago," the lieutenant began, his voice slow with fatigue, "a Panamanian-registered container ship docked at the Colombian port of Cartagena and off-loaded ten tons of a compound commonly called drilling mud. In fact, as determined by a combined Customs Department and Bureau of Alcohol, Tobacco, and Firearms investigation, the declared consignment of drilling compound conceals two tons of American-manufactured dynamite. The investigation began with the purchase of the dynamite by an Englishman who has acted in the past as an Iranian agent in the purchase of military ordnance for the war against Iraq. The investigation followed the dynamite from the United States, to Mexico, to Asia, then to South America.

"This dynamite has no military value.

"After the off-loading of the container at Cartagena," Stark pointed to the port on the Caribbean coast, then traced a highway running east along the coast, "a truck then transported the container of drilling compound east through the mountains. The DEA maintained surveillance of the truck from the moment the freighter docked to the time the truck parked at a jungle airfield fifty kilometers south of the town of Riohacha.

"The area exports coffee, tobacco, and bananas. There is now some oil exploration. However, the area is infamous for marijuana plantations and drug syndicates. The airfield was at one time used for planes carrying out loads of marijuana. DEA officers familiar with the airfield report a number of structures remaining from the time of gang activity."

"That's where the dynamite went?" Niles asked.

"Yes, sir."

"And that's where we'll be going."

"Yes, sir. Via Barranquilla. From Barranquilla, a transport plane will take us to San Juan del César. A helicopter will be waiting for us there. The helicopter will insert our squad a few kilometers from the airfield. The helicopter and pilot will wait on call while we remain in the field."

"And what role," Niles asked, "does the Colombian government have in this action?"

"No role. The government of Colombia will not be notified of our entry. Nor will they be notified of what we find. We will carry electronically encoded radios which make monitoring of our transmissions impossible."

"Encoded walkie-talkies?" Alvarez asked. "How do we decode ourselves?"

"The radio circuits encode and decode every transmission instantaneously. Any technician—of the government of Colombia or the enemy—will receive only static. Also, Sergeant Alvarez, as the squad electronics specialist, will carry a scanning unit capable of searching for and recording the transmissions of other radios. I will demonstrate the units during our flight."

Alvarez turned to the others. "Corps goes modern."

"We will wear civilian-market fatigues, use civilian-market equipment, and carry black-market weapons which I purchased from a dealer in Miami."

"Very interesting." Niles looked back to Vatsek and Alvarez. "This does sound like a covert operation, does it not?"

"This is serious." Alvarez nodded. "Marines getting twentieth-century radio equipment? Someone is serious."

Vatsek asked, "M-16s or Kalashnikovs?"

"New Colt Commando rifles," Stark answered. "One M-16 with an M-203 40mm grenade launcher."

"An over-and-under?" Vatsek reached out for the boxes. "That one is mine."

"All the Colt rifles have the new one-in-seven twist barrels. There are 9mm pistols. I can distribute the weapons for your inspection." He reached into a cardboard box and brought out a Colt Commando.

"I'll take that, Lieutenant." Niles jerked back the charging handle to confirm the empty chamber. "One question. The cablegram did not cover this. What do we do? What are the instructions from the colonel?"

"Observe and report. Also, there is an extraordinary threat involved. International sources reported a number of Palestinians in transit, via commercial airlines, to Colombia. It is believed—"

"Palestinians? From where?"

"That remains uncertain. The Europeans would not cooperate and the Latin nations did not have the resources to trace the backgrounds of the suspects."

"What about Iranians?"

"Possible. Again, no cooperation from the Europeans. It must be assumed Iranians will be involved. If you look at the map, you will see that the airfield is within easy flying distance of both the American embassy in Bogotá and the Canal Zone. Or the Guantánamo Naval Base on the south shore of Cuba. There is speculation that the Iranians—or their Palestinian proxies or the M-19—will attempt to strike on or before this Wednesday. The president will deliver his State of the Union address Wednesday evening. A major terrorist incident could cast a pall over the address, which is, of course, covered by the international press."

"A hit could upstage the president."

"Correct, Captain."

"Can't have that." Niles turned to the sergeants. "Gentlemen, you've heard the briefing. You wish to volunteer for this assignment?"

"Ready to go," Vatsek answered. "Payback on some Iranians is okay with me."

Alvarez nodded. "No Congressional debate, no United Nations resolutions. Fly in, do it. Fly out."

"And it may involve Iranians," Niles added. "What about that Farsi-speaking Marine, Lieutenant?"

"Waiting at Homestead Air Force Base, sir."

"Waiting?"

"For this plane. Didn't you intend for him to join the squad?"

"I want to talk to him before he goes with us."

"I brought his file, sir. And the comments of Colonel Devlin. The colonel personally interviewed Javenbach. And conducted a background check. You will read much more there than is usually found in a Marine's file."

Niles glanced through the collection of personnel records. He motioned for Vatsek and Alvarez to look over his shoulder as he read the typed sheets. "Ali Akbar Javenbach. Born 1963 in Hesar, a village outside of Tehran. Father imprisoned by Shah. Died in prison. Uncle imprisoned by Shah. 1979, freed uncle during riots—that's interesting. Older brother executed by Revolutionary Guards. Escaped with mother and younger brothers and sisters. Joined another uncle in the United States. Others in family disappeared during purges. Joined Marines on eighteenth birthday. Volunteered for Recon after one year in service. Qualified. Expressed intense ideological commitment to the ideals of the United States. Volunteered when offered Recon assignment—" Niles passed the folder back to the sergeants.

"I'll talk to him when he gets on the plane."

Guiding the Piper Cub over the grass of the narrow airstrip, the pilot steered for the trees. The moon-faced, acne-scarred Latin grinned at Kalaq. Waiting for the small plane to slow, Kalaq watched the onrushing green wall of trees and palms. The propeller chopped through the tall grass, bits of wet grass and leaves plastering the windshield. Kalaq saw the individual pale trunks of the trees and the tangles of hanging vines and he shouted out in Arabic, then Russian for the pilot to stop.

The pilot laughed and the plane spun. Kalaq hit the windshield. The pilot reached across him and opened the door. Hanging by his safety belt, Kalaq looked out at a waving field of grass. Latins and Palestinians in green fatigues watched from a few meters away.

Still laughing, the pilot told him in English to get out. Kalaq did not understand. The pilot pulled the latch of the safety belt and shoved Kalaq from his seat.

Dropping down to the dirt, Kalaq heard the engine rev behind him. Prop wind whipped the grass. The plane rolled away and in seconds lifted into the overcast sky. As the engine noise faded, he heard Arabic.

A young woman walked to him. Very young, slim, she looked like a teenager in her olive drab fatigues. She wore an Uzi slung over her shoulder.

"Iziz Kalaq?"

"Where are my fedayeen?" He studied the young woman, her pretty features, her short-cut hair, the smooth, untanned skin of her hands.

"You are the first of your group. Your men will come by truck or by plane. Today, tomorrow."

"Who are you?"

"They know me as Linda Gomez. Like you I am with the Popular Front. But I came on the ship with the explosives. I speak Spanish and I will translate for you to the Colombians."

"I want a rifle. And a uniform."

"Come."

Gomez led him to the trees. Trucks, trailers, and pickup trucks lined the end of the clearing, where the shadows and branches of the overhanging trees and palms provided concealment from airborne observation. Black-and-green-patterned camouflage netting covered the trailers.

At one trailer, two Palestinians opened buckets of gray clay. They pulled a black plastic bundle out of every bucket. Then they threw the buckets of clay into the jungle. Piles of black plastic bags surrounded the trailer.

"What is that?" Kalaq asked her.

"Dynamite. Two tons."

Kalaq looked at the airstrip—and instantly, he understood how the Iranians would strike. "With a plane. Two tons of dynamite in a plane. The Americans will not know of the attack until they are dead."

"Very imaginative, yes?"

"But why dynamite? It is trash. It is only good for making roads. Why did they not—"

Gomez laughed. "They did. That trailer, there. It came today. It is all C-four. Three tons of American C-four plastique. It will be an explosion like the barracks in Beirut."

Calculating the power of the dynamite and the plastic explosive, Kalaq imagined a plane hurtling out of the sky and a white flash. And he laughed with Gomez.

"They will die. So many of them will die. And all the world will hear of yet another victory."

Working by the headlights of trucks, Air Force technicians ran hoses from the fuel truck to the wings. Other technicians checked the engines. From the window of the jet, Niles watched the young Marine stride through the lights of the service vehicles.

"Here comes the new guy."

Lieutenant Stark spoke into the intercom telephone. Outside, the engines continued whining. "The door will be open momentarily."

Niles sewed the cuffs of his new Taiwan-made camouflage pants. He wore the shirt of his new fatigues and the faded and patched camouflage pants from Beirut. He looked around the cabin at the litter of boxes, plastic bags, beer bottles, and weapons. Vatsek slept in a VIP chair tilted back to horizontal, his new boots on the armrest of another chair, a beer bottle clutched in his fist. Across from Niles, Alvarez loaded magazines from two boxes, steel-tipped 5.56mm SS109 cartridges from one, tracers from the other.

"I don't know," Niles said to the others, "if that Marine will want anything to do with this squad. Covert unit or international trash detail—he will have a legitimate doubt."

"Sir, it's one thing to talk about payback—" Alvarez loaded magazines as he spoke. The brass of every cartridge glistened with oil—he had taken all the cartridges out of their factory-packed magazines, then wiped the brass with a clean rag soaked with lubricating oil. Now he tediously reloaded the magazines. "But this kid may be an extreme case. If he thinks he can put down the locos who wasted his brother or the others in his family, maybe we've gotta pass on him. Whether we need him for the language or not."

"Psychological problem?"

"They killed his people."

"His file didn't report any problems."

"Not many Revolutionary Guards hanging out at Parris Island. Can't unload on them if they aren't there. But if we go up against a unit of the Guards and the kid goes kill-crazy, no bueno."

At the door, Lieutenant Stark wrenched the release lever and motioned for the Marine to step into the plane. The young Iranian immigrant wore starched camouflage fatigues. As instructed, he carried nothing—no personal effects, no equipment. Standing beside Stark, Javenbach appeared slight. His head came only to the lieutenant's shoulder. He saluted the lieutenant:

"Corporal Javenbach."

Niles transferred the needle and thread and new pants to his left hand as he stood. He shook hands with Javenbach, then pointed to one of the seats. "I've read your file. You are a very outstanding young Marine. Excellent scores on every test you take. What exactly did the lieutenant tell you of this unit?"

"Nothing, sir."

"Nothing? And you volunteered?"

"Sir, Lieutenant Stark told me I would be needed as a translator. We did not discuss the unit, sir. We did not discuss the assignment, sir."

"Maybe we'll need a translator, maybe not. We don't know yet."

Woken by the voices, Vatsek lurched forward in his chair, spilling foam over his crotch. "Aggh, goddamn it—oh, sorry. We there yet?"

Niles and Alvarez laughed. Stark threw a towel to the sergeant.

"A few more hours," Niles answered. "Corporal, I read in your file that you left Iran shortly after the Revolution. Did you fight against the Shah?"

Javenbach hesitated. "Yes, sir."

"But then you left. Why?"

"The mullahs declared the Islamic Republic. The brother of my father—my uncle had been many years in the prisons. He told of the teachings of the mullahs and of their insanity, of the insanity to come to the nation, of the end of all hope for those who did not accept the words of the mullahs as the words of God. I knew but I did not believe. But after the return of Khomeini, they took my brother. He had been very brave. He had fought for the Revolution. But they shot him. Then I believed what my uncle told. My father was no longer living. I had the responsibility of my family. I could not wait and hope. One brother of my father had come here to the U.S.A. to escape the SAVAK. He accepted us. It was very difficult, but America is our home and our country now."

Niles finished the last stitches on his pants leg. Knotting the thread, he cut it with his knife. "Your file says you got your uncle out during the riots in Tehran. How'd you do that?"

"It was not difficult. It was the days of the fighting at Doshen and Farahabad. The fedayeen and the Mujahedeen were victorious at Doshen and they distributed weapons to everyone. And everywhere, there was fighting—the Javadan Brigade fought with the Mujahedeen and fedayeen and the cadets and the men in the streets and so forth and so on. I heard of attacks on Evin Prison. I thought Qasr would be next. I went to the prison and watched and waited. Mobs came and there was fighting and the soldiers and guards left the prison. I freed my uncle without firing my rifle. It was not difficult."

"You just waited?"

"Yes."

"How long?"

"Two days."

"And nights?"

"My uncle waited three years. My wait was nothing."

Niles grinned to Alvarez and Vatsek. Alvarez nodded, Vatsek leaned forward and asked:

"So you were with the fedayeen?"

"No, sir. My brother was Mujahedeen. He fought for

liberty and socialism in Iran. I only fought. My brother had hope but the fanatics murdered him. After that, I did not hope. I took my mother and brothers and sisters away."

"You've been through all these questions before," Niles said. "When you joined the Marines. When you talked to the colonel. Right?"

"It is difficult for Americans to understand what happened in that country. They ask many questions."

"And what if you went up against Iranians?" Niles finally asked.

"I hope there is never war between our country and Iran. The young men know nothing of the United States and go to the army only because the mullahs threaten the penalty of death. If they knew of America they would fight the mullahs and the fanatics of the Pasdaran."

"And what about the fanatics? The Revolutionary Guard?"

"They are the enemy of everything that America is. The old mullahs take young men with no education and no hope and make them martyrs. They took my friends who hated the Shah and hated the corruption and made them the Pasdaran. I hope it will never happen that I see my friends who are with the Guards. Because now they are the enemy."

After Javenbach finished, Niles and the others said nothing. Alvarez loaded cartridges, each round clicking against the thin steel of the magazine he held. Finally Niles asked the corporal:

"So you volunteered for this without knowing where we'd go or what we'd do?"

"Yes, sir."

"This is not a Marine Corps operation. We can't wear uniforms where we're going. Once we're in, we're on our own. Do you understand?"

"Yes, sir."

"Do you volunteer for this?"

"Yes, sir."

Niles turned to Stark. "We got any of these made-in-Taiwan fatigues for the corporal? And equipment? And a rifle?"

"I anticipated the corporal accompanying our squad."

Niles pointed to the boxes. "Assemble your gear, Javenbach. You're on your way to Colombia."

Mosquitoes droned against the netting. Smoking a Colombian cigarette, Iziz Kalaq lay in the darkness listening to the static of the radio frequency. He pressed the light on his wristwatch again. Minutes more to wait. He heard the voices of the other fedayeen in the night—cursing the insects and the heat, laughing of the coming strike against the Americans.

Kalaq felt sweat trickling over his face. Sweat ran through his hair. His sweat-soaked fatigues clung to his body. Reaching through the netting, he found the plastic jar and drank the warm water, hating the taste of the purification chemicals. He longed for ice and vodka. The crazy clerk Rajai had not included any alcohol in the supplies for the Colombians and Palestinians—no beer, no liquor, no cigarettes. Kalaq bought cigarettes from the Colombian guerrillas guarding the airstrip, but the tobacco tasted like burning wood.

Voices approached. He heard Spanish. Boots sounded on the rotting planks of the steps and a flashlight waved through the interior of the shack.

"Is there a message yet?" Linda Gomez asked in Arabic.

"No. We must wait for the time." Pushing aside the netting, Kalaq left the cot. His cigarette touched his pants and the ember hissed against the wet cloth. Two quick drags brought the glow back but one side of the cigarette remained soaked. "A few more minutes."

"Your men are complaining."

"It is very hot here." Kalaq went outside. The air seemed cooler. But the insects buzzed around his head. He flicked his cigarette into the night. Finding the repellent in his fatigues, he applied the chemical to his face, neck, and hands. He felt insects crawling on his sweaty skin. "In Lebanon and Syria, there was snow."

"Your men want beer and cigarettes. They want the Colombians to drive to a village to buy what they want."

"No. Buying for thirty or forty men would alert the police. That cannot be allowed."

"That is what Ortiz said. And look." Gomez put the

flashlight on the man standing with her. One of the guerrillas held a bloody cloth to his lip. Blood had stained the Colombian Army uniform he wore. "One of your men hit him. This is very bad. Ortiz had his rifle but instead he walked away. Some of your men are smoking marijuana. And they all have weapons."

Kalaq gripped the Colombian's shoulder. "Tell him I apologize. Identify the man who hit him and I will see him punished. After this is done."

She translated his promise. Pointing her flashlight toward the voices and laughter a hundred meters away, Gomez repeated her warning. "They are smoking marijuana. It is a danger to the action."

"Where did they get it? Who brought it here?"

"It grows everywhere."

"Ask how we can get them the cigarettes and liquor. Without betraying all of us."

"Only by sending a truck to Maicao or the coast. We talked of this. If the truck goes to San Juan, they will be seen. But if they go to the Riohacha or Maicao, they will be gone all the day."

"We have two more days here. If cigarettes and beer will stop this trouble, it is nothing. Send them tonight."

"That is not possible. There are many bandits. There are gangs. One man or two men cannot travel at night."

Laughter came from the night. Flashlights approached, the beams whipping wildly over the grass and vines covering the ground. The radio operator appeared. He carried a flashlight in each hand. His stupid laughter stopped when he saw the bleeding Colombian.

"Go to the radio," Kalaq told him. "It is time. Send the message I wrote."

The flashlights lit the interior. Kalaq heard a chair fall. A code sequence came from the radio monitor. After a moment, the operator keyed a response in code.

"We will get them what they want," Kalaq told Gomez. "Send the Colombians to that town. The town that is near."

"But it will alert—"

"Alert who? How can it betray us? If there are bandits and gangs, let the Colombians say they are another gang. Let them say they are buying for a month. It does not matter. We will be gone in two days."

"It is against instructions."

"Those are my instructions. Do as I say. Send a truck to get the cigarettes and liquor. Why make the time in this hell difficult?"

He heard the operator keying the coded message. Leaving the woman, Kalaq went to the radio. He watched the operator fumble through the two lines of letters and numbers. A quick response came. Laughing, the operator keyed the message again. Finally, a confirmation came. The operator scribbled down a message transmitted from Lebanon. Then they heard only the static.

Kalaq read the series of letter and number codes. The letters and numbers referred to the pages and lines of a phrase book he carried. Rajai had another book. Without the books, the codes meant nothing. Kalaq flipped through the pages of his book and found: All continues as scheduled . . . aircraft comes . . . two days . . . dawn.

"Very good," he told the operator. They left the rotting shack. Gomez and the Colombian guerrilla had gone. Kalaq walked with the operator back to the other fedayeen. "Tell me of the problem with the Colombian. Who hit him? Why?"

"Odeh speaks French. The Colombian speaks French. Odeh asked with great courtesy, as a comrade, if the Colombian or one of his comrades would take our dollars and buy a few items we did not receive in the supplies. But what is the answer? A lecture on security and discipline. We who have fought all our lives, lectured by a teenager. Odeh silenced him with a slap, as if he were a child."

As they neared the voices, Kalaq smelled the acrid marijuana. He had often smoked hashish in Beirut, but not the leaves of the plant. The voices of the men went quiet as Kalaq and the operator thrashed through the ferns and vines.

Though the shack had no floor or walls, a palm frond and sheet metal roof provided shelter from the sun and rain. Posts and thick cross-members supported the hammocks where the men slept. Canopies of netting covered the hammocks, sheets of netting hung in place of walls. Kalaq pushed through the sheets of mosquito netting and stepped into the smoke.

"Odeh! Where are you?"

"Here."

"Don't slap that boy again. He came crying to me and I had to hold his hand and call his mother on the radio."

The men laughed.

"And why did you not come to me about the cigarettes and beer? I have only one pack. How can I provide for all of you? Tomorrow, the truck goes to the village. If you had told me today, you would have what you want tonight. You must wait until tomorrow. There will be no ice or cold drinks, but be patient. We will be out of this jungle in two days. Only two days of work and we return to Lebanon."

As he walked out, his flashlight swept across a row of boxes. Wads of leaves covered one box. He saw what looked like a cigar rolled of white paper. He took it as he passed. Behind him, lighters flared and smoke clouded in the hammocks. The men talked and laughed again. Kalaq found the track through the undergrowth, kicking through the tangles until he stumbled up the steps of the shack.

Inside, the radio hissed with static. He gulped more of the chemical-stinking water and something living fluttered in his mouth. He spat the insect out. As he checked the water with his flashlight, insects flew at the beam. Beetles and moths walked on the warped walls of the shack. He went back to the cot, carefully closing the curtains of netting.

He examined the paper cigar, shining the beam of his flashlight directly on the paper. He saw words on the paper. Someone had torn a tissue-thin page from a Koran and used the page to wrap a wad of leaves. Kalaq laughed as he lit the hand-rolled cigar. Rajai had not included cigarettes and liquor with the supplies. But the Iranian clerk undoubtedly included a Koran.

The harsh smoke scorched his throat. But he pulled down drag after drag, filling his lungs with the intoxicant. He no longer felt the heat and his sweat-soaked fatigues. The static buzz of the radio became a distant sound, only one more insect in the swarms circling in the darkness.

Discipline. The discipline of his fedayeen. How could he maintain the discipline of his fighters in this hell? They had offered to give their lives in an attack against the Americans. Instead, Rajai sent them into a miserable jungle to work like common laborers, unloading cargo from trailers and cutting the brush growing on the landing strip. The buckets and crates contained explosives and the drums fuel for the plane—but what did that matter? Rajai had recruited Kalaq and his unit as fighters—not as labor. After traveling for two days and nights, from Syria, through Europe, then through Central American and South American airports, his men stepped from the trucks and went to work sweating in the tropical heat. And Rajai expected them to slave at the demeaning work without even the small comforts enjoyed by laborers.

So what if they demanded beer and cigarettes? So what if they smoked marijuana? If the drug kept his men laughing through this affront to their courage and devotion, let them smoke all night.

Tomorrow, Kalaq sent the Colombians for whatever his fedayeen desired. And for his vodka.

Rajai changed frequencies. In the predawn silence, the electronic hiss of the radio seemed loud. Rajai put the confirmation message from Kalaq in his briefcase with the code book. The next communication came in a few minutes. He went to the glass doors and looked out at the courtyard.

Snow swirled through the lights. Rajai listened to the hiss of the radio as he watched the snow falling through the bare trees of the villa. On the far side of the property, where the wealthy Sunnis who owned the villa had quartered their servants, a shadow moved. He saw the outline of a man with a Kalashnikov—one of his Revolutionary Guards pacing to warm himself in the last freezing hours of the night.

The wait started now. The coded report from Kalaq confirmed the movement of the explosives, the supplies, and the squads of Latins and Palestinians. Tomorrow the squads worked to assemble the explosives for the arrival of the aircraft. Then, the next day, as the sun rose in Colombia on the twenty-fifth of January, the plane landed at the airstrip.

In less than fifty hours, he learned of success or failure in the attack on the American target that the committee of mullahs and Revolutionary Guard commanders in Tehran would not yet reveal to him. Rajai knew he would not learn of the target until the victory.

And until the victory, or the failure, he remained in Baalbek. The committee in Tehran wanted the responsibility for the attack to fall on the radical gangs of the Bekaa.

Code interrupted his thoughts. He heard the dot and dash code identifying the Revolutionary Guard unit dispatched to Colombia. Returning to the radio, he keyed the response, then waited as the transmission flashed to the opposite side of the earth. Another sequence of electronic signals came. Rajai noted the letters and numbers. The radio man off the coast of Colombia then repeated the sequence. Taking the second code book from his briefcase, Rajai flipped through the pages and found the lines.

Leaving . . . ship . . . trucks . . . ready . . . Insallah.

Rajai tapped out the confirmation code. The radio went silent. Returning to the windows, Rajai looked out at the snow and thought of Kalaq, the loud and erratic leader of gunmen who talked of conquering Israel and driving America from the Middle East, who bragged of every petty murder of Lebanese or Jews.

Though Kalaq had waited all his life for glory, the braggart would never enjoy the fame of this attack. When the plane carried the explosives away, before Kalaq even learned what military base or embassy the plane destroyed, the role of the Palestinian ended—without recognition, without glory.

A joke, Rajai thought, a joke.

Warm rain in his eyes, Sayed stood at the door to the cabin, listening to the exchange of radio codes with their director in Lebanon. The wind carried an intermittent rain off the Caribbean. Despite the wind and night, the tropical rain felt hot. He held a plastic sheet over his pack and rifle, rain running over his face and arms, sweat running over his body. On the deck forward of the freighter's superstructure, he heard the voices of the other men in his unit. He thought of the Iraqi Front and prayed silently, Let us succeed, let me prove myself to the mullahs, let me win freedom from the Front, I want no other reward.

The radio buzzed with another sequence, The technician called out to him, "Sayed! The message is received."

"Then we go."

The technician turned off the power and disconnected the antenna wires. He slipped the portable transmitter into the padded, waterproof pack. Sayed lifted the heavy radio pack, holding it while the operator put his arms through the straps.

Sayed rushed down to the deck. Clutching plastic tarps over their shoulders, the Revolutionary Guards crowded the railing of the freighter. They watched the cargo launch rising and falling on the surface chop.

"Into the boat." He led the young men down the rusting steel stairs. The launch rolled with the wind chop. Judging the rise and fall of the deck, Sayed jumped, then went to the wheelhouse. The other Iranians jumped, their rifles and packs clattering. Speaking California Spanish, Sayed asked the boatman:

"Any patrol boats?"

The Colombian answered in fast, slurred exclamations. Sayed told him to repeat his answer very slowly.

"No patrols. My men saw no patrols."

Sayed saw the last man step off the stairs. He signaled the boatman.

The deck vibrated with the knocking of the motor. Wind chop bumped the launch against the steel of the freighter, then the launch moved away, water churning. Sayed watched the freighter disappear into the night as the launch pitched through the choppy water. Ahead, he searched the darkness for any sign of the coast.

Ten minutes later, the boatman spoke into a walkie-talkie. A voice answered, then lights flashed on and off—headlights. Two tiny yellow lights remained to guide the launch to the shore. The boatman turned to Sayed and explained in very slow Spanish:

"We do this many times. Beach to ship, ship to beach. Very good business. Much money. No problems."

In the rain, the coast of Santa Marta remained only an

irregular smear of darkness. The boatman steered for the yellow lights. A horn sounded ahead. The boatman switched on his running lights and Sayed saw a pier. At the bottom of a ramp, a floating dock rose and fell on the ocean swells. The launch thudded into the tires ringing the dock.

Sayed glanced at the luminous dial of his watch. Six hours to dawn—enough time to transit the coast road and start into the mountains.

Two men came down the ramp from the pier. The boatman threw ropes to the men and they lashed the launch to the dock. Sayed stepped over the railing onto the slick planks of the dock, then ran up the ramp. He saw the trucks at the other end of the pier. Twisting the sheet of plastic to cover his rifle, he pushed down the fire-selector and slowly pulled back the cocking handle to chamber the first cartridge.

Sayed wanted nothing to go wrong, not here on the beach, not on the highway, not in the mountains. His commander in Khorramshahr had recommended him for this action despite the doubts of the mullahs from Tehran. Arguing that Sayed had returned by his own decision from the United States, then proved his loyalty and courage on the Iraqi Front, his commander had told the mullahs to ignore the few years of decadence in California. If the mullah needed a loyal soldier who could speak English and Spanish, take Sayed.

And the mullahs did take Sayed away from the blood-drenched trenches of the Front to the calm of a long ocean cruise to Colombia. And the execution of the Palestinians? It would be nothing. He had killed in California, executing the old man who recognized him during a liquor store robbery—but no one in Iran knew of that murder. His commander knew only of his killings on the Front. Sayed killed as told, without question—Iraqi wounded, deserters from the Guard, civilians suspected of spying, whoever. The Palestinians and their Colombian allies had betrayed Iran, therefore they died—Sayed did not question how they had betrayed Iran or why or when.

This cruise to Colombia took him away from the Front. If he pleased his commander and the mullahs, perhaps he would not return to that madness.

Sayed wanted no problems. Tomorrow or the next day,

when the plane left the airfield, he killed the Palestinians and the Latins. Then they returned to the freighter for the long cruise back to Iran—another month.

In total, months away from the madness and horror of the Front. Though Sayed did not dare to ask, he prayed for a greater reward.

Never to return to the Front. Insallah.

16

A SWIRLING mist enveloped the helicopter. The skids scraped stone and Niles leaped out. The other Marines followed. In the translucent gray mist, Niles scrambled over the slabs of rock. He slid into a tangle of brush, slipped free, then dodged through the shadowy forms of trees. He threw himself flat on the matted forest debris. Above him, the DEA helicopter lifted away in an explosion of noise. The others formed a security star behind Niles, their boots touching, their eyes and their rifles covering the forest and the drifting mist around them.

The rotor noise faded into the distance. Niles waited, watching the forest, his ears still ringing. In the predawn light, he saw only the gray lines of tree trunks and the black splotches of foliage. Silence returned to the ridge. He heard drops of water splattering through the ferns as mist condensed on leaves. Birds dove from branch to branch, the air-rush across their wings loud. The Marines watched the forest.

As the minutes passed, the overcast sky paled with the unseen dawn. Birds called out in territorial shrieks and whistles. The Marines remained silent and motionless, waiting, watching, listening. Finally Niles rose on one elbow and saw that Sergeant Alvarez lay to his right. He kicked his boot.

The sergeant flicked the radio key-set to transmit a signal back to the DEA airfield at San Juan del César. A click-code reply from the DEA radio confirmed the radio link.

Without a word, Niles moved, taking point. He led the line

of men down the ridge line, pushing through the ferns and hanging vines with his left hand, holding his short Colt Commando in his right hand, a round in the chamber, his thumb on the safety, as he listened for sounds ahead. But he heard only the birds and the falling drops of condensation from the branches high above them.

His eyes scanned for signs of human passing. But he saw nothing—no trails, no trash, no tool scars on the trees. As more light filtered through the trees, he moved faster. The deep matting of rotting leaves silenced the footsteps of the Marines. Behind him, Niles heard the quiet sound of leaves on leaves as Vatsek used a fallen branch to sweep away the marks left by their boots.

Satellite-generated maps and high-altitude photos showed a low mountain with a long, snaking ridge line. From the rocky crest where the five Marines had left the helicopter, the forested ridge curved south for three kilometers before twisting to the west and descending into a valley several kilometers wide. A river cut through the dense forest covering the valley. On the opposite side of the valley, the steep hillsides rose to the crest of a high mountain ridge dominating the area. Ten more kilometers of forested hills separated the peak from the airstrip used by the Iranians and Palestinians.

Niles wanted to cover all the distance to the airstrip before dark. He maintained a quick pace. But with daylight, the humidity and temperature in the windless forest increased. Sweat poured down his body, soaking his fatigues, making the black plastic of his Colt rifle slick.

Coming to the western hook of the ridge, they followed the slope down into the valley, gravity speeding their pace. The forest changed to triple canopy. Thirty-meter-high trees and tagua palms shadowed a second level of treetops. Only spots of daylight broke through the two levels of trees and palms to fall on the ferns, wide-leafed plants, and spiny shrubs growing on the ground. Liana vines snaked over the earth and covered the twisted trunks of the trees. In the semi-darkness, the motionless air stank of rot. Insects buzzed around the Marines. Niles set a compass bearing and maintained the pace.

RECON

Three hours after the helicopter insertion, Niles felt water oozing into his boots. They had reached the center of the valley. Continuing, he looked for the river. The wet soil had rotted the roots of trees, causing trees to fall. Tangles of branches and arm-thick vines forced Niles to weave through areas of black mud and stagnant water. He felt insect bites on his hands and neck. Behind him, he heard one of the men slap at his fatigues. Niles pushed aside a branch—and slime-glistening leeches clung to his sleeve and his green-patterned hand.

Niles moved faster, cutting straight through the stinking pools, mud sucking at his boots with every step. Fallen trees blocked his compass bearing. Checking for snakes, he went over the rotting logs, sometimes sinking as deep as his knees in the water and putrid muck. Then, through the trees, he saw daylight reflecting from water. He rushed the last hundred meters.

The river looked like a wide, slow-flowing swamp meandering through the forest. Niles saw no banks or current. But fifty meters away, he saw brilliant white, long-legged birds picking through the shallows of the opposite side.

Hand-signaling the other Marines forward, he took a ten-meter coil of o.d. green nylon rope from his pack. Every man carried an identical coil. Niles whipped a bow-line around his waist, then knotted his rope to Stark's. The three other men watched the darkness of the stagnant mud flats behind them. Stark passed an end back to Alvarez. Niles watched Javenbach. The young man seemed nervous but not fatigued, tying two quick knots, then passing the coils to Vatsek.

Birds flapped away as Niles entered the river. The current became stronger with every step. The water cleared and he saw small fish streaking past his legs. As the water level passed his knees, he watched for a drop-off. He stepped carefully through rocks, then he walked in shallows again—to a sandbar, he thought. But a few steps farther, his boots sank into the rot and black mud of the shore.

Niles turned and signaled the four other men. They crossed as he coiled and unknotted the sections of rope.

Grinning, he whispered, "Sorry" as he passed back their ropes.

Vatsek answered, "Colombian white water adventure."

Continuing, Niles struggled through a few hundred meters of swamp, then felt dry earth under his boots. He walked uphill, leaving the humid darkness of the valley floor behind as the gentle rise became a hillside. Niles checked the compass bearing against the position of the river and his memory of the topographic map. He cut to the southwest.

The new bearing took them over the lower slopes of the mountain, allowing them to angle across the mountainside. After the oppressive heat and stinking semi-darkness of the valley, the shadowy hillsides felt cool. Niles set a quick pace through the forest, allowing noise in a trade-off for speed. At the end of the line of men, Vatsek worked fast, trying to obscure their tracks, pausing to sweep away a boot mark or rearrange leaves, then rushing to catch up. Niles knew they left some marks—their hurry and the crumbling earth of the mountainside made boot prints inevitable. But the total absence of other people in the area made the sounds and the scattered tracks an acceptable risk.

Niles looked back and saw all the men soaked in sweat. Yet they moved quickly and quietly, their eyes always scanning, their rifles gripped in their hands. They showed no fatigue. He maintained the pace, ignoring his own fatigue. After flying from the cold and snow of Lebanon to the tropical heat of the Colombian rain forest, then the sudden demand of the march on his limited physical conditioning, his endurance surprised him. He thought Alvarez and Vatsek—despite their youth—might be also suffering after their months of inactivity in the siege bunkers of Beirut, but he knew they would not complain or even admit it, not while an 'old man'—a twenty-two-year veteran—walked point. Stark had his youth and years of soccer competition. Javenbach had the recent conditioning of Parris Island. Before fatigue cut his stride, Niles wanted to make the ridge.

They climbed higher, passing the altitude of the first mountain. The forest changed, the trees thinning. Sunlight broke through the living canopy. Vines and grasses covered the ground. The growth concealed their tracks but made footing more difficult. The ferns grew larger, sometimes blocking their compass bearing with walls of spiked fronds—thrashing through the ferns meant hundreds of cuts. To gain altitude as he avoided the obstructions, Niles scrambled straight up the steep mountainside, slinging his Colt over his shoulder and clawing at the vines with his hands.

When he felt a wind cooling the sweat on his face, he signaled the others to wait and clawed his way to the ridge line. He stopped short, unslinging his rifle and advancing carefully, slowly, and silently to the top, then went flat and listened. He heard birds and the trees creaking with the shifting of the wind. Behind him, one of the Marines kicked loose a rock. He listened to the natural sounds for minutes, enjoying the rest, then stood and walked through the trees, scanning the ground for any signs of others.

He saw nothing. Hand-signing Stark, Niles continued to the downslope. There, through a gap in the trees, he saw the expanse of forest and mountains ahead.

The forest continued into the distance, unbroken, undulating with hills and valleys, shadowed by masses of drifting clouds. A crease suggested the line of a wide river appearing in the satellite photos, but Niles saw none of the smaller rivers marked on the map. On the horizon, he saw the vast green plain of the César Valley. Streaks of rising smoke marked towns along the highway running northeast to the Venezuelan border.

He did not see the airstrip or the dirt road. Squinting into the glare, he looked for a clearing or a line marking the path of the narrow dirt road leading to the airstrip. His visual search spotted nothing.

Looking behind him, he saw the others cross the ridge. They formed a loose circle and watched the area, holding their rifles with one hand, reapplying camouflage paint with the other. Stark pointed to the west and whispered:

"Airfield?"

Niles shook his head no. He pantomimed binoculars.

Stark shrugged off his pack and found his binocular case in two seconds. He offered the binoculars to Niles. Niles motioned for the lieutenant to look. Checking his compass, then setting the focus of the binoculars, Stark searched a specific sector with the optics. He found the airstrip. Pointing, he passed the binoculars to Niles.

The high-powered optics revealed a broken line of gray. From his position on the mountain, Niles could not see the long rectangle of the airstrip. But the slash in the forest had exposed the gray trunks of trees along the far side of the airstrip. Niles took an exact compass bearing, then unfolded his plastic-laminated map. With his fingernail, he plotted a route intersecting the access road. He hand-signed the bearing for the road, then led the squad down the mountainside.

Niles raced the sun. Only four hours thirty minutes remained until night. Striding downhill, he used gravity to accelerate the pace, pushing himself to cover the distance. He did not stop for breaks. He guessed at his body's consumption of water and gulped from his canteens without stopping. The younger men followed his example.

As the ground leveled, he maintained his stride through the shadowed forest, the matting of rotting leaves silencing his boots. The small ferns and leafy plants hid his boot marks. He made another kilometer before the sight of a shack stopped him. Dropping to a crouch, he waved the others back.

Trees arched over the shack. Years of leaves lay on the sheet metal roof, providing soil for weeds. Vines covered the clearing and Niles saw no foot trails. Vines grew over the rusting fenders of a derelict truck. Niles heard only birds and insects.

He saw no sign of occupation and moved ahead. Mounds of old trash—cans scorched by fire, broken bottles, slabs of melted plastic—forced him to pick his steps slowly. He walked behind the shack. The ruts of a road wove through the trees. Weeds and vines indicated no traffic for years. He signaled for Stark to bring the line forward.

Past the road, Niles saw overgrown rows of coffee bushes. Trees remained, but had been thinned—coffee requires shade from the tropical sun. The remaining trees also blocked airborne observation of the marijuana scattered among the coffee bushes. The tall, leafy plants had gone to seed and died, unharvested. The line of Marines hurried through the rows, seeds showering them every time they pushed branches aside.

But apparently the few plants in the coffee rows had grown spontaneously. A hundred meters past the road, they came to the marijuana fields. Rows of thousands of plants, neglected for years, had become an impenetrable tangle of branches and leaves and drying seed-clusters. Niles motioned the Marines to detour. He did not want to chance the fields—perhaps the gang had protected their crop with booby traps, perhaps the Colombian Army had closed the plantation with land mines. Staying in the coffee rows, they worked their way around the fields, then resumed the southwest march.

Throughout the next kilometers, marijuana appeared frequently. Roads no wider than a mini-truck or a motorcycle led to plots and fields. Plants grew in clusters or rows, screened from the air by overhanging trees. All the crops—and the shacks, water tanks, and wells—had been abandoned. Niles paused at the overgrown ruts, looking for tire marks or footprints. He found no marks of recent traffic. Between the quick stops, he broke into a jog, trying to make up lost time.

The heat increased in the last hours of the day. Drinking the last of his third one-liter canteen to swallow a salt tablet, Niles passed a whispered question along the line: "How much water left?"

Weight had limited the water they carried to four liters each. Stark returned the answers, signaling Niles with his index finger, One. The others, like Niles, needed to refill their canteens. He checked his watch. Only an hour and forty minutes until sunset. Darkness would come sooner. He no longer had the energy to run, but he somehow had the reserve strength to keep striding to the southwest.

Another road stopped him. Swaying with exhaustion, he looked down at the clear-cut tire tracks in the earth. He walked along the road, studying the tracks. A flat toad lay in the road, swarmed by ants and flies. Pushing aside a branch, Niles looked at the broken stems—the wilted leaves remained soft to his touch, not yet dried by the sun. He stepped back into concealment. The tires had different treads—two vehicles had passed. The tire marks and the leaves that had fallen on the road indicated the vehicles had not returned. Looking up to the overhanging trees, he saw broken branches higher than his reach. That suggested high-backed cargo trucks to Niles.

Niles pointed to Vatsek and motioned the sergeant forward. Vatsek had more experience with vehicles. Niles pointed to the tracks in the road and asked: "What went past here?"

Passing his M-16/M-203 over-and-under assault rifle and grenade launcher to the captain, Vatsek went flat on the road. He peered at the tracks. "One truck with bald tires. The other's got decent tires but it's got a front-end problem. A shimmy in the steering linkage. Maybe just lately because the front tires aren't scalloped out yet."

"How much weight are they carrying?"

"Not a full load. Can't tell. I'd have to walk for a ways, see if they bottomed out."

"No time." He returned Vatsek's rifle/grenade launcher. "Think the Colombian armed forces would have good tires on their trucks?"

"Maybe. But they'd have trucks of the same make. I think, I don't know. You think the Colombian Army's out here?"

"I don't know. But the trucks mean someone is."

"Dopers, Captain. We're in Strawberry Fields out here."

"I don't know."

"How much farther?"

"Two klicks, as the crow flies. But we ain't crows."

Niles dashed across the road. He continued as quickly as he dared through the forest and marijuana fields. This close to the airstrip, he risked encountering sentries or booby traps. Every flutter of a bird's wings, every click from an insect, made him pause. He avoided open areas and patches of ferns, but scanned those areas for the boot prints of the Palestinians. He saw no tracks until he reached the road leading to the airstrip.

Tire marks and boot prints marked the rutted dirt road. As

on the other hand, passing vehicles had snapped off the branches of overhanging trees—Niles knew the shipping container of dynamite had done that. Other tires indicated mini-trucks. The boot prints and a cigarette butt meant a patrol. Niles passed a one-word warning back:

"Enemy."

He watched the road for a minute, looking in both directions, studying the trees and brush where the road curved. He searched the shadows for sentries. No one watched this section. Finally, he took the five steps to cross the road. He turned and covered the other men, then cut toward the airstrip.

Moving a step at a time, he paralleled the road, his eyes never stopping as he scanned the pale, twisting trunks of the trees for movement. Shafts of sunlight angled through the trees, creating areas of light and semi-darkness. Birds called out around him. The bird noises reassured him—birds fly or go silent when outsiders enter their territory. He continued walking slowly and silently—watching and listening for the Palestinians.

Acrid marijuana smoke stopped him. Going flat behind a tree, he heard a man cough. He waited. Movement took his attention, then a light flared, the flame bright in a shadowed area. A man sat with his back to a tree, smoking a cigarette the size of a cigar. He wore camouflage fatigues. A G-3 automatic rifle—the standard issue of the Colombian Army—leaned against the tree. Niles watched him drink from a can, then throw the can away. The man walked back to the road, puffing on the huge cigarette.

Continuing, Niles heard voices speaking Spanish. Metal screeched. Other voices shouted out in Arabic. As he moved toward the airstrip, slashes of daylight appeared through the trees. He saw a rectangular form. Men argued in Spanish and Arabic, shouting at one another without comprehension about drunkenness and damage to a truck. A voice shouted out in Arabic for quiet. Niles signaled for Stark to wait, then shimmied forward on his elbows, finding concealment behind hundreds of empty shipping cans containing a residue of gray clay—drilling mud, Niles realized.

He rose to a crouch and watched sunburned, sweating men breaking open wooden crates. They took out plastic-wrapped packages and threw the crates aside. A man called out instructions in Arabic—and Niles recognized the curly hair, the mustache, and sharp features from the photos taken by Angelique Chardon.

Returning to the line of Marines, Niles whispered one word: "Kalaq."

Looking into the container transport, Iziz Kalaq saw only the bare steel interior. His fedayeen had stacked the tons of dynamite—still bundled in hundreds of black plastic bags—in a long pile alongside the container, ready to load on the plane. He crossed the rutted fields to the second container. Inside, a few crates remained. But two of his men worked continuously—despite the heat and flies, levering off the wooden slats of the crates. Another man took the heavy packages of American C-4 plastic explosive to a long rectangular stack. The stack looked like a wall made of wide, flat bricks.

"All will be done before night," one of the sweating men told him.

Kalaq looked to the west. The sun stood on the high mountain peaks. Starting back to his pickup truck, he called out: "Hurry. We cannot use lights."

Linda Gomez and the Colombians beat at the fender of the Japanese pickup truck, trying to bend the sheet metal away from the tire. They talked Spanish and gestured at the driver, Raman, a faithful middle-aged fighter from Gaza. Grinning with alcohol and marijuana, Raman sat in the grass, watching the Colombians struggle to repair their truck. They looked up as Kalaq approached, their voices going low as they spat out Spanish. From their expressions, he knew they cursed him. Let them. Tomorrow he left this place.

"Your driver is drunk!" Gomez told him. "If he had driven into the dynamite, there could have been an explosion!"

"Girl, you know nothing. The truck would do nothing to the dynamite but break it. Fire a bullet into the dynamite.

There is no danger." He took the battered G-3 rifle from the back of the pickup and thumbed off the safety. "You want to see? Then will you believe me?"

"No! No! You are a madman! Are you on drugs?"

"No, girl. I am not a madman. I am the commander of this action. Remember that. And keep these bourgeois teenagers away from my fighters. You cannot expect us to remain forever tolerant of their insults. There will be a penalty. Raman!"

"Yes!" Rising to his feet, Raman staggered to him.

"Is there another truck?"

"Another truck?" Raman looked in all directions. "A truck?"

"Now we inspect the work on the landing strip." Kalaq pointed to the men dragging the last of the saplings and high weeds from the landing strip.

"A truck? There is a truck!" Raman staggered toward the semi-truck and trailer that had carried drums of aviation fuel to the mountain airfield.

Jerking him back by his shirt, Kalaq pushed him in the opposite direction. "Not one of those trucks. You are drunk, my friend. We will walk." Laughing at his driver's antics, Kalaq slung the G-3 rifle over his shoulder.

Then the Colombians laughed. Turning, he saw Gomez speaking with the teenagers, undoubtedly translating his misunderstanding with Raman. Anger flashed through him. To ridicule Palestinian comrades for the amusement of foreigners, to ridicule her commander Iziz Kalaq behind his back—if she could sense his rage, she would not joke with the teenagers. Then he thought of the photos of the Frenchwoman, screaming, twisting, and struggling to escape the searing pain, escape impossible—and he laughed. Linda Gomez ridiculed him today, but tomorrow she returned to Lebanon. Now he must give the landing strip a final inspection.

The incoming transport plane required the removal of all the small trees and brush growing on the landing strip and a meter-by-meter inspection of the ground. For secrecy, the grass and weeds covering the strip remained. Kalaq and his fedayeen risked a confrontation with the Colombian Army if a patrol plane spotted the area cleared or burned off. Leaving the grass growing would not present a problem to the transport.

Kalaq wove through the knee-high growth. Under his boots, the earth felt flat and hard. The unknown smugglers who had prepared this field had done their work well, finding the plateau, cutting the narrow strip out of the jungle, then somehow packing the earth of the cleared field hard. Graded very slightly to the south, rainwater drained away without eroding the surface. Even after years of neglect and seasonal storms, the strip remained smooth under the even growth of the weeds.

Fedayeen with axes had cut the saplings and bushes off at the ground. Nothing remained to puncture the tires of the transport. Kalaq searched for stumps but found only scuffed earth and roots. And beer cans. The Colombians had returned early with a pickup truck loaded with cases of beer. Judging by the number of empty cans, every man drank a case. But what did it matter? The men had labored throughout a long, miserable day of tropical heat and stinging insects. Let the men enjoy the small comfort of the alcohol—there would be no combat here, only degrading and demoralizing labor. Their comfort and spirit came first.

As the day faded, Kalaq reached the far end of the airstrip. His men sprawled in the grass, silent with exhaustion. But they had finished. He went to the men and told them:

"Thank you for your patience today. You came to fight, yet circumstances forced you to work like peasants. I promise you this is the end of the indignity. I give you this promise, a promise to bring you joy. This is your last day and night here in this jungle. Tomorrow, we are gone."

In the last minutes of light, Niles snaked through ferns and vines. He inched toward the shack with the long, improvised antenna strung through the branches of overhanging trees. Alvarez followed two body lengths behind Niles. They carried only electronics and pistols. Niles had no intention of using any weapons tonight. Until the plane arrived at the airstrip, he wanted information only—recordings of names, dialects, and radio transmissions.

The Palestinians had not cleared a perimeter or even beaten down the grass. Brush, ferns, vines, and dense clusters of banana trees grew in tangled masses everywhere—against the slat-board shacks, near the open shelter strung with hammocks, to the edge of the grassy airstrip.

Niles expected booby traps or trip-flares. Flat on his belly, he crawled forward in stops and starts, searching the semi-darkness with his eyes, looking for wire or monofilament trigger-lines. Minute by minute, he lost light. Finally he moved through darkness. Ten meters ahead, he saw Palestinians walking by the yellow beams of flashlights. He heard men cursing the heat and insects. Others talked inside the shack with the radio. But Niles could not understand their conversation at this distance.

Cutting a fern frond with his thumbnail, he stripped the leaflets from the center stem. He continued forward through the seedlings and brush, waving the stem like an insect's antenna to feel for trip-lines. Turning over on his back, he passed the stem above him, checking for lines set high. Every time he advanced, Alvarez advanced. Alvarez carried the cassette recorders and the awkard tube of the microphone case.

Stark, Vatsek, and Javenbach remained a hundred meters back—they did not understand Arabic. Stark monitored the band scanning unit. He wore headphones and listened for walkie-talkie transmissions by the Spanish-speaking Latins working with the Palestinians.

A double-click signal alerted Niles. He plugged the earphone into his left ear and heard Stark whisper:

"They are placing sentries."

Niles clicked his radio's transmit key to acknowledge the warning. He heard Alvarez acknowledge also.

Shouting in Arabic startled Niles. Feet kicked through the brush. His hand went to the knife in his boot and then he heard laughter. Against the light of battery lanterns, a form staggered. An arm jerked and Niles heard metal clink on wood—a can. Four or five steps to his right, a Palestinian urinated. Trying to zip his pants, the man fell in his own urine. Men laughed. Niles watched the bright points of their cigarettes scratch the darkness as they laughed and gestured.

Flashlights approached. Voices spoke Spanish. The Palestinians went silent for a moment. In Arabic, one man talked of the playboy Colombian revolutionaries, with their hair styled in Paris and their politics from rock-and-roll music. In Spanish, the Colombians talked of the Arab clowns, risking the failure of the action with their drinking and marijuana smoking. The Colombians passed the Palestinians and walked into the trees. Niles keyed his radio to alert the other Marines.

Niles continued to the shack. He heard boots on the floorboards, the rotten wood creaking and sagging. A battery lantern lit the interior, the windows projecting rectangles of light onto the lush growth outside. Niles found trash littering the ground under the window. Listening to the voices inside, he carefully cleared a path through the trash, gently picking up bottles and cans and setting the trash aside.

The Palestinians talked of the heat and the Colombians. One voice called someone named Gomez a traitor to the Popular Front. Another man laughed as he told the story of crashing the pickup truck into the trailers and how Gomez panicked, screaming that the dynamite would explode. Niles crouched an arm's distance from the shack, concealed in the brush, listening to the Palestinians. Though they spoke quickly and slurred their words, he understood enough to follow their ridicule of Gomez.

Then a voice said—"Iziz, my commander. You tell me. Why were we dispatched to this boiling and infested place of suffering? Why did not they who conceived this action decide to load the aircraft in a city?"

"Because here, in this jungle, we are beyond the sight of the criminal CIA of the Americans. It is the need for secrecy. And I tell you this, I do not agree with every detail of this operation."

Niles recognized the voice from the tapes in the luggage of

Angelique Chardon. After the Frenchwoman's murder, he had reviewed the cassettes of her interviews, listening again and again to the tape of Iziz Kalaq mouthing the propaganda of his terrorist gang. Now he heard the same voice and the same propaganda—confirming his identification of Iziz Kalaq.

"Our Iranian comrades want to strike with the surprise and mystery of Allah. The Iranians want to deny the Americans the honor of revenge."

"The mystery is what we strike," another man commented. "When do we know?"

"Tomorrow, we know. And tomorrow we are gone. Gone to Lebanon to receive the welcome of heroes. We will know tomorrow at this time. We will know we have changed history."

"My commander," another man interrupted, "history is what is known. As you explained to us, what we will do here will not be known."

"The Iranians fear the revenge of the Americans."

"Do we?"

"No! Have I not told you we have nothing to fear from the Americans? Do you think I only speak empty words, like the dog Arafat?"

"No, my commander. I know you do not fear. You are my leader and the leader of all of us who are here. But is it not true we will remain anonymous?"

"I regret the secrecy. I rage against it. But is it not enough to know we are the men who struck out and defeated our enemies, that we are the men who changed history?"

In the light from the window, Niles saw Alvarez reach out to the rotting slat boards of the shack. The boards of the wall had rotted at the floorline. Light showed through cracks and spaces. Alvarez slowly pushed a black mini-microphone/transmitter through a crack. The mini-mike disturbed insects. Beetles ran over the green-and-black-patterned camouflage paint of Alvarez's hand. With one finger, he pushed the device into the shack, then withdrew his hand and shook off the insects. Alvarez held up his other hand to a shaft of light.

Inside a miniaturized receiver/recorder, a cassette turned. The spools paused as the voices inside paused. When the Palestinians spoke again, the voice-activated unit resumed recording.

Alvarez whispered the single word, "Wired."

Kalaq waited for the time of the radio transmission. He sprawled across his cot, a can of hot beer in his right hand, one of the Koran-wrapped marijuana cigars in his left. The amber power light of the radio console lit the interior of the shack. Outside, he heard the voices of his men.

He took a long, deep drag of the intoxicating smoke and thought of silence. The Iranians demanded that Kalaq say nothing of this attack. Tomorrow, when the radios and televisions and newspapers of the world carried the story of his strike against the Americans to the nations of the world, Kalaq could not step forth to the cameras and journalists to accept the glory. He could not claim responsibility or even admit a role.

Silence denied Kalaq glory. Without the broadcast of the claim of responsibility, no one profited by the attack. The United States had many embassies—destroy an embassy and they would only rebuild it. The profit came in the glory to the group responsible. If the attack remained a mystery, the Americans would threaten and investigate, but do nothing.

And if a leader took responsibility, the Americans would do nothing.

The year after Arafat ordered the execution of the American diplomats in Khartoum, the Americans allowed him to address the United Nations in New York.

And only weeks ago, after accusing President Hafez al-Assad of Syria of participating in the bombing of the Marines—Kalaq believed Assad provided the hexogene for the bomb—the grinning dog president of America declared Assad to be a leader who worked for peace in Lebanon. The peace of a Syrian conquest. A Syrian peace for a Lebanon reunited with Syria.

Kalaq did not fear the Americans. The cowards. As he

told his men, the Americans would do nothing—even if a brave leader of the revolution declared his responsibility for the strike.

What would they do if Kalaq announced the victory tomorrow as his victory? Nothing. Perhaps they would send journalists and cameramen. To record his statements for the televisions of America, so that decadent and fearful audiences could stare at the image of the fighter who slaughtered their Marines and killed their diplomats.

Let the Iranians keep silent. Let them remain the unknown architects of mass assassination. Kalaq wanted no more roles in mysteries.

Tomorrow he took his place in the leadership of the Palestinian struggle. His people must forget the defeated Arafat, the impotent Habash, the ancient Abu Daoud, the dreaming Abu Iyad—and follow Iziz Kalaq the Killer. The killer of Maronites, Israelis, and Palestinian traitors. Killer of the Marines in Beirut. Killer of American diplomats.

With this action, his silence ended. He announced to the world his role in the defeats inflicted on the enemies of his people. Forget silence. Tomorrow, when he returned to Lebanon, he declared himself the leader of this action. And also he made public his role in the slaughter of the Marines in Beirut. Why should Kalaq, the leader of the front-line fighters, remain silent?

He exhaled marijuana smoke at the orbiting mosquitoes. With the glory of the strike against America, his name became another word for fear . . .

"Kalaq! You clown!" Gomez shouted out as she rushed into the shack. "Your men are celebrating their victory already and you are taking drugs! Where is the discipline? The Colombian Army operates in this area. Agencies of the United States work with the army. We could be attacked at any moment and you and all your men are drunk. The Colombians cannot protect you. Control your men."

Thrashing through the hanging netting, Kalaq stood. "You forget that you speak to Iziz Kalaq, commander of this action. If my men want to drink their beer in this miserable place, I grant them that comfort."

"And tomorrow morning, will they work on the explosives and drink their beer? And smoke marijuana?"

"Of course not."

"Of course not, because they will drink it all this night."

"If they drink it all, I will send for more."

"No! No more."

"You will do as I tell you. I am the commander."

Gomez looked at her watch. "You are the commander? Kalaq, you are the leader of one squad of fedayeen. Drunken fedayeen."

"You question my authority?"

"We will question he who actually commands." She pointed to the radio.

"Rajai commands nothing. Rajai is only my clerk. He hides in Lebanon while we—"

"I will ask him. I believe he will instruct you to control your men—no!"

He shot her in the face. She staggered back, blood spurting from the wound. Kalaq fired again and again into her chest. She fell backward against the wall. Stepping over her, he aimed at the center of her short-cut black hair and fired again, blood and brains exploding back from the bullet hole to spray his face.

Kalaq holstered his pistol. With the hot beer, he washed the gore from his hands and face. Men ran to the shack. Looking through the door, they stared at the corpse of the young woman.

"Drag that traitor out. Throw it in the jungle."

A Colombian teenager crouched down. Blood continued draining from the wounds to the woman's head and chest. He touched her throat to feel if her heart still beat. Turning, he stared at Kalaq. The teenager pushed through the Palestinians at the door. They heard him speak into his walkie-talkie.

"Did you hear?" Kalaq shouted at his men. "Drag that out of here!"

Two hundreds meters away, Stark monitored the quick transmissions between the Latins. The Latins spoke very quickly in idiomatic Spanish but he understood that Kalaq had murdered Gomez. He understood the obscenities. The Latins questioned one another in a confusion of voices and obscenities, one voice finally forcing the others to remain silent. Stark listened to the Latin speaking slowly. That voice made the decision for the group. Stark listened as the other Latins agreed.

The walkie-talkie frequency went quiet. Keying the hand-radio to alert Niles and Alvarez, Stark waited sixty seconds by his watch before telling them:

"The gang is breaking up."

17

BLOCKING the light from the moon and stars, the dense interwoven canopy of branches created a night of depthless black. Ali Akbar Javenbach watched the darkness. He saw no movements or shapes other than the vague shifting forms generated by his own eyes as he stared. Only sounds broke the black—leaves rattling through branches, the scratching and rustling of insects, and the movements of the other Marines as they shifted in their sleep. From time to time, he heard animals pass, their small, quick feet unmistakable.

Sometime after dawn—the Marines had learned from a microphone—the plane would come.

After two years of training, Javenbach finally faced the enemies of his new country—Palestinian mercenaries sent here by the fanatics who had taken Iran from the Iranian people. The seizure of Iran had not satisfied the mullahs and their gangs of Revolutionary Guards. The fanatics wanted the world. Americans did not understand this. When they talked with Javenbach of Iran, they asked why the mullahs hated the United States, why young Iranians volunteered to die in suicidal attacks, why the people of Iran destroyed the dictatorship of the Shah only to surrender to the crueler, far more murderous regime of the Ayatollah. Americans did not understand the psychopathic hatred of the mullahs for any people or nation or faith offering escape from the prison of the Islamic Republic.

Americans talked of preachers in small towns terrorizing children with threats of hell. They called these loudmouthed and intolerant men 'fundamentalists.' But the traditions and

315

laws of the United States limited the power of men who claimed to speak for God. Americans did not comprehend the culture that produced the mullah and how the word 'fundamentalist' could never describe the ignorance, the obsessions, the twisted faith of the mullahs.

Javenbach thought of the aged and senile mullah who had denounced his father for educating his daughters. Scuttling through the streets in his gray robes, the mullah quoted lines from the Koran memorized in his youth as a response to any question—the marriage of a daughter, the payment of a debt, the books read by children. Javenbach remembered his father correcting the mullah's failing memory and interpretation. The mullah took revenge by telling ignorant and illiterate street boys—who could not read the Koran—to scream 'unbelievers' and throw stones at the Javenbach home. Javenbach saw the same response years later when the leaders of the revolutionary movements attempted to form a government after the exile of the Shah. The mullahs took power by denouncing as 'unbelievers' anyone who questioned their rule—but after the revolution, the mullah's gangs did not shout and throw stones, they murdered.

And as the mullahs gained power, the Dark Ages returned to Iran. Americans believed they faced a nation of conflicting factions. In truth, Javenbach told them, they confronted a disease. Americans negotiated and waited, believing the factions of Iran would agree to rejoin the modern world. But a plague does not negotiate. If Javenbach had believed the revolution would mature to a government of laws and reason, he would have stayed, even fought for change. But he saw no hope for Iran between the insanity of the mullahs and the attacks of the Marxists.

Now he had the duty of fighting one gang of killers dispatched by the mad priests. He must not fail his new country. He knew that the others doubted his loyalty. Any slip in his discipline, any hesitance to act, would confirm their suspicions. He could not fail. America deserved his courage and any sacrifice this duty required.

Only three years before, his family came with nothing—no money, no gold—from an enemy nation. At a time when thousands of Iranians paraded across television screens cursing the United States as Satan, Americans tutored the Javenbach family in English, taught them bus schedules, and arranged for college classes. Americans and their government expected the Javenbachs to work and improve themselves, but demanded nothing else—no one demanded they abandon their religion, no one forced Christian or Jewish holidays on them, no one broke into their home to enforce American customs. Even if his mothers and sisters had wanted to wear the chador, the symbol of enemy Iran, no policeman or Christian priest would have torn the veil away.

No American—born and living all his life in liberty—understood his debt to his new country. He had talked with immigrants from many nations—Russian Jews, Vietnamese, Nicaraguans, and Ethiopians. The other immigrants understood. After the oppression and fear of dictators of whatever ideology or religion, the immigrants valued freedom more than life.

Javenbach only wanted an opportunity to prove himself equal to the gift of freedom.

He thought of this as he watched the darkness. The lives of all the other Marines depended on his vigilance, and he never stopped in his search for movement or sound. Then his eyes fixed on a line. He saw the form of a tree, a black form against an almost black background. Looking at the forest canopy, he saw a few specks of reflected gray light, the first light of dawn.

The minutes passed, the forest emerging from the darkness.. He saw the forms of the other men sleeping in the brush around him, their boots near his, their rifles in their hands and pointed outward.

He had trained for the honor of fighting for America for two years. Trying to think of when he decided to be a soldier, he remembered a night in his first months in the United States when he watched the inauguration of the new president on the color television of his uncle. And with shame, he remembered the simultaneous release of the diplomats and embassy personnel held prisoner in Iran. He had understood all the Farsi insults and taunts screamed at the cameras. In contrast, the inauguration seemed so calm and sane, stately, a symbol of a powerful nation that he prayed would accept him despite his place of birth. He watched the ceremony and social events in the capital, marveling at the polite transfer of power from one group to the opposing group. Soldiers in fine uniforms had stood at attention in the background, rifles in their hands—but unlike in Tehran, they did not point their rifles at the people of the nation.

Since then, he had developed a fascination for television coverage of formal government events—the speeches of the president, the foreign receptions, the State of the Union speeches every January. And at every event, behind the dignitaries at the center of the screen, he watched the ceremonial guards.

The ever-present honor guards had sparked a fantasy in his mind—guarding the President of the United States. He imagined himself at attention in the background, his uniform perfect, his body and face rigid, his mind focusing on all the real and conceivable threats to the life of the president. From this fantasy came the idea of joining the armed forces. Perhaps the president personified the United States. When he later talked with recruiters, he never mentioned his dream of becoming a ceremonial guard—he knew they would suspect him of plotting to assassinate the president. Instead, he volunteered for the Marine Corps. He proved himself in the basic skills, then volunteered for Recon. He wanted to prove himself a trustworthy and brave man, an American, worthy of the rights and liberty of an American, even if born in Iran.

And often he thought of appearing in the ceremonies—a naturalized citizen trusted to hold a rifle in the presence of the President of the United States of America. But that would come later.

He realized that he would miss tonight's State of the Union address by the president. Perhaps his uncle would videotape the presentation for him, three thousand kilometers away in the jungles of Colombia.

The faint whirring of the miniature recorders interrupted his thoughts. Javenbach looked to the band scanner unit. Alvarez had used black tape to reduce the power lamp to a speck—only a tiny point of light glowed, indicating the circuits operated. The LED frequency readout displayed numbers. As instructed, Javenbach shook Alvarez awake: "Scanner."

In the graying light, he saw Alvarez touch the recorder linked to the scanner, then the receiver/recorder units monitoring the transmitters placed in the airstrip shacks. Alvarez put on the headphones. Then, muffled by the distance, he heard a man shouting in the airstrip shacks. Alvarez listened.

A shadow moved beside them. Captain Niles crouched beside them, hand-signing a question to the sergeant.

"This is it," Alvarez answered in a whisper. "Coded message coming in. El Goon Numero Uno calling for the radio operator. Captain, your Arabic is better—"

Niles put on the headphones. They waited in silence for minutes. Sunlight broke through the upper canopy, the branches glowing green. Vatsek and Stark sensed the movement of the other men and woke. Finally Niles whispered to the others:

"Radio man sending out code. Code coming back." A minute later, the captain smiled. "Radio man asked Kalaq for the code book. Kalaq carries the code book. We've got to get him and that code book. The radio man's reading out the message . . . Aircraft . . . come . . . thirty minutes . . . next transmission . . . in zone of operation . . . That's it. Alvarez, code it to San Juan. Gentlemen, we go to work."

During the thirty-minute wait, Kalaq readied himself for the responsibility of dispatching the aircraft at the Americans. He changed to clean fatigues. He combed his hair. Without a mirror, he could not see himself—another detail the clerk Rajai had overlooked. Finally, while he waited for the radio operator to return, he smoked a marijuana cigarette and drank a beer.

The radio operator stepped through the door of the shack at the moment the dot and dash code came from the monitor. As the operator wrote down the transmission from the incoming aircraft, Kalaq paced the rotting floor of the shack. He feared the next hours. Any one of a hundred obstacles threatened the operation—if the Colombian Army interfered with the loading and take-off, if the pilots forgot their vows of martyrdom, if the Americans somehow intercepted the aircraft before the target, Iziz Kalaq lost his rightful position in the leadership of the Arabic Revolution.

Flipping through the pages of the phrase book, the radio operator decoded the transmission: "The aircraft . . . comes . . . the zone of operation . . . five minutes."

"Our long wait ends. Now comes the time of glory." Kalaq emptied another can of beer down his throat. Taking a sack of smoke grenades and the heavy G-3 rifle, he left the shack. The rising sun shot lines through the ground mist. Across the hundred meters of weeds, he saw men still sleeping in their hammocks. He aimed his rifle at the tree-tops and fired three times, the booming of the heavy-caliber rifle shattering the silence.

Men staggered from the shelter with rifles. Others swung out of their hammocks. Kalaq called out, "The plane comes now! Assemble! A few hours of work and we return to Lebanon!"

Kalaq thrashed through the grass and brush of an over-grown road to the airstrip. Looking to the east end of the airstrip, he saw no one at the parked trucks. The Colombians had the responsibility of guarding the road and the airstrip. But he had not seen a Colombian since he executed Gomez. Perhaps the reality of an execution shocked them and they had fled to the safety of their discos and revolutionary cafés. Their desertion meant nothing—he and his fedayeen did not need security for their last few hours in the jungle.

Walking into the open ground of the long airstrip, he looked at the eastern horizon. No plane approached. He continued to the center of the airstrip and threw a smoke grenade. Red smoke billowed from the grass, clouding into the still air. He listened for the plane but heard only the hissing of the smoke grenade and the distant voices of his men. He waited a few minutes before throwing the next grenade.

Propeller roar came from the northeast. He ran to the edge of the cleared strip and watched the sky. The noise rose to a thunder, and an old four-engine airliner appeared above the trees, one wing tip tilted to the ground as the plane banked in a circle around the airstrip. Kalaq saw the forms of men through the cockpit windshield. Around him, his fedayeen ran through the high grass, waving their arms at the plane. The old airliner disappeared to the west. Kalaq waited for minutes—had the pilot lost his courage? Then he heard the noise of the engines returning.

Seeming to clip the treetops at the west end of the airstrip, the airliner came down for the landing. The tires cut into the grass, the propellers throwing clouds of debris, the plane shuddering. The Palestinians watched the plane roar past them, the wings vibrating and flashing with the sun. At the far end of the landing strip, the plane slowed to a stop. Slowly, ponderously, the plane pivoted, the tail section almost touching the parked trucks and trailers. The engines died.

The silence lasted only seconds. Another plane landed. The twin-engined commuter plane bounced over the grass, the propellers dissipating the last of the red smoke as the small plane whipped through a turn and taxied to the west end of the field. Two men left the plane. The pilot remained at the controls.

"Muhammed! Salah!" Kalaq pointed to the commuter plane several hundred meters away. "Take your rifles. Go ask their identity. I will be with the others, loading the dynamite."

Doors opened on the airliner, a passenger door behind the cockpit and a cargo door near the tail. Men in the plane called out to the fedayeen, shouting for them to make a loading ramp.

Kalaq walked to the east end of the airstrip. He did not hurry—as a leader, he must maintain the appearance of command. He watched the confusion, crewmen shouting directions to his men, his men searching for the means to improvise a solution.

Considering the position of the cargo door to the piles of dynamite and plastic explosive, Kalaq saw the problem. The pilot had not correctly positioned the plane. He went to the nose of the plane and shouted up at the white-haired pilot:

"You! Pilot! Move this aircraft! Did you not see the

material you are to load? Why did you turn the loading door to the wrong side?"

The pilot did not respond. At the back, Kalaq saw one of his men moving a truck and trailer. The man backed the trailer under the fuselage. Other men stacked crates against the trailer to form steps. Despite the confusion, the crewmen and his fedayeen managed to improvise a ramp to the cargo door.

"Kalaq!" a voice called out. "Is it you? Here?"

He turned and saw a man he knew only by the name Ghassan. A Palestinian of always-changing allegiances, Ghassan had trained for Black September in 1971. But the leadership had not assigned him to the justice units executing Arab enemies or to the teams striking against the Zionists in Europe. They passed over him again when they chose the team to strike against the Zionists at the Munich Olympics. Denied a role in that victory, Ghassan left Black September for the more radical Palestinian groups striking at Israel from the camps in Lebanon. He worked with the Syrians and the Iraqis on special projects—bombs, rockets, and remote-controlled detonators. After the evacuation of Beirut by the main-force PLO, Ghassan appeared in the Bekaa with the Iranian Fahkr Rajai, working on the design of the bombs to destroy the American and French barracks.

"We work together again." Kalaq embraced his comrade. "What is your assignment this time?"

"The gift." Ghassan smiled, pointing at the airliner. Unlike Kalaq, Ghassan looked like a soldier. He cut his hair very close. In Lebanon, he wore Syrian Army fatigues. Here, he wore slacks and a Hawaiian sportshirt.

Muhammed and Salah, the fedayeen Kalaq had told to question the men from the commuter plane, called out to him. Muhammed pointed to Ghassan. "He is one of us."

"But the other will not speak," Salah told him.

"I will question him. Help with the loading. Who is he who came with you?" Kalaq asked Ghassan, looking at the balding, middle-aged man who approached.

"That is Jean-Paul," Ghassan laughed, "who says he is French. But is not."

Above them in the airliner, the old, white-haired pilot

stood in the passenger door and called out in Farsi to the man called Jean-Paul. Kalaq studied Jean-Paul's features.

"He is Iranian. Is he not?"

"He will not say. He tells nothing to this technician. He says only, secrecy, secrecy. But I know he is not Arabic."

Jean-Paul and the old pilot argued in Farsi. Another crewman stepped into the doorway. The three men argued in shouts.

"Iranians. This is my last operation with them. Soon I direct my own actions."

"Kalaq, you are one of the fighters. And in the future, we fight together. But now, I must work for the Ayatollah and prepare the gift to the Americans."

"I will introduce you to the comrades. I am directing their work out here. But in the aircraft, they must know to take instructions from you."

"No, my friend. Secrecy. They are not to know my name or that I am wiring the charges. The comrades in the aircraft will assist me and relay my instructions. I am sorry to impose the difficulty, but I must do as the Frenchman tells me."

"The Iranian."

Ghassan laughed. "The man with the money."

Walking up the ramps of boxes, Ghassan stepped through the cargo door. Fedayeen and crewmen stood on the flat trailer, the groups of men talking and gesturing, pointing to the piles of explosive. Kalaq did not interfere in the arguments. Calm, he waited for his friend Ghassan to take charge of the aircraft crewmen. Then Kalaq would direct the labor of his fedayeen. Watching the men, he saw the old, white-haired pilot slowly, awkwardly stepping down the ramp of boxes.

A voice shouted in bad Arabic: "You! You who are doing nothing!"

Kalaq turned and saw that Jean-Paul shouted at him. Ignoring the Iranian, he started toward the other men. But the Iranian ran to him, shouting and shaking his fist:

"You! Stop! Do as I tell you. I need you to help the pilot."

"I am Iziz Kalaq, commander of the fedayeen. Who are you?"

"That does not matter. That man, that pilot—" Jean-Paul pointed to the white-haired pilot. "Assign men to guard him. And men to work. The pilot says there is a ditch in the field that must be repaired before he can take off."

"We inspected the field. There are no ditches."

"He says there is. He must inspect the field himself."

"How can he inspect it? He cannot walk."

Jean-Paul spoke quickly to the old pilot. To answer, the pilot walked away, slow but determined. "And he must be guarded. He is to be martyred in the action and he cannot be allowed to escape."

"An unwilling martyr. I will guard him myself. Allow me to start the men to work. I will return immediately."

On the ramps, a group of fedayeen formed a line. One man took a black-plastic bundle of dynamite from the pile and passed it to the next. The dynamite sped through their hands to the crewmen in the door. Then came the next bundle and the next. A crewman threw empty plastic bags out of the airliner. Kalaq walked through the sweating men, encouraging them—but they did not stop to listen. Another group of fedayeen rolled a barrel of fuel across the grass. A crewman walked onto the wing with hoses and a hand-pump with which to top off the plane's tanks. Kalaq returned to the Iranian. A hundred meters away, the pilot walked through the grass, peering down at the flat, hard-packed earth.

"All is in order. I am free to assist you."

"Then go! Go!" the Iranian told him. "Look there. He has already escaped."

"That old man?" Kalaq rushed after the pilot, laughing at the idea. "Don't escape, old man. You can't escape from this hell. You could walk forever and never escape. Fly your plane into the paradise of martyrs. Only then shall I receive the glory of your sacrifice."

Prone in the brush at the side of the airstrip, Javenbach stared at the McDonnell-Douglas DC-4. Images and memories juxtaposed in his mind: the obsolete propeller-driven DC-6 transport that carried his family from Karachi to Turkey, a map of the Americas in his citizenship class, a newspaper photo of an old prop-driven passenger plane that had flown from Colombia with tons of marijuana and landed on a highway in Kansas.

The four-engined DC-4 had a cargo capacity of several tons. With careful fuel use, the plane could fly to the United States—Javenbach had no doubt of that. The DC-6 transport plane from Karachi, loaded with tons of cargo and passengers, had flown for thousands of kilometers without a stop—Karachi to Kuwait, Kuwait to Istanbul.

If the Palestinians completed the loading of the explosives early in the day, the plane could fly the few thousand kilometers to Washington before the end of the State of the Union speech by the president, then crash into the assembled leaders of the United States, killing the representatives, the senators, and the president.

The assassination of the American government, televised to the world.

Javenbach shimmied backward into the brush. Ten meters behind him, concealed in the trees, Lieutenant Stark continued monitoring frequencies on the band scanner.

"I know the target," Javenbach whispered.

"Are there Iranians there? Did you overhear it?"

"The State of the Union speech. By the president. Tonight. It is only three thousand kilometers away. Two thousand miles. That plane can fly from here to Washington with tons of explosive."

Stark touched the hand-radio Javenbach wore on his webbing belt. "Talk to the captain."

The Palestinians threw the black plastic bags from hand to hand along the line of men. One of the bags broke, spilling sticks of dynamite. Men stepped back, startled by the sight of the explosive. A teenager snatched up the loose sticks and tossed the sticks to the relay line. The men shouted jokes to one another as they passed the individual sticks of dynamite through the cargo door of the old airliner.

Every shout boomed through Niles's head. He turned down the volume of the preamp on the shotgun microphone and tried to follow Kalaq as he ran after the white-haired pilot. But the noise and voices of the men working next to the airliner overwhelmed the microphone. He heard the voice of the Iranian called Jean-Paul, shouting Arabic at the Palestinians playing with the sticks of dynamite.

His hand-radio clicked. Glancing to Alvarez, he saw the sergeant cup his hand over the earphone he wore and listen. The sergeant keyed a confirmation. He turned to Niles and pointed from the hand-radio to Niles, hand-signing for Niles to talk. Niles shook his head no. Alvarez whispered the single word:

"Important."

"Watch Jean-Paul the Iranian," Niles whispered. "Try to record any talk with Ghassan. He might be the leader." Leaving Alvarez with the microphone and cassette recorder, Niles slowly slipped back through the discarded cans and gray clay to where Vatsek waited with their equipment.

"Strak-man and Teen-wonder worked it out," Vatsek whispered to him.

"Teen-wonder?"

"Javenbach."

Niles plugged in his earphone. Keying his radio, he whispered: "This is the old man. What's so important?"

"Captain, this is the corporal. I believe I know the target. That plane—"

"Lieutenant!" Niles interrupted. "Are you absolutely positive these radios cannot be intercepted?"

"Yes, sir. Absolutely, sir. Without one of our radios to decode the transmissions, anyone monitoring our frequency will hear only electronic noise. I tested the radios myself, sir. I'd stake my life on the security of the encrypting circuits."

"You are, your life and our lives. Continue, Corporal."

"Sir, that aircraft is very old, but it can fly to Washington in eight or nine hours. The State of the Union speech is tonight. The president. All the senators. The representatives. All of the leaders together on television."

"Of course . . ." Niles went silent for a moment, considering the simplicity of the attack. The combined technical resources of the Coast Guard, the DEA, and the Air Force stopped only five or ten per cent of the drug flights entering the United States. The converted airliner would fly north, then hide in the air traffic around Washington. Entering the restricted air space of the capital at maximum speed, at a hundred meters off the ground, the pilot would aim for the lights of the Capitol Building. The Secret Service would have less than thirty seconds to hit the airliner with Stinger missiles. But would a hit from a small missile stop the airliner? Thirty or forty tons of high-speed metal? Maybe not. Once the pilot started his straight-line kamikaze run, that airliner would not stop. They could do it. So obvious.

"Good thinking, Corporal. Maybe you guessed it. Heyzoot, you still there?"

Key clicks answered.

"I'll come up and take back the microphone. I want this information coded to San Juan for relay north. Also forward this information. Second plane brought an Iranian. Monitored conversation identifies him as paymaster of technical specialists now assembling explosives. Request permission to capture Iranian and technical specialist. Also, request permission to destroy the plane here. Repeat, destroy."

The propeller drone of the plane alerted Sayed. Exactly as his director in Lebanon had told him, the noise of the propellers came from the east thirty minutes after sunrise. He did not see the plane but he heard it circle the airstrip two kilometers to the south. A second plane landed a minute later. Sayed hurried through the camp, shouting out to the men:

"Into your squads!"

The Revolutionary Guards kicked out their cooking fires. Gulping the last of their tea, finishing their rice and canned meat, they threw down the aluminum dishes—they would not need their mess kits again. All nonessential equipment remained here. After the action, they carried only their weapons back to the ship waiting off Santa Marta.

Sayed shouted at the PKM gunners, "Call your men together. You are the leaders! You know your men."

The shouts of the four machine gunners added to the noise. With the heavy belt-fed PKM machine guns hanging by slings from their shoulders, the team leaders staggered through the trees, finding the men in their fire teams.

At the trucks, the Colombian drivers watched. They

smoked their first cigarettes of the day and watched the foreign militiamen. Sayed went to the drivers. In his bad Spanish, he told them for the tenth time:

"You wait here all day, understand me? We return before night."

"Of course, General. We will wait. But what if you do not return?"

Turning his back on the laughter of the drivers, he took Iradj aside. Suffering a chest wound early in the war against Iraq, the young man had never completely recovered. The voyage through tropical heat had aggravated the old wound and he had coughed blood. Sayed did not want the coughing to betray the other men as they infiltrated the airstrip. He had decided to leave Iradj with the trucks, watching the drivers.

"Do not take your eyes away from those men. Do not allow them to approach you. They are dishonest. They are criminals. If they try any tricks or they try to leave before night, shoot them. We will all depend on you."

"I shoot—" Coughing interrupted Iradj. He spat, then coughed again, doubling up as he hacked. He spat again. "I shoot them? But then how do we return to the ocean?"

"They are paid to wait until night. If they try to leave before night, shoot them. We will drive the trucks ourselves."

Sayed went to the four fire teams. Each team had five men, a PKM machine gunner and four men with Kalashnikov rifles. Three men in each group carried ammunition drums for the machine guns. The last man carried a replacement barrel for the PKM. All the men carried packs with rations and water for the day. Sayed hurried through the groups of Revolutionary Guards, checking the weapons and the walkie-talkies of the machine gunners. He found every detail in order—these men had all fought on the Iraqi Front, where errors meant death. Shouldering his own pack, with his rifle in his hands, he addressed the Guards:

"Remember! Silence and patience. In the next hours, we will take our positions. Then we wait. The damned Arabs are to complete their work. The aircraft is to go. But then, when the aircraft is gone, all Arab hirelings of Iraq die. Wait for my word and fire. Any Arab that we do not kill immediately, we must hunt down and kill. We cannot return to the ship and we cannot return to Iran until we kill every one of the lackies of the monster Saddam."

Sayed led the line through the shadowed rain forest. In total, his twenty men carried sixteen automatic rifles and four heavy machine guns—and they would strike by surprise, cutting down the Arabs and their Latin mercenaries in a murderous cross fire. Sayed expected—and the director in Lebanon demanded—total annihilation. The director had ordered that the Arabs and Latin mercenaries cease to exist. If an Arab escaped, if one of the Latins lived to tell the Palestinian Revolutionary Front of the attack in Colombia, then his unit had failed.

And failure meant Sayed returned to the Iraqi Front.

Rushing south to the airstrip, his body flowing with sweat after only a hundred steps, he refused to consider failure. He marched to victory. Freedom from the front.

Insallah.

Against the brilliant greens of the airstrip and the trees, the old pilot looked already dead. He had no color in his face, the skin dead white, his eyes lined by black sags. Kalaq followed him for hundreds of meters as the old man examined the earth of the airstrip. The pilot said nothing as he paced, staring at the earth, kicking aside the grass and weeds, looking at the trees at the edges of the airstrip.

Kalaq tried to question the pilot. "Do you speak Arabic? Can you tell me what the target is? Can you cast light on what the Ayatollah holds secret?"

The old man turned and walked away quickly. Kalaq watched him, incredulous. Did the old man dream he could run into the jungle? Finally Kalaq followed him. "Think you can escape? How can you escape the will of God? Is that not what you Iranians say?"

Glaring at Kalaq, his eyes sharp, his jaw clenched, the old pilot turned again. He continued toward the west end of the airstrip. He ignored Kalaq. A few meters later, he kicked something in the grass and pointed.

An automobile wheel lay in the grass. The work crews had

missed the wheel when they cleaned the airstrip. Kalaq saw that the tracks of the airliner's tires passed over the wheel. Kalaq jerked the tire out of the grass and weeds. Running, he rolled the wheel to the edge of the airstrip. The pilot resumed his inspection. Kalaq ran back, coughing and spitting. He lit a cigarette and paced behind the pilot.

"This must be one of the jokes of Rajai. No one knows the target. They can tell me nothing. But now I meet with he who does know the target and he does not speak my language. That clerk Rajai would think this funny."

The pilot stopped again. He stared at Kalaq. Then he looked back at the distant airliner. He walked a meter to one side. Replotting a straight line from the airliner to the west end of the airstrip, he altered his path.

Kalaq laughed. "Old man, you Iranian, you are only one more device of suffering in this hell. The heat, the insects, the Colombians, the secret. I ask you this, Iranian. Fly directly to your martyrdom. Do not permit the Colombians or the Americans to shoot you down. Let nothing stop you. For if you do not succeed, I will never know the answer. I will return to Lebanon and wait but never know, because until the television shows the flames and the dead, it will remain a secret, even to those who—"

"Quiet!" The pilot told him.

"What? You do speak my language. Now answer my question. What is the target?"

"I do not know." The old pilot stopped. Watching Kalaq for a response, he spoke in slow, halting Arabic: "Walk. If they see us stop, if they see us talk, it is suspicious."

"Talk, old man."

"Palestinian, I give you your life. Promise you will not interfere with that flight if I speak."

"Why do you accuse me of interference?"

"Listen to me. If I do not fly that airplane against the Americans, the fanatics kill my children and my grandchildren. But I think they kill my children and grandchildren even if many Americans die. Promise me there will be no interference and I will give you your life."

Kalaq stared at the old man. "I want this victory. I want

the strike against the Americans. Why would I interfere with the airplane?"

"The fanatics deceive you. You will not know. Never know. You do not return to Lebanon. They silence you. You will die."

"What? I am the leader of the fedayeen. I plotted this with the Iranian who commands the action. I am one of the leaders. They cannot—"

"If you are a leader, why do you not know the target? Do you think the fanatics will leave you—a gang of Palestinians—to tell the Americans who attacked them? Think, Palestinian. The fanatics want their secret. Death will silence you forever. That is why you die."

Niles converted his Colt Commando to a silent rifle. He dropped out the magazine, then slowly pulled back the charging handle to eject the cartridge from the chamber. He pushed in the magazine of reduced-charge Interdynamics rounds. Finally, he slipped the aluminum suppressor tube over the muzzle of the rifle.

Beside him, Vatsek loaded a 40mm high-explosive round in his M-16/M-203. He slowly closed the sliding barrel of the M-203 and set the safety. Vatsek and Niles waited, watching the Palestinians refuel and load the airliner.

Fifty meters away, a Palestinian pumped aviation gas from a barrel. A long hose from the hand-pump went straight up to the wing of the old airliner. A crewman crouched on the wing, holding the hose in place. Two other men rolled another barrel of fuel through the high grass.

At his web belt, Niles felt the click of his hand-radio. He clicked an acknowledgment and cupped his hand over his earphone. Stark told him:

"Request to destroy denied. Repeat, request denied by highest authority. Air Force will intercept threat. Colonel requests that we capture leaders for interrogation. He sends congratulations on mission accomplished."

Niles stared at the airliner, watching the gang loading the explosive. He thought of the arrival of the second plane after the airliner. Monitoring the conversations of Kalaq, he had identified Jean-Paul the Iranian and Ghassan the specialist. Ghassan called the Iranian the paymaster. Perhaps the Iranian led this action, perhaps he only paid the gangs working for the Iranians—either way, he worked with the commanders in Tehran. Niles knew—he would bet a month's pay—that the commuter plane would take the Iranian and the bomb specialist out before the airliner tried to get off the ground—which meant he lost the connection to Iran. Only Kalaq would remain. Kalaq had the code book, but Niles doubted he knew who had organized and funded the attack. Kalaq complained of knowing nothing.

Under the wing, he saw Jean-Paul the Iranian take a walkie-talkie from his pocket. The Iranian listened, then walked away from the loading of the plane. He called out to the men in the cockpit of the airliner. A man shouted down to him. Speaking quickly into the walkie-talkie, the Iranian hurried toward the west end of the field where the small plane waited. Niles felt his hand-radio click again. Stark told him:

"Captain, the scanner monitored a walkie-talkie exchange in Farsi. The corporal says the pilot of that Cessna informed the Iranian—his name is actually Minatchi, not Jean-Paul—that the airliner pilot is talking with Kalaq. They are alarmed because they did not know that the pilot spoke Arabic."

Niles clicked an acknowledgment. He watched the Iranian running for the other end of the airstrip and he realized—

Hit them now.

Taking his hand-radio from his web belt, he curled around it to cover his whisper. He clicked the key to alert the men. Despite Lieutenant Stark's assurances of the fail-safe encoding, he did not use the names of the other Marines. "Gentlemen, there is about to be a fuel transfer accident. Lieutenant, Corporal. I want you two in motion for that Cessna. I want you to capture the Iranian, that Palestinian Kalaq, and that white-haired pilot. If you get them, we can prove Iran is responsible for this shit. I want you in motion right now, go!"

"Yes, sir. Moving."

"Hey-zoot, Godzilla. Prepare to evacuate."

Niles screwed a hearing protector into his right ear, hoping the earphone in his left ear would give some protection. He pulled back the charging handle of his silenced Commando to chamber the first Interdynamics round. Raising the rifle, he sighted on the head of the crewman crouched on the airliner's wing. The crewman held the hose in the fuel port.

"Ready?" Niles asked Vatsek.

"Ready since October the twenty-third."

On the wing, the crewman leaned forward, looking inside the tank. The silent bullet punched into his skull and he fell forward and lay still, instantly dead. The fuel hose slipped out of his hand. Aviation gasoline spurted from the hose, gasoline flowing over the wing, then splashing onto the trailer where the line of Palestinians passed dynamite hand-to-hand.

"Now!" Niles hissed.

The launcher popped and the heads of the Palestinians whipped toward the sound. An instant later, the grenade exploded with a flat crack. High-velocity steel-wire shrapnel cut down men, others shouted out in panic as the gasoline flashed. Niles and Vatsek did not stay to watch.

A rifle fired, one of the gunmen raking the trash heap with full-automatic. Niles signaled for Vatsek to continue back. Chambering another Interdynamics cartridge, he snapped the silent shot into the face of the Palestinian. The gunman put his hand over his eye and staggered. The other men scattered, running from the flames.

Niles moved back fast, putting trees between him and the burning airliner. He felt his hand-radio clicking but did not stop. Rising to a crouch, he paused to scan the forest behind him—the tangles of seedling trees and ferns, the hanging liana vines, the deep shadows—then turned and sprinted.

Kalashnikov fire tore past him, his reflexes throwing him sideways and down as the high-cyclic-rate automatic fire of M-16 rifles answered the ComBloc weapons. Niles shimmied forward. A Kalashnikov fired and Vatsek's M-203 launched high explosive. The shrapnel left a wounded man screaming until another burst of M-16 fire cut him off. His hand-radio clicked and clicked until he answered.

Stark's voice came fast. "—says there's other Iranians operating out here. Scanner's picking up radios."

"No shit!" Vatsek answered. "We just killed five of the crazies."

"Lieutenant." Niles spoke over the others. "Stop talking and make those captures."

"Yes, sir—"

Niles crawled through a wall of thorny ferns and looked into the muzzle of Alvarez's rifle.

"Sorry, sir. Tried to warn you. A squad of Iranians walked into us—"

"Time to go, sergeant. Where's—"

Vatsek dodged through the trees, his M-16/M-203 in one hand, a Soviet PKM machine gun in the other. A pack hung over one shoulder. Despite the weight, the hulking sergeant moved fast. "Look what I found—"

"Drop it, Sergeant. No time for souvenirs. We've got to make distance."

"Ain't a souvenir, sir. Hey-zoot here. High explosive in the forty tube." Vatsek passed his M-16/M-203 over-and-under automatic rifle/grenade launcher to Alvarez. He slipped the pack over his head. The blood-soaked pack held another 250-round drum of heavy 7.62x54mm ammunition. "And look at this—"

Vatsek passed a walkie-talkie to Alvarez. Alvarez switched off the power and put it in his pack with the squad's long-range radio.

"Sergeant!" Niles hissed, pointing back at the airliner. "You got tons of burning av-gas and explosive back there. You waste time carrying that and you waste your life!"

"Captain!" Vatsek pointed into the rain forest with the muzzle of the PKM. "We got unknown numbers of Iranians out there. I don't carry this and they got us outgunned! Take the point, sir! Waiting for you, sir!" Vatsek jerked back the cocking to confirm the loading of the machine gun. A cartridge flew free. "Long life through superior firepower!"

18

PARALLELING the airstrip, Javenbach ran through the forest. He thrashed through tangled growth and vines, birds startling away. His rush and noise violated all the teachings of his instructors—but he continued running, knowing that he risked his life, trying to gain distance on the gang leaders. The far-off hammering of a heavy-caliber automatic weapon stopped him.

He turned and saw Lieutenant Stark pointing toward the airstrip. Javenbach veered through twenty meters of trees. At the edge of the open ground, earth movers had left mounds of soil. Years of matted grass covered the mounds. He went flat in the grass and ferns. Parting the weeds with his rifle muzzle, he scanned the open ground.

Fifty meters away, directly opposite him, the gang leaders—Kalaq the Palestinian and Jean-Paul Minatchi—stood with the white-haired pilot. They all watched the east end of the airstrip.

Flames rose from the airliner. In the distance, Javenbach saw men running. Shooting broke out, rifles firing bursts of full-automatic.

At the west end of the field, only two hundred meters away, the Cessna pilot sprinted for the twin-engine commuter plane. Javenbach went to one knee and sighted his M-16 on the Cessna's right engine. But he did not fire. He looked at Kalaq and Minatchi—if he shot out the engine, he alerted the men the captain had ordered him to capture.

"Corporal!" Stark crept from the trees. He still carried the backpack of electronics. Dropping down flat, the lieuten-

335

ant held out headphones. "Give me a quick translation of this . . ."

As he watched the Cessna pilot climb into the cockpit of the plane, Javenbach listened to a cassette tape of static-blurred Farsi voices shouting to one another over walkie-talkies. Javenbach recognized the voice of the leader telling the others to hold their fire. Then the leader called out again and again for Yusef. Yusef did not answer.

Electric starters whining, the props of the Cessna turned, the engines sputtering, then revving. Javenbach saw Kalaq and Minatchi run for the Cessna. The old pilot stood alone in the center of the airstrip, watching the airliner burn. Throwing off the scanner headphones, Javenbach raised his rifle again.

A flash lit the windshield of the Cessna. Javenbach snapped a glance to the airliner and saw a wing flipping away from a rising ball of flame. He sighted on the right engine of the Cessna and fired a burst as the earth-shaking roar of the explosion hit. The roar covered the muzzle reports.

But the prop continued spinning. Engines revving at full power, the Cessna bounced across the airstrip. Kalaq and Minatchi waved their arms to stop the pilot. Javenbach sighted on the head of the pilot.

Before his finger touched the trigger, glass sprayed from the cockpit. The pilot jerked sideways. The left engine sputtered and stopped. The Cessna veered to the left as the sheet metal of the plane's fuselage dented and flexed. Flame sprayed from the right wing. The plane continued in a wide arc, leaving a stream of burning gasoline in the grass. Metal screeched and the right propeller stopped.

In the sudden quiet, the hammering of machine guns drifted across the airstrip. Kalaq and Minatchi watched their escape from Guajira burning.

Stark keyed his hand-radio. "This is the lieutenant. Automatic weapon fire has destroyed the small plane here. What is the source of the weapon fire?"

Alvarez reported, "That gang of Iranians. They're wiping out everything that moves. Did you make the grab?"

"They're running this way!" Javenbach dropped down flat. Kalaq and Minatchi wove through the high grass, Kalaq sprinting erratic zigzags, the middle-aged and overweight Iranian lagging behind. Javenbach heard high-velocity bullets ripping through the grass. Bullets skipped off the earth and hummed over his head, cutting through branches.

Screaming with pain, calling out to Kalaq, Minatchi fell. Kalaq did not stop. Lieutenant Stark motioned Javenbach back into the trees. Stark pointed to himself then to the left. Javenbach nodded and crawled right, keeping his head below the top of the overgrown mounds. Bullets punched into the trees as the machine gunner hundreds of meters away tried to bring down Kalaq. Looking up, Javenbach watched the Palestinian sprint to the right, then cut left and smash through a tangle of brush only a few steps away.

Javenbach rose to one knee and scanned the sun-streaked shadows of the forest. He heard Kalaq coughing and stumbling. Steel clattered. Javenbach keyed his hand-radio and whispered, "This is the corporal. I am following Kalaq."

The explosion slamming his ears, Niles dropped flat. Fragments roared over him and he felt a wave of heat. He stayed face down as metal rattled down through the trees. Branches fell. Men screamed, others shouted out.

Raising his head, Niles saw a scene of flames and swirling gray smoke. The trees lining the east end of the airstrip burned. Forms moved through the smoke, staggering away from the fires. Looking back, Niles saw Vatsek throw aside a sheet of metal. Alvarez checked Vatsek's back for injury and the two Marines rushed forward to Niles, dropping prone beside him and looking for wounds.

"I'm okay," Niles told them. He pulled the hearing protector out of his ear. Despite the protector, he heard a high-pitched whine.

"Big bang," Vatsek commented, speaking next to Niles's ears but sounding far away. "Gang got their money's worth."

Machine guns fired from across the airstrip, heavy-caliber bullets tearing through the trees and palms.

"The Iranians." Alvarez shifted his position, crouching behind the protection of a meter-thick trunk.

Acrid smoke drifting from the burning trees and wreckage

blocked the light. The Palestinians shouted to one another in the smoke, a shout stopping with a grunt as a man took a bullet in the back. Others fired back blindly at the gunners. The Marines waited as the Palestinians retreated.

Niles pointed straight ahead. Vatsek flipped out the bipod legs of the PKM machine gun. Niles shook his head no. Checking his Colt Commando for damage, Niles sighted down the long aluminum suppressor tube—straight. He slapped the base of the Interdynamics magazine, then advanced through the semi-darkness, watching for the Palestinians. He felt his hand-radio click but did not stop. Behind him, Alvarez whispered into his radio.

Leaves and fragments continued falling around Niles. The ringing in his ears altered the small sounds, every sound becoming a threat. He depended on his eyes, scanning the smoky darkness for shapes and movement.

A Palestinian—a G-3 rifle in his hands—crouched near the edge of the airstrip, looking across the open ground to the opposite tree line. A voice called out in Arabic, asking if he saw the attackers. The Palestinian answered no, then turned back to watch the airstrip. Niles sighted the Commando on the back of the gunman's head and dropped him with a silent Interdynamics slug. He pulled back the charging handle to chamber another cartridge and moved forward. The voice called out again. When no answer came, the form of a second gunman appeared in the smoke.

Stepping back, Niles switched his grip on the Commando, putting the short rifle to his left shoulder as he eased around a tree knotted with lianas. He heard movement and stepped sideways, bringing up the rifle—and his boot caught on a vine. Twisting as he fell, he brought up the Commando.

The Palestinian turned. A beardless teenager, he wore baggy camouflage pants and a sweat-soaked T-shirt. He held a G-3 automatic rifle. The sight of the falling American startled him. He took two steps back as he brought down the muzzle of the heavy rifle.

Niles pointed the Commando at the teenage fedayeen's chest and snapped off the shot. But the underpowered Interdynamics slug hit the G-3 rifle, punching through the plastic front hand-guard and ricocheting from the steel barrel. The smashed slug slashed across the Palestinian's chest. Staggering back, blood spreading from the long, shallow wound, the Palestinian aimed his rifle at Niles and died as Vatsek triggered a long burst from the PKM.

Firing the heavy machine gun like an assault rifle, Vatsek rushed forward, holding the muzzle on line with the teenager's chest. The bullets tore through the boy's body, the impact of bullets flipping the rifle aside and throwing the boy back into ferns.

A pistol popped, a bullet zipping past Vatsek. The hulking sergeant dropped to one knee and raised the PKM to his shoulder. He tracked a form in the smoke and fired a three-round burst, a simultaneous burst coming from Alvarez. Niles saw a man spin back.

Alvarez crouched beside the captain. "They know we're here now."

A wild spray of 7.62NATO tore through the foliage as Palestinians fired their G-3 rifles at the sound of the Marine's weapons. Niles twisted the aluminum suppressor off his Commando and jammed it in his pack. He changed magazines, loading his rifle with full-powered cartridges, then sprinted to the west, dodging through the forest, Vatsek and Alvarez a few steps behind him, while the Palestinians continued wasting ammunition.

Niles stopped at a rutted and overgrown trail that had once been a road leading from the airstrip. At the other end, he saw the shack housing the Palestinian radio. He slipped back into the brush and signaled Vatsek and Alvarez to stop. Then he keyed his radio. "Lieutenant. This is the Old Man. You got those prisoners?"

"We're following Kalaq," the lieutenant answered. "He succeeded in running into the jungle. The other leader and the pilot did not."

The ringing in Niles's ears forced him to turn up the volume of the radio. "Which way is he moving?"

"We split up. I think they're going east along the side of the airfield."

"Back to the radio."

"Perhaps, sir."

"And the Iranians?"

"Machine gun fire destroyed the Cessna. I saw the Iranian leader fall. I don't know about the older pilot. He's somewhere on the airfield."

"Find them. We must get that Iranian. And Kalaq and his code book."

Niles signaled Alvarez. The sergeant crouched next to him. As Vatsek watched the area, Niles asked: "Do you have the frequency of the gang's radio?"

"Got it ten times."

"Louder. I'm having trouble hearing."

"Me, too. Wonder why? I got the frequency."

"You think you could fake a coded answer if Iran sends in another message?"

"They don't send coded messages. I think it's Morse numbers and letters. I think that code book's got lines of jive, indexed by numbers and letters. The two messages this morning were the same except for one sequence. They can't send information, but the system's good enough for what they're doing, you know, alerts and things like that."

Automatic weapons fired a hundred meters behind them. Niles heard the distinctive cyclic rate of Kalashnikov rifles. The G-3 rifles of the Palestinians returned the fire. Then came long bursts from a PKM machine gun. The Palestinians did not fire again.

"It's that E-rannie gang putting down the bomber gang—" Alvarez started.

Single shots from Kalashnikovs popped as the Iranians killed wounded.

"—and they are taking no prisoners. Try to figure this one out, Captain."

"Could you fake a message?"

"If I got that code book. What do you want me to say?"

"Nothing. I want a fix on their headquarters. Vatsek! You got forty millimeter flares?"

"Red star parachute."

"Give me one more high explosive and the red flare."

"Can't see the flare in the daylight."

"That so?" Taking the M-16/M-203 from Alvarez, Niles sighted on the shack. He put the high-explosive grenade through the door. The pop sent dust clouding from the windows and walls. Reloading the M-203 tube with the flare, he launched the flare into the interior of the shack. Red chemical glare lit the interior, smoke billowing from holes in the roof. Putting the second high-explosive grenade in the tube, he set the safety and passed the assault rifle/grenade launcher back to Alvarez.

"Oh, yeah." Vatsek nodded. "Pyro-action."

"That radio station is hereby off the air," Alvarez added.

Niles crossed the narrow road and signaled the others to follow. "Now we get that code book."

Corporal Javenbach heard fire fights hundreds of meters away. He rose from a crouch and took three slow and silent steps to the cover of a head-high palm. With the muzzle of his rifle, he shifted a frond aside.

Kalaq stood in a green expanse of broad-leafed plants. Blood streamed down his face as he stared at the shadows of the forest around him. He swept his heavy rifle in a semi-circle, aiming everywhere. Turning, Kalaq stomped through the lush growth. Javenbach saw the Palestinian slip behind the trunk of a tree and watch for a moment. Then he continued, his boots loud in the leaves and small plants.

As he moved away, Javenbach felt his hand-radio click. He did not risk a voice answer. He crouched and watched the forest. Clicking the transmit key, he plugged in the earphone and pushed it into his ear.

Captain Niles asked, "Corporal? Are you following Ka-laq?"

He answered with two clicks, yes.

"You're close?"

Two clicks, yes.

"Is he going back toward the buildings?"

Three clicks, no.

"He's running?"

Two clicks, yes.

A rifle blast shattered the silence. Javenbach dropped flat as Kalaq fired two- and three-shot bursts, the bullets ripping through branches and small trees. All of the bullets went in another direction.

"He shooting at you?"

"No, sir," Javenbach whispered.

"On our way. Stay close to him. You lose him, he's gone."

Hearing Kalaq run, Javenbach walked as quickly as the ground vegetation allowed, his eyes scanning shadows ahead. A slight wind swayed the higher branches, bringing the acrid stink of burning gasoline and rubber. He heard the clatter of plastic and metal—a rifle hitting a tree. Javenbach saw Kalaq suddenly illuminated by a shaft of light. Angling behind a tangle of brush, Javenbach rushed forward, gaining ten meters. He heard a hacking cough. He peered through the screen of leaves and saw Kalaq leaning against a tree, coughing and choking, spitting out long streams of mucus.

Javenbach moved fast. Timing his strides to the coughing, he circled the Palestinian. He heard boots cracking forest debris and froze, but too late. Thrashing through the brush, Kalaq wiped his face with one of his fatigue sleeves as he stumbled. Javenbach rushed him.

The noise of boots sprinting startled Kalaq. Panicked, he turned and looked back, then whipped around and saw the Marine but could not raise his G-3 before Javenbach straight-armed him, throwing him back against a tree. Javenbach jerked up a knee at Kalaq's crotch but Kalaq twisted, smashing the plastic stock of the G-3 across the Marine's ribs. Javenbach whipped the butt of his M-16 around and missed Kalaq's head, hitting the tree, the plastic and aluminum rifle bending where the stock joined the receiver. Javenbach swung again and again, beating Kalaq with the plastic stock. Kalaq tried to block the blows with his left arm. Javenbach beat down the arm and slammed him in the face.

Stunned, Kalaq fell. Javenbach hit him across the back of the head, finally snapping off the stock and buffer tube of the M-16. He crouched on Kalaq's back, forcing his face into the matted leaves, trying to wrench his arms behind him. Kalaq pulled his pistol and twisted, throwing Javenbach to the side as he tried to point the pistol. Javenbach grabbed his arm as he fired.

The 9mm bullet punched through Kalaq's foot. Screaming, Kalaq fired again, blindly trying to find the Marine with bullets. Javenbach fell to his side and kicked, his boot contacting Kalaq's hand and throwing the pistol meters away. Javenbach rolled onto the screaming man and drove a fist into his solar plexus.

Gasping, choking, Kalaq struggled to breathe. Javenbach hit him again, then turned him over and ripped his fatigue shirt off, knotting the torn shirt around his arms, binding his feet with the sling of the broken M-16. Pointing the G-3 rifle at Kalaq, Javenbach keyed his hand-radio.

"I took the Palestinian leader."

Niles answered from a few steps away. "Yeah, you took him." Going to the semiconscious prisoner, Niles checked the pockets of the Palestinian's fatigues. In his right thigh pocket, he found a notebook. Numbered, hand-written lines covered the pages.

"Shit!" Vatsek spat out. "It's in Arabic."

"Of course, Sergeant," Niles laughed. His laughter stopped when he saw an instant photo between the pages. The snapshot showed Angelique Chardon screaming against pain she could not escape. Niles returned the photo to the notebook. "Now let's get this prisoner back to the airfield. Alive."

On his belly in the grass, Lieutenant Stark searched for Jean-Paul Minatchi. He stayed flat, never raising his head, using his hands to probe ahead as he crawled over the flat, hard airstrip. Though the high grass concealed him, the grass offered no protection from bullets. If the Iranian force spotted him, he died.

Fire fights continued as the Iranian force swept from the east end of the airstrip around to the south side. He heard shots from the G-3 rifles of the Palestinians—but the Iranian force responded with overwhelming fire from their Kalashnikov automatic rifles and PKM machine guns.

He no longer heard the ripping sound of M-16 rifles. Minutes before, he had monitored the radio conversation between Captain Niles and Corporal Javenbach. While they pursued the Palestinian leader Kalaq, Stark had to find the Iranian paymaster of the terrorists, Jean-Paul Minatchi, before the Iranian execution squads started their final search of the area.

A man groaned and called out—Stark did not recognize the language but he veered toward the voice.

Flies and the rich smell of blood stopped him. His hand found clotted blood. Angling away from the voice, he followed the smeared blood to fly-swarming shoes and pants. Blood soaked the clothing of the dead man. Stark stayed an arm's length away as he circled around—a scab of clotting blood surrounded the corpse.

Minatchi had bled to death. A bullet from a PKM had destroyed his right thigh, severing the femoral artery and breaking the femur. Stark heard the other man groan again. Quickly, he searched Minatchi. He found a French passport, airline tickets, thousands of United States dollars in rolls of hundred-dollar bills, and a notebook of hand-written pages. All the personal effects went into his pack with the scanner unit. As a last detail, he turned the dead man's face to the side and took a photo for identification. Then he crawled toward the other man.

The white-haired pilot, a man approximately sixty years of age but looking older, lay where the bullet had dropped him. Blood frothed at his lips and from a hole in his chest. Waving away the flies on the pilot's face, Stark pressed his fingers to the carotid artery for a pulse—the man's heart fluttered. He checked the wound. He saw that a bullet had punched through the old man's chest and exited from his side, tearing through the right lung. Considering the man's age and bad physical condition, Stark wondered how the pilot had the strength to continue breathing.

Stark keyed his hand-radio. "Captain, this is the lieutenant. Bad news."

"What?"

"The Iranian is dead. The pilot is dying. Through and through lung wound, shock, pulse failing."

The old man blinked and turned his head to Stark. "Soldier . . . your country is America, soldier?"

"Sir, the pilot can speak English."

"Then talk to him. You got a recorder? We've got Kalaq and it's time to get out of here."

"Yes, sir."

"I was a pilot . . . for the airline of the Shah . . . I speak

English because I was a pilot . . . I tried to escape from the insanity of Persia . . ."

Shrugging out of his backpack, Stark found the scanner and disconnected the cassette recorder. He held the recorder close to the old man as he spoke. In a quiet, failing voice, the pilot told the Marine lieutenant of the prison, the threats, and the promise of life for his family if he gave his life in the Holy War.

Vatsek and Alvarez lashed together an improvised litter for Iziz Kalaq, tying the semiconscious prisoner—gagged, blindfolded—between long saplings. To the east, sporadic shooting continued. They no longer heard fire fights—only fire from individual rifles. Niles watched for the approach of the Iranian force, counting the minutes the sergeants took to prepare the wounded man for transport.

"Sounds like they've wiped out the gang," Alvarez commented.

"Isn't that too bad," Vatsek laughed.

"Yeah, it is. They'll come looking for us."

"Don't know we're here."

"Maybe." Alvarez hissed to the captain. "We're done."

Niles left his concealment. "Stark found the others. Only the pilot's alive and he's dying. Code out for extraction."

"Where will the pickup be?" Alvarez pulled out the long-range radio.

"Airfield. Extreme west end."

"They'll try to hit us, sir."

"Tell the pilot to bring all the smoke he's got. We can't carry this prisoner out if we got those Iranians behind us."

"If they know we're here." Vatsek pulled off his bandolier of 40mm grenades. "For the corporal."

"And this." Alvarez passed the captured walkie-talkie to the captain. "Maybe he can jive them somehow. Get them running around in circles."

"Get that helicopter." Taking the bandolier of shells and the Iranian walkie-talkie, Niles wove through the trees and vines to Javenbach. He praised the corporal in a low whisper: "Good work on the capture. Here—Vatsek took this radio from one of the Pasdaran squads."

Javenbach switched on the walkie-talkie. Only static came from the speaker.

"We're getting out of here immediately. I'm calling the helicopter down on the airstrip. I have no doubt that the Pasdaran will try to knock us down. Use your imagination, if there's any way to give us thirty seconds or so, that's all we need."

Nodding, Javenbach hooked the walkie-talkie on his belt webbing. The radio squawked and a voice spoke. "They are searching for more Palestinians. The leader asks if the machine gun was found."

Alvarez returned the long-distance radio to his pack. "Helicopter coming." He and Vatsek gripped the poles of the litter and started away.

"We're almost out of here. Monitor them, Corporal. Alert me if the situation changes."

Glancing at his compass, Niles took the lead, cutting back to the airstrip. He rushed ahead through the trees and brush, then stopped. He watched and listened for movement. The ringing in his ears had faded into a faint, metallic whine superimposed over the silence of the shadowed, windless forest. He listened for shooting in the distance, trying to determine the location of the Iranians. But he heard no more fighting—the Revolutionary Guards had annihilated the Palestinians. Niles continued, rushing ahead, stopping and watching, then advancing again.

In less than five minutes, Niles reached the airstrip. The Cessna had burned down to ashes and smoking metal. He did not see Lieutenant Stark. At the far end of the airstrip, shimmering with the morning heat, he saw flames rising from the masses of twisted metal that remained of the airliner and trucks. Blackened, blast-stripped trees surrounded the wreckage.

A skirmish line of men in camouflage green walked through the grass with rifles, searching the airstrip.

"Lieutenant." Niles whispered into his hand-radio. "You with that pilot?"

"No, sir, I'm on my way out. He's dead. This was absolutely an Iranian operation. The pilot—"

"Tell me later. We're running out of time. Get out of

there." Niles turned to the other Marines. He pointed to the west end of the airstrip. "There. Against the tree line. Alvarez, call the helicopter down so that the wreck gives us some cover. Tell the man to do a circle and throw out all the smoke, then come down right there. Javenbach, break in on their frequency and make things difficult. No matter what"—Niles pointed at Kalaq—"that shit goes out with us. He's the only connection we got left. Vatsek, I'm glad you picked up that souvenir. Think we'll need it. Go, gentlemen."

With a groan, the sergeants picked up Kalaq. The Palestinian twisted against the ropes, trying to free his hands. Niles gave the prisoner a light punch in his bullet-smashed foot. Behind the gag, Kalaq screamed. They carried Kalaq away.

Niles dropped prone on the old earth-mover mounds and watched the line of men search the airstrip. In the heat shimmer, the specks flowed and shifted.

Stark called out from the grass. "Coming in."

"Move it," Niles hissed.

Rotor-throb came from the east, the throbbing increasing by the second until the noise became an overwhelming, unending thunder. Olive-drab Hueys veered across the open sky of the airstrip. Stark scrambled over the mounds a few meters from Niles. Niles ran to him.

"Move," he shouted. "Our ride's here."

"Did you call the airborne?"

"Sir, I don't know who that is."

They ran along the tree line. One helicopter banked over their heads. Through the open side door, a crewman threw smoke grenades, one after another. White smoke clouded from the canisters, obscuring Niles's view of the Iranians.

Rifles and machine guns fired from the ground. Weapons answered from the helicopters. Niles angled across the airstrip, sprinting. He saw Vatsek and Alvarez run from the trees carrying the litter. Above them, the helicopter descended, the grass seething and whipping in the rotor-storm.

As the skids sank into the grass, Vatsek threw the litter inside. Alvarez and Javenbach climbed in and secured Kalaq. Vatsek ran around the nose of the Huey and dropped to a crouch, putting the PKM to his shoulder and searching for targets. In the deafening noise, Niles heard Alvarez shouting. He did not understand until a bullet smashed the Plexiglas of the side door.

Vatsek fired sweeping bursts, firing blind through the smoke. The others pulled him back and he sat in the side door as the helicopter lifted away, leaving the screen of smoke below. Niles and Stark held the sergeant's packstraps as he aimed down, ripping the tree line with the PKM.

Two Iranians left the cover of the trees to follow the helicopter with their rifles. Vatsek put the sights on a man and held the flashing muzzle steady. One man fell back. The other Iranian ran for the tree line, Vatsek following him with the sights, dropping him, then spraying the area, chopping branches, firing straight down as the helicopter left the airstrip behind.

They pulled Vatsek inside and slammed the bullet-shattered side door shut. Niles shouted to the American crewman. "Where'd the airborne come from?"

"Colombian Airborne," the American shouted back. A sharp-featured Chicano, he wore mirrored sunglasses and a Houston Oilers T-shirt. "Army commander at Barranquilla got some calls last night. Calls to the DEA. Calls to the police. Anonymous, but they had every last detail on the gang."

"I know who made the calls," Niles shouted back. "A gang of Colombians. The ex-associates of the gang down there."

"And we got a call from a general. Some colonel was stalling on acting on this airstrip. Could've been paid off. Happens all the time. General sent helicopters into San Juan at first light. We held up their fueling as long as possible. That's when we got your pick-up call. For once, it worked out right. And what you did to that gang looks great. Wish I'd brought a camera."

"We didn't do it. Fuel accident. Burned themselves up."

The DEA man laughed. "Whatever you say."

"Radio ahead. We need an immediate flight out."

"Already did. We got to get you hotshots out of here. You and your prisoner. Don't want any problems with the Colombians. Got all the problems we need already."

"Radio ahead to Panama. Request a flight to Washington. With a chemical interrogation specialist."

Niles crouched over Kalaq. He watched the Palestinian's chest heaving with the quick, shallow breathing of panic. His shoulders and arms twisted against the ropes binding him, as if he thought he could escape from the helicopter.

Of all the Palestinians and Iranians, Niles had only captured this one terrorist—this coward and loudmouth who had somehow participated in the bombing of 23 October with the Iranian named Rajai. He stared down at Kalaq and thought of the horrible death of the Frenchwoman. Did she die for working with Niles? Or for what she learned when she worked for Rajai?

Picking up one of the empty brass casings from the PKM, Niles pressed the base of the cartridge against Kalaq's temple, like the muzzle of a rifle. The Palestinian went rigid. Only his mouth moved. Niles pulled down the strip of cloth gagging him and heard Kalaq pleading for his life. Leaning down, Niles shouted the Arabic question into Kalaq's ear:

"Where is Rajai?"

Static hissed from the radio. Rajai stood at the filing cabinets, sorting through a year of accumulated papers documenting his operations with the militias and political factions of Lebanon. His appointment to his new office in the Foreign Ministry ended his work in Lebanon. After the conclusion of the aircraft bombing of the Americans, aides assumed the duties of recruiting agents, fighters, and technicians—his position in the organization no longer allowed him to risk capture and interrogation.

Now he culled through his files. Rajai did not trust others to read and evaluate each folder of information. Nor did he want to risk shipping the files through Lebanon and Syria to Iran. He must do the work today, while he waited for the reports from the units in Colombia. When he returned to Tehran, the files returned with him in his car.

He went through the hundreds of folders name by name. The files detailed the training, careers, and his personal evaluations of fighters and technicians who operated from units in Lebanon. He had employed some of these men in his operations—the training of the Hizbullah gangs, the assassinations of militia leaders opposed to Syrian and Iranian intervention in Lebanon, and the bombings of the Americans and the French. He wanted to employ the men in his future operations. Their files went into a box he would carry to his new office in the Foreign Ministry.

Other men had no further value to him. Reading the name of a Popular Front technician, he compared the fedayeen's name and age to the list of Palestinians dispatched to Colombia with Iziz Kalaq. The man's name appeared on the list. Rajai took one sheet from the folder—a sheet with identification photos, a detailed physical description, and a column of dates and assignments. He kept only the single page. He threw all the other papers from the man's folder into the box of discarded papers. Why maintain a complete file on a dead man?

Rajai checked the time and calculated the time in Colombia—only an hour after dawn. The fedayeen had not yet completed the loading of the aircraft—there would not be another coded transmission until the plane had taken off for its target.

Taking the box of discarded files, he stepped out of his office. The wind whipped snow through the bare trees of the villa. At the gate, a guard stood behind the shelter of the wall, his back to the warmth of a scorched and smoking oil drum. Rajai walked across the courtyard to the oil drum and dumped the hundreds of sheets of paper into the glowing coals. For a few seconds, flames rose higher than his head, carrying ash and burning paper into the wind. Rajai stepped back and watched the flames, staring as flames formed the images of flaming cities, then the fire receded to a mass of ashes in the blackened metal. When nothing of the papers remained to betray him, he returned to his office.

Only a hiss came from the monitor. Turning up the volume of the radio, he heard faint voices in the static. He listened but could not understand what they said. He checked the time again—four or five more hours remained until the plane left the airstrip in Colombia. Depending on the flight time to the target, Rajai had the remainder of the day to work. Soon he learned of the success or failure of the attack on the Americans.

Until then, he waited, reading through his files—assembling the personnel and squad leaders for a future attack.

Sprawled in a lush tangle of thorned ferns, his senses spinning, Sayed heard the throbbing of a helicopter. Blood flowed over his face. Flies flitted in his eyes and buzzed in the clotting blood. Waving the flies away, he searched for the wound. His fingers found a bullet gouge in his scalp. Looking at his watch, forcing his eyes to focus, he saw that two hours had passed since the explosion of the Palestinian plane.

Riflefire continued—but only from the M-16 rifles of the Colombians. Sayed did not hear his men firing back. He had not heard the popping of a Kalashnikov rifle since he regained consciousness. Colombians shouted to one another and he understood that they searched for men they called terrorists.

He slowly shifted his position. Pushing his rifle ahead, he snaked deeper into the ferns, enduring the scrape of thorns on his hands and arms, silently unhooking his fatigues from thorns. Flies found the blood clotting in his hair but he did not waste motion flicking the flies away. Deep in the center of the tangle, in the green shadows, he lost sight of daylight.

Clicking came from his walkie-talkie. Someone spoke Spanish and then the transmission stopped. The Colombians had found one of his fire team's radios. Switching off the power of his walkie-talkie, he set it aside. He could not risk trying to communicate with any of his men.

Spanish voices approached. Sayed heard boots kicking through the leaves and sticks matting the ground. An M-16 rifle fired, a long burst of high-velocity bullets tearing through the ferns. Sayed steeled himself and did not move as the soldier fired again, bullets ripping through the fronds. A man shouted and the soldier answered in the rapid Spanish Colombians spoke.

Sayed waited as the voices and riflefire of the soldiers continued into the distance. He lay without moving for almost an hour, listening and watching. He heard voices hundreds of meters away. But no soldiers remained in his area. Turning, he tried to rise to a crouch and his vision faded and he fell. He lay still again, only semiconscious.

The Colombians had destroyed the Palestinian unit and wiped out his own squad of Pasdaran. If he wanted any chance of escaping from Colombia, of returning to Iran, he must radio his director and tell him of the attack. He drank from his canteen and waited. When he regained his strength, he would return to the trucks.

In the cockpit of the executive jet, Niles crouched behind the pilots. A coil cord stretched from the encrypted radio to the headphones Niles wore. He stared out at the horizon-spanning blue of the Caribbean as Captain Niles spoke to Washington, encoding circuitry reducing the voice of Colonel Devlin to an electronic monotone.

"If you are absolutely certain this Fahkr Rajai is in Baalbek, I can argue hot pursuit. But I do not believe I can gain authorization for a search. Can I assure the National Security Advisor that this will be surgical? A quick and precise seizure? With absolutely no chance of exposure? Exactly as we discussed last month?"

Niles rubbed the days of beard stubble on his face. Green greasepaint and Colombian dirt came away on his hand. "Well, sir . . ." Glancing at the pilots, he saw them talking to one another. He spoke vaguely in case they listened to his conversation. "Ah, I don't know about absolute. But this is it. This fellow we picked up in Colombia answered all my questions. I got an address. I got directions. The man we want will be there for several more hours. Considering that I've been there, considering that your weatherman tells us there's bad weather, snow and all that, considering that we can call ahead for transportation in and out, I think I've got a chance of catching him while he's there. This won't be a noisy visit, if you know what I mean."

"You don't anticipate opposition?"

"Maybe he'll have two or three friends there. But there won't be a party. Not like the downtown office. That would be the Fourth of July."

"Then this will be as we discussed before? Infiltration. Seizure. Exfiltration."

"Yeah. We talked about it. And after my first look-see, I explained why I couldn't do it. But things have changed. We've got the address and we know the man is there. In fact, he's waiting for a message from us now."

"The message from the code book?"

"That's it."

"I will propose this exactly as we discussed. I don't believe there will be any hesitancy on his part to authorize. It was the advisor's proposal to capture this individual for interrogation."

"I'll be here. Next two hours."

Rajai glanced at his watch—eight in the evening Lebanese time, twelve noon in Colombia. The schedule dictated that the plane must leave in the next hour. But he heard only static from the radio.

Outside, his guards paced in the snow, walking to the heat of the fire in the oil drum, warming their gloves and coats, then returning to the darkness. Rajai had no more paper to dump into the oil drum. He had worked throughout the day and evening to reduce his files to only three cardboard boxes of folders. The boxes held a year of work in Lebanon and the start of years of work in the future as he exploited his contacts to form the cadre of new operations.

The guards left their concealment and stood at the wrought-iron gate. Headlights passed in the street, the tires of heavy transport trucks vibrating the tile floor. Light reflected on the chrome of an antenna as one of his guards—Akbar—walked out of the gate. Watching the street, Akbar spoke into the walkie-talkie.

Akbar talked with the other guards, then crossed the courtyard to the French doors of the offices. He knocked at Rajai's door. Only then did he see Rajai standing inside the door, staring face to face at him.

"Yes?"

"Our men at the checkpoint report Syrian reinforcements of antiaircraft crews. And ammunition trucks. There may be danger for you tonight."

"The Syrians fear for nothing. There will be no attack tonight."

Nodding, Akbar backed away. Rajai locked the door. So the Syrians knew, he thought. They feared attack by the Americans. They feared for nothing.

Only this one last night in Baalbek. Tomorrow he returned to Tehran to begin his assault on America—and his guards went to the Iraqi front. Alone with the hissing radio, he laughed at the irony of his reward for the loyalty of his men. But he could not risk betrayal. They knew of his year in Lebanon and they knew of his return to Tehran. Therefore they went to the front, to be martyred on their first day—a sacrifice to security.

Code interrupted his thoughts. He heard the alert series. An instant after the last click, he keyed the reply. Then came the sequence of page and line numbers.

The plane . . . flys . . . to the destination.

Rajai sent the confirmation. Now he waited.

19

ECHNICIANS in brilliant orange uniforms serviced and refueled the jet. Wearing a raincoat over his dirty camouflage fatigues, Niles waited at the cabin door, watching the approach of a royal blue Cadillac limousine escorted by a Dodge sedan. The cars followed the service vehicle lane through the lines of parked aircraft, then slowed to a stop at the steps to the jet.

Two men left the escort car. Tall, square-shouldered, their hair cut military short, they wore overcoats and gray suits. One man stopped Niles at the door to the limousine, but the door opened and Colonel Devlin motioned him inside. Niles sat on the rear-facing bench seat, his back to the glass partition separating the passenger seats from the driver.

"Captain Niles, this is Richard Todd. He works with the agency's Director of Special Operations." Niles shook hands with the thin, pale bureaucrat in a dark gray suit and black bow tie. "He has offered his resources for this mission."

"We got the authorization?" Niles passed a stack of cassette tapes to the colonel. "Sir, those are recordings of the interrogations of the Iranian pilot and Kalaq. There are also tapes of conversations between the Palestinians in the terrorist gang. We've got to move fast to exploit the information."

"First, however," Todd interrupted, "I would like to ask what happened in Colombia. You had received instructions to allow the plane to take off for the target."

"As I explained to the colonel, there was a fire during fueling. One crew was loading explosives into the plane

355

while another hand-pumped fuel from barrels into the wing tanks. The fire spread to the explosives and the plane went."

"A fire?" Todd repeated.

"Fire, then the explosion. Then the shoot-out with the Pasdaran. Apparently, Rajai wanted to liquidate all of the Palestinians involved with the plane. I imagine he intended to make the Pasdaran unit disappear also. Colombians did that for him."

"We will never know their intended target."

"We'll know when we bring back Rajai. We got that authorization?"

Devlin nodded. Todd continued questioning Niles. "You have a man with a truck waiting in Beirut. Can you contact your man again and give him a drop point if we provide a helicopter?"

"That would cut time. But we'd be risking the Syrians knocking us out of the sky."

"You'll be flying in a Soviet helicopter. Syrian markings."

Niles glanced outside at the guards standing in the rain—agency men. Todd explained their presence. And Niles knew that he and the other Marines now worked for Todd. But if he objected, he lost the chance to capture Rajai.

"The agency does have the good stuff. I'll work it out on a map and call ahead. What about the uniforms and identification?"

"All that is ready."

"A Soviet advisor's uniform? One that'll fit my sergeant?"

"That's right," the colonel answered.

"Mister Marvel comes through. Just like old times—"

"Captain," Todd interrupted. "You're confident you can enter the area in Syrian uniforms?"

"Bet my life on it."

"The colonel told me of your improvised operations in the Moslem sectors of Beirut on 23 and 24 of October of last year."

"Don't know what you're talking about," Niles laughed.

Todd smiled, his gray face twisting to show his perfect teeth. Then he laughed also, the sound mechanical, like an electronic replication of a laugh.

Red light flashed in the windows as a civilian ambulance stopped at the jet. White-uniformed medics went up the steps with a stretcher and carried Kalaq down.

"Be advised," Niles told Devlin and Todd, "that Iziz Kalaq is a sadistic, murdering son of à bitch. He's alive because we had to put questions to him. He deserves anything that happens to him."

"I'm sure you have the same opinion of Fahkr Rajai," Todd replied. "But we must have that man alive."

"I brought you Kalaq. We would have had an Iranian and the pilot of the plane, except that the Pasdaran squad shot them down. I will do whatever is necessary to bring Rajai back for interrogation."

"We trust you will. Remember however, this operation must remain covert. There is considerable troop movement in the area to cover your action. But if at any time, you believe you risk a confrontation, you are to withdraw."

"I'm no martyr. And I know what capture means."

"Only the extraordinary nature of this pursuit—and your qualifications as an individual soldier—motivated the colonel and me to seek authorization for this action. Good luck, Captain Niles. The men outside will help you with the equipment and uniforms."

"No heroes, Niles," Colonel Devlin told him. "If you don't capture him this time, we'll get authorization for another action."

"I'll hold you to your word, sir." Saluting, Niles stepped out.

Inside the limousine, Devlin and Todd watched the guards help Niles carry several heavy boxes from the trunks of the limousine and the escort car.

"File transfer papers documenting their reassignment to Honduras as trainers," Todd told Colonel Devlin. "Backdate the transfers two days. Prepare an accident report describing the crash of a helicopter. If we lose that squad of Marines in Lebanon, they died in Honduras."

A change in the vibration of the engines woke Niles. He lay in the aisle as the leather jump boots of the other men walked around him. Vatsek's voice called out:

"That's not Lebanon down there. What a difference civilization makes."

Hands shook him. Lieutenant Stark told him, "Captain, we've started the descent."

The pilot's voice came over the cabin intercom. "Marines. Be prepared—"

"We ain't Boy Scouts—" Vatsek shouted back.

"—to exit immediately. Your transport is waiting, rotors turning."

Niles stood up straightening his Syrian fatigues. He put on his Soviet-style greatcoat and turned up the collar. The coat covered him from his ears to his knees. His load-bearing web gear buckled over his coat. He walked back to the mirror in the door of the washroom and modeled the uniform for himself. Behind him, the other men assembled their gear and checked their weapons.

"Looking good," Alvarez commented. The sergeant wore an identical uniform—same coat, same webbing, same boots. "We look regulation. Syrians never looked this good."

"But we still look like Americans."

"Worked that night in Hay al-Sollom. And we got the winter working for us. Wear the helmet and a scarf, wear your face paint, wear gloves over your hands, you can pass."

"And don't talk," Niles added, "Come daylight or bright light, we got real trouble."

"Come daylight, we're out of there."

"Yeah. Niles squeezed a dab of brown camouflage greasepaint into his hand and rubbed it onto his face, darkening his skin. In the mirror, he saw Vatsek—in a Soviet uniform with the shoulder insignia of a radio-technical officer—pick up the PKM machine gun captured in Colombia. Niles went to the conference table. "Sergeant Vatsek, do you intend to go everywhere in the world with that weapon?"

"Yes, sir. It is my friend for life."

"Corporal Javenbach." Niles motioned the young man over to him. "Shaffik will be bringing a collection of fatigues and miscellaneous gear in the truck. You will be getting out of that uniform and becoming a Revolutionary Guard. The Revolutionary Guards man checkpoints around—"

Loud engine whine stopped his explanation. As the pilot took the jet down for a landing, Niles buckled himself into a seat. The lights of a town flashed past. He saw the scattered lights of hangars and then the tires skidded, a line of runway lights blurring past. As the plane shuddered to a stop, the pilot spoke again:

"Thirty seconds to your helicopter. Please be prepared to exit when this aircraft stops moving." Niles stood and slap-checked his Syrian web gear.

The plane finally rolled to a stop. Outside, Niles saw the silhouette of a bus-sized helicopter with jet engine housings forward of the rotor mast—a Soviet MI-8 troopship. He wrenched open the door. Frigid air struck him. Snow swirled. The low throb of rotors cut through the whine of the jet engines. Niles looked for the step-ramp—but saw no one in the area. He dropped down to the slick, icy asphalt, signaling for the other Marines to follow.

A flashlight waved from the side door of the MI-8. Niles jogged across asphalt, the blades cutting the air above him. A gloved hand reached out to him and hauled him into the interior. Niles shouted out, "Shalom!" But the crewman chopped his hand past his visor—no talking—and turned away.

Niles helped his squad through the side door. He gave the thumbs-up to the silent crewman and the helicopter lifted away, freezing rotor-storm blasting through the door. The crewman pulled the side door closed. Vibration and the turbine roar of the engines echoed in the metal interior. Leaning against a round window, looking through streaks of snow on the plastic, Niles saw the lights of apartments and streets flash under him, then he saw the darkness of the Mediterranean. The helicopter banked and dropped down to a few meters above the ocean.

Not speaking, each man alone in the darkness and noise, the Marines flew north. Niles slouched on the web-work bench and thought of a hundred ways to fail—the Syrians monitoring international calls, a map error by the pilot, a breakdown of the truck, the arrest of Hijazi at a checkpoint. And if his squad actually reached Baalbek, the kidnapping of the Iranian would be a miracle. The coded transmission to Baalbek five hours before had confirmed that Rajai waited at the radio. But did he still wait? Or had he left for Tehran? Niles had no way to know until they entered the villa.

A fist tapped his shoulder. Vatsek's square hand pointed to the coast, where the sprawl of lights marking Beirut glowed under storm clouds. The helicopter continued north another two minutes, then turned east, gaining altitude. Rising and falling, lurching, the helicopter followed the Jounieh highway through the mountains. A flashlight glowed, Alvarez cupping the flashlight in his hand to check his pack and the long-range radio. Then Alvarez held the light for Stark as he tested the scanner. Niles took out his hand-radio and clicked the transmit. He held the radio to his ear as the others shouted back through the encoded circuits.

The helicopter bucked and shuddered, flying through the absolute black of clouds. Niles left his seat and looked forward to the pilots. He saw a video screen of terrain-following-radar displaying the electronic topography of the mountains. Then the form of the crewman blocked his sight of the controls. Waving his flashlight over the Marines, the crewman pointed down.

As if on signal, the helicopter dropped out of the clouds, a gray landscape of hills and snow-pale fields appearing outside the round ports. Niles looked out at a line of headlights on the highway. They had reached the center of the Bekaa, where the east-west straightaway of the Jounieh highway intersected the highway to Baalbek.

"One minute!" Niles shouted out. He plotted an approximate compass bearing by the highways and looked to the northeast. He saw a gray smear on the storm clouds—Baalbek. "Hey-zoot! Any codes on his frequency?"

"Zero!"

"Strak-man! You got the scanner operating?"

Vatsek pointed at Stark. "That's you, Lieutenant!"

"Yes, sir!"

"What do you hear?"

"Arabic. Russian."

"—and Farsi," Javenbach shouted out. "The Iranians curse the Syrians and the Soviets."

"Why?"

"I don't know. They only curse."

The helicopter banked sharply. Below, Niles saw a parked truck flashing its headlights, the beams shining on a narrow, snow-covered road running along the railroad tracks—the same service road he and Chardon had used the night they escaped from Baalbek. Paralleling the main highway, the service road continued to within five kilometers of the town.

A point of searing red light flickered and red glowing smoke billowed up from the snow. Niles turned back to the other men. Holding up his Kalashnikov, he jammed in a magazine. The crewman threw open the side door as the helicopter descended.

Snow exploded as the rotor-storm swept the road, the lights of the trucks going gray with flying snow. Niles waited until the landing tires hit earth and he jumped out, coming down hard on the rutted, frozen earth. Jerking back his rifle's bolt handle to chamber a round, he rushed away from the helicopter and dropped down, the rotor noise and blowing snow making hearing and sight impossible. He stared into the wall of gray, swirling snow and heard the turbines shriek as the helicopter lifted away. The rotor throb faded to the west.

The headlights went off. Silence returned. The flare sputtered out in the mud of melted snow. Niles watched the night, looking for movement and listening. He heard only the wind. Turning, he saw no movement by the truck and he rose to a crouch.

"Hijazi! ¿Qué pasa?"

"Nada, Old Man!"

Niles ran to the cab of the truck. He glanced inside and saw the silhouette of the young Lebanese lieutenant. Rushing to the canvas-covered back of the stake-side truck, he swept his penlight over the cargo area. Boxes marked Marlboro, Johnny Walker, Smirnoff, and Levis stood against the sides. Then he waved the beam of the tiny light over the road. In the crusted snow, he saw the ruts of the tires and his own boot prints. He called out, "Into the truck!"

The other Marines left the snow. As they hurried past him, Niles questioned Hijazi. "What is all the traffic on the roads? This is two o'clock in the morning."

"There is a mobilization of Syrian forces."

"Is Israel attacking?"

"Perhaps the air force. I saw no armor. Only antiaircraft guns."

"Have they hit Israel? They expecting a counterstrike?"

"No, no attacks, no incidents, nothing. Who can know why the Syrians mobilize?"

"You brought the clothes and equipment?"

"Yes, but you came in uniforms."

In the back of the truck, Vatsek laughed. "Wow, check this out. All right! Smirnoff."

"Up front, Godzilla. Leave that vodka alone."

Shining the penlight on Hijazi, Niles saw that the young Lebanese officer wore a Syrian uniform. "One of my men will be dressed as a Pasdaran."

"Yes, they are on the roads also."

"How many? What are they doing?"

"Nothing. Syrians control all the checkpoints this night."

Vatsek climbed into the cab of the truck. "What's all that in back? Did we come to kill? Or party?"

"The cigarettes and liquor explain why I have this truck. I tell soldiers the liquor is for their officers and the soldiers ask no more questions."

"Thanks for coming, Shaffik," Vatsek said. "We couldn't do this without you. Now move it. Stop short of the highway. I'm going to need your voice."

Niles stepped into the rear of the truck. The truck lurched away, bumping over the rutted service road. Crouching down with the other men, he asked, "What's going on with the radios?"

"Nothing," Alvarez answered. "Zero in, zero out."

"Any Farsi on the scanner?"

"Yes, sir," Javenbach told him. "Outposts checking with their commander. Walkie-talkies only."

"Corporal, see these fatigues here? This equipment?" Niles pushed a box to him. He pulled tattered fatigues and a wool stocking cap out. "These clothes are your Revolutionary Guard uniform. Put that hat over your hair." He turned to Alvarez and Stark. "Okay, I want to try to determine if Rajai is there. Going through those checkpoints is scary and I don't want to do it if the man's gone. I'll have Hijazi make a voice transmission, in the clear, saying that they're fighting the Colombian Army."

"It won't sound right," Alvarez countered. "No distance."

"We'll put it through the walkie-talkies, then into the microphone."

"Sir," Stark interrupted. "Why don't you call him on the telephone? We've got his phone number."

"We'd have to go through the checkpoints to get to a phone."

"No, sir. Perhaps not."

"No?" Niles took out a folded satellite photo of Baalbek. "There's the town." He pointed to the bottom edge of the photo. "There's the highway and the Syrian checkpoint. There's no where to call from out there."

The lieutenant studied the photo as the truck swayed. "There are two industrial shops on the highway. This photo does not show the section of the highway to which I am referring. One was bombed out. But the other is still there."

Niles unfolded another photo showing the town and the countryside.

Stark pointed to the highway running south from Baalbek. "There. Perhaps a kilometer before the checkpoint."

"We'll try it. I don't want to chance those checkpoints until I know that man is there."

As the daylight faded, Sayed staggered through the trees. A root caught his boot and he fell, the shock making his head pulse with pain. He swatted the flies away from the wound and pushed himself to his feet. Despite his pain and blood loss, he forced himself to continue. He had hidden from the soldiers throughout the day, then escaped from the airstrip. But if he did not find the trucks before dark, he died in Colombia.

Sayed walked three steps across the ruts before he realized he had reached the road. Looking down at the dirt, he saw tire tracks. He broke into a run, stumbling and falling, dragging himself to his feet and continuing, following the tracks west.

The litter stopped him. Plastic tarps, cartons of food, and wooden ammunition boxes lay on the road. In the clearing, he saw the pans and plates from the meal that morning. Iradj lay in a scab of blood swarming with ants and flies. The drivers had somehow shot him.

All the equipment and provisions of his unit lay in the dirt. The drivers had taken nothing. They had left the rifle of Iradj, the few magazines of ammunition, the Turkish cigarettes, and boxes of Iranian tea. Then they had swept the trucks clean of trash and cigarette butts—leaving no evidence to link them to the Iranians. Desperate, panicking, Sayed kicked through the boxes and plastic tarps. He found the padded backpack containing the radio.

Taking the radio under the cover of the trees, he switched on the power. The indicator light glowed. He unrolled the antenna and threw it into the branches above him. Flipping through the code book, he scrawled the codes of phrases to communicate the explosion of the plane and the attack by the Colombian troops.

Through the cut in the canvas, Niles watched Hijazi and Javenbach at the gate. Snow swirled through the glare of the naked light bulbs hanging above the parked trucks and cars. His breath clouding in the air, Hijazi argued with the guard. Niles heard the guard explain that he could not allow strangers to enter the parking lot, and Hijazi demanded that the guard open the gate. Niles heard the truck's door open.

"Hey, Captain!" Vatsek hissed through the canvas. "That shit has no respect for a uniform. What do you do say we shoot him?"

"Sergeant. That man is doing his job. Give him a minute, he'll respond to persuasion."

Standing on the side-slats, Niles looked toward the Syrian checkpoint. Billboards and the curve of the highway blocked the soldiers' sight of the truck. Looking to the south, Niles saw only empty highway and darkness. No trucks, no cars, approached. Only troop trucks and transports moved during the Syrian mobilization.

"What we will do, is threaten to shoot him."

"Captain!" Stark punched a button on a cassette recorder as a static-scratchy code came from the scanner. "It's the Iranian frequency. Another transmission coming in."

A code series blasted from the monitor, the dot-dash sharp and free of static.

"That's the confirmation from the radio in Baalbek. Recording the message."

Niles knocked on the cab. Vatsek looked back through the rear-view mirror. Pointing toward the car repair lot, he hand-signed for him to call back Hijazi and Javenbach.

Words hissed from the monitor.

"Is that Arabic? Do you understand that?" Stark asked.

Vatsek shouted out in Russian. Turning up the volume, Niles listened to the voice. Distortion and static blurred the words. He understood nothing. "Not Arabic. And it can't be the Palestinian radio. We burned it."

"The Pasdaran unit?"

"Why not?"

Boots scuffed on the bumper and Javenbach climbed into the back. Niles knocked on the cab again and told Vatsek, "Wait."

Hearing the radio, Javenbach sat on the planks and leaned close to the monitor. The transmission alternated between voice and code. But no more code came from the radio in Baalbek.

"He is begging for an answer," Javenbach translated. "He is wounded, his men are dead or captured, he is alone, the Colombians deserted him, he begs for the director to send help to him. But there is no answer."

"He's calling the director?"

"But there is no answer."

"But there was an answer. The radio in Baalbek sent back a confirm. And now there's nothing. That's our man. If it was an office flunky, he'd radio for him to use code. But Rajai just pulled the plug. He's letting his man in Colombia talk into space. The shit, leaving one of his men out there."

"We're going in?" Alvarez asked.

"That's it."

Alvarez plugged a cassette recorder into the long-range radio, changed the band, and tuned the frequency to the faint voice screaming from Colombia. He started a second recorder. Then he switched the scanner back to the local frequencies. Farsi voices spoke. "I'm locking in on the Revolutionary Guard radios. If they're watching the man's street and they spot us, we'll know about—"

"Wait—they are calling for guards." Javenbach translated the communications. "They demand Revolutionary Guards and two trucks immediately. An emergency. They leave for Damascus immediately . . . the checkpoint leader refuses . . . and they tell him it is on the authority of . . . Rajai."

"There he is," Niles told the others. "Now we get him."

Racing the engines of the cars, wiping ice from the windows, his guards prepared for the drive to Damascus. Rajai carried the boxes of files from his office to the white Mercedes. Two boxes went into the trunk. The third went in the back seat. As Akbar shouted into his walkie-talkie, demanding an escort of Pasdaran and trucks to the Syrian border, Rajai took a seat in the warmth of the Mercedes and waited as the men folded the steel stocks of their rifles and buckled bandoliers of ammunition across their coats. Four men got into the second car, a dark blue Mercedes. Akbar and a driver got into the front seat of his car. Exhaust clouding in the cold air, they drove from the gate.

"At the checkpoint," Akbar told him. "Others will join us. In two trucks with heavy weapons."

"More guards? It is unnecessary."

"The Syrians think there will be fighting tonight."

Rajai said nothing and watched the dark streets of the town pass. Few lights showed in windows. No other cars dared the streets. The headlights of the Mercedes showed walls crumbling onto the trash-strewn sidewalks. All the wealthy families—of all faiths—had fled, Christian and Moslem alike. Only the poor remained in this place of fanatics and war. The idea of the Americans attacking this dying town, this slum, seemed a joke to Rajai—and he realized that the ignorance, incompetence, and arrogance of the Americans actually made the attack possible, if not inevitable.

Colombian soldiers had destroyed the plane. If they took Kalaq prisoner, if Kalaq cooperated, if the Colombians released the information to the Americans, if the Americans pursued an investigation in Lebanon, if the Americans somehow learned of Rajai's office in Baalbek, then came the attack. Grandiose and vainglorious, a military spectacle staged for the honor and televisions of the United States, costing hundreds of millions of dollars in lost aircraft, squandered munitions, and pilot casualties as the jets met a storm of antiaircraft fire.

To bomb an empty office.

Laughing at the joke, he took a last look at Baalbek, a town soon to be a focus of world attention as the fanatics of the Revolutionary Guard paraded the corpses of dead American pilots through the streets.

Tomorrow he began his work in Tehran. Despite the failure of the committee's operation, his future waited. His dreams, his actions, would shape the future of his country, bringing war with America and the cataclysm of Year Zero, when war and invasion and liberation destroyed Iran, cleansing the nation of culture, religions, and history.

Then began the rule of Rajai.

Kilometers away, the transport truck parked at the side of the highway. Javenbach monitored the walkie-talkies of the Iranians. Niles crouched with him, listening to the voices. From time to time, Arabic-speaking Hizbullah militiamen spoke on the frequency. The other Marines waited, ready, watching the highway for Syrian trucks or the cars of the Iranians.

Niles heard an exchange between two Arabic speakers— then another voice shouted over the transmission. Javenbach translated, "He's telling the Hizbullah to bring the car, they don't want to give up the car to the Revolutionary Guards. He says to stop the delay, the director cannot wait—"

"Cars coming!" Vatsek shouted out. "Civilian cars."

A transmission came from very near. "A Revolutionary Guard asks why the truck is not coming—"

"It's a Mercedes," Vatsek called out. "Two Mercedes and jeep with a recoilless rifle."

The cars sped past. Alvarez called out, "Look like Iranians."

Niles spoke into his hand-radio. "Go! Shaffik, put it in gear. That is them."

Engine whining at maximum rpm's, clashing the gears, Hijazi accelerated after the Iranians. Alvarez and Vatsek leaned out and looked ahead.

"Shit!" Vatsek kicked the railing slats. "What is this? We need a Corvette to chase those—hey! Captain! Tell Shaffik to kill the lights and make maximum speed."

As he relayed the instruction to Hijazi, Niles looked back and saw headlights gaining on them. "What—"

"Keep the radio on. When I give the word, Shaffik hits the brakes, hard." Nodding to the approaching Land Rover, Vatsek grinned. "Stand by, Lieutenant. I'll show you something they never taught at Parris Island."

Alvarez laughed. "Godzilla goes crazy!"

"Don't call me no Japanese lizard. Watch. Give me that pop-gun." Vatsek hung his PKM on the side slats and took the Kalashnikov from Alvarez. Palming down the safety-lever of the Kalashnikov, Vatsek called out to Stark. "Ready?"

"I understand." Hijazi spoke from the radio. "I wait for the signal."

The headlights gained on the truck. High beams flashed. Vatsek squinted into the glare, his left arm hooked through the side slats as he watched the open-topped Land Rover and the three Iranians riding in it. Two rode in the front, the third behind the pedestal-mounted Soviet PK machine gun. Vatsek's right hand casually held the pistol-grip of the Kalashnikov. Engine screaming, the truck almost kept ahead of the Land Rover. But the small, lightweight, four-wheel-drive Land Rover pulled up behind the transport, the driver peering ahead to pass.

"Hit the brakes!"

Even as Vatsek shouted, the tires screeched, the truck shuddering as Hijazi stood on the brakes. The Land Rover hit the heavy steel bumper of the transport truck and Vatsek fired down into the Iranians, killing the driver and passenger instantly, hitting the third Iranian with a one-handed burst as the man tried to grab the machine gun.

Hijazi maintained the skid, correcting from side to side as the heavy truck tried to sideslip on the slick asphalt. Jammed against the bumper, the Land Rover slowed with the truck. Vatsek held onto the side slates, watching and waiting as the vehicles lost speed.

"Got it!" Vatsek shouted out. He set the safety on the Kalashnikov and tossed it back to Alvarez. Dropping off the back of the truck, he went to the side of the Land Rover and pulled out the dead driver. Stark follow him. They dragged the bodies off the highway.

Niles hit the cab. "Go on."

The truck moved ahead. But the Land Rover stayed on the bumper. Vatsek and Stark ran after the Land Rover as Hijazi braked to a stop again. The bumper of the Land Rover had hooked over the trailer hitch of the truck. Vatsek squatted at the side of the Land Rover and gripped the bumper. He lifted the bumper free with the strength of his legs, then got in the Land Rover and stood behind the PK.

Sweeping aside the broken glass and blood, Stark revved the engine and shifted into first. Tires spraying, he passed the truck. Vatsek squinted into the freezing windrush and saw the taillights of the three cars. Checking the drum of cartridges, he jerked back the cocking handle and triggered a three-shot burst into the sky to test the weapon. He looked back and saw the truck falling back as Stark floored the Land Rover.

"Mister America to the Old Man," he said into his hand-radio. "Want us to stop the convoy?"

"Get point-blank to the one-oh-six." Niles meant the Land Rover mounted with the 106mm recoilless rifle. "Hit them, then stop the others. No fire into the Mercs. Don't know which one our man's in."

"Will do. Make speed, Lieutenant."

"Be advised," Niles added. "They are trying to call the dead Pasdaran on the walkie-talkies."

"Nothing we can do about it." Vatsek held the steel post of the machine gun mount as Stark gained on the Iranians. The road blurred past, every pothole and crack in the asphalt rattling the aluminum truck. Ahead, against the yellow fan of the other Land Rover's headlights, he saw a silhouette stand. The tube of the 106mm recoilless rifle swiveled. Vatsek jerked the PK off the pedestal socket and sat in the glass of the passenger seat. Punching out the shattered windshield with his gloved fist, he laid the machine gun on the dash. The walkie-talkie squawked Farsi at his feet.

At one hundred meters, a point of light blinked from the Iranian Land Rover. A bullet slammed the fender, another clanged off the steel pedestal shaft. Stark cut to the left, then swerved back to the right, weaving over the highway as Vatsek put the sights on the center of the Land Rover ahead and eased back the trigger, the heavy machine gun jackhammering against his shoulder.

The recoilless rifle flashed, the rocket shrieking past Vatsek, exploding twenty meters behind him, the blast and fragments spraying into the fields. He did not take his eyes off the Land Rover as he held the machine gun on line, counting off three tracers—no less than fifteen rounds—before releasing the trigger.

A form fell, arms and legs flailing as the man hit the road and cartwheeled. But the rifle fired again, and Vatsek felt glass slash across his forehead. He put the sights on the taillights of the Land Rover and squeezed off bursts as Stark zigzagged, swerving, braking, accelerating. Stark held steady behind the other truck for an instant and Vatsek fired a long burst, slugs tearing through the tailgate, shattering a taillight, a tracer streaking into a tire.

Lurching as the tire blew out, the Land Rover swerved to the left, slid sideways, then rolled, the Iranians flying from the flipping wreck. Stark cut to the edge of the highway to avoid the disintegrating tangle of metal. Looking back, Vatsek saw the transport truck clip the front end of the smashed Land Rover, sending it spinning from the road. Hijazi flashed his headlights and sounded the air horn.

Ahead, the two Mercedes sedans accelerated, flying along the straight highway. Stark kept the pedal to the floor, the tires of the Land Rover vibrating. But the sedans made distance by the second. Vatsek keyed his hand-radio: "Captain, we're losing them. We can't keep up with them. Let me put some rounds into the cars while they're in range."

"Do it," Niles agreed. "Put it in to both cars."

Vatsek set the PK's rear leaf sight at maximum range and aimed in front of the lead car, the white Mercedes.

In the truck, Niles stood on the slats behind the cab. He slashed the canvas cover with his knife and tore a wide hole. Alvarez passed the PKM machine gun up to the captain. He laid the machine gun across the roof of the cab. Wind tore at his sleeves and coat, flipping his Syrian helmet away.

Tracers arced from the Land Rover to the highway fifty meters ahead of the white Mercedes. Tracers skipped off the asphalt. Niles saw the line of tracers angle down as Vatsek adjusted his aim. Bullets hit around both of the sedans. Niles compensated for the extreme distance and fired, trying to drop the heavy slugs down on the cars.

Firing a long burst, he watched the tracers streak above the Land Rover, then arc down. But the phosphorus of the tracers burned out before completing the arc. Niles fired blind. Hooking a leg through the slats, he faced into the windrush and held the sights over the taillights of the first car, dropping bullets down on the Iranians, hoping to score hits by numbers and probability.

The white Mercedes hydroplaned through a flooded section of highway, waves of water flying high. The tires lost contact with the asphalt and the Mercedes drifted sideways. The driver overcorrected, losing control, the car spinning. The second Mercedes slowed and swerved to avoid hitting the first.

As Stark bore down on the spinning Mercedes, Vatsek shifted his aim to the blue Mercedes, triggering careful five-round bursts, seeing a tracer streak to target, then pausing and shifting aim and firing five more rounds as Stark slowed for the flooded stretch of highway. The driver of the white

Mercedes finally brought the car to a stop in the field at the side of the road. Wheels spraying gravel and mud, he tried to accelerate.

Aiming through spraying water, Vatsek fired a long burst into the fender, hoping to score on the engine. Stark continued past the Mercedes. Vatsek jerked the PK machine gun free of the shattered windshield and turned in the seat, firing back at the Mercedes, a tight burst hitting the fender and tire. But a rifle flashed from the passenger-side front window, slugs hammering the Land Rover, a ricochet humming past Vatsek's head.

The Land Rover skidded to the side, a tire flapping on the rim. Stark strained at the wheel, forcing the truck straight as he lost speed. Vatsek held onto the seat as the Land Rover shuddered and lurched, bumping to a stop.

"Vatsek! The other car!" Stark shouted out.

The blue Mercedes whipped through a turn. Vatsek found the PK machine gun between the seats. Jumping out of the Land Rover, he set the machine gun on the hood and fired at the onrushing Mercedes. The PK fired twice, then jammed. He jerked the cocking handle back and felt glass crunch.

Rifles fired from the windows of the Mercedes. Vatsek dropped down behind the tire as slugs punched into the Land Rover. Stark went prone on the wet asphalt and fired a Kalashnikov under the frame, aiming at the onrushing headlights. Tires skidded. Vatsek jerked back the cocking handle again and the machine gun ejected a cartridge.

Iranians threw open the doors of the blue Mercedes, stepping out as the driver braked to a stop. Vatsek rolled to the side and fired into the windows, glass exploding, the driver dying. Rifles returned the fire.

As the transport truck stopped, two rifles flashed from the stalled white Mercedes, bullets smashing through the windshield, slugs continuing through the cab and splintering the slats beside Niles. He put a burst low through the front door of the Mercedes. Men left the other side. Taking shelter behind the sedan, they raked the truck again. Niles fired a burst into the front of the car, a tracer ricocheting away, the men dropping down. Two hundred meters ahead, he saw

Stark and Vatsek exchanging fire with the Iranians of the blue Mercedes.

Niles pulled the PKM free of the canvas and followed Alvarez and Javenbach out of the transport. Hijazi dropped out of the door.

"Shaffik!" Niles shouted out. "You okay?"

"Okay, okay."

"You're bleeding."

"It is from glass. I am okay."

"Corporal, tell them they'll live if they surrender."

Crouching behind the steel bumper of the truck, Javenbach called out to the Mercedes. The gunmen answered with long bursts of full-auto, bullets hammering the truck, clanging off the bumper, shattering a headlight. Javenbach's leg kicked backward and he fell. Niles lunged out and grabbed him, pushing him against the tire. He found blood pouring from a through-and-through wound above the corporal's boot top. When he touched the leg, Javenbach gasped—shattered bone.

"Your leg's broken." Niles put Javenbach's Kalashnikov in his hands. "Stay here and shoot to wound. We want Rajai alive."

Alvarez lay prone behind the rear double wheels. He watched the Mercedes over the sights of his rifle. Niles dropped down with him and flipped down the bipod of the PKM.

"This is it," Niles told him. "We close them down now."

To the south, they heard a long burst from a machine gun. Flame mushroomed into the sky as the gasoline of the second Mercedes exploded into flame.

"Godzilla got serious."

"I'm taking their feet off, be ready to rush." Sighting on the space under the white Mercedes, he fired a long, accurate burst into the narrow space. He saw tracers skip off the asphalt, the front tires popped, a form staggered away, then he hit the back tires.

No one fired back. Alvarez ran around the back of the transport truck and sprinted for the Mercedes. Jerking the PKM off the ground, Niles followed the sergeant. Orange light from the distant gasoline flames flared from the glass and polished enamel of the Mercedes. Niles saw Alvarez jerk back and a rifle fired. Niles sprayed a burst high over the car and cut around the front.

An Iranian with a Kalashnikov, his legs and coat soaked in blood, fired a Kalashnikov one-handed, trying to hit Alvarez. A dead man lay in the mud. The wounded Iranian sat with his back to the Mercedes, his legs shattered, his right arm limp. But he still fought. Alvarez splashed through the mud and ice behind the Mercedes, staying in a squat, the trunk of the Mercedes blocking the fire of the Iranian. The Iranian snapped a last wild burst at Alvarez and the bolt slammed closed on the empty chamber. He jerked the trigger again, then dropped the rifle and reached for the rifle of the dead man.

Niles rushed forward, kicking the rifle out of the man's hand. He looked down into the scarred face of the Revolutionary Guard. The man twisted away. Niles pointed the PKM at him and shouted out, "Stop!"

A pistol fired, a bullet slashing past Niles's left arm and ribs, the Iranian rolling again and bringing up the pistol. Niles and Alvarez fired simultaneously, the bursts of slugs throwing the Iranian back into the mud, dead.

Alvarez looked inside the Mercedes. Niles threw the door open.

A small man lay curled in the footwell of the rear seat, his hands covering his head. Niles pushed aside a heavy cardboard box and pulled the Iranian out.

Niles recognized the beard and the styled hair. He had seen the small, elegantly groomed Iranian the night of 24 October, outside the theater in Hay al-Sollom where hundreds of Hizbullah fanatics chanted of death.

Blood soaked the Iranian's tailored pants and coat. His breathing rasped. Niles checked him and found blood flowing from a wound in his buttock. Somehow, a bullet had found him where he hid on the floor of the Mercedes.

"He's hit. Already in shock." Niles shouted across the highway. "Shaffik, get the truck turned around! Our man's wounded." Stark and Vatsek ran to the Mercedes. "Grab him!"

Carrying Rajai by his hands and feet, Niles and Vatsek took him to the truck. They laid him on the planks, then helped Javenbach up. "Question him," Niles told Javenbach. "Get something out of him. Tell him we'll take him to a hospital if he talks."

Starting the truck, Hijazi backed through a semicircle. The truck tilted to one side, the bullet-hit right front tire riding on the hard inner core designed to keep the truck rolling despite minor damage. He wrestled the steering wheel around, gunning the engine while he waited for the Marines.

Niles squatted on the bumper, watching and listening as Javenbach tried to interrogate the wounded Iranian. Vatsek pulled up Rajai's shirt and found an exit wound under his right shoulder blade. Pressing a compress pad to the wound, Vatsek put his ear to Rajai's chest and listened. Javenbach shouted questions but Rajai did not respond. Vatsek looked up, shaking his head.

"Bullet went up through his gut, maybe his kidney, then through his diaphragm and lung. Sounds like his right lung collapsed."

"Damn it!" Niles shouted out. "All this and our man takes a bullet in the ass."

"We got something." Alvarez heaved a cardboard box into the truck. "That box is full of papers, with names and faces."

"Code out for the helicopter."

Running to the Mercedes, Niles saw Stark opening the trunk. The lieutenant opened two boxes and looked at sheets of paper. "These look like personnel files, sir."

"Take it, move it." Niles grabbed one of the boxes and ran back to the truck. Stark followed. They pushed the boxes into the back of the transport.

Inside, Alvarez tapped out a radio message. The truck labored against the bullet-shot tire to pick up speed. Javenbach read the papers with a flashlight.

"These are his files—"

"You positive?"

"Of men, of their organizations, of the work they did for him."

A camera flashed as Stark took photos of Rajai, full-face and profile. Vatsek put his ear to Rajai's chest again. He slammed Rajai's chest with his fist, then listened again. He put his huge, square hand to Rajai's throat and felt for a pulse, then shook his head.

"This shit's dead."

"—here is one who worked against the Marines in Beirut. And here, a Palestinian from the United States."

"Sir." Stark held up a sheet of typed and hand-written entries. "This is the day-by-day documentation of his work."

"Yeah?"

"These files have more than we would have ever gotten from him through interrogation."

Niles looked at the thousands of pages in the boxes. "You see addresses there?"

"Addresses. Names, photos, technical skills, past actions."

"Well, how interesting," Niles commented. "Looks like we scored. Looks like we're coming back." He looked up to the men. "I got volunteers?"